The New Economy and Macroeconomic Stability

The past decade has seen many leading economies, especially the US, undergo profound structural transformations. Departing from the standard theories employed to explain this phenomenon, *The New Economy and Macroeconomic Stability* provides the first broad analysis of the New Economy. The book studies the interaction of key variables such as information technology, globalization and the increasing significance of intangibles and financial markets.

The New Economy and Macroeconomic Stability utilizes a 'neo-modern' perspective drawing on the complexity theory to advance the study of stability, and of the dynamic behaviour, of economic systems. Togati utilizes the Calvino labels to identify new empirical evidence and examines the implications for global stability based on New Classical Macroeconomics and Keynesian theory. The analysis developed in this book has important practical and policy implications for the New Economy. This book is essential reading for students, academics and practitioners in this field.

Teodoro Dario Togati is an Associate Professor of Economics at the University of Turin, Italy.

Routledge Frontiers of Political Economy

1 **Equilibrium Versus Understanding**
Towards the rehumanization of economics within social theory
Mark Addleson

2 **Evolution, Order and Complexity**
Edited by Elias L. Khalil and Kenneth E. Boulding

3 **Interactions in Political Economy**
Malvern after ten years
Edited by Steven Pressman

4 **The End of Economics**
Michael Perelman

5 **Probability in Economics**
Omar F. Hamouda and Robin Rowley

6 **Capital Controversy, Post Keynesian Economics and the History of Economics**
Essays in honour of Geoff Harcourt, volume one
Edited by Philip Arestis, Gabriel Palma and Malcolm Sawyer

7 **Markets, Unemployment and Economic Policy**
Essays in honour of Geoff Harcourt, volume two
Edited by Philip Arestis, Gabriel Palma and Malcolm Sawyer

8 **Social Economy**
The logic of capitalist development
Clark Everling

9 **New Keynesian Economics/ Post Keynesian Alternatives**
Edited by Roy J. Rotheim

10 **The Representative Agent in Macroeconomics**
James E. Hartley

11 **Borderlands of Economics**
Essays in honour of Daniel R. Fusfeld
Edited by Nahid Aslanbeigui and Young Back Choi

12 **Value, Distribution and Capital**
Essays in honour of Pierangelo Garegnani
Edited by Gary Mongiovi and Fabio Petri

13 **The Economics of Science**
Methodology and Epistemology
as if economics really mattered
James R. Wible

14 **Competitiveness, Localised
Learning and Regional
Development**
Specialisation and prosperity in
small open economies
*Peter Maskell, Heikki Eskelinen,
Ingjaldur Hannibalsson,
Anders Malmberg and Eirik Vatne*

15 **Labour Market Theory**
A constructive reassessment
Ben J. Fine

16 **Women and European
Employment**
*Jill Rubery, Mark Smith, Colette
Fagan and Damian Grimshaw*

17 **Explorations in Economic
Methodology**
From Lakatos to empirical
philosophy of science
Roger Backhouse

18 **Subjectivity in Political
Economy**
Essays on wanting and choosing
David P. Levine

19 **The Political Economy of
Middle East Peace**
The impact of competing trade
agendas
Edited by J.W. Wright, Jr

20 **The Active Consumer**
Novelty and surprise in
consumer choice
Edited by Marina Bianchi

21 **Subjectivism and Economic
Analysis**
Essays in memory of Ludwig
Lachmann
*Edited by Roger Koppl and
Gary Mongiovi*

22 **Themes in Post-Keynesian
Economics**
Essays in honour of Geoff
Harcourt, volume three
*Edited by Claudio Sardoni
and Peter Kriesler*

23 **The Dynamics of
Technological Knowledge**
Cristiano Antonelli

24 **The Political Economy of
Diet, Health and Food Policy**
Ben J. Fine

25 **The End of Finance**
Capital market inflation, financial
derivatives and pension fund
capitalism
Jan Toporowski

26 **Political Economy and the
New Capitalism**
Edited by Jan Toporowski

27 **Growth Theory**
A philosophical perspective
Patricia Northover

28 **The Political Economy of
the Small Firm**
Edited by Charlie Dannreuther

29 **Hahn and Economic
Methodology**
*Edited by Thomas Boylan and
Paschal F. O'Gorman*

30 Gender, Growth and Trade
The miracle economies of the postwar years
David Kucera

31 Normative Political Economy
Subjective freedom, the market and the state
David Levine

32 Economist with a Public Purpose
Essays in honour of John Kenneth Galbraith
Edited by Michael Keaney

33 Involuntary Unemployment
The elusive quest for a theory
Michel De Vroey

34 The Fundamental Institutions of Capitalism
Ernesto Screpanti

35 Transcending Transaction
The search for self-generating markets
Alan Shipman

36 Power in Business and the State
An historical analysis of its concentration
Frank Bealey

37 Editing Economics
Essays in honour of Mark Perlman
Hank Lim, Ungsuh K. Park and Geoff Harcourt

38 Money, Macroeconomics and Keynes
Essays in honour of Victoria Chick, Volume One
Philip Arestis, Meghnad Desai and Sheila Dow

39 Methodology, Microeconomics and Keynes
Essays in honour of Victoria Chick, Volume Two
Philip Arestis, Meghnad Desai and Sheila Dow

40 Market Drive and Governance
Reexamining the rules for economic and commercial contest
Ralf Boscheck

41 The Value of Marx
Political economy for contemporary capitalism
Alfredo Saad-Filho

42 Issues in Positive Political Economy
S. Mansoob Murshed

43 The Enigma of Globalisation
A journey to a new stage of capitalism
Robert Went

44 The Market
Equilibrium, stability, mythology
S.N. Afriat

45 The Political Economy of Rule Evasion and Policy Reform
Jim Leitzel

46 **Unpaid Work and the Economy**
Edited by Antonella Picchio

47 **Distributional Justice**
Theory and Measurement
Hilde Bojer

48 **Cognitive Developments in Economics**
Edited by Salvatore Rizzello

49 **Social Foundations of Markets, Money and Credit**
Costas Lapavitsas

50 **Rethinking Capitalist Development**
Essays on the economics of Josef Steindl
Edited by Tracy Mott and Nina Shapiro

51 **An Evolutionary Approach to Social Welfare**
Christian Sartorius

52 **Kalecki's Economics Today**
Edited by Zdzislaw L. Sadowski and Adam Szeworski

53 **Fiscal Policy from Reagan to Blair**
The Left veers Right
Ravi K. Roy and Arthur T. Denzau

54 **The Cognitive Mechanics of Economic Development and Institutional Change**
Bertin Martens

55 **Individualism and the Social Order**
The social element in liberal thought
Charles R. McCann, Jr

56 **Affirmative Action in the United States and India**
A comparative perspective
Thomas E. Weisskopf

57 **Global Political Economy and the Wealth of Nations**
Performance, institutions, problems and policies
Edited by Phillip Anthony O'Hara

58 **Structural Economics**
Thijs ten Raa

59 **Macroeconomic Theory and Economic Policy**
Essays in honour of Jean-Paul Fitoussi
Edited by K. Vela Velupillai

60 **The Struggle Over Work**
The "end of work" and employment alternatives in post-industrial societies
Shaun Wilson

61 **The Political Economy of Global Sporting Organisations**
John Forster and Nigel Pope

62 **The Flawed Foundations of General Equilibrium Theory**
Critical essays on economic theory
Frank Ackerman and Alejandro Nadal

63 **Uncertainty in Economic Theory**
Essays in honor of David Schmeidler's 65th Birthday
Edited by Itzhak Gilboa

64 **The New Institutional Economics of Corruption**
Edited by Johann Graf Lambsdorff, Markus Taube and Matthias Schramm

65 **The Price Index and its Extension**
A chapter in economic measurement
S.N. Afriat

66 **Reduction, Rationality and Game Theory in Marxian Economics**
Bruce Philp

67 **Culture and Politics in Economic Development**
Volker Bornschier

68 **Modern Applications of Austrian Thought**
Edited by Jürgen G. Backhaus

69 **Ordinary Choices**
Individuals, incommensurability, and democracy
Robert Urquhart

70 **The Labour Theory of Value**
Peter C. Dooley

71 **Capitalism**
Victor D. Lippit

72 **Macroeconomic Foundations of Macroeconomics**
Alvaro Cencini

73 **Marx for the 21st Century**
Edited by Hiroshi Uchida

74 **Growth and Development in the Global Political Economy**
Social structures of accumulation and modes of regulation
Phillip Anthony O'Hara

75 **The New Economy and Macroeconomic Stability**
A neo-modern perspective drawing on the complexity approach and Keynesian economics
Teodoro Dario Togati

The New Economy and Macroeconomic Stability

A neo-modern perspective drawing on the complexity approach and Keynesian economics

Teodoro Dario Togati

Routledge
Taylor & Francis Group

LONDON AND NEW YORK

First published 2006
by Routledge
2 Park Square, Milton Park, Abingdon, Oxon OX14 4RN

Simultaneously published in the USA and Canada
by Routledge
270 Madison Ave, New York, NY 10016

Transferred to Digital Printing 2006

Routledge is an imprint of the Taylor & Francis Group, an informa business

Typeset in Baskerville by
Newgen Imaging Systems (P) Ltd, Chennai, India
Printed and bound in Great Britain by
Biddles Ltd, King's Lynn

British Library Cataloguing in Publication Data
A catalogue record for this book is available from the British Library

Library of Congress Cataloging in Publication Data
A catalog record for this book has been requested

ISBN 10: 0–415–33876–X
ISBN 13: 978–0–415–33876–9

To Smart Father and his two little monkeys
Alessandra and Giulia

Contents

Preface   xix

Introduction   1

Aims of this book 1
Optimistic views of the NE 1
Sceptical or pessimistic views of the NE 2
The key question addressed in this book 4
Macroeconomic data are insufficient for the study of stability 5
The crisis in current economic theory 6
The limitations of neoclassical theory 6
The limitations of Keynesianism 7
A neo-modern alternative 8
Complexity theory 9
Calvino's labels 9
Our modelling strategy 10
The generality of Keynesian theory 11
Plan of the work 11

PART I
Alternative approaches to stability   13

1 Equilibrium without structural change   15

Key aspects of neoclassical methodology 15
Stability as an article of faith 17
Limitations of the stability assumption 18
Can we demonstrate that the economy is stable? 21

2   Instability and dynamic equilibrium   23

Harrod and Keynesian growth theory 23
The neo-Ricardians 25
Kaldor, Robinson and Minsky 26
Non-linear dynamics 26
New Growth Theory 29
Limitations of growth models 31

3   Structural change without equilibrium   35

A theory of reasoned history 35
Techno-Economic Paradigms 37
Critique of aggregates 38
Analysis of interactions and complementarities 38
Instability 40
*Limitations: the dangers of technological
    determinism 41*
*The dangers of disregarding macroeconomic
    equilibrium 42*

PART II
Stability analysis and the neo-modern
perspective   47

4   The crisis in economic theory and the neo-modern
     perspective   49

Modernism 50
Post-modernism: general features 52
Post-modernism: its implications for economics 54
The neo-modern alternative 55

5   Complexity theory   58

Vision 58
Light theory 60
Dynamic versus structural simplification 61
Elements of 'realism' 63
The complementarity view 64
Inductive approach 67
Stability 68
Limitations to the SFA 70

The lack of systemic dynamic laws 70
Failure to account for complex patterns 71
Lack of explanatory power 73

6 **Our approach to stability: structural change and**
   instantaneous equilibrium   74

   Some general features of our meta-model 74
   Focus on complex historical patterns 74
   Institutions as generating functions of complex patterns 76
   Macro models and interpretations of complex patterns 78
   The key steps in our simplification strategy 79

PART III
The two basic macroeconomic paradigms   81

7 **The neoclassical macro model**   83

   The key causal factors 83
   The gap between pure theory and actual phenomena 84
   Friedman's attempt to overcome the gap 85

8 **Keynes's macro model**   88

   Keynes and the complexity approach 88
   The generality of the General Theory *90*
   The distinction between primary and secondary variables 93
   Primary and secondary variables in the basic macro models 95
   Is there a 'philosophical' justification for the causal ordering
   *   in the* General Theory? *96*
   The irreducibility of expectations: a critique of psychologism 98
   Keynes's broader notion of essence 100

9 **Some key differences between Keynes**
   and the 'Classics'   104

   Keynes's alternative to psychologism and institutional determinism 104
   Institutions as exogenous data 105
   Keynes's macro and the institutions of the modern economy 106
   Keynes versus standard dynamic approaches 108
   Keynes and stability 108
   Keynes's informal dynamic method 109
   Stability and the instantaneous equilibrium model 112
   Beyond Keynes 113

PART IV
**A preliminary account of stability of
the New Economy**   117

10 A broad definition of the New Economy   119

The NE as consisting of a number of key factors 120
Interrelations among economic factors 121
The overlap between the economic and socio-institutional spheres 123
Micro–macro features 126
Acceleration of certain key trends 128
The five empirical laws of the NE 130

11 Multiplicity   131

A new division of labour 132
Market unification 132
Negative externality effects 133
Fragmentation of structural conditions 134
Reduced autonomy of national economies 135
Instability due to the plurality of models 136
*Problems in the governance of the
    world economy 137*
Lack of convergence 138

12 Rapidity   140

Productivity growth 141
Acceleration of positive feedbacks 142
Greater flexibility of the goods market 143
Greater flexibility in the labour market 144
More rapid obsolescence 145
*Problems due to the nature of contemporary
    knowledge 146*
Technological unemployment 146
Product differentiation 146
*Greater heterogeneity in structural
    conditions of the household 147*

13 Lightness   148

Extension of the market logic 149
Broader concept of value and capital 150
Faster expansion of financial markets 151

Problems in the quality of goods 152
Instability due to deregulation 154
Erratic behaviour of financial markets 155

14 Precision   158

More data and better measurement techniques 158
*A more important role of 'formalist' values
    in economics 159*
Attempt to improve forecasting 160
Measurement problems 161
Modelling problems 162
Forecasting problems 163

15 Visibility   165

Monetary policy rules 166
Pragmatic monetary policy 169
Fiscal policy rules 170
Pragmatic fiscal policy 171
Rules for markets 173
Pragmatic structural policies 176
On the limits of general policy rules 177
Lack of a general model to guide monetary policy 178
The inflation target may be too low 178
Uncertainty about the potential growth rate 178
Macroeconomic problems beyond inflation 179
The risk of moral hazard 179
Crowd-in effects may be weak 179
Instability due to expenditure cuts 180
Instability due to tax cuts 181
The limits of setting rules for markets 181
On the limits of pragmatic policy 182

PART V
The New Economy and macroeconomic theories   185

**16 New Classical Macroeconomics and the
New Economy: an overview**   187

The NE and the 'deep' parameters 188
The 'normal' working of the economy 188

Economic fluctuations 190
A general view of the NE 192

17 New Classical Macroeconomics and the key features of the New Economy 195

Multiplicity 195
Rapidity 198
Lightness 200
Precision 202
Visibility: general remarks 205
Monetary policy 206
Fiscal and structural policy 208
NCM and instability due to visibility 209

18 Keynesian theory and the New Economy: an overview 212

The NE and Keynes's broader notion of essence 212
The 'normal' working of the economy 214
A broad view of economic fluctuations 215
The endogenous nature of business cycles 215
'Global' versus 'local' imperfections 216
Business cycles and institutional changes 219
The analysis of long-run trends 220
A general view of the NE 221
The Keynesian model and specific features of the NE 224

19 Keynesian theory and multiplicity 226

Growing interdependence between individuals and countries 227
Winners and losers 228
Governance of the world economy 229

20 Keynesian theory and rapidity 230

Technological change and labour market flexibility 231
Wage flexibility: dynamic versus static analysis 232
The nature of contemporary knowledge 234
*Greater heterogeneity in structural conditions
    and agents' behaviour 236*

21 Keynesian theory and lightness

237

The quality issue 237
Deregulation and financial innovation 239
Erratic behaviour of financial markets 240

22 Keynesian theory and precision

244

Management by numbers 244
Conventional methods and indicators 245
The widening gap between theoretical and empirical progress 246
Predictive failures 246

23 Keynesian theory and visibility

248

Growth as a condition for stability 248
The intrinsic limits of pragmatism 248
A new discretionary policy stance 249
Monetary policy 250
Fiscal policy 252
Structural policies and rules for markets 255

Conclusion

258

The neo-modern perspective and the building of scenarios 258
The generality of the Keynesian scenario 259
The dynamic stability of the NE 261
The structural stability of the NE 262
Macroeconomic theories and the features of the NE 263
Policy implications 264

Notes 267
Biliography 285
Index 299

Preface

Several parts of this book have benefited from discussion and debate at seminars and conferences. In particular, some of the ideas developed here were first presented at the meetings of the Evolutionary Association of Political Economy (EAEPE) held in Siena and Maastricht. Further stimulus for writing this book came from my participation in the NESIS (New Economic Statistical Information Systems) project, financed by the European Commission. I heartily thank all of the participants at these events for their stimulating discussions and insights. Many of the ideas contained in this book have also evolved over the years through the exchange of views with numerous colleagues and scholars. It is impossible to thank them all, but I would like to offer particular thanks to Victoria Chick and Terenzio Cozzi for their constant encouragement to develop my ideas about Keynes. I would also like to thank the following people for comments on parts of this book: Fabio Bagliano, David Colander, Andrea De Panizza, Clark Eustace, Maurizio Franzini, Eva Hagsten, Paschal Preston, Deo Ramprakash, Paolo Riguzzi, Graham Room, Mauro Visaggio, Adrian Winnett, Teun Wolters and Tony Clayton.

Finally, I wish to thank Laura McLean who has helped me to improve my English style and Robert Langham of Routledge for his patience and kind encouragement throughout the stages of the book.

Introduction

Aims of this book

The New Economy (NE) – defined here as the transformation that has been taking place in leading economies (especially in the US) since 1995 – is a phenomenon that has attracted enormous interest and given rise to numerous comments and debate both in the media and in academic journals. Much of the literature on this topic focuses on specific aspects of the NE, such as the effects of the new technologies on corporate management and productivity, or the way customers can benefit from the Internet. In contrast, this book analyses the implications of the NE for macroeconomic stability, taken in a very broad sense as encompassing both cyclical and growth issues. The rationale for this choice is that we subscribe to the view held, for example, by Rostow (1990: 428–31), according to which cycles are simply the historical form that growth takes, and that to treat them separately is a form of intellectual violence that rules out the very heart of the problem of both cycle and growth (see also Archibugi 2000: ch. 2; Freeman and Louçã 2001: chs 1–4).

These issues seem to be even more relevant now that the NE has completed its parable from boom to depression than a few years ago, when the NE still held the spotlight. The passage of time allows us to form a more balanced interpretation of the phenomenon and of the main opinions surrounding it. While most authors agree that the term NE refers to the important shift in the US economy that took place in the 1990s, opinions differ as to the nature of this shift.[1] For the sake of simplicity, we shall refer to the two broad lines of interpretation appearing in the literature as the 'optimistic' and 'pessimistic' stance.

Optimistic views of the NE

The optimistic stance has been expressed in a variety of ways. The first, which thrived in the euphoric atmosphere of the late nineties and which was widely touted by the media (especially in newspapers and magazines such as the *Wall Street Journal* and *Fortune*), very simply declared that computers are changing everything about the economy. In particular, it heralded the NE as the onset of a Golden Age in which the business cycle would disappear and the laws of old economics would no longer apply (e.g. Weber 1997; Kelly 1998). These authors clearly held a very optimistic, techno-centric vision of economic growth, where the future of the NE was envisioned as a linear development of the current technical potentialities and where stability problems would never arise because technological progress is virtually unstoppable.

Another view, analytically much more robust than the previous one and quite widespread among economists, holds instead that the NE does not abolish the business cycle but amplifies the relative stability already achieved by the US economy following 1945. In particular, several authors point out that the new technologies moderate the business cycle by reducing transaction costs, improving information and allowing new inventory management methods (e.g. McConnell and Perez-Quiros 2000), accelerating financial innovation and deregulation (e.g. Kose *et al.* 2003) or even allowing the system to approach the perfect competition model (e.g. the *Economist* 1–4–2000).

Sceptical or pessimistic views of the NE

The second broad stance, which has gained favour since the recent stock market crashes and strong economic slowdown in all major countries, holds instead that the beneficial impact of the NE on the macro economy does not really justify the kind of revolutionary hopes garnered in the early years. For many, enthusiasm for Information, Communication and Technology (ICT) just went too far, although the excessive optimism of the 1990s should not give way to excessive pessimism now (e.g. Baily 2002: 18–21). Other claims regarding NEs (e.g. in 1929 and in the 1960s) have always been proven wrong in the past, and the recent NE is no exception (see e.g. Shiller 2000: ch. 6; Boyer 2004). In particular, the phenomenon of the business cycle persists, with at least qualitative continuity in its mechanisms and effects, despite immense structural changes (e.g. DeLong 1999: 19–20; Baily 2002: 18).

But the authors expressing this moderate and, at this point, practically undisputed claim do not stop here. They also put forward further views concerning the nature of the NE. Strictly speaking, one can note two main broad opinions within this group. The first is to suggest that since the NE fails to abolish the cycle, then it must have only a rather modest impact on the macro economy. Indeed, as Baily argues, macroeconomists have reason to be sceptical about the term NE.[2] This view is expressed in several different, though often not mutually exclusive, ways:

- by stressing that the main effects of the NE appear at the micro or structural level and that it is difficult to link these to the business cycle and the macro level (see e.g. Cohen *et al.* 2000: 3);[3]
- by pointing out that while the NE certainly caused a significant revival of productivity, the increase is not exceptional by historical standards and has a rather limited impact on the economy's potential income and long-run growth. Gordon notes, for example, that: 'virtually all the progress has been

concentrated in the durable manufacturing sector with surprisingly little spillover to the rest of the economy... There are no sign of a fundamental transformation of the US economy' (Gordon 2002: 18–9);

- by arguing that the NE, and especially the US economic miracle, is not the inevitable result of structural changes induced by globalization or ICT but is due to exceptional factors or sheer good luck (e.g. Krugman 2000; Stiglitz 2002b). In this vein, Stock and Watson (2003) suggest that the recent lower output volatility is mainly the result of smaller macro shocks;

- by considering the moderation of the business cycle in recent decades to be the result of improved policy-making, such as the introduction of automatic stabilizers and the reduced volatility of public expenditure (e.g. Blanchard and Simon 2001; Auerbach 2002) or the important lessons learnt about how to better conduct monetary policy (see, e.g. DeLong 1999, 2003; C. Romer 1999; Clarida *et al.* 2000; Blanchard and Simon 2001; Banerji 2002; Baker 2003; Bernanke 2004; Martin and Rowthorn 2004). DeLong stresses, for example, with reference to the US, the 'FED's greater success at maintaining its balance: at acting pre-emptively and maintaining an appropriate balance between price stability and maximum purchasing power, rather than careening from one objective to the other...' (2003: 2), as well as 'the swift reaction of the FED to 1987, to 1998, to 2001 shocks' (ibid.) (i.e. stock market crashes and financial panic).

The second opinion is more pessimistic. It underlines that the NE does not improve macroeconomic performance or simply leave it unaffected but that it also implies some new dangers for macroeconomic stability. According to various authors, while the recent business cycles were induced by restrictive policy,[4] the NE implies instead that relatively more dangerous business cycles driven by changes in animal spirits have returned. This is recognized by Baily (2002: 18), for example, who emphasizes that the recession in 2001, which involved large swings in inventory and investment, resembles old-style pre-Keynesian recessions (see also DeLong and Eichengreen 2001; the *Economist* 10–3–2001).[5] Moreover, as Baily (2001: 250) points out, information technology has not improved our capacity to foresee the economic future. In the end, neo-Schumpeterian authors like Perez (2002) and Freeman and Louçã (2001) (see also Louçã 2003) regard the NE as a new Techno-Economic Paradigm that brings about major structural changes which may have rather negative effects at the macroeconomic level, such as persistent structural unemployment and speculative bubbles leading to major downturns and recessions.

To summarize the key characteristics of this second stance, we can refer to a representative contribution such as Zarnowitz's brilliant 1999 paper making five main points.[6] First, the concept of instability is not obsolete in the NE. The NE is not necessarily more stable than the old economy; neither improved inventory control nor a shift towards services nor deregulation *per se* grant greater stability.

Second, the NE is a complex phenomenon; it consists of a number of interrelated features, not just ICT. The greater expansion of financial markets, globalization, and the liberalization of markets are also important.

Third, Zarnowitz stresses what we call 'duality', namely the fact that these features are two-edged swords: they tend to have dual effects, both positive and negative. There is reason to believe, for example, that although globalization may reduce cyclical instability for a number of reasons, it can also bring about increased vulnerability.[7]

Fourth, Zarnowitz endorses an endogenous view of business cycles, in contrast with the believers in the inherent stability of market economies, who attribute recessions to policy errors and external disturbances. In particular, he criticizes the view that business cycles in the NE, as in the old economy, can be accounted for primarily by productivity shocks induced by ICT. The latter will not *per se* assure greater macroeconomic stability, as most technical changes are gradual and localized. To understand the business cycles in the NE, one should take into account a number of interrelated factors. Zarnowitz stresses, for example, that 'recessions originate mainly in market developments: overconfidence, over borrowing and over-investment' and that an 'endogenous approach focuses on . . . links between profits, investment, credit, stock exchange, inflation and interest rates; these interactions are central to process of economic fluctuations and growth' (1999: 72). In the end, Zarnowitz emphasizes that discretionary government macro policies may reduce or end cyclical instability, although incorrect policies can also destabilize the economy.

The key question addressed in this book

These two basic views represent the background for our analysis. Briefly, the question at stake is whether the NE implies more or less real instability, that is, whether the observed relative stability in traditional macro data is due to greater stability of the private sector or to smarter economic policy. This book suggests that to come to definite conclusions concerning this issue we must not rely on a priori views but should make a preliminary step (which, in principle, economists of all persuasions can agree upon), namely, to identify the largest number of potential sources of instability and to assess to what extent they are real. In other words, we should draw stability conclusions based on a comprehensive account or map, so to speak, of the relevant endogenous and exogenous mechanisms involved in order to determine the overall performance of real economic systems.

In particular, we have to assess to what extent the NE is characterized by either dynamic or structural instability, that is, whether it implies slower convergence towards a given state of equilibrium or important changes in agents' qualitative behaviour giving rise to shifts from one equilibrium to another (for an analysis of this distinction see, for example Vercelli 1991: 30). In the light of this object of analysis, the key premise underlying this book is that the best way to study stability is to adopt – much in the spirit of Zarnowitz – a full-blown approach to the complexity of the NE that takes into account the interactions between its key factors.

Macroeconomic data are insufficient for the study of stability

In order to develop our analysis along these lines, two major problems need be solved: first, what is the relevant empirical evidence, and, second, what are the appropriate methods to use? These problems arise because the standard macroeconomic tools and data are either insufficient or inadequate. For example, it can be argued that, despite their obvious usefulness, standard indicators such as Gross Domestic Product (GDP) or employment or labour productivity do not fully allow us to distinguish between stable and unstable outcomes. They fail to tell us a complete story for a number of reasons.

First, these aggregates are influenced by macroeconomic policies and the existence of automatic stabilizers. For instance, it is true that, as macro data show, there has been a recovery in the US economy after 2001. However, it would be quite hasty to conclude that this economy is stable. As many recognize, this recovery is not a 'spontaneous' product of market forces but is undoubtedly due to a large extent to expansionary, monetary and fiscal policy.

Second, these aggregates provide an insufficient early warning system for policy-makers. While the recent macro performance of the US is reassuring to policy-makers, they should probably not be so complacent. Things look quite different when one acknowledges that the US recovery coexists with (or is even bought at the expense of) huge structural imbalances (e.g. the so-called twin deficits in public finance and current account of the balance of payments and huge private debt), casting serious doubts on the future prospects of the US economy.

Third, standard aggregates are becoming much less significant, as the NE economy is characterized by important dimensions of qualitative change, such as the greater weight of services and intangibles in the GDP, which are extremely difficult to quantify and are often overlooked by statistical systems. Focusing on the standard aggregates does not appear to be enough to capture the peculiarity of the NE and the new stability problems it faces. For example, recent productivity data alone do not characterize the NE; industrialized countries have already experienced major productivity gains before (e.g. in the 1960s).

These problems suggest that identifying a new set of indicators that go beyond the standard ones for assessing instability is not a straightforward task. It is certainly not a purely empirical issue that can somehow be 'fixed' by using pragmatic devices in applied research. What we need instead is to devise a set of new methodological 'rules of the game' to help us examine the NE without encountering these problems. For example, if we want to grasp the peculiarity of the NE, it would be useful to define it in terms of a few irreversible trends, such as the acceleration of technological change and to evaluate it in terms of corresponding new pieces of empirical evidence, such as Moore's law (according to which computing power doubles every eighteen months).

The crisis in current economic theory

Before going into detail about such rules, we must be aware that the problem faced by the analysis of stability is not only with data. Standard macroeconomic methods are also unsatisfactory for studying this issue. As pointed out by DeLong, for example, there is a gap between theory and descriptive accounts of the business cycles in the tradition of Wesley Mitchell's approach:

> Observers of the business cycles have long felt that this approach contains profound truth – yet it has never been well-integrated into old Keynesian, new Keynesian, monetarist, or new classical business cycle theories. Just what is it about the structure of capitalist market economies that causes real economic activity to rise and fall in ways that seem to show certain empirical regularities?
>
> (DeLong 1999: 21)

We suggest that similar considerations apply to growth theory. Strictly speaking, it is true that the gap between theory and empirical analysis underlies all branches of economics so that it is appropriate to speak of a general 'crisis in economic theory'. However, this gap appears particularly serious in the analysis of the dynamic behaviour of economies, given the strange dichotomy we face in this field. On the one hand, we find pretentious academic attempts at uncovering a few of 'God's equations' governing the evolution of a complex economy. On the other we see more practical minded people and institutions building rich and well-informed scenarios concerning the tendencies of real-world economies. These, however, are often based only on an intuitive or informal (i.e. not explicitly derived from economic theory) grasp of the interactions among key phenomena. In our view, the key explanation for this gap is that current macroeconomic theory is unable to provide a satisfactory stability analysis along the lines described earlier.

The limitations of neoclassical theory

To make this clear, let us refer to the two basic paradigms in macroeconomics, that is, neoclassical and Keynesian theory, which broadly correspond to the two interpretations of the NE summarized earlier. For neoclassicals, the market economy based on full price flexibility is intrinsically stable, unless institutional factors or policy-makers disturb it in some way. In their view, the NE confirms this basic insight because they take it for granted that phenomena such as globalization and technological change would have mostly beneficial effects.

This stability assumption has some obvious limitations for the kind of analysis we want to pursue here. First, it constrains neoclassical theory to provide an account of short-run instability only in terms of rigidities and market imperfections (e.g. lagged adjustment in prices and expectations). This account is inadequate for a number of reasons. Suffice it to note that it fails to consider endogenous mechanisms. This is because it relies on a range of exogenous or *ad hoc* factors that are dealt with in a partial equilibrium fashion, that is to say, in such a way that each factor alone appears to be responsible for unfavourable outcomes, such as recessions.

Second, it provides an explanation of long-run instability emphasizing supply-side factors. Following its use of production functions to analyse growth issues, neoclassical theory holds that countries that face sluggish growth of income or productivity have an insufficient endowment of productive factors, such as labour force or various types of capital.

Moreover, production functions deal with these supply-side factors in a reduction-ist way. They are bound, for example, to consider them as independent rather than interrelated, as they often are in the real world (see e.g. Freeman 1988; Fine 2003: 210–11). As noted by Fine (2003), for example, in the statistical work associated with New Growth Theory (NGT), which is often used to deal with the NE, it is recognized that more than a hundred variables will affect endogenous growth, from R&D expenditure to levels of democracy and trust or indeed any variable that might be deemed to affect economic performance. But he rightly points out that

> it is scarcely credible that the hundred or more conditional variables are inde-pendent of one another and in their effects on growth. So a full model of interaction ought to be laid out...(but) such a model is mathematically intractable and the simple ad hoc device of adding variables to the regression has been used in the absence of any rationale other than to test for them.
>
> (Fine 2003: 210–11)

In the end, standard models focus on relatively narrow co-movements, ruling out phenomena which do not behave like stationary stochastic processes (see e.g. Vercelli 1991: 141).

The limitations of Keynesianism

Let us now focus on the Keynesian camp. Keynesians seem generally better equipped to deal with stability problems than their neoclassical counterparts. They in principle emphasize the role of both endogenous and exogenous mechanisms and supply and demand factors in both short and long-run analysis. They have a priori views that the private economy is unstable and that policy is needed to keep it on track. In other words, stability is not a property inherent in the market economy or the interaction of atomistic individuals, it is a property of the system as a whole, once institutions and the intervention of the state have been taken into account. Their interpretation of the NE fits this view. As already noted, Keynesians regard phenomena such as globalization and technological change as having both positive and negative effects and suggest that relative stability is due to smarter policy intervention.

However, there are some powerful obstacles in the way of a full-fledged Keynesian approach to stability. The major one is that Keynesian theory and its key principle of effective demand is seen by most economists as applying only to the short-run. This view is especially popular among Schumpeterian economists, according to whom:

> Keynesianism...did not deal with deeply rooted, long-run sectoral problems. Geared to demand-side management...Keynesians neglect such factors as technology and developments in particular industrial sectors...within the Keynesian system there was no room for productivity, no way to stimulate or spur it...
>
> (Rosenof 1997: 146)

This view is so widespread that many Keynesian macroeconomists simply take the long-run neoclassical equilibrium concept and its underlying stability assumption for granted. Another obstacle to the successful extension of Keynesian analysis in the long run is that previous attempts in this direction, such as those by Harrod, or by Hansen with his stagnationist approach, have emphasized particular mechanisms (e.g. the instability principle or exogenous shocks such as population increase or technological change) as the key, neglecting the interrelations between a number of phenomena.

A neo-modern alternative

In the face of the two basic problems arising in the analysis of the NE – namely the need to single out both a more refined set of indicators to capture instability and a modelling strategy capable of overcoming the gap between current macroeconomic methods and reliance on informal scenarios – the main aim of our analysis can now be stated more completely. This book proposes a solution to such problems by developing a full-blown analysis of interactions inspired by what we call the 'neo-modern' view.

This view amounts to suggesting that the best way to address a long-run issue, such as stability, is not to rely on a priori views or formal approaches seeking to demonstrate the operation of particular mechanisms. It is better to proceed, so to speak, in an *ex post* fashion, that is, to assess and compare the stabilizing and destabilizing factors that occur in actual economies. It must be noted, however, that we are not proposing a purely empirical or a-theoretical stance. According to the neo-modern perspective – which reflects the attempt to overcome the limitations of both modernist and post-modernist canons that have exercised a deep influence in many areas, including economics – models have a limited but useful role to play in the analysis of complex dynamics.

In particular, unlike modernists stressing unifying, all encompassing theoretical projects (such as the general equilibrium approach), neo-modernists regard models as singling out only partial causal stories, like pieces of a puzzle. However, in contrast with post-modernist views ultimately implying the fragmentation of economics, neo-modernists do not give up unifying visions altogether. They suggest that models can be meaningfully combined or integrated to complete the puzzle.

In other words, the task we try to accomplish in proposing this new neo-modern label is to help economists derive scenarios more rigorously than they currently do. In short, neo-modernism consists of a general attempt to extend the boundaries of science into areas, such as stability analysis, which are badly covered by current standard methods.

Complexity theory

Fortunately, this enterprise need not start from scratch. In our view, the complexity theory is one of the approaches that fits this neo-modern perspective. We believe that, despite its many shortcomings, 'the complexity concept holds much more potential for reconstructing economic theory than is currently being exploited by economists' (Viskovatoff 2000: 130). We suggest that the complexity theory can also be useful for the purposes of this book. In particular, it is quite relevant for macroeconomics and global stability analysis, because it proposes a powerful vision of the economy as a whole, stressing, for example, that the idea of pluralism of systems and the evolution of economic forces are cumulative and time irreversible. It presents phenomena, such as positive feedbacks, increasing returns, self-organization nonlinearities, path-dependence and lock-in (see e.g. Arthur 1994; Colander 2000a,b; Comim 2000: 155, 183; Pryor 2000: 63), which seem relevant for the NE.

Moreover, this approach does not seek to provide a unified, all encompassing, theory. It demotes theory to a lower level, especially when compared to general equilibrium analysis (the archetypical instance of 'hard theory'). In the complexity view, theory appears to be 'light', that is, it no longer appears as a purely deductive and self-contained sphere. Much more emphasis is placed on the knowledge of economic history and the history of economics.

Especially relevant for our purposes is that complexity theory – as developed especially by the Santa Fe Institute and by a number of authors stressing an institutional view of complexity (e.g. North 1990; Prasch 2000a,b; Viskovatoff 2000) – provides useful insights on the two key issues we have identified, namely the identification of new indicators and of an appropriate modelling strategy for dealing with stability.

Calvino's labels

As for the first issue, complexity theory can be seen as a good source of inspiration for the 'rules' that allow us to describe the NE and identify the major sources of instability. Following these rules, we can describe the NE in terms of a few key patterns or empirical 'laws' concerning the economy as a whole which are able to reflect what Pryor (2000) calls 'dimensions of structural complexity', that is, the main structural changes brought about by the NE. The patterns we have in mind refer to the acceleration of certain processes, such as globalization, technological change, the weight of finance and services, the focus on data and forecasts, the role of the state and so on, which seem to characterize the NE in all major countries. These patterns are of an historical–institutional kind, because they are shaped to a large extent by institutional factors. There is a strict link, for example, between the acceleration of globalization and a certain institutional set-up (e.g. liberalization of markets, anti-monopolistic laws, trade agreements and exchange rate regimes) that allowed the 'creation' of continent-wide and inter-continental markets in the past decades.

In principle, these patterns can be expressed in different ways. In this book, we have chosen to group the main features of the NE under a few broad categories or labels ('multiplicity', 'rapidity', 'lightness', 'precision' and 'visibility') which were first suggested by the Italian post-modern writer, Italo Calvino, during his Norton Lectures at Harvard University, to characterize the last century in general (see Calvino 1993).[8] Among the key advantages of this classification system, the most prominent is that it fits our effort to account for interactions between a number of economic phenomena and institutional factors.

Our modelling strategy

The second contribution of the complexity approach is that it broadly inspires our modelling strategy for dealing with the stability of the NE. First, like this approach, we subscribe to the 'light theory' canon. This means that we do not rule out theory as such, but we narrow down the potential of current macroeconomic theories – that is, both the neoclassical and Keynesian paradigms – to a weak notion of equilibrium, such as instantaneous equilibrium. In other words, we believe that while 'light theory' rules out stationary long-run equilibrium states and deterministic laws of long-term evolution of complex systems, it is not necessarily inconsistent with instantaneous equilibrium. This plays the role of benchmark in the analysis, as it shows the key factors playing a causal role at any given moment in time.

On this basis, we underline two major points in this book. First, we suggest that the two basic macro paradigms highlight different causal factors, in view of the fact that they rely on alternative visions of the economic process or what can be more precisely regarded as the 'essence' of it. While neoclassical theory stresses the key or essential role of productive resources and atomistic preferences, Keynesian theory emphasizes instead aggregate propensities and monetary factors that determine aggregate demand. It should be clear, however, that it does not simply ignore resources. Rather, it regards them as 'secondary givens' that can play a role only by affecting the causal factors. For example, a technological breakthrough, such as ICT, does not determine outcomes *per se*, but it does play a role by influencing the propensity to invest.

Secondly, in line with complexity theory, we do not seek to replace existing theories, but to integrate them: we believe that the Keynesian and neoclassical approaches both have a role to play in stability analysis. In particular, they can be used to construct something like a 'meta-model' or perhaps even a new branch of macroeconomics. The contribution of these basic paradigms is twofold. The first is in highlighting specific causal mechanisms that account for the main stabilizing and destabilizing forces at work. The other is in deriving a perspective on global stability or a scenario of major trends by considering the various mechanisms in a coherent picture. In our book, we shall derive two scenarios from the basic macro paradigms and then draw a comparison between them in order to derive more general conclusions on stability.

The generality of Keynesian theory

It should be clear that this meta-modelling approach does not neutralize the theoretical differences between the two paradigms; the 'Keynes versus Classics' dispute is revitalized, although at a different level. It can be shown that Keynesian theory actually represents the most general framework.

The claim to generality concerning Keynes's theory is justified for two reasons. First, Keynes provides the most general account of instantaneous equilibrium, following the fact that Keynes adds a new dimension to neoclassical analysis. While the latter stresses self-interest and competition, Keynes holds that the 'mutual interest' dimension, which reflects the existence of a basic interdependence among economic agents, must also be considered as a real determinant of behaviour. This view, which finds analytical expression in concepts such as the paradox of saving or the multiplier, underlies his belief that macroeconomics is an autonomous discipline based on systemic principles (i.e. which transcend the individual agent).

Second, the Keynesian paradigm also provides the most general scenario. Unlike its neoclassical counterpart, it relies on changeable parameters, such as those underlying the aggregate demand function. Based on the distinction between causal factors and secondary givens, this paradigm actually shows that the principle of effective demand can be used to account for the effects on stability of structural changes, such as those induced by the NE. In particular, changes in the secondary givens (e.g. technology, population and forms of the market) influence the stability of the economy by determining changes in agents' propensities. It can be argued, for example, that the rapidity of technological progress and the diffusion of intangibles determine a shortening of investors and consumers' horizons, with sizeable effects on the stability of aggregate expenditure.

Plan of the work

The analysis of the macroeconomic stability of the NE is developed in three basic steps. The first step – which is carried out in Parts I–III – consists in discussing stability from the methodological and analytical standpoint. In Part I, from Chapters 1 to 3, we provide an assessment of the existing approaches to stability in economic theory. In Part II, from Chapters 4 to 6, we then clarify the main features of our neo-modern approach, placing it in the context of the debates concerning modernism and post-modernism, on the one hand, and complexity theory as developed by the Santa Fe Institute on the other. Finally, in Part III, from Chapters 7 to 9, we compare the two basic macroeconomic paradigms, clarifying the reasons why it is justified to regard Keynesian theory as being more general than its neoclassical counterpart.

The second step is developed in Part IV from Chapters 10 to 15 and concerns a broad definition of the NE and an initial preliminary account of its stability. Chapter 10 singles out the new methodological criteria that help us to single out the new patterns or 'dimensions of structural complexity', taking many factors simultaneously into account and seeking to integrate historical and institutional factors in the analysis. This analysis shows that these patterns can be summarized by Calvino's labels. The prima facie account of stability in the remaining chapters is carried out by taking stock of various causal mechanisms that are emphasized by several commentators of the NE, whether or not they are explicitly derived from macro models.

The third step of the analysis, carried out in Chapters 16–23 of Part V, is to develop a more formal discussion of stability by deriving alternative scenarios concerning the NE. The purpose here is to start from the two basic theoretical frameworks we have singled out (New Classical Macroeconomics (NCM) and Keynesian theory) and account for their strengths and weaknesses in terms of the explanatory power of the key features of the NE.

Part I

Alternative approaches to stability

Part I of this volume examines a number of approaches to the analysis of stability. As noted in the introduction, it is not enough for our purposes to rely on mere observation of macroeconomic indicators, for these incorporate policy moves and, thus, may obscure structural change. We have also argued that a fully satisfactory approach to stability issues has to include structural analysis concerning the sources of qualitative change arising from the interplay of a number of key phenomena, while operating within the context of a relatively weak notion of macroeconomic equilibrium.

What follows is an attempt to determine how well the existing approaches fulfil this ideal. As shall be seen, none of them is entirely successful, despite the valuable insights they provide. Neoclassical theory, dealt with in Chapter 1, adopts a strong notion of equilibrium but neglects to consider structural change. Instead, the relatively heterodox theoretical perspectives discussed in Chapter 2 combine a concern for certain forms of instability with weaker notions of dynamic equilibrium. Finally, the neo-Schumpeterian approach, discussed in Chapter 3, stresses structural change without equilibrium.

The overview provided in Part I is not intended to be exhaustive. Other approaches to instability, such as those by Minsky and the theory of transformational growth (e.g. Nell 2002), have not been included because they can be seen as akin or complementary to the Keynesian perspective defended in this book. They will therefore be addressed more explicitly in later sections, along with a discussion of Keynes' theories.

1 Equilibrium without structural change

In this chapter we focus on how neoclassical theory, with its strong roots in the tradition of general equilibrium economics, treats the issue of stability. Since analysis of the NE inevitably implies reference to some notion of equilibrium, it seems only natural to assume that the standard concept of general equilibrium intrinsic in much of current macroeconomics might serve as a good starting point for the study of stability. However, this would be a very hasty conclusion. Given that it considers the system to be inherently stable, both dynamically and structurally, standard general equilibrium theory is clearly not suited for the task.

Key aspects of neoclassical methodology

It is worth noting from the start that the assumption of stability underlying neoclassical theory does not derive from sheer neglect of complexity. Nor does it stem from the a priori ruling out of particular variables and their interrelations. For example, neoclassical theory acknowledges the existence of a range of factors capable of influencing economic growth; moreover, in its analysis of the NE, it readily admits the existence of factors other than ICT, such as globalization or finance. Rather, the premise of stability in neoclassical theory is the inevitable outcome of how general equilibrium theory deals with this multitude of variables and their interrelations. Above all, it is a result of the reductionist approach adopted by standard theorists that leads them 'to remove anything that could create inherent instability from their models' (Tvede 2001: 164). This is accomplished by adopting a number of key assumptions (e.g. linearity, perfect competition and negative feedback mechanisms) and analytical tools (e.g. production functions and representative agent devices) as the basis for the macroeconomic and econometric models used to study fluctuations and growth.

Let us take a closer look at the particular features of standard models that allow any assumption of instability factors to be ruled out. First of all, theory within the general equilibrium tradition is taken to be a purely deductive and self-contained sphere or 'closed system' (see e.g. Lawson 1997; Dow 2002; Chick 2003). One implication of this stance is that standard models admit a clear-cut definition of exogenous and endogenous variables and accept the 'economicist' view that 'the boundaries of the economic sphere are objectively defined' (Freeman and Louça

2001: 110). Having defined the maximizing behaviour of atomistic agents as the canon of rationality and the 'first principle' of economic analysis, standard theory holds that one can endogenize, that is, explain in terms of rational behaviour, certain factors such as state intervention, social institutions or cultural characteristics. Indeed, according to Gary Becker's approach, for example, phenomena such as education and skills, crime, the household and even addiction can be 'treated as if [they were] the outcome of rational (utility maximizing) behaviour by individuals, albeit in what often are non-market contexts' (Fine 2003: 214).

Second, standard theory takes the view of economies as cumulative and linear processes. The assumption of linearity allows a facile solution to the complexity of interrelations. Standard models tend to focus on a small number of variables and to group related factors together under some exogenous residual random term. For this purpose, these models 'assume linearity somehow and then brush off the remainder as statistical noise' (Freeman and Louçã 2001: 109; Tvede 2001: 186). In particular, production functions and growth accounting exercises treat technological change essentially as an exogenous shock or residual. Technological change is, therefore, regarded as having simple, linear effects on the economy under artificial conditions (perfect or unbounded rationality, free competition, full availability of perfect information, etc.), introducing the concept of what can be referred to as 'technological determinism'.

Third, neoclassical theory is based on a mechanistic view, according to which it is possible to reason in terms of atomistic relations, or relatively isolated sub-sets of the complex socio-economic system. Thus, for example, standard theories rely on the *ceteris paribus* condition, following Mill's approach. While they do take into consideration a wide variety of factors, these are dealt with separately, as though independent. The individual causal factors analysed in isolation from all other factors can then be – ideally – combined with them once all theorizing is complete. In other words, analysis is carried about before synthesis (see Viskovatoff 2000: 151). A mechanistic view also implies that it makes sense to isolate pure market forces from their institutional context, which can be taken as a given. The implicit assumption is that markets tend to perform the task of allocation no matter what kind of shocks or institutional context are at work in the economy.[1] For example, despite the enormous institutional differences between countries, competition is assumed to bring about certain outcomes – such as international price uniformity – as implied by the law of one price or the purchasing power parity theorem.

A fourth factor is that standard models used in the study of growth and cycles are intrinsically rooted in the concept of equilibrium – in the sense of a permanent dynamic property prevailing in the markets – and the rocking-horse metaphor introduced by Wicksell and Frisch (see e.g. Louçã 1997; Freeman and Louçã 2001: 60; Tvede 2001: 149–50). According to the equilibrium paradigm

> the economic system tends spontaneously to equilibrium; cycles are exogenous perturbations produced by random shocks which trigger an endogenous propagation mechanism with stabilising properties. This provides the rationale

for separating growth and fluctuations, that is for decomposing the movement of an economic system into trend and cycle. Trend is conceived as the *loci* of equilibria – a moving centre of gravitation – while cycle is restricted to the analysis of the stochastic error term and to the properties of the equilibration mechanism.

(Reati 2001: 109)

It is important to note that detrending – namely the view that the trend (the growth of the economy) and the cycles (the acceleration and deceleration of growth) can be dealt with as if they were unrelated phenomena – implies ruling out the effects of cycles on the trend. As a result, structural factors that are likely to influence the longer-term evolution of productive forces come to be defined as merely exogenous. This, in fact, is a crucial aspect of Solow's standard growth model, which assumes that the natural rate of growth depends on the growth of the labour force and labour productivity (as determined by technical progress), and that these are exogenously determined, as implied by the assumption of diminishing returns to capital (see e.g. Thirlwall 2002: 20–8).[2]

It is also worth noting that emphasis on equilibrium implies a corresponding emphasis on stationarity and the irrelevance of the passage of time. This means that economic variables are expected to stabilize around some imaginary permanent level or constant rate of growth. In other words, standard theory relies on the 'ergodic assumption', resting on the belief in long-run equilibrium independent of initial conditions (see e.g. Davidson 1982–3), the neglect of uncertainty and, thus, acceptance of the deterministic nature of empirical phenomena.

As a result, the descriptive potential of equilibrium models is limited to recurrent phenomena characterized by a high degree of quantitative regularity (see e.g. Vercelli 1991: 141). Neoclassical macro theory thus concerns itself with 'universal laws' conceived as 'event regularities', that is, stable patterns among data series identified with the aid of econometric techniques, such as the link between money and prices in Friedman's version of the quantity theory of money (see e.g. Lawson 1997, 2003; Dow 2002: 138).

Stability as an article of faith

The stability assumption can also be seen as a counterpart to economic mechanisms that, for neoclassical theory, grant the attainment of equilibrium. As for dynamic stability, neoclassical theory focuses on the role of market-clearing prices. The efficiency of the price mechanism is guaranteed by the existence of negative feedbacks, which are thought to return the system to a unique point of equilibrium whenever it has deviated from it. In particular, the presumed universal presence of diminishing returns assures that the system will gravitate towards a unique and stable equilibrium (see e.g. Prasch 2000a: 220).

It should be noted that this conclusion, which underlies much of current macroeconomics, does not follow from scientific demonstrations based on dynamic accounts (involving out-of-equilibrium processes) of how equilibrium comes about. Strictly speaking, the competitive static equilibrium underlying standard theory implies an a priori view concerning stability:

> All economics has been able to do for the last fifty or one hundred years is to look at systems with very strong attractors, not even talk about how an equilibrium point is reached but simply point out that there is an equilibrium and that if we were there, there would be a tendency to stay there.
>
> (Arthur 1994: 64)

This is no mere coincidence. It has been clear for some time that attempts to demonstrate dynamic stability have failed, not only in the context of standard general equilibrium models, but also within the context of more recent developments in 'pure theory', including game theory (see e.g. Vercelli 1997: 290).[3] Indeed many theorists have concluded that

> the two main classes of models which were consecutively taken to embody the most 'fundamental' economic theory – general equilibrium theory and game theory – suffered from the same basic problem: they could not demonstrate the stability or uniqueness of the equilibrium which their logic seemed to require.
>
> (Viskovatoff 2000: 129–30)

Rather than dropping the assumption of general equilibrium because of lack of proof, many mainstream macroeconomists seem to take stability almost as dogma. This can be seen in the following statement by a prominent economist (reported by Fisher): '[T]he study of stability of general equilibrium is unimportant, first, because it is obvious that the economy is stable and second, because if it isn't stable we are all wasting our time' (1983: 4; quoted in Vercelli 1991: 30–1).

In terms of structural stability, commitment to the uniqueness of equilibrium forces general equilibrium theorists to assume that the structure of the economy is fixed and immutable, that it is a given prior to the interaction of agents within the market. As underlined by Prasch, this 'assumption allows prediction and removes market processes from the study of economics' (2000a: 218); in particular, the market process, the price relations, must not feedback on the structure of the economy, that is, either demand or supply schedules, otherwise the possibility of multiple equilibria cannot be ruled out.[4]

Limitations of the stability assumption

Strictly speaking, the ubiquitousness of the stability assumption in standard macroeconomics does not necessarily lead to the ruling out of negative outcomes, such as depressions or sluggish growth. Claims about the possible instability of real-world economies can be found in the literature, in textbooks and research articles alike. However, the lack of attempts at stability analysis in standard macro theory undermines the quality of its explanations and makes it subject to a number of serious limitations. First of all, it leads the theory to dismiss the scientific relevance of unstable equilibria, which are considered to be ephemeral and unobservable states (see e.g. Vercelli 1997: 287).

Second, standard theory regards negative outcomes as being ultimately generated not by the internal workings of the economy but by anomalies, exogenous disturbances to the private sector (e.g. productivity shifts and institutional rigidities) or through sheer error (e.g. confusion about relative prices or between permanent and transitory prices or policy mistakes, such as unjustified changes in the money supply of the central bank) (e.g. Tvede 2001: 160–1). In other words, it can be argued that neoclassical theorists rely on the distinction between external impulse, or shock and propagation (the inherent equilibrating mechanism) made by Frisch (1933) with his 'stick and rocking horse' metaphor:

> The fact that neoclassical theorists assumed that markets were rational and efficient did not mean that they pretended that business cycles didn't exist. It would be absolutely coherent to assume that markets are efficient and people rational and at the same time observe business cycles if these were caused by series of external shocks. The shocks were like Ragnar Frisch's 'stick'. The basic assumption was that shocks that were external to the market place itself caused the fluctuations.
>
> (Tvede 2001: 163)

Third, it provides an explanation of long-run instability emphasizing supply-side factors. Following its use of production functions to analyse growth issues, neoclassical theory holds that those countries that face sluggish growth of income or productivity have an insufficient endowment of productive factors, such as labour force or various types of capital.

In the end, the stability assumption invites many macroeconomists to accept a peculiar sort of dichotomy between short-run and long-run analysis. This occurs when the notion of stability of equilibrium is only accepted with reference to the long run, as is the case with many Old and New Keynesians. While NCM insists that the economy is always in perfect market equilibrium, this influential group of Keynesians accept that the economy may be in disequilibrium in the short run (i.e. at variance from full employment equilibrium), with the adjustment process taking place only rather slowly due to various types of market imperfections.

Blanchard's recent macroeconomics textbook is a good instance of this approach. Several times throughout the book, Blanchard mentions the current lack of visible endogenous adjustment mechanisms in many European economies. However, he explains that in his view this is either a short- or a medium-run phenomenon and does not call into question the 'economics of the long-run' based on the stability assumption (see Blanchard 2003). This approach reveals an internal consistency problem, as it amounts to suggesting that alternative principles are relevant in explaining the same circumstances. Old and New Keynesian macroeconomics also fail to completely harmonize short- and long-term equilibrium, leaving a gap between the economics of the short- (or medium-) run concerned with business cycle issues and that of the long run where growth issues are discussed. While the former is based on Keynesian insights into effective demand problems that impair adjustment, the latter instead takes for granted that these problems will disappear and that the transition to long-run equilibrium will inevitably occur. However, there is no convincing analytical bridge between the two.

It can be argued that it is precisely this dichotomy that is responsible for two major shortcomings in standard macroeconomics. The first is that it provides only rather mechanical theories of growth isolated from the more 'realistic' analysis of fluctuations. This is the case with Solow's neoclassical model as described previously: the natural rate of growth depends on the growth of the labour force and labour productivity and both are exogenously determined. The second shortcoming stemming from the dichotomy in short- and long-term analysis is that it undermines the quality of analysis of fluctuations, creating a gap between descriptions of business cycles and theory. In fact, while business cycle phenomena have often been accurately described since they first started occurring, only very rarely has economic theory been able to furnish adequate explanations, instead resorting, in most cases, to rather contrived or *ad hoc* theories instead. This gap between theory and description was pointed out by DeLong in reference to Victor Zarnowitz's influential contribution in the tradition of Wesley Mitchell's approach:

> Observers of the business cycles have long felt that this approach contains profound truth – yet it has never been well-integrated into old Keynesian, new Keynesian, monetarist, or new classical business cycle theories. Just what is it about the structure of capitalist market economies that causes real economic activity to rise and fall in ways that seem to show certain empirical regularities? My assessment at least is that economists will not be able to claim that they understand the business cycle until they have successfully integrated Zarnowitz's approach – which is Wesley C Mitchell's approach as well – with that of other, currently more popular approaches.
>
> (DeLong 1999: 21)

It may be that this gap arises because the lack of true stability analysis leads standard macroeconomics to overlook the duality of phenomena that lies at the heart of the business cycle. In fact, if we accept that the business cycle is made up of alternating periods of boom and depression, a proposition implying that adjustment will occur in any case does seem rather misleading.

In the analysis of the NE, the gap between theory and description can be seen quite clearly in the reaction of the early proponents of the beneficial effects of the NE to the stock market crashes and recession in the US and elsewhere. Although such events are difficult to accommodate within the conventional paradigm, these economists stop short of calling into question the basic assumptions of their models. Instead, to save face as economic analysts, they prefer to temporarily suspend theory (at least until better times come along) and take a sudden interest in the duality of phenomena at the descriptive level, for example, by making a list of the pros and cons of various features of the NE.[5] To characterize this form of 'pragmatic' behaviour, Godley and Izurieta (2002) point out a swift, silent volte-face they describe as follows:

> Barely a year ago, it was widely accepted...that the US growth rate had been permanently raised, the business cycle had been abolished...fiscal policy should never be used as an instrument of policy, the budget should always be in surplus, and judicious adjustments to short-term interest rates by the Federal Reserve were all that was needed to keep non-inflationary growth permanently on track...consensus has been downright confuted...by the course of events. But no one is saying he is sorry. There has been...no statement of what went wrong that is *other than descriptive*, and no sense has been conveyed that the *system of ideas* that might be held to underlie the previous orthodoxy has come under threat or require modification.
>
> (Godley and Izurieta 2002: 48–9, emphasis added)

Can we demonstrate that the economy is stable?

Frank Hahn's approach

A second approach to stability analysis, which shares some of the methodological premises of general equilibrium analysis, is to reject the concept of stability as an article of faith or as an obvious and intrinsic property of real-world economies. Stability is instead regarded as a potential feature of the economy which must be rigorously demonstrated within the context of 'realistic' out-of-equilibrium adjustment processes, capturing at least some of the basic mechanisms of real-world markets. A common point of departure for the various analytical efforts carried out in this direction is to take a full-blown version of general equilibrium theory, such as the Arrow Debreu model, as the benchmark for analysis and then to drop some of its most stringent assumptions (e.g. the complete market hypothesis, perfect competition or knowledge). By doing so, one obtains a more flexible and realistic notion of equilibrium that allows for a wider range of outcomes, such as the possibility of multiple equilibria.

One of the most significant attempts to theorize about disequilibrium states has been carried out by Frank Hahn. Hahn criticizes New Classical theorists like Lucas for relying on the assumptions of uniqueness and stability of equilibrium despite the fact that they cannot be shown to derive from the first principles of rational behaviour. He points out that Lucas's model only considers situations in which the invisible hand has already accomplished its task, and objects that this is only half the story. He reproaches Lucas for not providing a theory derivable from the first principles to explain how Walrasian equilibrium comes about. In particular, there is no theory of price and wage formation, even if prices are flexible:

> They are not properly endogenous to the fundamental theory, because there is no theory of the actions of agents that explains how prices come to be such as to clear Walrasian markets. It is an article of faith...they always do so.... But

I do not find it helpful to have a central problem of economic theory, and indeed of economic policy, treated in this way. However, I also readily admit that it is easier to live by faith, and that at the moment a fully worked out theory of price (and wage) formation is not to be had.

(Hahn 1982: 49)

Limitations to the Hahn view

As pointed out in the passage in the previous section, the lack of theory of price and wage formation explains why efforts to demonstrate stability on the grounds of the first principles have not been successful. One of the problems undermining the development of an endogenous theory of prices concerns the modelling of expectations formation and learning processes in terms of the rationality axioms. The quest for a formal model of knowledge and learning has proved elusive (see e.g. Sent 1998; Dow 2002: 85).[6] More in general, complicating factors which reflect instability in real-world economies, such as path-dependence (or hysteresis) and indeterminacy (multiple equilibria), are difficult to include in an all-encompassing approach based on 'first principles' capable of combining dynamics with equilibrium.

These types of problems explain why this approach to stability, while in principle much sounder than previous ones, has failed to provide an alternative foundation for macroeconomics, which continues in large part to rely either on the a priori assumption of continuous perfect market equilibrium or on that of long-run equilibrium. They also help explain why 'progress' in macroeconomics over the past few years has consisted in manipulating these complicating factors in such a way as to leave the stability hypothesis intact. An example can be found in the rational expectations hypothesis, which was initially heralded as a true revolution in economics. Yet while allowing for a certain degree of uncertainty, this hypothesis quite simply assumes that agents are knowers of the only true model of the economy.

2 Instability and dynamic equilibrium

A second approach to stability analysis is to construct models that account for the potential instability of real-world economies by relying on weaker concepts of dynamic equilibrium than those underlying the neoclassical tradition. Various approaches have been taken in the attempt to reconcile instability and equilibrium. The first is that of traditional Keynesian growth models based on the notion of steady growth. Another is the restatement of Keynesian views on the basis of non-linear dynamics. A third approach is represented by endogenous growth theory.

Harrod and Keynesian growth theory

In order to assess the traditional Keynesian theory of growth based on the notion of steady state, we shall begin with a brief analysis of macroeconomic debate following the publication of the *General Theory*. Keynes's theory was generally considered applicable only to the short run. In fact, his book lacks virtually any reference to long-period analysis in the 'modern' sense of the term. Indeed,

> the various statements to be found in the *General Theory* about long-term problems... are not based on any formal analysis of changes that are likely to take place over time. There is no attempt to link a sequence of short periods and to trace the changes from one to the other that lead to growth and to cyclical movements.
>
> (Asimakopulos 1991: 121–2)

Moreover, Keynes altogether rejected the use of mathematical formulas to account for sequences of short periods, owing mainly to his belief that long-term expectations cannot be modelled on the basis of past data. This view is evident, for example, in his critique of Tinbergen's study on the statistical testing of business cycle theories.[1]

In the late thirties, these aspects of Keynes's analysis were considered to be major flaws. That is why, after the *General Theory* was published, 'with the use of modelling as a common language, economists attempted to represent Keynes's ideas on business cycles in a variety of mathematical forms' (Jarsulic 1997: 377).

Many theorists turned to macroeconometric models employing linear stochastic equations; however, in doing so, they tied themselves to a severely limited dynamic framework lacking 'an endogenous economic account of business cycle behaviour' (ibid.: 377).

These limitations were eventually overcome by authors such as Harrod and Kalecki (followed later by Joan Robinson, Kaldor, Goodwin and Pasinetti), who sought to extend Keynes's short-period analysis to consideration of accumulation over time. This they accomplished by providing a formal account that very much resembles modern growth theory (see e.g. Asimakopulos 1991; King 2002; Thirlwall 2002). Kalecki developed a mathematically determinate business cycle theory drawing on the dual relation between profits and investment and changes in capital stock.[2] Harrod, instead, set out to demonstrate that the business cycle is but one aspect of the growth process. His dynamic approach stemmed from the view that positions of static equilibrium cannot be taken as a starting point for the correct analysis of cyclical phenomena but that these phenomena 'should be regarded as oscillations around a line of steady growth' (Harrod 1951: 261). Harrod thus criticized the *General Theory* for being static (as it focuses on levels of income, not on rates of growth) and limited to the short period (it neglects changes in productive capacity), arguing that it needed to be complemented by a dynamic equilibrium theory concerning rates of growth.[3]

Harrod initially focused on the relationship between the multiplier and the accelerator, a topic which had attracted the interest of various scholars, including Hansen and Samuelson (see e.g. Samuelson's classic 1939 paper). He then tried to extend Keynes's static equilibrium analysis by asking the question 'if the condition of static equilibrium is that plans to invest must equal plans to save, what must be the rate of growth of income for this equilibrium condition to hold in a growing economy through time?' (Thirlwall 2002: 12). Seeking to answer this question, Harrod developed an analysis of moving equilibrium based on his fundamental growth equation describing the normal 'warranted' rate of growth (dependent on the saving rate and on a given capital requirement per unit of output). If this rate prevails, aggregate demand equals productive capacity. One of Harrod's main conclusions is that, even if this growth rate exists, it is not stable. For this reason, he posited an instability principle meant to provide a fundamental explanation for the business cycle: any deviation of the actual rate of growth from the warranted growth path would be accentuated over time, and the system would be cumulatively unstable. In other words, economies appeared to be poised on a 'knife-edge'. Any departure from equilibrium, rather than self-righting, would be self-aggravating.

The relation between the actual rate and the warranted rate is a short-run problem. However, Harrod also considered the problem of long-run instability in terms of the relationship between the actual rate and the 'natural' rate of growth, as determined by the rate of growth of the labour force and the rate of growth of output per worker, which represents the potential rate of growth of the economy. Thus, if all labour is to be employed, the actual growth rate must match the natural rate. Again, this equilibrium too turns out to be unstable (see e.g. Asimakopulos 1991: 138, 165; Ruttan 2001: 24; King 2002: 56–8; Thirlwall 2002: 14–15).[4]

As Jarsulic pointed out, one of the key implications of Harrod's theory is that 'investment should be self-reinforcing and that this would produce instability in any aggregate demand system' (Jarsulic 1997: 338). Moreover, Harrod's theory indicates that the accelerator may be somewhat weakened by the presence of a substantial level of autonomous investment, unrelated to the current level or rate of change of income. Monetary policy and a programme of public works, while perhaps of some help, may still prove inadequate in offsetting the effects of a relatively high warranted rate and the resulting tendency for the system to relapse into depression before full employment is reached in a boom: 'Stagnation might therefore be the normal state for mature capitalism' (King 2002: 59).

The neo-Ricardians

For the sake of brevity, we will not provide a detailed account of the debate following Harrod's contribution to Keynesian growth theory as to how to overcome the problem of the knife edge (i.e. the Cambridge, UK, flexible saving-ratio model versus the Cambridge, US, variable capital-ratio model) or the capital theory debate.[5] However, we shall outline the major developments of the Keynesian stance.

On the one hand, some Keynesians followed the neo-Ricardian tradition based on 'real' analysis without money, rejection of the neoclassical value and distribution theory and reliance on alternative models of income distribution, especially the classical surplus approach. These theorists insisted that the principle of effective demand should be coupled with a relatively strong notion of long-run equilibrium, which was regarded as the centre of gravitation (e.g. Eatwell and Milgate 1983; Garegnani 1983; Bortis 1996). Neo-Ricardians '...stress the importance of long-period analysis. Normal prices are supposed to be stable in the long run and are consequently seen as centres of gravity, around which short-period or temporary market prices fluctuate' (Eatwell and Milgate 1983: 5). Uncertainty and money are not considered significant in the long run, where normal prices are determined by the technological and institutional environment instead. For neo-Ricardians, one implication of this view is that 'it is not sufficient to develop a theory of fluctuations. A theory of the long-term trend is also required' (ibid.). Such a theory is necessary for the analysis of stability 'since it matters whether fluctuations are around trends implying lower or, in contrast, higher level of persistent unemployment' (ibid.).

A distinguishing characteristic of this approach is that it is able to account for structural change. This is especially apparent in Pasinetti's contributions to the theory of growth in a multi-sector economy (e.g. Pasinetti 1981). Whereas Harrodian models imply a form of equilibrium over time in terms of steady-state balanced growth, with the economy changing only in terms of increased size, Pasinetti presents a model of equilibrium over time coexisting with continuous structural change brought about by differences in the rate of technological change and the income elasticities of demand in the various sectors.

Kaldor, Robinson and Minsky

In juxtaposition with the neo-Ricardian tradition, post-Keynesian theorists such as Kaldor and Robinson progressively abandoned steady growth theory as the foundation for discussing stability issues. At first, these authors insisted

> upon defining as a basis of their argument a steady growth process and elucidating the circumstances under which this process can be maintained. They also conclude, more or less in passing, that the maintenance of steady growth is difficult if not impossible under capitalist processes.
>
> (Minsky 1975, quoted in King 2002: 113)

Later, however, these theorists were to drastically modify their views. As noted by King, 'Robinson and Kaldor began their career as equilibrium economists. They ended up as severe critics of both the concept itself and of its relevance to any actual capitalist economies' (King 2002: 77). Equilibrium analysis, in their view, was best replaced by historical analysis, where history is taken to be a sequence of short-term events. This implies that the long run has no independent existence (Harcourt 1981: 5).

In line with this view, Minsky, another important post-Keynesian figure, took no interest in the analysis of production, the operation of product markets, pricing theory or Sraffa's critique of neoclassical theory, all of which had attracted the attention of the Cambridge Keynesians instead. In particular, Minsky believed that 'Growth without cycles...was simply impossible, "real" analysis without money was futile, paradoxes in capital theory and alternative models of income distribution were at best amusing academic games' (King 2002: 113). On the grounds of his financial instability hypothesis (see e.g. Tvede 2001: 205–10 and Chapter 18), he even suggested that

> once you define the financial institutions of capitalism in any precise form then the normal path of the economy is intractably cyclical and the problems...of macroeconomic theory is to spell out the properties of the cyclical process...within a cyclical perspective uncertainty becomes operational... without a cyclical perspective uncertainty is more or less an empty bag.
>
> (Minsky 1975, quoted in King 2002: 113)

Non-linear dynamics

Building on the seminal contributions of Keynes, Schumpeter, Harrod, Kaldor and Goodwin, a more recent class of models (e.g. Goodwin 1990, see also for reference Vercelli 1991; Jarsulic 1997) refute the view typically emphasized by neo-classical economists (see e.g. Samuelson 1939) that the structure of the economy is linear and invariant. For example, as Vercelli pointed out (1991: 38), economic systems are non-linear and cannot be safely approximated by linear models. A number of theorists have suggested that recent developments in natural sciences and mathematics (e.g. chaos theory and other forms of non-linear dynamics),[6] according to which the universe is becoming more complex and potentially more unstable (see e.g. Prigogine and Nicolis 1989), may also be applicable to economic systems. In fact, both chaos theory and Keynesian theory are anti-determinist and anti-reductionist, revealing an important link. In other words, both hold that you cannot analyse non-linear system as you do with linear ones, by breaking the system into details which are analysed one at a time. Non-linear systems have to be understood in their entirety (Tvede 2001: 198; see also Vercelli 1997: 288).

In order to understand the connection between these new formal tools and growth theory, it should be noted that it was immediately clear to some Keynesians, such as Kaldor, that the language of linear dynamic systems underlying Harrod's work was inadequate to the tasks he had undertaken. Kaldor (1940) produced a synthesis of Harrod and Kalecki's ideas, introducing non-linear methods into Keynesian cyclical analysis. Other important models, such as Goodwin's (1951), were also produced along these lines. The usefulness of such models is that

> they show that the positive feedbacks generated by aggregate demand, rep-resented by an investment accelerator, can easily produce unstable aggregate equilibria under economically reasonable assumptions. When the dynamics of the system are constrained by non-linearities, which in the Goodwin case stand for 'floors' and 'ceilings' to investment demand, self-sustaining cycles are the outcome. Thus the models suggest that empirically reasonable depictions of economic behaviour can produce, independent of external shocks, at least part of business cycle dynamics.
>
> (Jarsulic 1997: 380)

Several versions of such Kaldor–Goodwin models were developed, based on various specifications of the investment function, time lags and, more recently, the introduction of financial factors affecting investment decisions (e.g. interest rates or liquidity constraints). Although these models have been successful in demon-strating that instability usually results from multiplier-accelerator sources and that there are many instances in which endogenous cycles result, they are fraught with serious limitations; in particular, their behaviour is too regular, when there are no external shocks.

Recent developments in the mathematics of non-linear dynamics may offer new insights into such problems, however (see e.g. Vercelli 1991, 1997; Jarsulic 1997; Tvede 2001). The discovery that simple, deterministic non-linear systems are 'messy', that is, capable of producing extremely complex dynamics, is seen by many as having important implications for stability analysis and for economics in general. For example, chaotic, dynamical systems show sensitive dependence on initial conditions, that is, the so-called butterfly effect. This implies unpredictability about dynamical paths (see e.g. Jarsulic 1997; Tvede 2001: 188–9).[7] Moreover, these systems defy classic determinism, in the sense that 'the property of chaotic systems imposes the use of stochastic methods for analysing and forecasting their dynamics' (Vercelli 1997: 288). They may eventually prove to have multiple, alternative, dynamic equilibria, the so-called 'attractors', or in other words, competing gravity centres which could exert pull in a system (Tvede 2001: 192).[8]

However, this does not mean that the study of business cycles is an inherently futile task. On the contrary, while these approaches do imply that the system cannot be understood according to a few, simple rules and that 'the behaviour of the system when you start to combine your rules could be much more complicated than formerly anticipated' (Tvede 2001: 200), they also suggest that mechanisms penetrating the complexity of many feed back systems can be found. One example is mode-locking, a phenomenon that

> happens when a number of initially uncorrelated processes lock into each other's rhythm to create a strong, aggregate movement. Given a vast multitude of processes in the economy that can contribute to instability, you would end up with something very similar to random noise, if it were not for mode-locking. Because of mode-locking, a boom can spread from one sector to many...the business cycle is a movement in the aggregate; when the economy moves, almost everything moves in the same direction because of mode-locking...
>
> (ibid.: 201)

Although non-linear dynamics 'is unlikely to produce many practical tools for economic and financial forecasting' (ibid.: 199), it does increase our understanding of the nature of some economic and financial systems. As noted by Freeman and Louçã for example,

> Nonlinear systems and models question the traditional definition of endogenous and exogenous variables, differentiate the impact of external perturbation according to the state of the system, produce mode-locking behaviours, model structural instability and dynamic stability in the same context, and interpret complexity.
>
> (2001: 117)

As a result, non-linear approaches are becoming more common in the field of cycle analysis, technological change and the evolution of institutions, and it even seems to encourage reconciliation between alternative heterodox perspectives, such as those by Keynes and Schumpeter (see e.g. Vercelli 1991, 1997). Furthermore, non-linear systems increase the plausibility of active policy moves, because a model that describes an unstable system is useful in explaining the interventions meant to stabilize it (see e.g. Vercelli 1991: 36). Another aspect of this approach is that it contributes to the development of Keynesian theory, for it shows that

> simple, deterministic non-linear economic models can produce time series behaviour which is dynamically complex, non-quite-periodic and extraordinarily resistant to prediction. This sounds like the business cycle behaviour

with which empirical economists are concerned, and which Keynes was trying to explain. Non-linear Keynesian macroeconomic models can in many cases be shown to produce dynamic complexity. This has been done analytically and by means of computer simulations by several authors...

(Jarsulic 1997: 382)

New Growth Theory

Another approach to instability and growth issues is endogenous growth theory, or NGT. NGT has become popular over the last few decades to account for a number of key phenomena conflicting with the Old Growth Theory (OGT) underlying the neoclassical stance. One example is the lack of convergence between rich and poor countries. The main purpose of NGT is to provide an internal mechanism for long-run growth; in other words, it seeks to endogenize what OGT takes as exogenous. Whereas OGT considers the natural rate of growth to be dependent on the growth of the labour force and labour productivity (determined by technical progress), which are both exogenously determined, NGT takes into account other factors involved in growth, such as investment.

Although the literature on endogenous growth includes many different models,[9] it can be argued that they all share a shift in focus from a notion of the economy based on a perfectly working market to one riddled with market imperfections. By introducing such imperfections, NGT rules out the neoclassical assumption of diminishing returns to capital which are necessary to OGT's conclusions concerning the exogenous nature of growth. This step involves some significant methodological divergences from the standard model.

First, it signifies a move away from Becker's 'imperialist' approach to an alternative approach to microfoundations and the relationship between economics and other social sciences. As Fine points out

the new microfoundations treat the economy as subject to imperfections to which non-market responses are a rational, if not necessarily efficient, response. In this light, institutions, norms and customs are seen as the path dependent, collective response to market imperfections. As a result, institutions etc. are neither taken as exogenous nor reduced to an as if market approach characteristic...

(Fine 2003: 214)

Second, it involves placing the emphasis on such key phenomena as increasing returns to scale (the bigger the economy, the higher the level of productivity) and positive externalities. Emphasis on such microeconomic imperfections is not new. For instance, Marshall chose to treat increasing returns as externalities in order to reconcile competitive equilibrium with dynamic phenomena at the level of industry (Thirlwall 2002: 31). However, NGT is unique in that it transforms micro-imperfections into a macro influence on the growth rate.[10] By extending Marshallian thinking to the aggregate level, NGT theorists assume that constant returns to scale hold for individual firms, while positive spillover effects – due, for example, to education, invention, learning and networks such as industrial districts – spread individual gains more widely throughout the economy as a whole, eliminate diminishing returns to aggregate capital and account for endogenous growth. In principle, any market imperfection can be used to generate a model for NGT, so long as it generates increasing returns; the analytical highway from market imperfections through increasing returns to endogenous growth has many lanes (Fine 2003; Stiroh 2003: 730).

A particularly relevant example for the analysis of the NE can be found in Romer (1986), where research and development (R&D) spillovers are seen to produce this result. That is

> each firm might face constant returns to scale and diminishing returns to capital, but its R&D effort could spill over and affect the aggregate stock of knowledge that is available to *all* firms. This would endogenize the evolution of the level of technology.
>
> (Stiroh 2003: 731)

In other words, rather than being exogenous, technology reflects the choices of firms who expend resources on R&D in the hope of reaping profits. This means that 'as long as there is sufficient incentive for firms to undertake such expenditures . . .' (ibid.: 735). In addition, 'the lower the cost of R&D, the more innovation and the faster the growth. This contrasts sharply with the neoclassical model, where savings rates do not affect long-run growth and there is no explicit role for innovation' (ibid.: 735).

Third, like the standard model, NGT is organized around the notion of steady-state balanced growth as equilibrium. This means that it asserts the existence of a supply-determined output path of the economy, towards which the actual output path of the economy is attracted in the long run. The generation of externalities in NGT models does not rule out competitive equilibrium.[11] However, 'the mathematical models for NGT are sufficiently complicated and diverse that they can . . . generate both multiple equilibria and complex, not necessarily stable, paths out of equilibrium' (Fine 2003: 208). Arguably, the existence of external effects may account for a certain degree of instability, such as underinvestment (see e.g. Stiroh 2003: 733). In general, market equilibrium is bound to be suboptimal, since firms do not consider the external effects of the accumulation of knowledge when making production decisions (Ruttan 2001: 25).

In addition to these considerations, a certain class of NGT models – such as those focusing on the role of innovation (and heterogeneity of capital) either in the form of a greater variety of products (e.g. Romer 1990) or in the form of higher quality products (e.g. Grossman and Helpman 1991; Aghion and Howitt 1998) – account to a certain extent for Schumpeterian long waves of structural change and structural unemployment. These waves are also analysed in the literature on General Purpose Technologies (GPTs). GPTs, such as steam engines, electricity and semiconductors, differ from other technologies in the range of their applicability. They can be applied to a wide range of sectors and lead to widespread gains in productivity throughout the economy as the new innovation diffuses and as complementary innovations in related industries lead to sustained productivity growth (e.g. Bresnahan and Trajtenberg 1995). However, as pointed out by David (1991) and Lipsey and Bekar (1995), GPTs require significant economic and social restructuring and adjustment, and the process of implementation should not be expected to be smooth.

Ultimately, NGT models suggest a meaningful role for government intervention. For example, given that the incentive to enhance the quality of human and physical capital may cause a permanent increase in the long-run rate of growth in per capita income, government intervention, perhaps in the form of an active technology policy, may permanently improve the rate of economic growth and not just the level of per capita income (see e.g. Ruttan 2001: 28).

Limitations of growth models

While the various approaches summarized in this chapter undoubtedly provide some valuable insights into the instability and growth problem, they cannot be regarded as sufficient to account for actual business cycles and growth. The next section examines some of their shortcomings.

One overall criticism is that all of these approaches can be accused of being what Keynes referred to as a 'simplified propaedeutic' for the real world economy. Keynes recognized that when dealing with the latter 'allowance must be made for the interactions among the independent variables of his analysis ... the complexity of these interactions means that the analysis of changes over time cannot be adequately handled by mathematical equations' (Asimakopulos 1991: 136–7). In particular, Keynes's critique of the accelerator hypothesis is also applicable to many of the models described. What Keynes objected to was the mechanical nature of the accelerator and its implicit derivation of long-term expectations from the calculation of the rate of change in output. He criticized this type of model because

> given the parameters and initial conditions ... it can be entirely worked out. It is what Shackle ... calls an engine of theory which depends 'for its whole cycle of phases, its whole pattern of movement, on a single principle of design'. There is no learning, no alteration of the way expectations are formed ...
>
> (Chick 1986: 291)

Similarly, despite their obvious utility, dynamic models, including those by Harrod and non-linear dynamics, are limited by their reliance on a single equation and by their inability to detect more than one or two key impulses or mechanisms. As a result, they disregard the complex interactions potentially taking place among the key variables and neglect to fully integrate monetary and real aspects. Moreover, some of the theoretical constructs, such as Harrod's warranted rate, require special conditions (e.g. perfect foresight), if they are even to be considered *possible* (see e.g. Asimakpulos 1991: 165).

In other words, such models fall short of clearly depicting the overall behaviour of real-world economies, often overlooking some of their most crucial aspects. Tvede (2001), among others, has noted that there are at least five different non-linear categories of feedback phenomena – that is, those phenomena that either push the economy away from a smooth trend movement (positive feedback) or pull it towards a smooth trend (negative feedback) – which are not easily accounted for even by non-linear models. Tvede makes reference to mechanisms such as positive feedback loops, cascade reactions, echoes, lags and disinhibitors.[12] Bearing these mechanisms in mind, he underlines that it has now become 'increasingly clear that to understand business cycles, it is not enough to pile more and more mathematical rules for the economy on top of each other' (ibid.: 166).

In addition to these general considerations, the models considered here are subject to more specific criticism as well. The notion of equilibrium itself is a major issue of concern. Despite the gradual shift away from neoclassical tradition to a weaker notion of equilibrium, and even though several of the models accept the concept of unstable equilibria or attractors, most of them continue to make reference to steady states of balanced growth acting as the centre of gravitation for actual output paths and to suggest the need for separate theories of growth and cycles. In particular, all of the mainstream growth models from Harrod to NGT consider the natural rate of growth – referring to the rate of growth of productive potential of an economy – to be exogenously determined by supply factors. As noted by Thirlwall:

> In all mainstream growth theory, the natural rate of growth (composed of labour force growth and labour productivity growth) is treated as exogenously determined, unresponsive to the actual rate of growth or the pressure of demand in an economy. It is exogenous in Harrod's original model...it is treated as exogenous in the neoclassical response to Harrod, as in the original model of Solow (1956), for example...it is treated as exogenous (by and large) in the post-Keynesian response to the neoclassical as in the original models of Kaldor (1957) and Joan Robinson (1956). Paradoxically, it is even treated as exogenous in new endogenous growth.
>
> (2002: 79–80)

It is especially important not to misconstrue the actual implications of NGT. While it does consider growth as endogenous, this is true only in a certain sense, that is, 'in the sense that investment matters for the growth rate, because the assumption of diminishing returns to capital is relaxed, not in the sense that labour force growth and productivity growth respond to demand and the growth of output itself' (Thirlwall 2002: 80). Indeed, as noted by Setterfield, NGT denies aggregate demand even an indirect influence on growth. Not unlike the neoclassical model, what NGT actually provides is a supply-side account of the growth process:

> [T]he Solow model and the NGT theories are similar in their treatment of growth as an essentially supply-side process. Since savings creates investment,

effective demand failures are impossible, and autonomous changes in aggregate demand can only impact the utilization of resources in the short-run as long as expectational errors or nominal rigidities – both of which are held to be transitory phenomena – interrupt the otherwise neutral (in terms of their impact on real variables) adjustment of prices. Meanwhile, the supply-determined output path of the economy – towards which the actual output path of the economy is attracted in the long run – is conventionally assumed to be independent of variation in demand and the transitory differences between actual and potential output to which these give rise.

(Setterfield 2002: 3–4)

A number of objections can be made, especially to the NGT, regarding the neglect of aggregate demand. First of all, it implies that even if unemployment were allowed, as is the case in certain neo-Schumpeterian models, such employment would be essentially structural, as opposed to being the consequence of aggregate demand failures.

Moreover, NGT models rely on economies that have a single output for consumption and investment. Although some models may foresee a separate sector for education or R&D, or whatever area represents a source for increasing returns to scale, the single output feature raises doubts as to whether NGT is capable of adequately capturing, let alone explaining, the patterns of growth and economic and social change associated with development (see Fine 2003: 208).

A third objection is methodological. While it is true that NGT takes a broader view of factors affecting growth and accounts for education and innovation and other elements in the economic and social infrastructure that contribute to increases in productivity,[13] it is equally true that it deals with them on the grounds of arbitrary assumptions. It can be argued, for example, that NGT models carry out an unjustified extension of the production function concept, which was originally used to express a precise relationship between input and output within productive processes. NGT takes phenomena that do not lend themselves to modelling and seeks to reduce them to precise quantitative relationships. More specifically, the assumption in NGT of a precise relationship between investment in resources, human capital, R&D and growth results is unfounded, for technological progress is only partly due to economic choices; while many forms of learning linked with production are endogenous, other historical, institutional or cultural factors cannot be endogenized (see e.g. Boggio and Seravalli 2003; Fine 2003).

But even granting that a wide range of state interventions can be measured more or less precisely, the use of production functions and the statistical work associated with NGT – such as the so-called Barro-type regressions – imply that the factors under consideration are completely independent. Indeed, as Fine points out, in the typical applied work associated with NGT

the regression is augmented by any number and combination of variables – a hundred or more – from R&D expenditure to levels of democracy and trust or indeed any variable that might be deemed to affect economic performance but it is scarcely credible that the hundred or more conditional variables are independent of one another and in their effects of growth.

(2003: 211)

In principle, the analysis of large numbers of factors should proceed on the grounds of theoretical models. However, this is not how applied economists proceed. They prefer to rely instead on *ad hoc* methods:

So a full model of interaction ought to be laid out, but such a model is mathematically intractable and the simple ad hoc device of adding variables to the regression has been used in the absence of any rationale other than to test for them. To put it bluntly, once Barro-type regressions are in use, it is far from clear how they depend upon theory at all. At a deeper analytical level, growth as a process of development involving complex interactions between the factors attached to economic and social transformation are being flattened and separated out to satisfy the need of the regression.

(ibid.)

In the end, NGT models, just like their OGT counterparts, focus on proximate sources of growth rather than more fundamental ones. As Ruttan (2001: 98) points out, both approaches have neglected the institutional sources of economic growth in a utopistic attempt to find a general theory of growth that applies at all times and in all places.

3 Structural change without equilibrium

In this chapter we focus on those approaches to stability analysis that emphasize structural change without considering the role of equilibrium as an organizing concept. An important part of this group is made up of approaches based on the evolutionary paradigm. In particular, we shall consider the so-called neo-Schumpeterian views that underlie several approaches to stability issues, including the 'reasoned history approach' and the related 'Techno-Economic Paradigm' (TEP) approach.

A theory of reasoned history

One way to deal with stability is to focus on the structural change occurring in actual historical processes. One of the theories attempting to do so is the so-called 'reasoned history approach' which figures strongly in the contributions of several neo-Schumpeterian authors, such as Freeman, Perez, Dosi, Soete, Louçã and Verspagen. This approach has several distinct features. First of all, it rests on the organic and evolutionary metaphor, according to which

> in real economic series non stationarity and time dependence do matter, economic variable do evolve (and)...do not stabilize around some imaginary permanent level or constant rate of growth...evolution is nothing more than the creation of variety and novelty and *a fortiori* no fixed attractor or strictly unchangeable mechanism can represent the process. Irregular waves do exist, and they cannot be studied under the diktat of the *ceteris paribus* conditions: time is turbulence.
>
> (Freeman and Louçã 2001: 118)

Second, it suggests that the concept of 'coordination' is more suitable for the analysis of evolution than that of 'equilibrium':

> Coordination, as a social process subjected to complex interactions – and not equilibrium, which is a state – explains the existence of attractors in growth patterns, the weight of social institutions, and the relation between the economic system and other parts of society.
>
> (ibid.: 120)

In particular, 'social and economic coordination...the economic behaviour dubbed as 'equilibrium', i.e. the dynamic local stability of the system ...' (ibid.: 127) is granted by key social, institutional and political factors. As noted by Freeman and Louça, the fact that coordination exists 'does not imply that there is harmony or equilibrium, either in the ideological sense of a general feature of capitalist economies or in the precise sense of a permanent dynamic property prevailing in the markets' (ibid.: 122).

Third, the reasoned history approach involves an interdisciplinary vision emphasizing 'the complexity of the interactions between the various subsystems of society' (ibid.: 135). Strictly speaking, this vision is not altogether new. For example, it underlies the theories of Marx and of other social thinkers (e.g. van Gelderen) who study 'capitalism as a whole'. Within the theory of fluctuations, it was postulated by Kondratieff (e.g. Freeman and Louça 2001: 79). Indeed a large part of neo-Schumpeterian literature seeks to provide a modern reformulation of Kondratieff's long-cycle or wave hypothesis. But a similar interdisciplinary approach has also been suggested more recently by Kuznets:

> If we are to deal adequately with processes of economic growth, processes of long term change in which the very technological, demographic, and social frameworks are also changing – and in ways that decidedly affect the operation of forces proper – it is inevitable that we venture into fields beyond... economics proper...it is imperative that we become familiar with findings in those related social disciplines that can help us understand population growth patterns, the nature and forces in technological changes, the factors that determine the characteristic and trends in political institutions.
>
> (Kuznets 1955: 28, quoted in Freeman and
> Louça 2001: 118)

Unlike previous formulations, however, the reasoned history approach is more sensitive to the methodological and epistemological implications of the interdisciplinary approach. As Freeman and Louça make clear, traditional analytic methods are unsuitable for the study of the relevant interactions. Hence, their approach 'denies the extreme assumption about self-contained models and methods, and looks for integrated theories that will be incomplete and not definitive, explanatory and not predictive, historical rather than simply economicist, and evolutionary rather than mechanistic' (Freeman and Louça 2001: 117).

Like Kondratieff, these authors emphasize a holistic and organic view, according to which all cycles are part of the same process and there is no strict separability of irreversible and reversible movements. Moreover, they endorse arguments against detrending, namely that the trend (the growth of the economy) and the cycles (the acceleration and deceleration of growth) are quite simply one and the same phenomenon (ibid.: 83). On these grounds, they are led to emphasize the effects of cycles on trend. Thus, for example, structural factors that are expected to influence the longer-term evolution of productive forces may be defined as merely endogenous consequences of the cycle itself.

However, Freeman and Louça depart from Kondratieff on several important points. In particular, they are sceptical as to whether it is possible to determine general internal laws as advocated by Kondratieff, according to whom, for example, 'the explanation of the long cycles and in particular those of prices must be looked for in the character of the mechanism and the internal laws of the general process of socio-economic development' (quoted in Freeman and Louça 2001: 109). Indeed Freeman and Louça criticize the theoretical requirement of universality in Kondratieff's tradition, stating that it

> amounts to (1) that only 'endogenous models' are valid and (2) that all relevant factors of all kinds must therefore be modelled as endogenous variables. As a consequence, the scope of the model is defined in such a way that it must include all social, economic, political and institutional realities.
>
> (Freeman and Louça 2001: 109)

In their view, this ideal of an all-comprehensive endogenous model capable of generating the cycles cannot be achieved, and 'amounts to the search for the Holy Grail' (ibid.: 111).

Thus, the search for a single best research strategy to account for complex dynamics continues. On the one hand are the standard models, which are generally limited to a small number of variables and are 'by this sole fact forced to ignore most of the relevant factors which are finally condensed under the form of some exogenous residual random term' (ibid.: 109). On the other are broader theoretical frameworks which define capitalism as a concrete historical process. These do not admit a clear-cut distinction between exogenous and endogenous variables, embracing the view that 'the boundaries of the economic sphere are not objectively defined and it is not possible to endogenise artificially such factors as state intervention, social institutions or cultural features' (ibid.: 110). While it is possible to capture the contradictions of capitalism by 'the concrete economic analysis of production and distribution...others remain outside the scope of each model' (ibid.: 110). In particular, the reasoned history approach makes a distinction between five subsystems of history which are relevant to the study of economic growth: the history of science and of technology, economic history, political history and cultural history. The point of this distinction is that 'the economic subsystem is partially and conceptually autonomous from the other social and political spheres, where independent processes may develop.' The theory must therefore address both 'their relative autonomy and their interconnections' (ibid.: 110).

Techno-Economic Paradigms

In principle, the 'reasoned history approach' is a rather general research programme. It seeks to provide the grounds for a new synthesis between the various contributions on the historical evolution of economies, such as those by the neo-Schumpeterians, Boyer and the Regulation school, Gordon and Maddison (ibid.: 95). In order to provide a modern reformulation of the long-cycle or wave hypothesis, the neo-Schumpeterian authors (particularly Freeman and Perez) developed a more specific type of 'reasoned history' referred to as the TEP approach, in which the NE is regarded as a new TEP (for a comprehensive assessment see Preston 2001: 38–41; for analysis of the NE along these lines, see also Verspagen 2000, 2002).

In line with Schumpeter, they insist that an understanding of booms and depression requires more than focusing on short inventory or investment cycles, as standard macroeconomists do. One should focus instead on 'long-wave' cycles (typically lasting approximately fifty years and divided into sub-periods of 'boom and bust'), concerning phenomena, such as the rise and decline of entire industries, major infrastructural investment, changes in the international location of industry and technological leadership and other related structural changes, such as those in the skills and composition of the labour force.

Critique of aggregates

One of the key features of this approach is the implication that an understanding of stability in the long-term context calls for more than a focus on a few aggregates. Moreover, in contrast with the early literature on long cycles, the neo-Schumpeterian authors are sceptical about the existence of quantitative macroeconomic regularities. Perez (2002), for example, argues that such regularities fail to emerge, as a result of the difficulties incurred in constructing constant money series or indexes and in comparing money values at different points in time. Furthermore, long-run aggregate series are meaningless, mostly because technological change brings about quantum jumps in productivity growth and radical changes in the relative price structure. On the other hand, the sort of disaggregated statistics that are related to the inner workings of the economy behind aggregates and that would be appropriate for testing the long-wave hypothesis are rarely available, and Perez is aware of this. She therefore shifts the focus of attention from measurement to qualitative understanding of the complex tensions and forces triggered by technological revolutions. This stance does not imply, however, that the search for simplification and regularities concerning business cycles is an impossible task. Theorists can still attempt to single out regularities of a qualitative kind.

Analysis of interactions and complementarities

One element of regularity is the paradigm itself. The neo-Schumpeterian authors divide the history of capitalism into five paradigms corresponding to major technical and organizational innovations, such as water-powered mechanization, steam-powered mechanization, electrification, motorization and computerization of the entire economy.

Another regularity is that the TEP concept places the emphasis on the set of complementary social, institutional and economic factors associated to technological revolutions in a given historically contingent context. Indeed, each TEP is characterized by a collection of economic factors, such as a certain type of raw material, labour force structure, consumption pattern, business organization, industrial and financial structure (see e.g. Freeman and Perez 1988: 59). Thus, for example, ICT constitutes a new TEP, for it is a general-purpose technology giving rise to a new range of products, services and industries and affecting almost every other branch of the economy by changing the input cost structure and conditions of production and distribution throughout the system.

Moreover, according to the TEP concept, an understanding of major transformations such as the NE requires more than a focus on the economy. 'Long-wave' phenomena should be understood as society-wide processes. In order to explain the long-run sequence of 'good and bad times', and chaos and the return to prosperity, one must consider wider-ranging social and institutional factors and not just the working of markets. This means that the new technologies in each TEP are tightly associated to a set of complementary institutions. Thus, for example, while regarded as crucial for the previous paradigm based on mass production and Fordism, consumer credit, oligopoly, trade unions, the welfare state and Keynesian policies are no longer considered viable or of such great significance in the current paradigm based on ICT (see e.g. Freeman and Perez 1988: 56–7).

It is clear that by stressing this element, the TEP approach overcomes the tendency towards empty generalization typical of standard economic theory and represents a clear advance over Schumpeter and the earlier literature on long cycles. While the latter attempted to confine the analysis of long waves within narrowly defined economic systems and to search for endogenous causes of business cycles, these neo-Schumpeterian authors instead deem a purely economic explanation legitimate only for the shorter inventory or investment cycles. In particular, while many neo-Schumpeterians and the previous literature on long waves or Kondratieff cycles narrowly focused on technological change alone, the TEP concept implies a broader perspective based on the consideration of two types of interaction.

First, it justifies a systemic view of technological change, according to which, on the one hand, the innovation process is at least partly explained by context and, on the other, technological change shapes society. As for the first influence, the TEP has strong ties to the 'National System of Innovation' (see e.g. Freeman 1988; Nelson 1993), which stresses the role of institutions, such as universities and public R&D, among the determinants of innovations. Therefore, these appear not as sudden breaks in the routine, but as phenomena occurring under special conditions that must be created and continuously reproduced. As for the second influence, Perez stresses that institutional change is necessary for the accommodation of technological revolutions: the establishment of a network of services (infrastructure), cultural adaptation, institutional enablers involving rules and regulations, education and financial innovation (e.g. consumer credit was important for the development of mass production) (2002: 41–2).

Second, the TEP stresses the interaction between financial capital and the upsurge of new technologies. This point has been of particular interest to Perez, who notes for example: 'Though technology takes pride of place in the explanation, it is as much determined by social and institutional factors and by the economy and finance as it, in turn, influences them' (2002: 160). The crucial role of finance appears quite clearly in the third element of qualitative regularity in long-wave phenomena captured by the TEP. As Perez points out, this consists in the sequence of events (hidden under many layers of unique factors, events and circumstances) that characterizes all industrial revolutions and recurs about every half century: irruption of the new technology, the frenzy phase based on the predominance of finance and the formation of structural tensions such as the stock market bubble, the mismatch between aggregate demand and supply and political unrest, the turning point usually in the recession that follows the collapse of the financial bubble and the synergy phase when all conditions are favourable to the full flourishing of the new paradigm (see Perez 2002).

Instability

In general terms, the 'reasoned history approach' provides an insightful analysis of instability. Following in the tradition of Marx and other social thinkers like van Gelderen subscribing to the organic and evolutionary metaphor, it regards the coordination process of 'capitalism as a whole' as the outcome of tendencies and counter tendencies, that is, of conflict. As Freeman and Louçã mention, the evolutionary metaphor requires the incorporation of the concept of 'morphogenesis', or the study of structural crises in economic history:

> Morphogenesis implies two essential features: changes and control, or rupture and continuity. Both coexist and are interdependent and inseparable: the one-sidedness of the analysis of a single term of the social process is indeed responsible for most of the relativist trends in economics, the extreme examples of theories of continuity being those defined by an assumption of perfect rationality and the general equilibrium paradigm.
>
> (Freeman and Louçã 2001: 119)

At the same time, the 'reasoned history approach' also tries to account for the fact that the instability in real-world economies is not extreme. The concept of coordination, for example, explains why 'disequilibrium processes exist but are constrained...why structural instability persists but does not drive the system towards explosion' (ibid.: 118).

In general terms, according to this approach, instability is due to processes of change, and crises are conceptualized in terms of a gap between the potential for growth and realized growth (ibid.: 127). This gap may arise essentially because the five social subsystems generate a large number of irregular fluctuations, that is, cyclical and wave-like movements with different periodicities. These fluctuations can be caused either 'by specific subsystem cycles (political business cycles, technological trajectories, cultural movements, life-cycle of products and industries) or by the lags and feedback in the inter-subsystem connections' (ibid.: 121), that is to say, because of the lack of synchronicity and harmony between the key social, institutional and political factors.

This general view is elaborated upon in the TEP approach, which sees instability arising because 'there is a basic mismatch between the technoeconomic possibilities and the existing social structures' (Louça 2003: 770). According to these neo-Schumpeterian authors, it is the mismatch between technological innovation and the (old, slowly adjusting) institutional infrastructure which is responsible for the tensions leading to economic cycles (see also Perez 2002: 25). More specifically, what underlies the deeper crises and long-term cyclical behaviour is the need for reforms and the inevitable social resistance to them. Indeed there is 'a sort of inertia and time lag involved in the changing embedded socio-cultural practices and norms across a wide range of institutions' (Preston 2001: 40). From this standpoint, the recent NE with the advent of ICT does not represent a unique event in the history of capitalism; a similar pattern of events and mismatch have been generated in the past by other technological innovations.

In addition to these considerations, the TEP has also made a significant contribution to the understanding of structural imbalances within the economic sphere that render the economy unsustainable and eventually lead to recession. Among these one can distinguish between those occurring at the macroeconomic level – such as the mismatch between the profile of demand and that of potential supply, the rift between paper values and real values generating a gigantic process of income redistribution and the tension between the socially excluded and those reaping the benefits of the bubble (see e.g. Perez 2002: 43) – and those due to market forms. As for the latter, one can note that in this neo-Schumpeterian literature,

> the crisis on the fourth long wave is often addressed in terms of the dampening effect of oligopolistic competition in the face of maturing technologies and consequent upward pressure in wages and prices and the inefficiencies of large corporations which tended to exhaust the scope for productivity gains.
>
> (Preston 2001: 40)

Limitations: the dangers of technological determinism

The account of the evolution of actual historical processes based on the TEP concept, despite its obvious utility, does not seem to be sufficient alone to single out new indicators of instability or to provide the basis for policy recommendations. A few major limitations can be noted here. The first is that the TEP concept fails to overcome all the dangers of technological determinism. As noted, for example, by Boyer (1988: 67), this turns out to be a salient feature in the present revival of neo-Schumpeterian ideas (see also Elam 1994; for an account of the debate on this issue, see Preston 2001: 40). Despite being an improvement over the old Kondratieff cycle approach and being much more flexible than other approaches,[1] the TEP approach still places technological change at the centre of the NE. In particular, although it also emphasizes other economic and social factors, such as institutions, finance, globalization and policy, it still regards them as being causally related to technology. This is made clear by Perez in the description of her informal model based on the sequence of events characterizing the evolution of various paradigms, from their rise to their decay. She argues that this sequence 'has been stripped of all those events not causally related to the absorption of technologies, which leads inevitably to streamlined simplifications that hardly ever occur as such' (Perez 2002: 49). In dealing with the financial system, Perez places the emphasis on the financial instruments that enable innovation, and on the financial bubble which derives from it.

A few problems can be noted with this approach. In the first place, it fails to consider that the key factors mentioned in the sequence are also, at least partially, autonomous. For example, major financial crises and economic recessions may develop because of the influence of other factors quite unrelated to innovation. Similar remarks apply to other important relations, such as that between technology and globalization. Second, while acknowledging in principle the relative autonomy of the socio-institutional sphere with respect to technology, in practice, the TEP actually establishes too rigid a link between the two (for a different perspective on this point, see Preston 2001: 40). Strictly speaking, there is no doubting that the TEP is right to stress the need for systemic analysis and to point out that history demonstrates several different modes of development and 'regulation' as opposed to a single universal mode. However, this approach ends up by positing a predominant causal link between the technological and socio-institutional spheres, as revealed by its tendency to overemphasize institutional change from one paradigm to the next. In particular, it can be argued that a sharp break did not really occur between the previous and current paradigms. While it is true that consumer credit, oligopoly, trade unions, the welfare state and Keynesian policies were crucial for the previous paradigm based on mass production and Fordism, these institutional elements are of continued relevance in the NE as well, although they have undergone some important changes in form. For example, Keynesian policies are still implemented, and trade unions (although in a different form from previous decades) still provide strong incentives for innovation. In the end, the TEP approach advocates systemic analysis solely for innovation and technological change. It fails to consider that other key economic factors should also be analysed in a systemic fashion.

The dangers of disregarding macroeconomic equilibrium

Another weakness of the TEP approach is that it fails to provide a full-blown macroeconomic analysis. Strictly speaking, this is not to say that there are no macroeconomic implications following from TEP analysis or that such implications are neglected. For instance, when describing the current process of turbulent change and adaptation to the NE, wherein some new industries are experiencing rapid growth while others are declining or stagnating, neo-Schumpeterian authors emphasize that the combined outcome of these contradictory tendencies may vary (in different countries, times etc), resulting in a quite uncertain net effect in terms of GDP growth and employment (see Louçã 2003: 790). Moreover, reference is made, at least implicitly, to Keynesian or non-orthodox macroeconomic policy views, for example, when criticizing the failure of neoliberal policies to provide the required direction in terms of industrial policy and coordination across policy areas (e.g. Freeman and Perez 1988).

We suggest, instead, that the TEP approach fails to integrate the analysis of structural change with macroeconomic *theory* and, in particular, fails to refer to an equilibrium concept that provides the basis for stability analysis, including normative assessments and policy recommendations. In most neo-Schumpeterian contributions, no clear reference is made to macro theoretical frameworks. On the one hand, standard neoclassical theory is sharply rejected. As Freeman and Louçã clearly point out

> [t]he orthodox view...ignores structural change and views the economies as cumulative and simple processes, driven by unexplained technological change and under artificial conditions (maximizing rationality, free competition, full availability of perfect information, etc.). In this framework, realism and the definition of distinctive periods of history are considered to be irrelevant or illogical. Of course, the long wave research programme...establishes an alternative evolutionary approach where the abstraction of the representative agent is completely ignored, where diversity and the creation of novelty are considered the main factors of economic change, and where time matters and morphogenetic processes are identified to describe the real economies.
>
> (2001: 94)

On the other hand, Keynesian theory is seen as applying only or mainly to the short run. Strictly speaking, neo-Schumpeterian authors such as Freeman and Louçã do not neglect the significance of Keynes's key contributions, such as his view of 'the complexity of the interactions between the various subsystems of society' (Freeman and Louçã 2001: 135), his emphasis on long-term expectations as semi-autonomous variables which are not 'compatible with the deterministic view of causality...and that...represent the organic synthesis of network causality and complexity (ibid.: 57). Moreover, in their view, Keynes's critique of econometrics showed his awareness of the 'fundamental importance of qualitative change' (ibid.: 123),[2] and his philosophy 'suggested the notion of organicity and therefore liberated him from the stringency of the concept of equilibrium' (ibid.: 60).

Nevertheless, the fact that 'he was not able to incorporate these notions into a dynamic approach' (ibid.) is Keynes's major limitation. In their 1988 contribution, Freeman and Perez stress, for example, that, while in the *Treatise of Money* Keynes endorses Schumpeter's view of innovation, it is surprising that 'neither Keynes nor the Keynesians followed up this recognition of the crucial role of technical innovation'. In the *General Theory*, Keynes's neglect of technology can be seen in his artificial view of the decline in the marginal efficiency of capital unrelated to the actual changes in techniques and capital stock. This justifies Schumpeter's critique of the *General Theory* that it is limited to the short run: it focuses on factors that govern the degree of utilization of industrial apparatus, not on changes of it. For this reason, it 'excludes the salient features of capitalist reality' (Schumpeter 1954: 1144; see also Freeman and Perez 1988: 44; Freeman and Louçã 2001: 55–6).

The lack of explicit macro frameworks in these contributions means that they take macroeconomic outcomes for granted, as if they were completely determined by the interaction between institutional features, on the one hand, and by structural changes on the other. Perez's book, for example, focuses on the description of the process of structural adjustment occurring at the sectoral level, that is, behind aggregates. She makes no attempt to bridge the gap between the two levels of analysis. While making reference to possible causes of instability, such as the mismatch between the profile of demand and that of potential supply, Perez then fails to provide a thorough discussion of the economic adjustment mechanisms involved, based on a clear benchmark or equilibrium notion (e.g. she does not answer questions such as the following: What can we do to get rid of unemployment? Shall we just wait for price changes to clear the markets? And if institutional changes are needed, what kind of changes should we pursue?). In her view, it is mainly institutional reforms, rather than traditional Keynesian policies, that are able to redress these kinds of imbalances.

This approach impedes a complete analysis of stability because it disregards the impact of technological change on the macroeconomic drivers of economic change, that is, the agents' behaviour. While it is obviously useful to describe the 'objective' changes that the new technology introduces (e.g. the fact that computers undoubtedly allow for more flexible production processes, etc.) it is also important to take into account the 'subjective' changes, that is, to address the issue as to whether the agents' behaviour (e.g. their propensity to consume or invest) is affected or not. If one is concerned with stability analysis, it would be erroneous just to assume, either implicitly or explicitly, that this behaviour is not undergoing change, or to expect that the new technology will have a certain effect. In our view, it is here, in the widespread behavioural changes brought about by the accelerating trends described previously, that the peculiarity of the NE lies.

In other words, while it may be true that a sequence of events broadly resembling past events may occur over the long run, as illustrated by the TEP approach, this does not suffice for today's assessment of the NE or for the drawing of policy implications. We cannot simply presume that adjustment will take place in due course, as it did with past technologies. While such an approach might be adequate for a historian's 'long-run' perspective, rules of conduct for the short run are required in order to advise policy-makers. But for this purpose, the mechanisms that grant adjustment at the macroeconomic level must be specified. These are questions that call for macroeconomic theory and the equilibrium concept as the basis for normative judgement.

Moreover, another reason that reference to the TEP concept does not provide sufficient grounds for studying macroeconomic stability is that it places too much emphasis on the sequence of recurring events which characterizes each technological revolution. Among the problems this raises we can mention the following. First, while useful for relating the reasons why booms and depressions occur and for highlighting some of the key causal mechanisms at work, the sequence approach may lead social scientists to regard 'historical laws' as determining the current state of affairs and to neglect possible changes in behaviour. Second, the sequence involves abstraction from other cycles; it reflects the long wave induced by technological change. Yet this is only one component of the actual dynamics deriving from the intersection of waves of various lengths (short- and medium-run cycles) induced by a number of other relatively autonomous factors, such as globalization, finance and policy moves.

Third, the long-cycle sequence involves abstraction from other non-cyclical qualitative movements of capitalist dynamics, such as empirical laws asserting the irreversible character or the acceleration of some key phenomena which characterize not just one TEP but the whole complex capitalist evolution since at least the turn of the last century. In a sense, they constitute a neglected link between the various TEPs. More in general, as pointed out by authors such as Maddison, Boyer and the Regulation school, even if one ackowledges the existence of historical periods, it is still possibile to doubt the adequacy of concepts such as cycles or waves (see Freeman and Louçaça 2001: 94–5).

In the end, the TEP's emphasis on the sequence of recurring events prevents it from capturing the essence of the NE. To declare that 'the events characterising the NE have occurred before' (Perez 2002: XVII) is simply not enough.

Part II

Stability analysis and the neo-modern perspective

As noted earlier, a full-blown stability analysis ideally requires a method capable of dealing with the complexity of combined dynamics. In other words, we need a method that provides a clear picture of the system's overall behaviour that relies on simultaneous treatment of a number of causal mechanisms rather than on their separate treatment justified on the basis of the 'everything else being equal' clause.

In general, the survey of the various existing approaches to stability presented in Part I leads us to one main conclusion, namely, that neither purely empirical nor purely analytical methods alone seem adequate for carrying out stability analysis. On the one hand, mere observation or description is insufficient because there is no equilibrium concept on which to build a coherent rationale or to individuate a hierarchy of factors. On the other, despite their usefulness in the analysis of static problems, standard analytical methods appear to be ineffective tools for the analysis of dynamic issues such as stability. In particular, they tend to rely on relatively strong notions of equilibrium that seek to determine the behaviour of the economy over time, according to a number of well-defined 'laws of motion'. However, these laws – when not utterly misleading – can only provide us with limited insight, for they are obtained not on the grounds of a full-blown mathematical model of interactions but by building elaborate models that assume the independence of the key factors and that, therefore, single out just one or two for analysis.

In Part II of this book, we propose an alternative approach to stability analysis, which can be referred to as 'neo-modern', in an attempt to overcome this impasse. To be fully appreciated, this approach needs to be understood in the light of the two main trends in current methodological debate. The first is the growing dissatisfaction with orthodoxy and with the abuse of formalistic approaches by some economists. In Chapter 4, we have chosen to tackle these issues by considering the debate between modernism and post-modernism, out of which the neo-modern perspective quite naturally arises. This perspective suggests that the best strategy for the study of stability is to rely on 'light theory'. In particular, this implies rejection of the quest for dynamic laws of the economy and commitment to the view that theory is not self contained but needs to be integrated with historical and institutional factors.

The second broad trend in methodology is the emergence of evolutionary thinking and complexity theory as major alternative frameworks for economics. Chapter 5 focuses on complexity theory, with particular attention to its links to the neo-modern perspective. Finally, Chapter 6 will provide an account of our own approach, which can be understood as an attempt to combine selected features of the complexity approach with the basic macroeconomic paradigms.

4 The crisis in economic theory and the neo-modern perspective

The obstacles to a successful analysis of stability are symptomatic of a broader crisis in standard economic theory. A number of vehement attacks on formalism have recently appeared in the literature and elsewhere (see e.g. the student-led post-autistic economics movement). In particular, there is a growing feeling that the use of formal methods has been unduly extended and that their repetitive applications is rather sterile (see e.g. Lawson 1997, 2003; Fulbrook 2003).

It should be clear, however, that this crisis is not simply a matter of the use of mathematics *per se*. What is at stake in debates among economists also concerns the proper role of theory in economic analysis, the extent to which it is legitimate to rely on abstraction, the relation between universal concepts, historical specificity and institutions and so on.

If these are some of the issues to be dealt with, some clues as to how to carry out stability analysis can be gleaned by making reference to recent methodological debate. In particular, the clash between modernism and post-modernism is a useful starting point, for two main reasons. One is that post-modernist ideas have been used to account for the effects of information technology on the stability of the NE. As noted by Kevin Kelly, a guru of the optimistic, techno-centric vision of the NE,

> As network rise, the centre recedes. It is no coincidence that global network appear at the same time as the post-modern literary movement. In postmodernism, there is no central anteriority, no universal dogma, no foundational ethic. The theme of postmodernism in the arts, science and politics . . . results in fragmentation, instability, indeterminacy and uncertainty. This also sums up the net.
>
> (Kelly 1998: 159)

The second reason is that the contrast between the two movements is extremely relevant to our views on stability. Our analysis takes as its starting point the belief that economics, like other disciplines, seems to be going through a transitional phase resulting from the overlap of several conflicting elements, such as the end of modernism and the full development of the post-modernist parable from success to crisis (or even implosion). There is now significant reason to believe that this phase of transition is likely to lead to a new and more advanced stage, which can be labelled as 'neo-modern'. In our view, it is within this context that a new perspective on stability can be fruitfully developed.

This claim obviously needs substantiation. By 'neo-modernism', we intend the recent broad cultural movement or methodological stance that attempts to combine aspects of both modernism and post-modernism. In a nutshell, it consists in the general attempt to extend the boundaries of science, on the basis of a new awareness for the need of combining an inductive stance with the proper role of theory. The use of the 'neo-modern' label is explicitly acknowledged by sociologists like Alexander (1994) and cultural theorists like Kumar (1995). But similar views have also been advanced by economists advocating a 'new synthesis' between those two movements (e.g. Chick and Dow 2001; Dow 2001, 2002; Hodgson 2001; Louçã and Freeman 2001). In particular, as we shall see in Chapter 5, we regard complexity theory as belonging to the neo-modern perspective. But to understand this 'neo-modern' view, the meaning of modernism and post-modernism must first be clarified. That is the goal of the present chapter. As we shall see, this is no easy task, for a full definition of these cultural movements is difficult, and the relationship between them is certainly not linear, either in historical or conceptual terms.[1] After giving a very brief definition (we really cannot do more than just hint at the main issues here), the chapter then introduces the neo-modern project in very general terms.

Modernism

'Modernism' refers to a vast cultural movement that flourished between the end of the nineteenth and the early decades of the twentieth centuries, and that criticized the trend towards modernization. Strictly speaking, it is also a heterogeneous movement. On the one hand, as noted by McCloskey (1986), it is related to the age of Enlightenment and its positivistic methodology (inspired by philosophers such as Descartes, Hume and Comte) and was concerned with establishing the foundations of knowledge and certainty (we can label this as 'official' modernism). Among its leaders, McCloskey lists Russell and Hempel (see also Boylan and O'Gorman 1995: 39). On the other hand, modernism also includes quite different (i.e. non positivist) landmarks, unsurpassed in Western culture, such as the critique of old rationalism, positivism and utilitarianism carried out by Nietzsche, Freud, Weber and Keynes in philosophy, psychology, sociology and economics, the musical innovations produced by Schoenberg, the Cubist revolution in the arts, the international style in architecture and the subjectivist turn in literature where writers such as Strindberg, Ibsen, Pirandello and Brecht, for example, emphasize that individuals do not possess a unifying character but exhibit a multiplicity and contradictory nature of levels of conscience (see e.g. Kumar 1995: ch. 4).[2] In regard to these contributions, we can speak of 'high modernism'.

Despite this heterogeneity, however, 'official' modernism has prevailed in the literature, that is, the label has been associated mainly with positivist views justifying the emphasis on linearity, stability and steady progress, rather than on the possible 'negative' or distorted effects of key phenomena. For example, McCloskey (1986) suggests that modernism is anti-historical in its preoccupation with foundations or certainty, endorsing scientism in holding that the boundaries of genuine knowledge coincide with those of science, relying on old-fashioned paradigms of physics, and the understanding of science in axiomatic terms, with a primary focus on prediction, control, observation, experimentation and measurement. Among the commandments of modernist methodology, McCloskey also includes explanations in terms of covering laws and a clear distinction between ends and means (see also Boylan and O'Gorman 1995: 39).

It is important to further clarify some of the key implications of these commandments (see e.g. Dow 2001: 64, 2002: 122). First of all, there is a need to distinguish between appearances and reality: 'reality is not as it presents itself' (Klamer 1995: 319). There are contingent or transient elements and fundamental invariant or deep structures that underlie appearances. The early modernists were experiencing 'a world in which "all that is solid melts into air" ... in which old certainties were lost.... This experienced ephemerality of reality motivated the search for the invariant structure that underlies that reality' (ibid.: 321). In general, both artistic movements and scientific theories tried to focus on the latter. For this reason they tend to rely on abstract and formal tools, starting from axioms referring to the smallest elements. Formalism is considered the best language for representing discovered truths (see e.g. Klamer 1995: 319; Cullemberg *et al.* 2001: 26). It is important not to regard this approach as being unrealistic *per se*. As Klamer again points out:

> Representation of the invariant structure required, it was believed, the development of abstract and formal methods. If the abstract, geometric paintings of Piet Mondrian and Malevitch seem removed from reality, they actually are intended to be realistic in the sense that they probe and represent 'deep' reality. Far from retreating into an abstract world removed form the real one, these early modernists were utopian... strove for ideals of emancipation and liberation and worked for a better world.
>
> (1995: 321)

Another implication is that theories tend to be a-historical, in that their objective is to identify universal laws of nature (or society).[3] Moreover, they express a monist vision of reality; in particular, reality has an objective existence and unifying forces await discovery. Finally, theories need to be assessed rationally, in terms of their logic and on the basis of empirical testing independent of how the ideas originated. There is no doubting that the most well-known application of these modernist principles in economics is the general equilibrium approach, which insists on the dogma of stability. As clearly stated in Samuelson's 1947 contribution, the aim of the general equilibrium approach is to build a universal model around the unifying principle of maximization under constraint (see e.g. Klamer 1995; Dow 2001: 67).

It must be noted, however, that 'high' modernism has also been interpreted as having a counterpart in economic analysis. As observed by Phelps (1990: ch. 1), for example, Keynes's emphasis on the sharp rejection of Classical doctrines, the irreducible multiplicity of perspectives, the end of 'objective truth' and the system's disequilibrium are in line with the contemporary revolutions in science, arts and philosophy.

Post-modernism: general features

As already mentioned, post-modernism is extremely difficult to define; the term is associated to a plethora of meanings (see Cullemberg *et al.* 2001: 9; Preston 2001: ch. 5; Dow 2002: 124).[4] It is therefore subject to numerous interpretations, each of which has rather significantly different implications for economics. For example, it has been said that 'Keynes is sometimes seen as the archetypical modernist and sometimes as a postmodernist' (Dow 2002: 124; see also Amariglio and Ruccio 1995; Dow 2001: 73). Bearing this in mind, we start by pointing out that post-modernism can be seen in broad terms as the cultural correlate of a post-industrial society, in which knowledge has become the principal force of production (see Lyotard 1984: 5; also Preston 2001: 82). It can be regarded as the antithesis of 'official' modernism (see e.g. Dow 2001: 61).[5] In contrast, the break between post-modernism and non-positivist modernist views is much less clear cut.

One major point of divergence between 'official' modernism and post-modernism is that the latter provides a philosophical foundation for duality and can therefore, at least in principle, accommodate the stability issue. More specifically, post-modernism is committed to an emphasis of the 'negative' aspects of phenomena from the start, asserting that they do not possess linear or simple outlines in our society, and that simple accounts for them may not hold.[6] Post-modern theorists, for example, criticize the notion of progress,[7] arguing that modern science and technology contribute possibly as much to 'barbarism' and destruction (e.g. the atomic bomb) as they do to the betterment of human life and the natural environment (see Cullemberg *et al.* 2001: 9).

At the analytical level, the emphasis on duality leads post-modernists to reject the 'official' modernist ideals of scientism, determinism and formalism. Instead, they place the emphasis on indeterminacy, fragmentation (i.e. the disowning of the concepts of totality, homogeneity and unity) and deconstruction (i.e. the critique of canons and dominant codes, such as the notion of 'Man' or the unified, rational agent). As noted by Dow, for example, this means not placing the concept of 'Man' at the centre of the analysis; in post-modern philosophy 'individuals themselves are, on the one hand, an integral part of their social context, and, on the other, fragmented. Individuals are not themselves independent entities with given information sets (Dow 2002: 124).

Two remarks are in order here. First, there is no clear divide between post-modernism and 'high' modernism on these issues. It is on this basis that several important authors, including Lyotard, Bauman and Huyssen, suggest that post-modernism may actually be profitably viewed as the 'acceleration', or latest stage of modernism, and as the full realization of its potential (see e.g. Kumar 1995: ch. 5).[8]

Second, post-modernists accept that there is a trade off between duality and generality of theories, and reject the notion that general theories (what Lyotard labels as 'grand metanarratives'), such as liberalism and Marxism, can provide a set of universal laws of motion of capitalism, regardless of the local context (e.g. Lyotard 1984: 71–2). They focus instead on case studies of local communities,[9] acknowledging that people live in a variety of psychological and social states and positions and that social inequality persists (see Cullemberg *et al.* 2001: 9–10). Moreover, post-modernism also rebukes 'essentialism', which is basically a summary of such crucial aspects of modernist science as the distinction between appearance and essence, the attempt to discover an order that lies beneath the chaotic surface, the scientific critique of common sense and the view that language is to a large extent representational (words correspond to the world they intend to describe). The point is that post-modernism rejects schemas and logic, relies on the notions of juxtaposition and simultaneity, refuses to establish hierarchies of elements (i.e. the distinction between appearance and essence or between cause and effect), appreciates 'depthlessness', that is, elements that comprise pure surface (i.e. the view that 'surface is everything') and contrasts the use of discourse analysis as a search for meaning (inevitably context dependent) with the positivists' rationalist programme of searching for truth. In particular, for post-modernist authors such as Roland Barthes, no fundamental reality exists outside language and discourse. Indeed, as aptly stated by Preston, for these authors 'everything which we encounter or experience as 'reality' is only (or primarily) a matter of languages or texts or discourses – that is, essentially forms of information – rather than external things (there is no 'out there', as it were)' (Preston 2001: 87).

These considerations have crucial implications. First, since each context is particular and generates its own knowledge, the focus on discourse involves incommensurability: the concepts and language used to account for each situation may have different meanings when applied from one situation to the next, and there is no independent means of determining which account is 'best'. Second, the focus on discourse also involves the critique of formalism. If there are no truths to be discovered, models are just one type of discursive means with no other better access to underlying essential truths than any other such means (see e.g. Cullemberg *et al.* 2001: 24–6; Dow 2001, 2002: 123–5).

This refusal to embrace the unifying agenda of modernism explains why post-modern authors tend to endorse eclecticism and call for a syncretism of styles and fields of enquiry. There are two major implications to this stance. First, it tends to generate an extension of disciplines outside their traditional boundaries.[10] Indeed, whereas modernist social science regards society as being sufficiently differentiated to proceed to autonomous analysis of its subsets based on different principles,[11] post-modernism claims that the lines of demarcation between various realms of society or between nature and society or culture have broken down. This can be seen, for example, in the increasing role that advertising plays in contemporary culture, in the increasing influence of cultural industry in advanced economies and in the fact that 'nature is gone for good' as Jameson (1992) puts it.[12] Second, it leads post-modernists to refuse clear-cut distinctions between the present and the past. In their view, the past is not rejected or imitated but is used to enrich the present and develop 'synthetic' or hybrid constructions (see e.g. Kumar 1995: ch. 4).

Post-modernism: its implications for economics

With these considerations as a background, the consequences of post-modernism for economics are easier to understand, even if they are not always straight-forward. In principle, one of the most significant is the rejection of the fiction of the 'rational economic man'.

> The postmodern condition may be said to open up a very different research agenda for economic scientists should they choose to disown what many regard as the necessary 'fiction' (defended by many, in the end, for contain-ing more than just a grain of truth about human subjects) of the unified self and move, instead, to a different fiction (but one supposedly more in tune with contemporary reality), the decentered self.
>
> (Cullemberg *et al.* 2001: 13)

However, it is quite evident that the majority of economists have not followed this path so far. Most quite simply stick to standard neoclassical theory and the 'official' modernist canon. Nonetheless, it would be erroneous to conclude that the neoclassical agenda is still viable or that post-modernism has not had a major impact on economics. On the contrary, one can mention several recognizable post-modern developments in our discipline, although they do not go far enough to involve revolutionary changes of the kind previously mentioned. The most signif-icant developments are those concerning the crisis of the two 'grand theories' of general equilibrium and Keynes's macroeconomics, ongoing since the late 1970s.

As for general equilibrium, the influence of post-modernism can be seen in a series of seemingly contradictory moves. In recent times, macroeconomics has been dominated by NCM, which is based on a clear eclectic tendency (well in line with the general equilibrium tradition) to combine new formal tools with past the-oretical beliefs. At the same time, however, several post-modern developments seem to undermine this very same tradition. For instance, much of current eco-nomics (including mainstream economics) is characterized by a certain amount of fragmentation and can no longer be classified in terms of general equilibrium (see e.g. Dow 2002: 123). While it is true, in general, that macroeconomists have not dismissed the standard assumption of rationality, most of them apply it in piecemeal fashion in a variety of contexts, quite outside any unifying logic of a Walrasian kind. This is especially evident in two strands of the literature. The first concerns the search for the micro-foundations of macro. This has led many to emphasize a variety of partial equilibrium stories based on a plethora of special assumptions which defy generalization, or to attempt to build all-encompassing theoretical frameworks, such as Hahn's alternative general equilibrium model (see e.g. Blanchard and Fisher 1989: 27–8).[13]

The second is the literature concerned with policy-making. It can be noted for example that the continuing failure of vast multi-equation macro models to perform satisfactorily (e.g. they make huge forecasting errors) in recent years has led to new developments, such as the coordinated use of a range of small models, as complementary lines of enquiry (see e.g. Dow 2002: 30–1).

Also undermining general equilibrium theory is the tendency of the NCM to consider its general equilibrium models as 'tales' rather than representations of the economy, in line with post-modern thought and the so-called 'rhetorical' approach to understanding economics developed by McCloskey (1986). In other words, it is possible to see NCM models as reflecting a 'linguistic' or technical turn, according to which what matters is not representation or the attempt to grasp the essential mechanisms of the real world economy, but simple internal consistency or the technical ability to construct tales.

On these grounds, it would therefore seem that general equilibrium theory, although it still exists, has a more limited role and is gradually being replaced in practice either by a plethora of precise but disjointed small-scale models capturing partial aspects of reality or by broader models which are relatively contentless.

As for Keynesian macroeconomics, it can be argued that post-modernist ideas have inspired the rejection of several aspects of Keynes's vision, such as his emphasis on macroeconomics as an autonomous discipline with respect to microeconomics and his optimistic belief that governments are able to steer the economy. The key point is that if universal laws do not exist, then there is theoretically much less justification for government intervention and much more reason to pay attention to local decision making. As Dow points out (2002: 123–5), postmodernism thus justifies the new wave of liberalism resulting in a shift from demand management towards the privatization of public sector activity. It also validates the challenge made by the rational expectations theory of the idea that government has superior access to knowledge that would warrant government activism and also allow it to be effective. Moreover, the revival in interest in neo-Austrian economics, which rejects macroeconomics and the use of aggregates in favour of microanalysis, has likewise been stimulated by post-modern trends.

The neo-modern alternative

In the light of this general overview of modernism and post-modernism, we can now clarify the key suggestion of our book: namely, that in order to build up a more general understanding of the economy and investigate its stability, we should make a neo-modern turn. This amounts to recognizing that, despite their limitations, both modernism and post-modernism have important lessons to teach us and need be accommodated. To do so requires combining features of these two apparently conflicting points of view, in order to create a kind of new synthesis.

We can start by noting the various incontrovertible merits of post-modernism. Dow mentions, for example, its concern in avoiding any demarcation between science and non-science and its plea for tolerance and open-mindedness to different meanings arising from different contexts (see Dow 2002: 125–6). Another post-modern feature we need to retain in our approach is its emphasis on the end of the relative autonomy of various spheres implied by the mechanistic view, subsequent to the increasing overlap, or contamination, between culture, economics and nature in the NE. Moreover, for our purposes, the post-modernists' emphasis on duality and the rejection of linear and unified modernist perspectives is crucial. Indeed, if it is true that stability should no longer be taken for granted but analysed, the possibility of instability must be allowed for. In this regard, the decentring of the canon of 'Man' by post-modernists and the distinction between social context and fragmentation of individual behaviour (or, in other words, the tension between homogeneity and differentiation) seem particularly useful. While the representative agent underlying standard theory can only justify the stability assumption, this distinction allows us to see the origins of the instability problem.

On these grounds, it may therefore appear that by emphasizing duality, post-modernism can provide the foundations for an alternative approach to stability. One should be wary of this conclusion, however. There is a significant limitation to post-modernism remaining to be overcome if its insights are to be fully developed by the social sciences, and by economics in particular. This is the belief that the focus on duality necessarily implies an almost complete rejection of theorizing as such, as if it were a completely modernist enterprise to be eliminated. Indeed, as already noted, the fact that post-modernism is the pure antithesis of 'official' modernism implies a number of rather 'negative' or 'destructive' claims. These include the out-and-out denial of methodology, the rejection of any form of essentialism or the notion of 'truth' following the view that 'reality' is only a matter of language, as opposed to external things, the incommensurability of knowledge and the lack of grounds for choosing one theory over another. This obviously makes theorizing about social and economic scenarios rather difficult (see e.g. Dow 2001).

In other words, if one takes post-modernism at face value, there is no basis for discussion of any kind of methodological rules concerning how economics should be conducted, and the whole agenda of building an alternative approach to stability analysis breaks down.[14] Many critics maintain that these rather nihilistic views are not actually sustainable (see e.g. Dow 2001, 2002: 167) and account for the still limited impact of post-modernism on economics. In particular, they explain why economists remain deaf to the post-modernist siren and why post-modernism has not yet resulted in the abandonment of the standard assumption of rationality or the whole general equilibrium project but only in the weakening of some of their properties and implications.

But all is not lost. The post-modern enterprise can still be saved from pure 'nihilism' by combining it with those aspects of modernism that are inevitably involved in theorizing, such as abstraction, causality and essentialism. It is here that the neo-modern stance enters the picture. It is important to note that this is not a completely novel proposal; to a significant extent, it already underlies the work of many scholars, although it has been referred to in different ways. Thinking along these lines, Dow (2001, 2002: 166), for example, proposes what she labels the 'synthetic approach', incorporating much of what is good in post-modernism without accepting the radically negative views just mentioned. She provides at least two critical arguments in support of her proposal. One is that the synthetic approach is implicit in most heterodox schools. The other is that it is not really foreign to post-modernist contributions either; in particular, it almost inevitably emerges when the post-modern approach is applied to a specific field, such as economics or literature.

On the other hand, it should be clear that rejection of the most radical post-modernist claims does not imply a simple return to modernism. If it is true that what we are suggesting here amounts to retaining some key modernist categories of theorizing, it is also true that it implies the firm rejection of other modernist claims. In particular, the neo-modern view recognizes the validity of the post-modern critique against general or universal theory, although it stops short of rejecting it completely.

The novelty of the neo-modern stance can thus be stated as follows. First, it emphasizes 'light theory'. Neo-modernism recognizes that theory still plays a crucial role in the understanding of the economy and in the guidance of policy-makers. For example, only 'high order' or systemic macroeconomic theory based on some of the previously mentioned modernist canons can help us avoid getting lost in the plethora of partial equilibrium models produced by the post-modern turn, particularly evident in the micro-foundations and policy-making literature. It can provide us with a set of arguments for choosing among theories, for combining them and for incorporating different types of knowledge. For instance, suggesting the criteria for selecting appropriate models and indicators can be useful in the development of 'discretionary strategies' for central banks.

For the neo-modern view, however, the scope for theory building on the basis of a pure, highly formalized, deductive approach or for making 'de-contextualized' general claims about the working of the economy, is much reduced. In other words, neo-modernism stresses the role of 'light theory', which amounts to recognizing that a truly universal and self-contained theory (i.e. one that seeks to achieve precise, internally consistent and definitive results), cannot exist or is bound to fail. In particular, there are no deterministic laws of evolution of complex systems.

A second novel implication of the neo-modern view is that it advocates a primary role for empirical evidence. Placing the emphasis on light theory is equivalent to the pursuit of a more inductive approach, opening the way to a better integration of theory with institutional and historical factors. As we will try to demonstrate, this involves much more than simply making often heard but vague claims, such as that 'history or institutions matter'.

Third, the neo-modern approach promises to be of great use in the field of stability analysis. Advocating 'light theory' means that we cannot hope to account for stability in a priori terms and that the entire argument of stability cannot be mathematical. In other words, advocating light theory means to deny the existence of laws of evolution of complex systems. We must therefore devise a method of dealing with complex dynamics and the stability issue based on a new combination of abstract/formal argument and historical method.

5   Complexity theory

The literature describes several research strategies that are consistent, at least in theory, with neo-modernism and which might be useful in understanding the NE. For the scope of this book, however, reference to complexity theory seems the most appropriate. We believe that, despite its many shortcomings, 'the complexity concept holds much more potential for reconstructing economic theory than is currently being exploited by economists' (Viskovatoff 2000: 130). In particular, it proposes a way out of the impasse of standard theory over the stability issue.

At least two reasons can be offered to justify this claim. First of all, complexity theory proposes a powerful vision of the economy as a whole that seems particularly relevant to the conceptualization of the NE. This is one of the reasons behind the recent emergence of a broadly defined mode of 'evolutionary thinking' (of which complexity theory is part) as an important alternative framework for economics (see e.g. Hodgson 1993, 2001, 2004a; Lawson 2004). Moreover, for the purposes of this book, given that the stability issue cannot be dealt with in partial equilibrium terms, a global vision is required. Second, complexity theory is consistent with three features characterizing the neo-modern approach: (a) it implies a more limited role of theory, that is, light theory; (b) it promotes an inductive turn in economics away from the standard deductive approach; (c) it provides analytical tools for the conceptualization of stability.

Vision

Complexity theory is not so much a unified theory as a vision, or conceptual framework, which seems especially relevant for macroeconomics. As Colander has observed, 'complexity provides a general framework within which to think about complex systems that is quite different than the conventional approach and is worth considering' (2000a: 4–5). The basic view it suggests is that the economic forces in complex systems evolve, are cumulative and time irreversible. They present phenomena such as positive feedbacks, increasing returns, self-organization (the system has properties out of which order is produced from disorder) and non-linearities (i.e. aggregate behaviour cannot be deduced from the mere sum total of individual behaviours. Because agents are expected to interact, interaction is expected to influence aggregate behaviour), path-dependence (i.e. previous results influence the subsequent trajectory of the system) and lock-in (i.e. once individuals have adopted a certain strategy there are obstacles to leaving it) (see e.g. Arthur 1994; Comim 2000: 155, 183; Pryor 2000: 63).

Moreover, the vision underlying complexity theory also seems relevant for interpreting the NE. Many scholars emphasize, for example, that competition involves a constant flow of new products and technological change and that technological change in turn offsets the natural tendency towards monopoly. Thus, from this point of view, technological change appears to be fully endogenous to the competitive process, rather than exogenous.

Strictly speaking, however, the complexity approach is not defined by the issues it examines. In fact, the emphasis on complexity is not new. Many themes in the current research on this topic were addressed by great economists, including Smith, Marshall, Keynes, Sraffa, Kaldor, Robinson, Schumpeter, Goodwin, Shackle and Hayek (see e.g. Colander 2000d: 125; Comim 2000: 155; Prasch 2000a: 217). Likewise, a variety of issues, such as path dependence, evolution, increasing returns and lock-in, have recently been taken up by conventional and non-conventional economists alike, including Aghion and Howitt, Baumol, Crafts, Krugman, Simon, Nelson and Winter.

Current complexity theory is therefore not defined by its objects of study, but by its methods, that is, by the approach it takes to understanding the economy, which inevitably influences the method of analysis it adopts (see e.g. Brock and Colander 2000: 73). However, the definition according to method is not unambiguous, given that there are many complexity approaches that can be followed. Among these, the Santa Fe Approach (SFA) is perhaps the most popular.[1]

For the sake of simplicity, we shall refer mainly to the SFA in what follows, because it provides richer insights into complexity than the alternatives. It places the emphasis on chaotic and non-linear dynamic processes in complex macroeconomic problems, in line not just with great economists of the past but also with the most recent advances in science.[2] As noted, for example by Wible (2000: 23), there are similarities between the SFA conception of complexity and the views of scientists, such as Prigogine and Nicolis (1989), who stress the themes of evolution and instabilities in modern biology and physics (i.e. quantum mechanics and relativity theory have taken a 'temporal' turn) and who hold that many fundamental processes shaping nature are irreversible and stochastic rather than reversible and deterministic (Wible 2000: 15–16).

We can draw several important inferences from these views, although the analogies between economics and natural science need to be handled with care.[3] First of all, they emphasize the idea of pluralism of systems, meaning the existence of various levels of partially autonomous systems of phenomena. Furthermore, each level may be made up of many partially autonomous systems functioning side by side. For example, the organs making up the human body are sufficiently autonomous to be identified as separate entities. The complexity approach extends this notion of multi-layered ontological complexity to a pluralistic view of the physical world, which is thus imagined as a compendium of many systems and sub-systems rather than as a single grand unified order or system of order. This pluralism of complexity lies in contrast to the reductionism of Newtonian mechanics, which likens the world to a grand clockwork mechanism (see e.g. Wible 2000: 18).

Second, complex dynamic systems require the development of a new conception of order besides equilibrium. This involves the adoption of a non-mechanical vision and a sharp distinction between microscopic and macroscopic terminology. In a mechanical system, where either no motion exists or where the motion occurs in a path that is reversible in time, equilibrium occurs when all the forces of the system sum to zero. In a non-mechanical system, instead, an order or pattern is defined as a steady state, which is a macroscopic property of the entire system and not a property of its constituent entities (e.g. a thermal steady state). It follows from this that complex systems may be in states far from equilibrium. Such states, which may persist indefinitely, are referred to as states of non-equilibrium (those in which self-organizing new patterns may emerge). Non-equilibrium is pervasive (it concerns most social processes) and thus seems to be a much more general case than mechanical equilibrium, which appears in quite limited and very rigid contexts (see e.g. Wible 2000: 18–19).[4] But this is not all. The analogies with physical sciences suggest that complex systems may also be characterized by chaos, which can be described as the appearance of turbulence in the system. Chaotic, turbulent behaviour is irregular and non-periodic and depends upon the initial conditions of the system (ibid.: 15).

On these grounds, it is not surprising that the complexity approach has been called 'a rallying cry for a variety of economists dissatisfied with neoclassical economics' (Pryor 2000: 63). As it is not a unified theory, the complexity view is compatible with a number of heterodox perspectives, including those of post-Keynesians, institutionalists and the Austrian school (Colander 2000a: 6; Prasch 2000a: 217, 2000b: 178).

Light theory

Various factors can be cited in support of the claim that the complexity approach involves 'light theory'. In very general terms, it can be argued that it does not seek to provide a unified, all-encompassing theory. Moreover, it demotes theory to a lower level, especially when compared to general equilibrium analysis (the epitome of 'hard theory'). In other words, the complexity view breaks with the tradition of theory as a purely deductive and self-contained sphere, placing much more emphasis on the knowledge of economic history and the history of economics.

It would be wrong to believe, however, that the complexity approach completely abandons the notion of 'grand theory' as such. In fact, it is often portrayed in the literature as a scientific breakthrough that is extending the boundaries of science by adopting the view of the economy as a complex system following the same laws as all complex systems. This seems to make it quite inconsistent with post-modern or relativistic canons. As noted by Colander, 'the complexity approach is an absolutist theory with a twist: i.e. it sees economics as having a grand theory and sees the purpose of economic science as to find that theory' (2000b: 33–4).

So how does the complexity approach differ from the standard general equilibrium model, which was also supposed to be a major instance of grand theory? At least three main differences help explain why the complexity approach can actually be regarded as 'light theory'.

Dynamic versus structural simplification

Both the complexity approach and the general equilibrium model consider science as the search for simplicity, or in other words, a process of data compression. However, unlike standard histories of economic thought, complexity theory advocates no single best way of achieving this; on the contrary, it allows the possibility of multiple potential patterns of simplification exploiting either formalized or informal knowledge. The main difference between the complexity approach and conventional economics lies in the type of simplification being sought: is it structural or dynamic? In the first case, as in the general equilibrium model, simple relationships are sought in order to reduce data into an analytically solvable model and then find the reduced form of that model (e.g. Einstein's equation). In contrast, complexity theory relies on iterative processes based on non-linear dynamic models. Whereas standard theory makes a leap of faith and assumes that the economy is subject to linear methods and relies on structural simplification, complexity theory advocates dynamic simplification instead.

As remarked by Colander (2000a: 2–4, 2000b: 32–3), structural simplifications are useful but not always satisfactory. Linear and static models are limited in some aspects, despite the potential merit deriving from their application. Generally speaking, such models work better in the natural sciences, whereas they overlook important elements in economics, such as path dependence, increasing returns, multiple equilibria and technology and the key insights arising from informal knowledge. For this reason, in Colander's view, 'economic theory has not been especially successful at finding simple structural laws that describe our economy' (Colander 2000a: 3).

In order to achieve dynamic simplification and extend the boundaries of science, complexity theorists also make a leap of faith. They assume that all complex phenomena are subject to similar forces, and that as complexity increases, transformations occur in which large numbers of interactions take place simultaneously, giving rise to an otherwise unpredictable pattern. They study the general development of these patterns and then apply the results of that general study to specific cases. In order to carry out this task, the complexity approach needs to be highly mathematical and statistical; it differs from conventional science in the nature of the mathematics and statistics it uses. Instead of seeking a formal analytical model with a formal solution for these complex phenomena, this approach looks for patterns that develop when non-linear processes are repeated over long periods of time.[5]

Having made these considerations, we can now turn to two major factors of 'lightness' in complexity theory. First, by focusing on iterative processes based on non-linear dynamics, it develops open models that lack a unique deterministic solution. In such models, many solutions are possible; which one is arrived at depends upon the initial conditions and the path the model follows.

Second, the simulation of dynamics on the computer diminishes the value of theories, in that it implies both a move away from deductive theory and a lack of commitment to a unique theory, that is, a pluralistic stance. This is easier to understand if one bears in mind that, in a certain sense, the complexity approach is a product of the NE:

> Developments in computers have made it possible to deal with models that are far more complicated than those that previously could be dealt with. One can simulate and, through rote computer power, gain insight into models with no analytic solution. Thus computers and simulations are the foundation of the complexity approach... [this] involves an enormous technological change in the way economists do economics... ultimately it is mathematics that will provide the formal insights into the institutions and history that are needed for economics to be a science.
>
> (Colander 2000a: 5)

Colander then offers the analysis of production as an example of how complexity economics differs from standard economics. While the latter would rely on a simple analytically solvable function, say the constant elasticity of substitution (CES) production function, the complexity approach would rely on computer simulation of hundreds of variations on non-linear models, many with no deterministic solution, to determine which model fits best the data. In this context, whether or not the models have analytic solutions would not serve as the relevant choice criterion of models as it does now. Instead, the relevant criterion would be whether it 'fits with the data'; elegance and solvability are de-emphasized. And this trend will continue as computing costs fall. Although complexity theorists are aware of the limits in what we can discover through simulation, their approach involves a stronger focus on mathematics and statistics than does standard economics. However, Colander believes that this does not make the complexity approach any less compatible with heterodox approaches. The point is that low-cost computing has led to a situation where the relatively a-theoretical exercise of singling out patterns is what comes first: 'The complexity approach demotes theory to a lower level and replaces it with conjectures and patterns that temporarily fit' (Colander 2000a: 6). It is only at a later stage that theory is needed and where heterodox approaches may also have a role to play:

> Determining whether these patterns are meaningful requires a knowledge of economic history and of the history of economics. Whereas in standard theory the latest theory is thought to include the best of the past, in complexity economics patterns can fluctuate and a variety of theories will be constantly tested.
>
> (ibid.)

Elements of 'realism'

The second reason why the complexity approach, unlike general equilibrium, involves 'light theory' is that it seeks to account for several elements of 'realism' – such as agents' heterogeneity, institutions, different layers and organizational levels, continual adaptation, emergent and perpetual novelties and out-of-equilibrium dynamics – by showing that they arise from the agents' interaction. Lightness means that consideration of these elements reduces the scope for pure deductive theory based on a few axioms alone. Strictly speaking, the complexity approach relies on models of artificial intelligence, referred to as adaptive non-linear networks or complex adaptive systems, which are not realistic in a descriptive sense. They are very general logical constructs that allow interdisciplinary analyses in that they can refer to widely disparate objects, such as ice, ants or economic agents.

However, these networks or systems can be seen as metaphors of dynamic real-world economic structures (Comim 2000: 157–8) and have properties which imply a departure from three canons of neoclassical economics: the universalizing concept of rationality, the view that the economy has no structure and the belief that explanation consists in finding unique outcomes (see Colander 2000d: 130). As for the first point, models of artificial intelligence allow the complexity approach to depart from the universal axioms of utility maximization by introducing empirical heterogeneity and cognitive foundations into economics. In contrast with representative agent models, which imply that individuals are identical, the complexity approach envisions the market as a population of heterogeneous and rival expectations, governed by the same principles of natural selection driving the process of biological evolution. Moreover, while the standard model assumes strong or substantive rationality, complexity theory embraces bounded rationality. As noted by Colander, the advantage of considering economics as the result of a number of iterative processes involving non-linear dynamics is that 'the complexity of the economy precludes the far-sighted rationality assumed of individuals in conventional theory' (Colander 2000c: 33).

As for the issue of the economy's structure, the emphasis on iterative processes and bounded rationality in networks of interaction allows a more direct account of increasing returns and institutions than does standard theory. While in the latter, institutions figure as external constraints and agents as atoms, in the complexity approach, instead, the agents' actions have structural foundations shaped 'by emergent social roles and by socially supported procedures, that is by institutions' (ibid.). Indeed once the agents' bounded rationality is considered in a complex environment, the interaction between agents and institutions quite naturally develops: '[P]eople will develop institutions to deal with the world, and these institutions will change their behaviour' (ibid.).

As for the third point, as already noted, the complexity approach calls into question the standard method of equilibrium, which focuses on unique outcomes and the goal of prediction, and shifts the emphasis to the analysis of 'process and emergence'. Lightness here essentially amounts to taking an anti-deterministic view. Complexity theorists are aware that the SFA model does not furnish an analytical understanding of the system over all time or allow prediction of the future. This stance can be stated in two ways: either by ruling out equilibrium altogether, by arguing for example that an evolutionary system does not arrive at a state of rest unless it were to stop evolving (e.g. Arthur 1994: chs 1–3) or by accepting weaker notions of equilibria and suggesting that many alternative equilibria are possible for a given process.

In any case, this anti-deterministic view implies a radical change in what economists consider as the key issues. For example, the concern is no longer that of getting the prices right but of understanding the varying roles that prices are playing. Moreover, although very complex dynamics can be generated on computers that mimic the most important features of real life economic processes, prediction still cannot be achieved for most individual events and patterns.[6] Complexity theorists thus tend to subscribe to the view held by economists like Hayek or Keynes, according to which theory should not concern itself with prediction but with explanation of the principle or the central factors that grant to a systematic pattern its characteristic appearance. Indeed, in economics, as in climatology, biology and geology, one should conduct a 'search for and an assessment of "major forces at work," study the emergence of structure (hurricane or species) and provide research with compelling explanations as to what has occurred and what can potentially take place' (Prasch 2000a: 216; see also Wible 2000: 19–23).

The complementarity view

Finally, the complexity approach, unlike general equilibrium, involves 'light theory', also because it does not seek to build a unifying, all-encompassing framework based on a reductionist perspective. The SFA model, for example, is not meant to replace existing theories but to complement them by revealing their elements of validity and weakness:

> [C]omplexity science is not a replacement for standard science; it is a supplement. It does not say that standard science is not a reasonable approach to take. It simply states that there may be other approaches that offer insight into areas that standard reductionist science has not been able to crack.
>
> (Colander 2000a: 3)

As already noted, these areas especially concern large composite systems, that is, systems of interacting entities. Colander then goes on to emphasize that this two-part approach (the one reductionist and the other studying large composite systems) is typical of science in general. For example,

> physics has a separate branch called solid state physics, which analyzes how certain aspects of reality are understood without appeal to first principles. They appear, and are, in some way connected to first principles, but the connection is too complex for us to understand or model. The complex systems have emerged and exist, but cannot be understood through reductionism.
>
> (ibid.: 3)

As noted by Wible, the complexity perspective is especially useful for accommodating different theories because of its reliance on the notion of levels of organization. At one level, we find models of a neoclassical kind which present a view of the economy as 'conservative, mechanistic social processes or systems. Such systems are real, they do exist, but they are far from a complete picture of the economic phenomena' (Wible 2000: 26). At a different level, we find theories that regard economic processes as self-organized dynamic evolutionary systems in sustained patterns of non-equilibrium. Indeed, it is thanks to the different levels of organization in complexity theory that conservative and dissipative systems can exist side by side:

> This suggests a conception of fundamental complementarity between mechanistic systems and life processes in a social science like economics. If this is so, then neoclassical and evolutionary approaches to economics might be complementary to each other in some fundamental way. Perhaps the neo-classical models focus more on the rigid and deterministic aspects of existing economic processes, while the non-neoclassical alternatives focus on those evolutionary processes which take economic activity in new directions to unfathomed levels of social, economic, and cultural achievement.
>
> (Wible 2000: 26)

On these grounds, the complexity perspective is able to account for a number of important features of the discipline of economics. First of all, it suggests that the current fragmentation and variety of schools and approaches may be a reflection of the different kinds and levels of complex phenomena being studied in the economy.

Second, and most importantly, it justifies the separation of the fields of micro and macroeconomics in that they refer to two different levels of complexity. In doing so, the complexity approach challenges the standard explanation for macro phenomena, implying that explanation of macro patterns based on theories and evidence from another level of complexity is untenable. Attempts to discover the deductive micro-foundations of macro phenomena thus appear to be fundamentally misdirected. As Colander points out, 'in a complex economy the connection between micro and macro that economics has been searching for cannot be discovered' (2000d: 33). It means that offsets made up of smaller elements cannot be broken down and must be treated as single entities rather than the sum of their parts. As complex systems evolve, new patterns can emerge and these patterns can take on an existence and a life of their own.

Third, complexity theory accounts for the existence of models based on different levels of abstraction, degree of formalization and completeness. Brock and Colander (2000: 75–6) distinguish between abstract Walrasian general equilibrium models providing a specific world view of markets (the so-called right price view) and 'light', much more informal models, used specifically for policy considerations. The latter are not merely simplified versions of the Walrasian model; they tend to reflect a more sophisticated view. They rely on an *ad hoc* combination of empirical observation and principles drawn from the general equilibrium theory, but the form they take is determined by the specific context at hand.

Casual observation reveals that multiple models are used in the difficult art of actual policy-making, but, as Brock and Colander suggest, the complexity justifies the use of such informal models. Policy cannot rely on all-encompassing models of the economy because they simply do not exist. Light or informal models may be sufficient

> to make policy recommendations within the complexity worldview one does not need a complete formal model of the economy, that is beyond our current understanding. But one can have an informal model of the economy that temporarily describes the current economy, and suggests what effect a certain policy will likely have on it.
>
> (Brock and Colander 2000: 79)

Complexity theorists argue that, because they are more pragmatic than general equilibrium based views, the impact of complexity theory on actual policy models tends to be quite limited. Policy models already reflect history and institutions, and policy is determined by real people dealing with real problems.

However, it would be wrong to assume that complexity is just a descriptive approach or a sort of a neutral catch-all for differing perspectives. It also has normative implications concerning the nature of economic modelling, including existing policy models that, while are laudable instances of light theory, need to be purged of unnecessary links with 'high brow' theory. Just as macro cannot be derived from micro, neither can policy models be derived from general equilibrium theory:

> [W]hat complexity does is to take away the backdrop of deductive theory for practical policy models and replace it with a broader, more inclusive worldview ... complexity theory removes the implicit belief that these policy models need to be connected to ... high theory. It is OK to find patterns and to base policy on patterns. Standard economics tries to connect theory and policy in explicit formal ways. The complexity vision suggests that that connection cannot be made formally – that the best we can do is an informal connection.
>
> (ibid.: 86)

It is important to note that this view applies to the majority of pre-1980s Keynesian and monetarist macro models (e.g. various versions of the IS-LM model), which were policy models. Brock and Colander argue that in the 1980s these were wrongly discarded, not because they were useless but because of the gap between practice and the stated methodology. The stated methodology held that formal models based on adequate micro-foundations were preferable to informal models. They thus conclude that

> ironically, complexity theory, which is itself highly mathematical, provides a kind of theoretical foundation for the type of practical economic work that policy economists have always done. Before, such policy work was seen as

hack work; in the complexity vision it is seen as the backbone of policy analysis, it is the large abstract deductive models that fall by the wayside.

(ibid.)

Inductive approach

As already noted, unlike purely deductive theory, the complexity approach involves a less important role of abstract theory and a more important role of knowledge of economic history and of the history of economics. This stance has to do with the existence of patterns. Indeed, determining whether a pattern exists is a statistical and historical problem. However, it is also clear that the complexity approach is not just about descriptive statistics or historical analysis: it studies the general development of these patterns and then applies the results of that general study to specific cases (Colander 2000c).

We shall now analyse some key properties of these patterns. First, its focus on patterns implies that the complexity approach has rather modest claims in terms of aims. It does not seek truth but a statistical fit that can be of at least temporary use in our understanding of the economy. If a fit proves good, then we can develop a law; however, laws can change according to the period. Through this inductive approach to establishment of laws, it is possible to remedy the flaws of standard economic theory, which has not yet successfully identified simple structural laws to describe our economy (Colander 2000a: 3).

Second, as noted by Brock (2000: 34) the study of patterns provides a simple means of distinguishing micro from macroeconomics. For example, whereas new macro patterns can appear at different levels of aggregation due to emergent phenomena, this cannot happen in micro patterns.

Third, the study of complexity tries to understand the forces, that is, the generating functions and iterative processes that underlie the patterns (Brock 2000: 34). It attempts to establish whether these patterns have a property of universality about them, that is, the so-called scaling laws.[7] Universality must be understood in the sense that similar patterns hold true for many different types of phenomena and over many different time scales. The same patterns can be found in finance, for example, as in sand-piles and statistical mechanics.

Fourth, in theory, patterns could be found for a broad range of macroeconomic issues. It might be possible to derive macro models with realistic heterogeneity amongst agents with different expectations by designing various types of simulation exercises concerning issues such as monetary policy, Okun's Law, Phillips Curve instability, wage setting institutions, Lucas' critique, fine tuning and oil shocks (see e.g. Brock 2000: 46).

One of the most significant experiments conducted to date concerned financial markets (i.e. Arthur 2000; Brock 2000). The attempt was to show how endogenous price formation occurs in an artificial financial world. The emphasis was on inductive processes and on how people depend on induction when they interact. Investors operating in these computerized markets could not assume or deduce expectations from some a priori rule, such as the rational expectations hypothesis, but had to work them out on their own (see Arthur 1994, 1995; Prasch 2000: 217). Complexity theorists have shown that artificial agents create and exploit multiple market hypotheses of what moves the market price and dividend.

Stability

What we have said about the SFA so far suggests that the complexity approach provides important insights for stability analysis. First of all, the SFA makes no a priori assumptions of stability. This should come as no surprise in view of the *prima facie* links between complexity and instability established by mathematicians and natural scientists, such as Prigogine, who stress that as the complexity of systems increases so does the probability of its being unstable.

Moreover, the lack of an a priori stability assumption can be seen in two closely related key features of the SFA. One is its overall vision of the economy. As Arthur (2000: 26) points out, the complexity approach is helping to address phenomena of market instability in that it portrays the economy not as deterministic, predictable and mechanistic but as process dependent, organic and always evolving.[8]

The second feature is the concept of equilibrium. Strictly speaking, the SFA rejects the emphasis on competitive static equilibrium underlying standard theory and its a priori view concerning stability:

> All economics has been able to do for the last fifty or one hundred years is to look at systems with very strong attractors, not even talk about how an equilibrium point is reached but simply point out that there is an equilibrium and that if we were there, there would be a tendency to stay there.
>
> (Arthur 1994: 64)

The SFA argues for a depiction of realistic and genuine processes of change where there are no attractors or where the attractors may change, meaning that processes have no definable end states. As Colander points out,

> the Santa Fe approach focuses on the competitive process, not the state of competitive equilibrium. In it, the competitive state is something that is almost never even closely approached: long before an industry moves to a competitive state, a technological change will change the industry, creating a further disequilibrium.
>
> (2000d: 130)

As noted by Comim (2000: 159), according to the SFA the focus of attention must shift from the search for equilibrium to ever-changing trajectories.

The SFA, however, is sensitive to the fact that, given the pervasiveness of the equilibrium concept, the complexity view (especially when being taught to students) can be made consistent at least with the notion that multiple equilibria are possible: '[T]he concept of long-run equilibrium will not be so confining if there is not a unique long-run equilibrium... [with] the concept of multiple equilibria, students will recognize the importance of institutions and conventions in choosing among equilibria' (Colander 2000d: 131).

The notion of multiple equilibria is consistent with a dynamic picture of the economy and stability analysis. The point is that, in this context, equilibrium is not a 'metaphysical' concept to be treated in a priori fashion along with various types of adjustment mechanism, but simply a temporary point of rest. The economy may be regarded as passing from one state to the other, stimulated by shocks or other drivers. In this view, the choice of equilibrium and the conditions of stability, that is, what causes a particular equilibrium to last a relatively long time, are not a matter of deductive theory but of 'empirical factors', such as initial conditions, initial positioning and institutional structure (i.e. the so-called path-dependency issue). In general, it can be argued that the notion of multiple equilibria shows why history matters from the point of view of complexity.

Let us take for example the arguments for and against laissez faire. In its rejection of the assumptions of unique and stable equilibrium, complexity theory rules out any a priori guarantee that the market will always lead to the most desirable equilibrium. In other words, deductive theory cannot provide a basis for the defence of laissez faire. Whether free markets actually benefit society is an empirical question: it may be possible to defend laissez faire on the grounds of the ignorance argument à la Hayek (the state lacks sufficient information to implement successful activist policy) or the historical argument that activist policies have already failed in particular contexts (e.g. Brock and Colander 2000: 79–83; Prasch 2000b).

On these grounds, we can conclude once again that the complexity view involves 'light theory': namely, according to this approach the scope for a deductive general theory based on first principles is limited. If stability is an empirical issue, the focus of abstract deductive theory should be on the smaller questions: accepting that the economy is in a particular position (e.g. a temporary equilibrium), and discuss how policy might influence the movement away from that position. In order to deal with these issues, however, complexity theory suggests that existing institutions should be incorporated in the models: 'policy suggestions should be made in reference to models incorporating such institutions, rather than in reference to an abstract model that does not incorporate such institutions' (Brock and Colander 2000: 79). When stability is no longer presumed, institutions in the real world, where positive feedbacks occur, can play a stabilizing role. In this context, activist policies may be needed (e.g. policies that disrupt or dampen positive feedback loops or stabilize incomes in the case of a downward spiral (see Prasch 2000b: 184)).

The SFA also allows the conceptualization of duality and structural instability. By modelling the economy as a complex adaptive system through the use of computer simulations, the SFA manages to show that a relatively stable structure can develop in a remarkably short period of time out of the interaction of individuals with limited knowledge. These models demonstrate true evolution, in the sense that structure depends upon specific relationships that emerge. They also show that structure is not reducible to a representative agent, which means that the system is genuinely complex. The complexity approach thus supports the view that the behaviour of agents in groups follows a logic that is quite different and irreducible to the behaviour of rational individuals taken in isolation.

In this context, one can see the origins of the sudden changes that may occur in structure and the possibility of dual outcomes. Since strategies are partially predicated on the beliefs and strategies of others, agents will change their strategies as their environment evolves. This explains why, given certain dynamic relations, certain patterns can develop and be subject to sudden changes. Let us take for example the patterns that emerge in financial markets. Simulations show that the characteristics of these patterns will differ, especially in terms of stability or instability, according to the value of the parameters reflecting empirical features and the characteristics of the environment, such as the rate at which agents update their hypotheses. If the rate of updating is low, the diversity of expectations collapses quickly into homogeneous rational expectations; but if the rate of the updating of hypotheses is increased, a complex regime results and the market displays several of the anomalies observed in real markets, such as unexpected price bubbles and crashes, high volatility and heavy use of technical trading (i.e. trades based on the recent history of price patterns).[9] It develops a rich 'psychology' of divergent beliefs that do not converge over time (see Arthur 2000: 24–5).

Limitations to the SFA

The SFA is characterized by a number of strengths, and, in fact, we have taken it as the starting point for our analysis of the stability of the NE in this book. Our approach can be regarded as a generalization of the SFA that we developed because, in our view, the SFA cannot be applied to the analysis of the NE in a straightforward manner. Despite its many strengths, a number of changes need to be made to its modelling strategy because, while not taking stability for granted, it fails to provide a global stability analysis. This could be pointed out as symptomatic of a more general problem undermining the SFA, namely the fact that 'application of the complexity approach to empirical problems . . . is fiendishly difficult and proves the ultimate stumbling block for the general acceptance of this approach into our science in but a limited number of cases' (Pryor 2000: 66). Before we can set out our own approach, we need to address this statement.

The lack of systemic dynamic laws

One major weakness of the SFA is that, even though it involves light theorizing, it still subscribes to a form of 'grand theory'. Unlike other neo-modern approaches, it therefore neglects to take into account post-modern criticism of any ambition of 'grand theory'. It can be argued that this perspective casts a doubt not only on general theories of society, such as Marxism but also on any general economic theory of 'dynamics' involving the attempt to model the behaviour of the economy over time. In fact, the SFA can be regarded as one such attempt. Although it rejects all-encompassing structural models of the economy that take stability for granted, the SFA still aims at uncovering 'general' laws of evolution, that is, patterns that occur in various domains and in the economy as a whole, on the grounds of mathematical practices borrowed from the natural sciences. In our view, it is doubtful that such dynamic laws, especially those at the systemic level, can actually be found.

At least two major factors undermine the SFA's project regarding 'grand theory'. First, by seeking to uncover general patterns, the SFA relies on analogies between economics and the natural sciences. Like all complexity theories, it focuses on new metaphors to gain understanding of previously opaque phenomena in a departure from the Newtonian model of science (see e.g. Pryor 2000: 64). Now, as emphasized in particular by Louçã (1997: chs 1–2), while biological and physical analogies are certainly useful as tools for creative thought, they are also quite limited. In particular, analogies cannot be extended beyond a certain point, because the logical relation of causality cannot be translated from biology or physics into economics. A general vision is one thing, but a precise causal mechanism is quite another.[10] Second, it is not clear as to whether purely economic dynamic laws even exist. As already noted, the attempt to find regularities in business cycles (e.g. Kondratieff cycles) has failed (see e.g. Perez 2002).

It is important to note, however, that these doubts do not amount to denying the scientific nature of economics altogether. The discipline indeed has a scientific basis, although it does not consist in the kind of dynamic simplifications sought for by the SFA. Moreover, the objections made do not imply that the SFA is useless. On the contrary, we shall see that our approach can be derived by analogy from it. This is not odd, for, after all, complexity approach is a general understanding of the economy that does not consist merely in singling out dynamic patterns. As Viskovatoff points out, many of the SFA papers contained in Arthur *et al.* (1997) present insights that do not derive from mathematical and computational modelling but from more conceptually oriented theorizing. One of the most significant instances of the latter is provided by Leijonhufvud's paper on the relation between macroeconomics and complexity (Leijonhufvud 1997), in which the author shows how the complexity vision based on adaptive behaviour and bounded rationality is able to capture a number of phenomena which appear as 'anomalies' or 'surprises' from the standpoint of general equilibrium theory (e.g. the disappearance of intertemporal markets or excess relative price variability in a high inflation context).

Failure to account for complex patterns

The second reason for the difficulties in applying the SFA to empirical issues and global stability is that it does not directly account for patterns of complex phenomena such as the NE. As already noted, the complexity approach places great significance on induction. It looks to models of artificial intelligence as good metaphors for real-world economic systems and for the interaction of agents with other agents and the environment, in line with the bounded rationality view. The SFA thus holds that relatively 'simple' patterns or regularities concerning rather specific macroeconomic issues or markets emerge out of the interaction of multiple agents. However, this approach seems unable to give a direct account for 'complex' patterns, such as the NE. There are a variety of factors that explain this drawback.

First of all, while these simple patterns help us appreciate 'duality', they are not adequate for addressing the global stability of the NE. This is partially because the NE does not merely consist of just one new leading sector, such as ICT but involves the interaction of several key factors. In order to address the NE, patterns of 'complex' phenomena based on the interaction of several aggregates are thus needed. It is unclear, however, how these can be obtained through computer simulations. In other words, as noted by Viskovatoff, the SFA has maintained the mechanistic tradition of orthodox political economy, according to which individual causal factors can be analysed in isolation from all others, to be ideally combined with them once all theorizing is complete. For the SFA therefore

> complexity [is] not a characteristic of how causal processes are connected to each other, but a characteristic of the behaviour of the time series of a given variable... economic theorizing can proceed in the same way as before, with one model being introduced after another each being intended to shed light on one putative causal mechanism of interest by being able to mimic it through a carefully chosen set of assumptions... chosen à la Friedman....
>
> (Viskovatoff 2000: 150)

Viskovatoff then compares the SFA with alternative approaches to complexity, such as that inspired by Niklas Luhmann. He points out for that in Luhmann's view complexity means that phenomena cannot be analysed one by one, as is instead held by standard theory, but can only be understood in their concreteness, by examining how the various causal structures and processes interact over time to produce the final result in any particular case (ibid.: 150).

Second, despite the fact that the SFA stresses a multi-layered approach and refuses reductionist explanations, it focuses mainly on individual patterns based on actual data and the statistical level of analysis. Again, this is not enough to allow analysis of the stability of NE. Common econometric methods cannot distinguish between the different types of interaction that would allow us to identify the causal factors in a complex system (see e.g. Pryor 2000: 67). For example, they do not allow us to verify whether actual outcomes are influenced by policy or are spontaneous. Moreover, the NE is characterized by a number of qualitative elements which do not easily show up at the level of macro data. A thorough assessment of stability of the NE therefore needs reference to quite a different layer of reality.

Third, as emphasized by Pryor (2000: 65–6), complexity theory is too narrow. It needs to be supplemented by a more systematic view of organizational structures, rather than focusing almost exclusive attention on processes. Pryor points out, for example, that the SFA fails to address various phenomena concerning the complexity of a structure (the so-called 'dimensions of structural complexity') such as the direct information requirements for a system, the increasingly greater internal interaction within a given organization or system and the rising heterogeneity of a system.

Lack of explanatory power

Another major factor that undermines the application of full-grown complexity theory to actual problems and global stability analysis is its relative lack of explanatory power. As Pryor puts it:

> The complexity approach can explain almost anything and, therefore, it can explain nothing ... By tweaking one or two parameters, we can also obtain all sorts of interesting results such as bubbles ... or cycles. In fact with suitable adjustment of the parameters we can obtain almost any results that we want. But proving that some weird event is possible does not really explain why it has occurred since such results can be obtained by other models as well.
>
> (2000: 67)

We suggest that a major reason for this flaw is the ambivalent stance taken by the SFA towards contemporary models of economics. On the one hand, the SFA should be thought of as a complement to these models. The problems it focuses upon embrace only a part of the entire range of problems studied by economists: in particular, those which are not dealt with effectively by the standard methods. On the other, the SFA suggests a role for standard structural models in interpreting the patterns that emerge from simulations.

It can be argued that the overlap between these two aspects raises some doubts about the nature of the SFA *vis-à-vis* standard theory. In particular, the SFA seems to fall between two stools. It is neither a standard theory, as it focuses on areas where this does not apply, nor is it an entirely alternative theory, because it relies on contemporary theories to interpret the patterns that emerge from its simulations. It is perhaps better to regard it mainly as a kind of vision or 'meta-model' that is in principle able to indicate clearly both the limits and the validity of existing structural models.

Even given this interpretation, however, the SFA is not without weaknesses. In particular, while its criticism of standard models is convincing, it fails to indicate how standard models can nonetheless be useful or in which domains they apply. More specifically, the complexity approach criticizes general equilibrium models and suggests that simplified macro models should not rely on it. However, it does not clarify what is left of these models once they have been purged of general equilibrium, nor does it explain what is their lasting contribution in terms of analysis of causal mechanism, or on what grounds we can choose between the causal stories different macro models tell. This relative silence about the causality issue also accounts for the kind of neutral stance the SFA takes in policy matters.

6 Our approach to stability

Structural change and instantaneous equilibrium

We are now in a position to clarify our approach to the analysis of the stability of the NE. The basic challenge is to overcome the limitations of standard approaches to complexity by developing a method that can cope with multiple interrelations between key variables. In what follows, we will focus upon our meta-model, that is, our set of instructions for conducting stability analysis. These instructions address important issues such as the kind of patterns to be considered and the role that existing macro models play in the interpretation of these patterns.

Some general features of our meta-model

Our approach is consonant with the neo-modern paradigm and draws on the broad view of complexity underlying the SFA. Despite its limitations, the SFA provides a very useful benchmark for our conceptualization of the NE. Indeed, the best way to present our methodology is to point out its similarities and differences to the SFA. Let us start by noting that we subscribe to the same canon of 'light theory' underlying SFA and, therefore, do not seek to build an all-encompassing dynamic model of the economy.[1] Moreover, we agree that existing macroeconomic theories have a role to play in the analysis. We also share the view that the real-world economy and economic methodology have many different layers. Indeed, the basic contribution made in this volume is to take full advantage of this argument, pushing the frontiers of knowledge in the realm of complexity even further. Our approach amounts to suggesting that the study of macroeconomic stability calls for consideration of a new layer of complexity, both in terms of actual real-world phenomena and methods of analysis. We shall now try to justify this claim.

Focus on complex historical patterns

In saying that our approach to stability analysis involves attention to another distinct layer of reality we mean, among other things, that the patterns we take into account when describing the main features of the NE are quite different from those emphasized by the SFA. We take into consideration more than actual statistical data, such as aggregate time series, or the iterative processes of computer simulations. By and large, these sources generate instances of 'simple' patterns (e.g. the short-run non-proportionality of consumption and income or the behaviour of a particular type of financial market). Instead, in dealing with the NE, we also need to consider 'complex' patterns referring mainly to the structure of the system, rather than to iterative processes; in other words, we have to focus on what Pryor (2000) calls 'dimensions of structural complexity'.

It is important to note that the formation of such complex patterns, unlike SFA patterns, cannot be studied on the grounds of non-linear dynamic models or statistical techniques. In particular, we hold that probabilistic laws concerning such patterns cannot be found, for such laws are based on the assumption that the causal structure is stable. But as pointed out by Dow, very few and relatively simple aspects of life

> such as mortality rates or incidence of damage to houses...are the areas where frequency distributions can be constructed and probability statistics calculated...these are then used as the basis for our insurance premiums. Even then premiums change with changing patterns of health or weather. This is the closest we get in real life to deterministic laws, albeit with a substantial stochastic variation.
>
> (Dow 2002: 144)

On the basis of this view, and in line with post-modern criticism, we call into question any ambition towards 'grand theory' underlying the SFA. However, we do not abandon all attempts at simplification, whether at the descriptive or theoretical level. In fact, we simplify the description of the NE by singling out a few empirical generalizations or patterns that seek to capture significant qualitative features of our economies linked to the processes of change and evolution. The empirical generalizations we have in mind are 'not numerical laws but "stylised facts": generalizations that do not hold exactly, and which are typically not established by any formal statistical procedure' (Backhouse 1997: 104) or reference to *ceteris paribus* clauses. Alternatively, these patterns could also be regarded as 'tendencies' or 'empirical laws' concerning the economy as a whole, that is, systemic empirical laws.[2] In this book, we view the NE as consisting of a number of patterns linked to the acceleration of certain processes, such as globalization, technological change, the weight of finance and services, the focus on data and forecasts, the role of the state and so on, which seem to characterize the NE in all major countries.

In conclusion, the stylized facts relevant to our stability analysis are broader than those normally considered by the SFA or the standard economic literature. In particular, as shown in Chapter 10, ideally they should be able to shift our focus from recurrent phenomena to irreversible trends, from simple data concerning macro aggregates to wider micro–macro features, from isolated phenomena to interrelated phenomena and from simple economic factors to complementary institutions. However, we shall find that establishing these broad stylized facts is no simple task and that it can only be carried out by developing an appropriate methodology.

Institutions as generating functions of complex patterns

First, however, we need to clarify some other aspects of these empirical laws. More precisely, we have to take up the issue of what the generating functions, or foundations, of these laws consist in. Given that they cannot be accounted for by statistics or probability theory, where do they lie? We suggest that such laws are rooted in certain institutional factors, broadly intended as encompassing 'not simply organizations, such as corporations, banks and universities, but also integrated and systematic social entities such as money, language, and law' (Hodgson 1998: 179). For example, at the root of the recent acceleration of the globalization trend we find institutional features, such as regulations and treaties that unify markets and promote trade, as well as new technologies.

This is not to say that institutions determine everything. We strongly disagree with attempts to explain the emergence of institutions on the basis of given individuals alone, as implied by the methodological individualism underlying neoclassical theory and the so-called 'New Institutional Economics' (see e.g. Schotter 1981; Williamson 1985; for a critique, see for example, Hodgson 1998: 176; Hollingsworth 2000: 602). But this does not imply that the opposite is necessarily true. As Hodgson points out:

> It is simply arbitrary to...say 'it is all reducible to individuals' just as much as to say it is 'all social and institutional'...neither individual or institutional factors have legitimate explanatory primacy. The idea that all explanations have to be solely and ultimately in terms of individual (or institutions) is thus unfounded.
>
> (2003: xv)

What is true, of course, is that 'institutions are formed and changed by individuals just as individuals are shaped and constrained by institutions.' (Hollingsworth 2000: 603). However, in order to avoid an infinite regress problem, a choice must be made. We choose to emphasize the view that 'human activity can only be understood as emerging in a context with some pre-existing institutions' (Hodgson 2003: xvii), and 'that institutions not only constrain but also shape individuals' (Hollingsworth 2000: 603). Various research projects linked to this view (see e.g. Hodgson 2003 for an overview) are being carried out. One can first focus on the effects of institutional constraints and downward causation and then seek to understand how the interaction between individuals gives rise to new institutional forms. For example, one can attempt to develop a theory of economic and institutional evolution along Darwinian lines.

Our macroeconomic standpoint leads us to emphasize mainly the first causal link, that is, how institutions constrain agents' behaviour and give rise to new perceptions and dispositions within them. Indeed, as many institutionalists hold, 'to take the institution as a socially constructed invariant – or emergent property – is a basis for consideration of macroeconomic dynamics and behaviour' (Hodgson

1998: 189).[3] This view reveals a crucial divergence from standard macro theory that considers institutions as external constraints that limit but do not influence or shape individual behaviour in view of the key assumption of exogenous preferences.

The idea that institutions shape individual behaviour and preferences is well rooted in the history of economic thought. One need only recall, for example, that the emphasis on malleability of individual preferences underlies a broad evolutionary approach to economic analysis and in particular 'old' American Institutionalist economics, from Veblen to Galbraith and their modern counterparts, including Hodgson (e.g. Hodgson 1998, 2001, 2003, 2004b). As Hodgson states 'Wesley Mitchell argued that the evolution of money cannot be understood simply in terms of cost reduction and individual convenience... the evolution of money changes the mentality, preferences and way of thinking of individual themselves' (2003: xvi). Moreover, 'Mitchell thought of business cycles as a phenomenon arising out of the patterns of behaviour generated by the institutions of a developed money economy... it is institutions that create the regularities in the behaviour of the mass of people that quantitative work analyses' (Rutherford 2001: 177).

For our purposes, it is important to note that this view also underlies more recent theoretical developments, including modern reformulations of evolutionary views (e.g. Nelson and Winter and their followers) and the complexity approach. In particular, it underlies the work of those authors who emphasize an institutional view of complexity, such as North (1991), Prasch (2000a,b) and Viskovatoff (2000). All of these contributions are of relevance for us in that they address the role played by institutions in economic growth. As Nelson and Sampat (2001: 39) have remarked, institutions affect what most economists regard as the 'proximate' factors behind productivity growth and increased standards of living, such as 'technological advance, physical capital formation, education and the efficiency of the economy and the resource allocation process' (ibid.). Moreover 'institutions influence the ways in which economic actors get things done' (ibid.).

More precisely, North effectively describes the positive role of institutions in granting stability as well as in generating structural patterns and growth. Once having defined institutions as 'the rules of the game in society or... the humanly devised constraints that shape human interaction' (North 1990: 3) and having observed that they consist of 'both informal constraints (sanctions, taboos, customs, traditions and codes of conduct) and formal rules (constitutions, law, property rights)' (1991: 97), North argues that:

> Throughout history, institutions have been devised by human beings to create order and reduce uncertainty in exchange... Institutions provide the incentive structure of an economy; as that structure evolves, it shapes the direction of economic change towards growth, stagnation or decline.
>
> (ibid.)

Moreover, following the view that economic history over time can be understood as a series of stages from local autarky to specialization and division of labour, where each successive step represents increasing specialization and division of labour and continuously more productive technology, North points out that 'spontaneous' passage from one stage to another does not necessarily occur. Without certain institutions, inefficient forms of exchange, the Suq for example, will not disappear:

> What is missing in the Suq are the fundamental underpinnings of institutions... these include an effective legal structure and court system to enforce contracts which in turn depend on the development of political institutions that will create such a framework. In their absence there is no incentive to alter the system.
>
> (North 1991: 104)

Macro models and interpretations of complex patterns

Now that we have specified the new kind of empirical laws that will be considered in this book, we shall examine our other claim that this approach to stability involves the development of a new method or branch of macroeconomics. In other words, we acknowledge that descriptive simplification based on the identification of empirical laws underlying the NE is only a first step. Some kind of theoretical simplification is also required; in particular, we have to show that the institutional approach to complexity being endorsed here makes it possible to perform a feasible analysis of stability. As our approach abandons the search for dynamic patterns of simplification on the basis of mathematical and statistical tools, we must also propose an alternative method of achieving simplification.

Strictly speaking, this does imply having to give up the use of formal models altogether. While we subscribe to the view that the economy is an 'open' system and we therefore seek to account for a plurality of relations, we also believe that simplification calls for some kind of modelling approach (see e.g. Chick and Dow 2001; Chick 2003). As noted by the SFA theorists, a lot of data can be compressed into models, thus making them undeniably useful in dealing with a large number of variables in a compact way, as in our macroeconomic analysis. However, it is also true that there are 'better' and 'worse' models, more or less 'general' models, models that are more or less capable of accounting for the complex patterns we have singled out and so on. Our suggestion, which follows from the 'light theory' canon, is that the use of dynamic models, in an attempt to summarize the complex evolution of the economy within the outlines of a simplistic formula, needs to be abandoned.

This critique, however, does not automatically carry over into the familiar structural 'static' macroeconomic models, such as IS-LM. In what follows, we shall see that these can also play a role in our stability analysis. Indeed, like the SFA, our approach is not meant to replace all existing methods or theories. On the contrary, it acknowledges the role of the major macro theoretical paradigms in achieving the simplification required by a manageable approach to stability.

However, we make the important claim that this contribution is limited. Indeed, neither SFA nor existing macroeconomic theory alone is sufficient to successfully cope with the global stability issue. In order to understand this claim, a few points need to be considered. First of all, in our view, theories are explanatory devices. In what follows, we shall maintain an 'essentialist' scientific realist perspective, according to which the aim of science is 'to discover the hidden essential mechanisms causing the observable events' (Boylan and O'Gorman 1995: 62).[4] This point reveals an important difference with respect to the SFA. As pointed out by Pryor (2000), one weakness of the SFA is that its main aim is to demonstrate that certain events can occur. However, in our view, this is not enough; one must also try and explain why they occur and establish what major causal mechanisms are involved.

Second, we believe that the macroeconomic reality is so complex that no single model can really hope to achieve a full understanding of it. In particular, it is difficult to imagine how one can model the interactions between the key trends of the NE that we have singled out. A large number of causal mechanisms seem to be operating simultaneously; these can be considered as different aspects of a full account of stability, like pieces of a puzzle.

Third, the puzzle metaphor also allows us to see how existing macro theories might be applied for our purposes. To carry out stability analysis, we need to follow a two-stage strategy in order to complete the puzzle. In the first stage, we take inventory of all the different parts, that is, the various causal mechanisms, revealed by existing macroeconomic theories. In the second, we try to piece them together according to a certain pattern. In principle, there are as many potential patterns as there are theories.

The key steps in our simplification strategy

On these grounds, we can now outline our strategy for simplification aimed at providing a manageable account of the stability of the NE. A number of steps can be identified. The first is to consider only two basic macro paradigms: neoclassical and Keynesian. The rationale for this move towards simplification is that both paradigms are in line with our essentialist scientific realist perspective and can be regarded as singling out two contrasting sets of essential causal factors at play. Most of the many other approaches or variants available in macroeconomics can be shown to differ from the two basic paradigms only in incidental factors. In other words, the distinction between essential and incidental factors enables us to simplify the range of possible interpretations of the puzzle.

The second step of our simplification strategy is to view both paradigms as capable of conceptualizing instantaneous equilibrium and identifying the causal mechanisms operating at any given point in time. In line with our refusal of any ambition towards grand dynamic theory, we narrow down the potential of both theories to this weak notion of equilibrium. We believe that while the 'light theory' canon rules out stationary long-run equilibrium states and deterministic laws of long-term evolution of complex systems, it is not necessarily inconsistent with instantaneous equilibrium. Whereas the SFA regards economic science as consisting of the isolation of universal patterns of dynamic simplifications, we identify this notion of equilibrium as the scientific core of economics and suggest that the necessary simplification is to be found in static analysis. Instantaneous equilibrium plays the role of a benchmark in our analysis, as it shows the key factors playing a causal role at any given moment in time.

The third step in simplification is to create a single 'map' of all the possible causal mechanisms at play. This helps us describe what is going on in the NE in terms of stability and instability factors. This map, which can be regarded as a new layer of macroeconomics, can be drawn by combining the insights of the two basic paradigms concerning the possible effects of specific NE trends such as globalization, rapid technological growth and so on. This move – which follows from the view that description is 'theory laden' (see e.g. Boylan and O'Gorman 1995: 77–8) – makes sense because these paradigms are, in a certain, sense complementary. What constitutes a primary or causal factor for neoclassical theory turns out to be merely a secondary factor in Keynes's theory and vice versa. In principle, this means that they tend to identify alternative sources of stability and instability. What causes instability for one theory may be seen as a stability factor in the other. This third step should make it obvious that our approach does not consist so much in elaborating a new theory as in combining the insights of already existing theories into a meta-model. The individual insights are treated in isolated fashion, like the pieces of a puzzle.

The last step in our simplification strategy is to devise a plausible broad account of stability, referred to as a 'meta-interpretation of the NE', by comparing the alternative scenarios proposed by the two paradigms. The two paradigms tend not only to suggest specific causal mechanisms but also to provide contrasting global interpretations of the 'NE map'. Each theory thus builds a kind of scenario in which some tendencies described by the map are bound to prevail over others. The aim of our comparison is to try to overcome the one sidedness of each account of the NE by singling out criteria for assessing their relative plausibility. We contend that plausibility is linked to the explanatory power of a theory and regard 'the notion of explanatory power as distinct criterion for theory choice' (Boylan and O'Gorman 1995: 91). Other criteria, such as predictive power, need to remain in the background, because, as noted long ago by John Stuart Mill and by many other theorists since (see e.g. Lawson 1997), the multiplicity of causal factors operating in the economic world implies the absence of significant invariant empirical regularities in non-experimental situations (see Boylan and O'Gorman 1995: 95).

Part III

The two basic macroeconomic paradigms

Part III of this volume deals with the first two steps of our strategy for simplification aimed at making the otherwise unwieldy analysis of stability more manageable. We shall start by examining the neoclassical and Keynesian paradigms in some detail, for these two basic macroeconomic approaches play an important part in our account of the NE. Both can be interpreted in essentialist terms, or in other words, as singling out some of the essential causal factors at play. Moreover, both rely on the notion of instantaneous equilibrium and identify causal mechanisms operating at a unique point in time. However, as we shall see, the two models differ in the essential factors they deem relevant. After singling out and comparing the relative contribution that each model provides to stability analysis, we claim, on the basis of a number of a priori arguments, that Keynesian theory is more general and has greater explanatory power than the neoclassical approach.

7 The neoclassical macro model

We broadly define the neoclassical macro model to include all approaches accepting the Walrasian paradigm (especially in its temporary equilibrium version, from Hicks' *Value and Capital* to Lucas's works). We suggest that, despite its limitations, the model singles out some essential aspects of economic reality, such as self-interest and competitive behaviour. For this reason, it can play a useful role in our stability analysis. It is important to note that our aim here is not to provide a survey of the model's main analytical building blocks. That we shall do in later chapters dealing with interpretations of the NE. Our main focus here is on the determinants of the notion of instantaneous equilibrium underlying the neoclassical model.

The key causal factors

The key causal forces underlying the notion of instantaneous equilibrium in neoclassical theory are referred to as 'deep parameters' and include preferences, technology and resource endowments in general. These are the ultimate determinants of the system of relative prices that assure consistency in agents' plans in all markets. This overall picture underlies both standard micro and macroeconomics. In the Walrasian approach, it also serves as the basis for studying the dynamic behaviour of the economy. The price adjustment mechanism guarantees that equilibrium will prevail in the long run, no matter what shocks or changes in the parameters occur, thanks to a number of assumptions, such as those of stability and rational expectations.

As already noted, the complexity approach calls into question this basic scheme. In view of the dynamic properties of the real-world economy (e.g. increasing returns, path-dependence, continuous change in preferences and technologies), it drops the assumption of stability, asserting that there is no guarantee for the attainment of anything like a state of long-run equilibrium. Dropping the concept of 'equilibrium over time' obviously has drastic consequences on standard macroeconomics: it disallows the formulation of the basic macroeconomic laws, based on the constant conjunction of events, such as the quantity theory of money asserting that in the long run an increase in the quantity of money is associated with inflation.

For this reason, the complexity approach advocates purging the neoclassical model of the notion of general equilibrium. To be more precise, it suggests getting rid of the unwarranted generalizing tendency implied by the stability postulate, whereby equilibrium is not seen as merely temporary but as a lasting feature of both reality and of the standard model. What is left of the model without stability? This is an important question that the SFA does not pose. In our view, what remains is evidence of causal mechanisms that are real but that do not uniquely determine actual outcomes; strictly speaking, standard macro models can only indicate 'tendencies' as opposed to 'universal laws'. While universal laws are supported by empirical evidence, tendencies may fail to show up in observed data and may thus survive the possible lack of stability in real-world economies.

The gap between pure theory and actual phenomena

This claim calls for some justification. What sort of tendencies does the neoclassical model capture? To what extent do they influence the final outcome? To answer these questions, it is useful to recall that awareness of the gap between actual phenomena and the laws of economic theory is nothing new. Ever since the foundation of political economy as an autonomous science, economists have tried to explain this gap in terms of the lack of stability in real-world economies. Mill, for example, believed that it was due to the operation of countervailing forces and disturbing factors. In his view, the established laws of political economy

> provided an accurate account of how specific causal factors operated, but they were not universal laws. Rather, they represent statements of tendencies. But since these tendencies were subject to numerous 'disturbances' or 'interfering causes' which cannot all be specified in advance, then *ceteris paribus* clauses that allow for these disturbances will play a crucial role in the formulation of these tendency 'laws'. Economics explores the implications of these established laws, but given the influences of the disturbing causes, these implications will not always be realized.[1]
>
> (Boylan and O' Gorman 1995: 11)

But many other prominent theorists have acknowledged the limitations of standard theory. One of them, Carl Menger, is a particularly relevant example for our purposes because of his philosophical stance, to which we will turn in the discussion concerning the status of standard economic theory.[2] Menger was a realist and essentialist. In line with Aristotelian views, he regarded entities as identifiable in terms of a few distinct characteristics that represent their essence. On these grounds,

> he maintained, in an Aristotelian manner, that the attempt to understand and explain real economic phenomena must reach behind the superficial appearances and attempt to understand the underlying essences. Further, the chosen concepts should represent that which is typical and exclude the superficial and accidental in the phenomenon under scrutiny.
>
> (Hodgson 2001: 80)

Menger's approach was based on two key principles: the so-called 'method of isolation', whereby it was possible to isolate the essential aspect of the phenomenon and to disregard the incidental and the attempt to break down the essential reality into its simple, typical and most enduring components (e.g. Lawson 1997: 113–27; Hodgson 2001: 82). For Menger, the fundamental unit of analysis and the enduring theoretical foundation for economics was the economizing individual. By this he meant that economics should focus on the particular aspect of human life concerning 'the manifestation of self-interest in the efforts of economic humans aimed at the provision of their human needs' (Menger 1885, quoted in Hodgson 2001: 82). While admitting the possibility of other motives, including 'public spirit' and 'love of one's fellow man', Menger simply 'consigned the study and incorporation of these other motives to other social sciences' (ibid.). According to him, based on the premise that individuals act on self-interest alone, it is possible to derive all 'exact laws' of pure economic theory and to seek to explain national and institutional phenomena in terms of the purposeful individuals within them. The fact that these laws capture only one aspect of the actual motives of behaviour and phenomena explains why they do not emerge in strict event regularities in the social realm:

> Theoretical research seeks to ascertain the *simplest elements* of everything real, elements which must be thought of as strictly typical just because they are the simplest. It strives for the establishment of these elements...without considering whether these in reality are present as *independent* phenomena...in their full purity. In this manner theoretical research...arrives at results...which, to be sure, must not be tested by full empirical reality (for the empirical forms here under discussion, e.g. absolutely pure oxygen, pure alcohol, pure gold, a person pursuing only economic aims, etc, exist in part only in our ideas). However, these results correspond to the specific task of the exact orientation of theoretical research and are the necessary laws and presupposition for obtaining *exact laws*.
>
> (Menger 1985, quoted in Lawson 1997: 115–6, emphasis in the original)

Further significant examples of awareness of the distinction between laws of pure theory and actual phenomena can be cited. For instance, both Robbins in the thirties and Hahn in recent times are of the 'view that the supposed empirically grounded propositions of economics are all formulated only at a very general level' (Lawson 1997: 96) and 'doubt whether concrete quantitative laws of economics can be practically derived' (ibid.). According to Robbins, this is partly because there are usually a large number of determinants of economic phenomena, and partly because 'certain factors, especially individual valuations and technical conditions, will be changing over time' (ibid.).

Friedman's attempt to overcome the gap

Issues concerning the congruity of theory and real phenomena have not stood in the way of standard macroeconomists willing to derive straightforward policy conclusions from their models. Friedman, for example, has tried to reconcile the dictums of neoclassical theory with empirical evidence by recurring to 'as if' or instrumentalist strategies. In particular, in his famous methodological contribution of 1953, Friedman calls attention to the predictive success of economic theory, rather than to the realism of its assumptions or their explanatory power. In his view, real economic agents can be regarded as if they were performing the necessary calculations to maximize their profit or utility. The fact that they do not actually behave in this way does not really matter, he says, because 'the only relevant test of the validity of a hypothesis is comparison of its predictions with experience' (Friedman 1953: 8–9). In Friedman's view, neoclassical theory is successful from this standpoint, and he alludes to the 'repeated failure of its implications to be contradicted' (ibid.: 22).

However, as several have noted (e.g. Maki 1986, 1992; Hausman 1992: 163), Friedman's methodological stance is often contradictory or inconsistent; in certain aspects it is even in line with scientific realism. Boylan and Gorman point out that 'Friedman...continues to be all things to all methodologists. His piece has...other dimensions, namely that of scientific realism ...' (1995: 115). This realist dimension is expressly stated by Friedman, who regards, for example, any scientific theory, 'as a body of substantive hypothesis designed to *abstract essential features* of complex reality' (Friedman 1953: 7). In line with the essentialist view, he seeks the hidden structures or essences of reality:

> A fundamental hypothesis of science is that appearances are deceptive and that there is a way of looking at or interpreting or organizing the evidence that will reveal superficially disconnected and diverse phenomena to be manifestations of a more fundamental and relatively simple structure.
>
> (ibid.: 33)[3]

Friedman's point is that the neoclassical model is false only at the descriptive level, and that it actually does capture the essence of what is going on in the economy. In particular the maximization axiom, while descriptively false, nonetheless reveals the essence of the economic behaviour of agents. For instance, according to this view, 'business firms are really, ultimately, at rock bottom, nothing but maximizers as characterized by neoclassical theory' (also Mäki 1992; Boylan and O'Gorman 1995: 127).

It should be noted, however, that although it justifies the neoclassical assumptions of rationality and perfect competition, Friedman's approach does not by itself guarantee the empirical success of his theory; it does not guarantee, for example, that laws such as the quantity theory of money are actually validated by econometric tests. Indeed, as many have recognized and as appears to have become even truer in the present NE, the simple fact is that 'significant invariant event regularities...have yet to be uncovered in economics...Econometricians continually puzzle over why it is that estimated relationships repeatedly break down' (Lawson 1997: 70).

On these grounds, one can conclude that a plausible interpretation of standard macroeconomic theory, such as that implied by Friedman's monetarism, provides an aggregate representation of the invisible-hand view according to which the simple forces of self-interest and competition bring about an optimal outcome for the economy as a whole. The strong assumptions of rationality and perfect competition that underlie monetarism are not arbitrary or 'false', but seek to capture the essence of key real-world causal mechanisms, such as self-interest and competition.[4] From this standpoint, despite differences in analytical and methodological style, neoclassical theory can be seen to express some of the key features of the conception of classical political economists, such as Adam Smith or even Marx. The neoclassical approach is unique in that it seeks to achieve reductionist explanations, on the grounds of those strong assumptions, to account for all phenomena and all layers of economic reality (i.e. micro and macroeconomics), including actual observable outcomes. However, the lack of stability in real-world economies continues to preclude the realization of this goal. The mechanisms of self-interest and competition that the neoclassicals refer to can, therefore, only give rise to tendencies rather than to 'universal laws'.

8   Keynes's macro model

We now turn to Keynes's macroeconomic model and his concept of instantaneous equilibrium. As already mentioned, a survey of the main analytical building blocks of the model is not provided here, but is reserved for later chapters dealing with interpretations of the NE. Instead, in this chapter, we show that the Keynesian concept of equilibrium is more general than its neoclassical counterpart and can therefore provide a valuable contribution to stability analysis. We argue that justification for this claim cannot be made in terms of empirical assumptions or expedient short cuts, but requires a series of more profound philosophical considerations. Ultimately, it rests on Keynes's broad view of the essence of the economic behaviour of agents. Rather than completely ruling out the neoclassical view, in which self-interest is seen as the driving force, Keynes integrates it with an additional dimension reflecting the interdependence or 'mutual interest' of agents. This dimension proves to be a key concept underlying Keynes's major analytical innovations.

Keynes and the complexity approach

There are a number of ways in which Keynes's vision of the economy resembles that underlying the complexity approach (Colander 2000b: 40; Wible 2000: 27). First, as has often been noted, despite the limitations of his static model and the lack of clarity in many of his methodological statements, Keynes focuses on a number of themes common in the literature on complexity, including the instability of equilibrium, the role of expectations, the peculiarity of the behaviour of agents in groups, the fallacy of composition and the role of positive feedbacks in economics (e.g. Comim 2000: 155; Prasch 2000a: 219, 2000b: 179–81; Foster 2004: 10–13), the questioning of econometrics and the non-ergodicity of the economy (e.g. Colander 2000b: 40). Moreover, non-linearities, path-dependence and lock-in are implicit in his model.

Second, the research programme pursued by complexity theorists consists in, at least to some extent, the development of some of Keynes's insights. As noted by Prasch (2000a: 219–20), for example, Arthur's model of belief formation in the stock market is a useful restatement of Keynes's insights into the formation of expectations in financial markets based on the interaction of many heterogeneous agents. Similarly, the complexity view accounts for the possibility of anomalies and inefficient outcomes emphasized by Keynes, such as the lack of future markets (see e.g. Leijonhufvud 1997).

Third, it can be argued that Keynes's approach and complexity theory complement one another. Keynes's simple structural model internalizes emergent properties and variables reflecting iterative processes over time, such as the multiplier based on the principle that 'we are all each other's customers' (e.g. Prasch 2000b: 179). His aggregates can be seen as the end states of iterative processes where 'learning' has temporarily ceased. Furthermore, both views claim the existence of different layers of economic reality, such that not everything can be explained on the grounds of the same principles. Given that they consider different kinds of layers, taken together, they provide a more complete picture of the economy. Keynes's macro theory appears as a particular layer where it is legitimate to take for granted some of the institutions and rules of the game that complexity theorists would like to account for on the grounds of computer simulations. Indeed simulations reveal the formation of certain patterns or conventional views which Keynes's structural model 'compresses' behind its equations.[1]

On the other hand, complexity theory seems to require integration with aggregate macro models, such as Keynes's, to deal with certain issues. In particular, computer simulations appear to be insufficient in dealing with macroeconomic issues such as stability. While helpful for understanding the evolution of particular markets or industrial sectors, they provide only limited insights into the evolution of the economy as a whole. What they lack is the necessary force of abstraction; a structural model capturing the key factors and market interactions thus seems to be indispensable for interpretation and development of policy guidelines.

Fourth, like complexity theory, Keynes's views are consistent with key tenets of the neo-modern research programme based on a combination of universal claims and more historical and contingent claims. For example, Keynes's approach is consistent with the notion of light theory. He made rather modest assertions concerning capitalist dynamics. Not only did he rule out the long-run equilibrium concept and the stability assumption underlying neoclassical theory, but he was also quite sceptical about the possibility of modelling disequilibrium or of building models focusing on paths or convergence processes towards equilibrium. As already noted, in contrast with complexity theory, Keynes's model identifies the determination of instantaneous equilibrium as the core of scientific efforts concerning 'universal' theoretical claims. All we can do in theory, his work seems to suggest, is to focus on 'fragile' equilibrium points. In particular, equilibrium states should not be understood as predefined positions towards which the system inevitably tends but 'as positions of *conditional or provisional* equilibrium ... positions which do not possess the mechanical stability property of conventional equilibria, and/or which may not be indefinitely reproduced over time as "states of rest" ' (Setterfield 2002: 4 emphasis in the text; see also Caserta and Chick 1997).

In addition, as can be seen in the final chapters of the *General Theory*, Keynes also sought to complement the focus on instantaneous equilibrium with consideration of historical factors that are bound to affect the evolution of capitalist economies.

In other words, Keynes's model seeks to combine the generality of theoretical claims and the specificity of historical evolution, thereby avoiding the extremes of a general, a-historical, all-encompassing theory on the one hand, and a mere historical-descriptive account of evolution on the other.

The generality of the *General Theory*

On these grounds, we are now able to see why Keynes's theory can be considered as more general than neoclassical theory in their limited field of application, that is, instantaneous equilibrium. The issue of generality has been the subject of heated debate in macroeconomics ever since the publication of Hicks's 'Keynes and the Classics'. We do not wish to recapitulate the entire debate; nevertheless, we argue that the analysis developed in this book helps shed new light on it. One convenient way of illustrating this is to assess some of the most recent exchanges on the issue, making reference to contributions by Hodgson (2001, 2004b), Davidson (2004) and King (2004). All of them have the merit of tackling the generality issue thoroughly and explicitly, and of examining some of the presumed weaknesses in Keynes's contribution. We shall try to show not that it 'is all in Keynes', but that Keynes did actually achieve what he claimed in his book. Moreover, we shall argue that he made several mistakes that partly account for the distortion of his key contribution in much of later 'Keynesianism', although they are not the same mistakes pointed out by many of his critics.

We start by considering some of Hodgson's claims. Hodgson subscribes to a certain consensus view currently emerging among economists of all persuasions, including many like Hodgson himself who are broadly sympathetic to the *General Theory*. According to this view, Keynes's theory is not truly a general theory, and the title of his book was misconceived. Hodgson asserts that a truly general theory is an all-encompassing and comprehensive theory that fits all circumstances, including other forms of economies such as barter or feudalism, while Keynes's theory was built upon a combination of highly specific institutional conditions and universalistic psychological foundations. Therefore, Keynes's 1936 book

> did not provide a general theory of the nature and level of employment in all past, present or possible human societies. What Keynes analysed was the quite specific relationships in modern capitalism between employment, expectations and effective demand. Rather than providing a truly general theory of interest or money, Keynes explored the quite specific, capitalist type of system in which 'money is the drink which stimulates the system to activity' (Keynes 1936: 173). Money has existed for thousands of years but it did not become such an elixir of production until the rise of modern capitalism. Keynes favoured the 'general theory' rhetoric but always ended up exploring the particular circumstances of the contemporary capitalist system. Absent in the *General Theory* is a truly general theory of employment, interest or money. Keynes's book applies to modern capitalism, and not to all forms of economic society.
>
> (Hodgson 2001: 222)

On these grounds, Hodgson criticizes the defenders of the generality of Keynes's theory, such as Davidson, according to whom this theory always applies – to new and old forms of economies alike – because it relies on a few basic postulates concerning the unique properties of money (which involve the rejection of key principles of standard value theory, such as the gross substitution axiom). In Davidson's view, Keynes's theory can alternately apply to different types of economies simply by adding further restrictions.

> Keynes's *General Theory* is meant to explain a modern, money using, market economy. If one wishes to analyze (explain, discuss) feudalism, or the economies of biblical times, one must add additional restrictive axioms to Keynes's general theory to obtain a special case theory of feudalism, or of biblical economics, etc. Nevertheless, a common general theory will underlay all these specific cases of historical economies.
>
> (2004: 3)

However, Hodgson criticizes Davidson for not clearly specifying what this 'common general theory' is or whether it is based on 'psychological laws' like Keynes's theory, or not. He also neglects to indicate which 'additional restrictive axioms' must be added to Keynes's theory to adapt it to the analysis of feudalism or earlier socio-economic systems.[2]

In our view, these observations are well founded. Keynes certainly did not set out to build a 'general theory' covering all conceivable circumstances and forms of economy, as he wanted to focus on 'modern capitalism' (see also King 2004). Nevertheless, we see two major problems with Hodgson's approach. The first is that his definition of 'general theory' lacks validity as a benchmark for assessing macroeconomic theories. The second is that other notions of 'general theory' seem more relevant to both Keynes and the 'Classics' than the one sustained by Hodgson.

Let us start from the first point. Hodgson's definition of 'general theory' is so stringent that no theory could satisfy it. Indeed, as Hodgson himself points out, no theory, at least in the social sciences, can possibly account for all circumstances, owing to tractability and computational limits (Hodgson 2001: 4, 16). In the case of macroeconomics in particular, restrictions of some kind are practically inevitable. Hodgson is therefore not mistaken in pointing out that general equilibrium theory is also not a general theory, because it 'fails to incorporate key phenomena, such as time and money' (ibid.: 225).[3] The problem is, however, that the restricted nature of Hodgson's definition leads him to remain sceptical concerning the claims of generality made by the two theories. He notes, for example, that 'overall, it is difficult to say whether the classical or the Keynesian theory is more general' (ibid.). In other words, Hodgson's definition of generality is problematic in that it fails to discriminate between theories or to make sense of macroeconomic disputes.

The second point raises the issue of possible alternatives to Hodgson's definition of generality. While undoubtedly correct in recognizing that Keynes's focus was on a broad entity such as 'modern capitalism', Hodgson rules out the possibility that a general theory concerning *at least* this form of capitalism may exist. Instead, this is precisely the type of theory we argue that Keynes actually tried to achieve. Hodgson follows Schumpeter's interpretation here, according to which the *General Theory* was not truly general because it carried 'meaning only with reference to the practical exigencies of the unique historical situation of a given time and country' (1936: 792, quoted in Hodgson 2001: 224). Thus, in Schumpeter's view, the *General Theory* does not quite apply outside the conditions of the US in the 1930s. It is important to note that he also provides an explanation for this lack of generality, one which Hodgson does not mention. For Schumpeter, the key point is that the *General Theory* focuses on the 'short-run', thus leading Keynes to abstract from the essence of the capitalist process consisting in the long waves of technology break-throughs and structural change. Indeed, in his view, Keynes's aggregative approach

> keeps analysis on the surface of things and prevents it from penetrating into the industrial processes ... It invites a mechanistic and formalistic treatment of a few isolated contour lines and attributes aggregates a life of their own and a causal significance which they do not possess.
>
> (Schumpeter 1939: 44)

Although Hodgson does not subscribe to Schumpeter's distinction between surface and essence, he does accept a few key implications of his view. First, following Schumpeter, he considers Keynes's policy conclusions not to be valid outside the unique conditions of the great depression:

> [T]he genuine defect that Schumpeter recognised was that Keynes simultaneously revered a 'general theory' and attempted to derive quite specific policy conclusions from such an edifice. For instance, the scope for govern-mental management of the level of effective demand would depend crucially on the economic institutions of a particular country and the nature and extent of its engagement with world markets. An entirely 'general theory' can tell us little of these vital but specific details. In this respect, Schumpeter's criticism hit home. It may be possible to regard Keynes's work as a framework for viable analyses that addressed such specific circumstances, but Keynes himself did not lay down guidelines for the development of historically sensitive theories.
>
> (Hodgson 2001: 225)

On these grounds, Hodgson is thus led to conclude that Keynesian policies are obsolete and should not be adopted in the NE (ibid.: 224). Second, like Schumpeter, he suggests that Keynes's theory is, at least to some extent, responsi-ble for the neglect of historical factors in economic analysis and the rise of abstract modelling approaches in modern macroeconomics:

> Keynes's use of the 'general theory' term to analyze what were highly specific historical circumstances helped to obliterate all consideration of the problem of historical specificity from economics. Furthermore, it helped to create the post-war synthesis between the neoclassical general equilibrium theory and post-war macroeconomics.
>
> (ibid.: 227)

In the face of these claims, our views can be stated as follows. We subscribe to an intermediate stance between the two polar interpretations of Hodgson and Davidson. On the one hand, we hold that Keynes's theory is not universal, as Davidson seems to suggest. We believe that his theory is limited in two specific ways. First of all, it is limited in the sense of the object of analysis to which it applies, that is, the modern economy. It is not just money that distinguishes this economy from other types of economy and marks the difference between Keynes and the Classics. As we shall see in what follows, the principle of effective demand makes sense only within a broader, although quite limited, set of institutions, such as developed capital markets and trade unions. Second, the scope of the *General Theory* is also limited from the standpoint of its explanatory power. Indeed one of the key advantages of Keynes's theory is that, unlike its neoclassical counterpart, it does not imply a concept of equilibrium over time or try to model the evolution of the economy.

On the other hand, unlike Hodgson we believe that, given these limitations, it is still possible to regard Keynes's theory as being quite general and, above all, more general than neoclassical theory. While Hodgson is right in suggesting that Keynes's theory is not a universal, all-encompassing model of the economy, he is wrong in believing that it lacks any generality, or that it fails to explain any common features between different economies, that is, that it cannot be general in a narrower sense, such as that defined by our 'light theory', which refers only to modern capitalism and is based on the concept of instantaneous equilibrium. We hold, instead, that it is precisely in this context that the claim to generality in Keynes's book can be assessed and the comparison with general equilibrium theory can be made in a meaningful way.

In particular, we make two major claims. First, Keynes's theory applies not only to the US in the 1930s, but also to several different countries in different times that can be considered forms of 'modern capitalism' or 'modern economies' in that they share a common set of features with the US. Moreover, we claim that Keynes's theory is still a valid and useful source of policy advice today, since – as we shall see in the following chapters – the NE can actually be regarded as having accelerated some features of the modern economy, rather than having overhauled it completely.

Second, we argue that Keynes manages to highlight more causal mechanisms potentially at work in the economy than the neoclassical model, even if they are not observable or do not give rise to regularities. In other words, we agree with Hodgson in asserting that, in Keynes's battle with the 'Classics', only the concept of generality in the *intensive* sense (rather than the extensive sense advocated by Hodgson) matters: 'the claim made . . . by Keynes was that his "general" theory would embrace and explain more phenomena within the single "economic society in which we actually live" ' (2001: 220).

The distinction between primary and secondary variables

As a first step in demonstrating the generality of Keynes's analysis in the context of 'light theory', one must have a proper grasp of the differences between Keynes and the Classics. The view taken by standard macroeconomics concerning these differences is, in our opinion, completely misguided. Typically, standard macroeconomics considers the two basic theories as sharing the same basic model of the economy, as described by general equilibrium theory, and differing mainly in their empirical assumptions. Such differences lead Keynesian theory, for example, to depart from the neoclassical norm because of special values of parameters, price rigidities on particular markets, money illusion or asymmetric information, all of which impair the adjustment process to full employment equilibrium. What we find particularly misleading is the familiar textbook view suggested by the post-war Neoclassical Synthesis (e.g. Modigliani, Samuelson and Patinkin), according to which Keynesian theory applies to the 'short-run', disequilibrium aspects of the economic process, while neoclassical theory applies to the 'long-run' growth processes. Even more objectionable is the similar distinction made by Schumpeter and, in more recent times, by Lucas, between the Keynesian analysis focusing on the surface or 'phenomenic' reality, and other kinds of analyses dealing with structural phenomena or 'essential' reality and based on the so-called deep parameters.[4]

It is important to note that in order to get a more balanced view of the 'Keynes versus the Classics' dispute, it is not enough to suggest, as do most post-Keynesians, that Keynes's novelty rests in his consideration of various structural features of a modern economy neglected by the Classics, including uncertainty, the fact that production takes time and the key role of money and expectations. While these are undoubtedly important features of the *General Theory*, one can question whether they constitute the uniqueness of Keynes in and of themselves. For after all, even the neoclassicals claim to take these issues into consideration; for example, they include money and expectations in their models and seek to account for uncertainty. Indeed, at some level of abstraction, the two models can be seen as relying on a common set of elements. In our view, this means that the crucial differences between them should be sought in another direction, namely in the role these common elements play in each model. But then a few questions naturally arise: how should these different roles be assessed? How can the theories be identified?

In order to answer these questions and draw definite conclusions concerning the generality issue, a first major step to take is to draw new distinctions between the possible variables included in a model that go beyond the familiar distinctions (e.g. between exogenous and endogenous). More specifically, capturing the difference between the two basic theories also requires the creation of finer distinctions between different types of exogenous variables, particularly in terms of their ability to influence income. One reason for this is that, while both the Keynesian and the neoclassical models can, in principle, accommodate an exogenous money supply and are thus similar in terms of the exogenous/endogenous distinction, they nonetheless appear quite different if one examines the role played by money in each of them. It is one thing to let money affect income as in the Keynesian model, but it is quite another to let it remain neutral as in the Classical one (at least if one thinks in terms of instantaneous equilibrium). A similar conclusion holds for exogenous expectations.

On these grounds, variables that can directly affect outcomes that represent the true determinants of the level of activity and which account for equilibrium at a given point in time are referred to here as *primary* or *causal* variables, whereas the others we label *secondary* variables. The latter can be taken as 'constant' or 'given' when dealing with the problem at hand. It should be noted, however, that the secondary factors are not completely irrelevant. For example, they may play an indirect role by affecting the primary variables.

Primary and secondary variables in the basic macro models

One crucial point to stress concerning this distinction is that the causal/secondary variables in the two basic models we are considering here are diametrically opposed. On the one hand, neoclassical theory regards atomistic preferences and resources (e.g. technology, size of labour force) as the truly irreducible causal factors, determined by nature or psychology before agents enter the market. Such a theory inevitably treats money and expectations as secondary variables instead. While a full justification of these claims and a more detailed account of the neoclassical model will be provided in Chapter 16, suffice it here to note that changes in these variables are 'neutral' in instantaneous equilibrium in that they do not distort 'real' variables, such as employment, real income and relative prices.

On the other hand, the causal variables stressed by Keynes are those that account for the key role of effective demand as a determinant of the level of activity: namely, money and expectations underlying the aggregate functions of consumption and investment. The causal variables emphasized by neoclassical analysis – preferences and resources – are not ruled out altogether in the *General Theory*, but appear among the secondary variables. Keynes himself makes this clear in chapter 18 of his book, where he makes the distinction between given factors, independent variables and dependent variables of his system, which is broadly similar to our distinction:[5]

> We take as given the existing skill, the existing quality and quantity of available equipment, the existing technique, the degree of competition, the tastes and habits of the consumer, the disutility of different intensities of labour and of the activities of supervision and organisation, as well as the social structure including the forces, other than our variables set forth below, which determine the distribution of the national income. This does not mean that we assume these factors to be constant; but merely that, in this place and split context, we are not considering or taking into account the effects and consequences of changes in them.
>
> Our independent variables are, in the first instance, the propensity to consume, the schedule of the marginal efficiency of capital and the rate of interest, though ... these are capable of further analysis. Our dependent variables are the volume of employment and the national income (or national dividend) measured in wage-units.
>
> (Keynes 1936: 245)

A few lines below this passage, Keynes notes that

> the rate of interest depends partly on the state of liquidity-preference (i.e., on the liquidity function) and partly on the quantity of money measured in wage-units. Thus we can sometimes regard our ultimate independent variables as consisting of (1) the three fundamental psychological factors, the psychological propensity to consume, the psychological attitude to liquidity and the psychological expectation of future yield from capital-assets, (2) the wage-unit as determined by the bargains reached between employers and employed, and (3) the quantity of money as determined by the action of the central bank.
>
> (ibid.: 247)

Is there a 'philosophical' justification for the causal ordering in the *General Theory*?

It is important to note, however, that not everything is settled by the distinction between primary and secondary variables. The two basic macro theories seem to be contrasting but symmetric (or even complementary). In order to be able to affirm the generality of Keynes's theory, we must take a second step. We must provide a broader 'philosophical' justification for the inversion of causal factors occurring in the *General Theory* with respect to standard theory. After all, it is here that the greatest and seemingly endless misunderstandings concerning Keynes's major work have quite likely arisen. In particular, two main, related, problems need to be solved. First, on what grounds does Keynes make the distinction between primary and secondary variables? Is it simply a matter of pragmatic choice given the problem at hand (i.e. something which is in the nature of an expedient or a 'short-cut' devised to solve a particular problem and can thus be accommodated or tolerated within the basic neoclassical paradigm for reasons of convenience rather than of principle) or do more fundamental factors account for it? The second is: what are the ultimate foundations of Keynes's aggregates? Is it all a matter of expectations dominated by irrational factors and psychology or are different forms of rationality and objectivity at play?

We hasten to point out that there is no clear-cut answer to such questions. There is leeway for different interpretations here because Keynes himself actually fails to clarify these strategic points in his *General Theory* and, at times, he even makes contradictory claims which do not fit any single interpretation. It should be clear, however, that two kinds of answers have historically prevailed in the Keynesian literature and macroeconomic textbooks, namely, that the distinction is pragmatic and reversible and that the ultimate foundations of Keynes's aggregates is psychological, as he refers to the 'laws' of human nature in general (see e.g. Hodgson 2001). It is not difficult to see that these two answers completely undermine any attempt at demonstrating the generality of Keynes's theory. One need only observe that psychology is the ultimate determinant of behavioural functions in standard theory as well. It therefore cannot account for Keynes's 'inversion', except as a short-run variant of standard theory justified by the criteria of expediency or by factors which are external to the theory, such as institutional rigidities.

We assume a different stance on both issues. First of all, in our view, the distinction in question is not at all of a pragmatic kind but is 'absolute' and 'irreversible'; it is rooted in a basic conception of the essence of economic behaviour, which is not reducible to the standard approach. Strictly speaking, however, this claim is not easy to demonstrate. Keynes, himself, seems to endorse a pragmatic view instead. He stresses, for example, that the given distinction is somewhat arbitrary in absolute terms and should therefore be carried out with reference to such factors as the relative speed of adjustment of various variables:

> The division must be made entirely on the basis of experience, so as to correspond on the one hand to the factors in which the changes seem to be so slow or so little relevant as to have only a small and comparatively negligible short-term influence on our quaesitum; and on the other hand to those factors in which the changes are found in practice to exercise a dominant influence on our quaesitum.
>
> (ibid.: 247)

Moreover, Keynes proposes this distinction for the explicit purpose of analysing the determination of level of activity. He does not regard it as appropriate for dealing with all problems (see e.g. Lawson 1985: 923). For example, he does not object to the standard analysis of individual firms aiming at determining their market shares. This view stands in stark contrast to the universalism of the Classical model, where the division between primary and secondary factors is permanent, that is, it is not determined by the question at hand.

Two remarks are in order at this point. First, the fact that the distinction stated is not 'absolute' or 'universal' in the *General Theory* is not necessarily or exclusively a sign of pragmatism. It indicates instead that Keynes's approach is consistent with the 'light theory' perspective, according to which there are various layers of economic reality (each with its own specific determinants), and modelling long-run evolution is not a feasible task. Indeed, in contrast with standard theory, the scope of Keynes's approach is limited. Not only is it inappropriate, for example, to discuss the distribution of market shares within a certain industry, but it also rules out the possibility to model growth, that is, the behaviour of 'slow' variables, such as the productivity and size of productive factors. Keynes focuses only on the behaviour of the 'fastest' variables and thus regards instantaneous equilibrium as the only scientific core of macroeconomics. This means, however, that within the limits of this equilibrium context his choice of causal variables is 'absolute' and opposed to the standard approach. In other words, in Keynes's 'light theory' perspective there is no room for neoclassical causal variables, because he does not consider the context of long-run equilibrium (where they make sense) as viable for macroeconomics. Only later, and thanks especially to the models of the neoclassical synthesis, does the Marshallian distinction between short-run and long-run equilibrium become a common means of reconciling the two basic paradigms: while it is legitimate to rely on Keynes's framework to study what determines income in the short run, one has to rely on neoclassical theory instead for dealing with problems in a long-run context, such as accumulation of capital and growth.

The second remark is that Keynes's distinction can be shown to be rooted not in psychology, but in a different view of the essence of economic behaviour that brings into sharp focus causal factors typically neglected by neoclassical theory. In order to clarify this point, we have to tackle the issue of the foundations of his aggregates. Before doing so, however, it must be recognized that Keynes's relative silence and his lack of emphasis of the need to distinguish between pragmatism and 'light theory' or between psychology and alternative objective forms of rationality or 'essence' can be regarded as a strategic mistake, as it generates confusion and authorizes all sorts of interpretations.

The irreducibility of expectations: a critique of psychologism

Let us turn to the question of the ultimate determinants of Keynes's aggregate functions and thus of expectations. As already noted, many authors tend to reduce Keynes's analysis of expectations to a matter of animal spirits or irrational moves (e.g. Shackle 1967: 129–34) or to emphasize that he actually accepts psychologism, that is to say, the view that psychological states are the only exogenous variables permitted beyond natural givens (e.g. Boland 1982: 94; Hodgson 2001: ch. 15; for a critique, see Lawson 1985: 923). Now it would seem that these stances are not completely unjustified in the light of Keynes's own terminology. For example, as shown in the quotations previously, he often refers to his aggregate data as 'psychological'. In our view, however, it would be a mistake to regard expectations in Keynes's analysis as the expression of mere subjective or psychological moves about which hardly anything can be said except that they are spontaneous (e.g. the so-called animal spirits). In particular, we suggest that expectations cannot be fully reduced to other given factors, such as individual preferences (and their psychological determinants).

Although Keynes's use of words is not always consistent, there is enough evidence to suggest that, in general, for him convention, not psychology, is the ultimate foundation of expectations. For example, in Keynes's theory, expectations appear directly in the form of aggregate data, rather than individual data as in neoclassical theory. Moreover, he links expectations – at least to some extent – to an objective anchor. This is a necessary step if theory is to generate determinate – though not deterministic – conclusions. It is vital to recognize that Keynes singles out quite a different type of objective anchor from that in standard theory, according to which expectations end up by converging at observed outcomes.

To make this clear, let us take a closer look at Keynes's writings. After pointing out in chapter 12 of his book that in estimating the prospects of investment, we must consider certain psychological factors such as 'the nerves and hysteria and even the digestions and reactions to the weather of those upon whose spontaneous activity it largely depends' (1936: 162), he is quick to remind us that 'we should not conclude from that that everything depends on waves of irrational psychology' (ibid.).

An important part of Keynes's account of expectations is also devoted to uncovering their objective determinants. In order to identify them, it is worth referring to his 1937 article 'The General Theory of Employment', in which he considers the various types of conventions that agents rely upon in order to make decisions in the face of uncertainty. Among these, he places emphasis on the fact that agents

> endeavour to fall back on the judgement of the rest of the world which is perhaps better informed. That is ... (they) endeavour to conform with the behaviour of the majority or the average. The psychology of a society of individuals each of whom is endeavouring to copy the others leads to what we may strictly term a conventional judgement.
>
> (Keynes 1937: 114, emphasis in original)

It seems plausible to suggest that what Keynes is arguing here is that, in forming their opinions or expectations about the future, agents tend not simply to act according to 'mass psychology', as if they were in a stadium, or to follow simple erratic rules of behaviour. They also make reference to their cultural and professional milieu and the familiar representations of reality which it generates, that is, what we might call 'popular' models. To copy others is to copy others' thoughts; the links among individuals concern beliefs or theories. In other words, it is arguable that Keynes recognizes the independent role played by 'theory' in shaping agents' expectations.

In order to show that such remarks by Keynes actually imply a sharp departure from psychologism, it is interesting to note their connection with the views of philosophers and social scientists in general who have dealt with similar issues and emphasized the role of theories as objective elements capable of influencing agents' behaviour. Keynes's stance seems to be in line, for example, with Karl Popper's 'world-3' conception, which admits the existence of 'theory' as an autonomous aspect of reality which must be sharply distinguished from the worlds of physical things and observed events (world-1) and mental states (world-2) (see e.g. Popper 1979: 154 and Togati 1998: 69–80 for a comment). Reference to world-3 allows us to state more clearly the way in which Keynes departs from standard analysis, and in particular, from the rational expectations approach. In principle, this approach also holds that theories might influence expectations; however, it also implies that, at the end of the day, theories are not an autonomous dimension of reality, because expectations eventually tend to coincide with observed data, that is, world-1 objects. As already noted, Keynes's long-term expectations defy this kind of reductionism instead, that is, they are fully autonomous. In terms of the Popperian conception, we can argue that the reason for this is that they are related to theories that are truly world-3 objects, that is, they are irreducible dimensions of reality that do not converge to the other dimensions.

An important implication of this distinction is that while rational expectations imply that people know the 'true' model of the economy (which is considered true in the strong sense that agents' subjective expectations converge to the objective probability distributions of events), for Keynes instead agents' confidence is 'artificial', as it is not grounded in adequate knowledge and a true model of the economy in the above 'strong' sense but in 'popular models' that are true only in the weak sense that they are widely agreed upon. Thinking along these lines, it can be seen, for example, that 'shared errors' on the stock market (e.g. pessimism/optimism or speculation) arise from the fact that traders do not know the external 'true' fundamental returns (as implied by the efficient market view and the rational expectations hypothesis) but rely on criteria or theories of stock prices which are intrinsic to the market and difficult to rank on a priori grounds; it can be argued, for example, that following technical analysis is no less rational than fundamental analysis for agents.

But this is not all. An even more significant link can be found between Keynes and Douglass North. In particular, both authors share a very similar 'institutionalist' approach to complexity. Like Keynes, North calls into question the standard view of rationality and stresses the significance of objective factors such as agents' 'shared mental models' and institutions to make sense out of the diverse performance of economies and polities. In a paper written with Denzau, he stresses, for example, that ideas matter, and the way by which ideas evolve and are communicated is the key to developing useful theory which will expand our understanding of the performance of societies both at a moment of time and over time:

> At a moment of time, the argument implies that institutions and the belief structure are critical constraints on those making choices and are, therefore, an essential ingredient of model building. Over time, the approach has fundamental implications for understanding economic change. The performance of economies is a consequence of the incentive structures put into place; that is, the institutional framework of the polity and the economy. *These are in turn a function of the shared mental models and ideologies of the actors*...systems of mental models exhibit path-dependence such that history matters, and...sub-optimal performance can persist for substantial periods of time.
>
> (Denzau and North 1994: 27, emphasis mine)

Keynes's broader notion of essence

On these grounds, one can now begin to understand Keynes's claim to generality. It rests on the fact that, by addressing the issue of agents' behaviour in the face of uncertainty, he singles out a new causal mechanism lacking in neoclassical analysis. Keynes's emphasis on conventional behaviour amounts to calling into question the standard view of the Rational Economic Man capable of pursuing self-interest and making autonomous choices by performing Benthamite calculations. Keynes's objection is not to deny that the forces of self-interest and competition are real determinants of behaviour but that they are not sufficient to understand it in full. Indeed, the major implications of agents' reliance on conventions is that, in order to pursue their interests, they *also* need to cooperate or coordinate their efforts. In other words, what Keynes singles out is the dimension of agents' interdependence or 'mutual interest' as opposed to simple self-interest.

In the *General Theory*, this basic interdependence between economic agents finds analytical expression in the view that macroeconomics is an autonomous discipline based on systemic principles (i.e. they transcend the individual agent), such as the fallacy of composition, the multiplier, the fact that 'we are all each other's customers' and that firms need to take into account the fact that wages are not simply a cost factor but also a key source of consumer demand (see e.g. Prasch 2000b: 179).

In line with the essentialist standpoint endorsed here, this view can also be expressed by stating that Keynes manages to define the essence of real-world economies in broader terms than the neoclassicals. This move appears to be consistent with neo-modernism; as already noted, the latter does not imply the rejection of the concept of essence, but its reformulation. In this regard, one need only note that Keynes rejects the standard conception of the Rational Economic Man as being too narrow. It amounts to considering only rather abstract, supposedly universal and invariant, features of behaviour, such as the fact that agents have preferences and try to pursue their self-interest in atomistic fashion, as the truly important ones. Other aspects of behaviour, such as their reliance on conventions, are quite incidental or contingent and need be reduced to the more fundamental, invariant properties.

Keynes's suggestion is not to reject the distinction between an invariant essence of economic behaviour and its more contingent characteristics altogether, but to shift the boundary between the two. The point is that there is also an element of generality or invariance involved in what the neoclassicals consider as incidental forms of behaviour. While conventions, for example, may take different forms, the element they have in common is the agents' reliance on some external reference point in order to make decisions, that is, what we have labelled as the 'mutual interest' dimension. In other words, Keynes's generality does not lie in building theory on the smallest number of assumptions (e.g. the axioms of rationality) as implied by the criteria borrowed from formal logic and adopted by general equilibrium theorists, such as Samuelson. It lies in broadening the realm of science by detecting new determinants of actual behaviour.

Keynes's broader notion of essence implies the rejection of any reductionist perspective. Being an essential form of behaviour, the dimension of 'mutual interest' cannot be reduced to self-interest, as implied by the micro-foundations projects or by more recent developments in standard economics, such as game theory. On the contrary, it is not existing conventions that need be accounted for on the grounds of the interaction between rational agents; rather, conventions actually 'come first', as they help agents carry out decisions concerning their own welfare or satisfaction. This justifies Keynes's reliance on aggregates, such as the propensity to consume or invest, as primary givens capable of internalizing this complex relationship.

Not surprisingly, due to the consideration of this new, autonomous, dimension of behaviour in macroeconomics, the conclusions Keynes draws about the rationality of behaviour differ sharply from neoclassical theory.[6] While in Keynes's view it is rational for individuals, for example, to follow an upward trend in the stock market so long as this is justified by some kind of theoretical view, it instead appears irrational on the grounds of the standard model. This difference has important analytical implications. The narrow conception of behaviour underlying standard theory ultimately explains why it can be regarded as systematically omitting all the notions which rely upon agents' interdependence and interaction, such as the multiplier and increasing returns as due complementarities. In order to account for these phenomena, it is necessary to give up the reductionist project based on the notion of Rational Economic Man as the essence behind the surface of complex wholes.

The differences between Keynes and the Classics should now be clear. Keynes's view amounts to suggesting that the reason why the laws of neoclassical theory are not fulfilled or supported by actual data is that it holds too narrow a conception of the forces governing agents' behaviour. It can be used to represent the implications of one force alone, that is, self-interest; it shows what would happen if this force were the only relevant one. Indeed standard theory focuses 'upon the aspect in question as though it existed in isolation – and typically as though it were free of internal instability as well' (Lawson 1997: 234). But self-interest does not operate in a vacuum. Keynes's critique does not deny that self-interest rules the economy, but avers that it is not sufficient to account for agents' actual behaviour. Therefore, it should not be dealt with separately or cast in terms of axiomatic maximizing behaviour as has become customary in standard macroeconomics based on representative agents' models.[7] Keynes's major contribution is to show that behind the violation of the *ceteris paribus* clause that impairs the actualization of the tendencies stated by neoclassical theory, there are not just 'imperfections' but other essential coordination mechanisms beyond the market mechanism, such as the 'popular models'.

Keynes's essentialist conception is strongly reflected in Denzau and North's approach. They start by arguing that 'it is impossible to make sense out of the diverse performance of economies and polities if one confines one's behavioural assumption to that of substantive rationality in which agents know what is in their self-interest and act accordingly' (Denzau and North 1994: 27). Something 'essential' is missing from the neoclassical picture. What is it? In line with Keynes, Denzau and North answer that to find out that we need to open the black box of rationality. However, they provide a modern answer that draws on recent advances in scientific knowledge. Denzau and North argue, for example, that once the box is opened 'we encounter the complex and still very incomplete world of cognitive science' (ibid.). As already noted, they then explore some of the implications of the way in which humans attempt to order and structure their environment and communicate with each other and emphasize the essential role of 'shared mental models' or structures of beliefs in society:

> Cultural learning in pre-modern societies not only provided a means of
> internal communication but also provided shared explanations for phenom-
> ena outside of the immediate experience of the members of the society in

the form of religions, myths and dogmas...such belief structures are not confined to primitive societies but are an *essential* part of the belief structure of modern societies.

(ibid.: 15, emphasis mine)

It can be therefore argued that these shared mental models are that part of reality not captured by the standard rationality view. Denzau and North make it clear that the reason these models are used by agents and must be considered in the analysis is that the working of the economy is not based on self-interest alone.[8] They reflect another dimension of agents' behaviour – one that Denzau and North refer to here as 'coordination' – that resembles our 'interdependence' or 'mutual interest' labels:

Mental models are shared by communication, and communication allows the creation of ideologies and institutions in a co-evolutionary process. The creation of ideologies and institutions is important for economic performance, as there exist gains from trade and production that require *coordination*...a market economy is based on the existence of a set of shared values such that trust can exist. The morality of a business person is a crucial intangible asset of a market economy, and its non-existence substantially raises transaction costs.

(ibid.: 20, emphasis mine)

9 Some key differences between Keynes and the 'Classics'

In this chapter, we elaborate on the conclusion drawn in Chapter 8 that Keynes's theory is more general than its neoclassical counterpart. As evidence, we demonstrate that, thanks to his broad notion of essence, Keynes managed to depart from standard neoclassical analysis on several key points, including the consideration of the role played by historical and institutional factors and the approach taken to dynamic and stability issues.

Keynes's alternative to psychologism and institutional determinism

One major point worth exploring in Keynes's approach is the extent to which it can be said to account for historical and institutional factors. This proves to be another rather controversial issue. According to Hodgson, for example, it represents one of the weakest aspects of the *General Theory*. In his view, there is a trade-off between Keynes's claims to generality and his concern for historical specificity. As he puts it:

> Keynes did little to ground his theory upon historically specific economic institutions. Although institutions, such as the joint stock company and the stock exchange, inevitably protrude into his narrative, he did not start from the specific institutions of capitalist society and then develop a theory that illuminated their principal causal processes and relations.
>
> Instead, Keynes...appealed repeatedly to 'fundamental psychological factors' as the foundation for his theory. His invocation of supposed psychological factors in his discussion of economic processes is more prominent than any discussion of historically specific institutions. Specific institutions appear casually in the *General Theory* as the mechanisms through which seemingly ahistorical psychological forces express their power. Keynes attempted to develop a 'general theory' that would apply to a number of different types of socio-economic system. He conceived of this general theory as having a universal and psychological foundation.
>
> (Hodgson 2001: 221)

Once again, we remain sceptical of this argument. In his account, Hodgson stresses two key elements: psychological factors and historically specific institutions. It is as if one or the other were the crucial determinants of the level of activity. However, this picture is misconstrued. In this account, not only is there a clear trade-off between the generality of psychological foundations and the specificity of the institutional context, but Keynes's theory also appears to be caught in a kind of impasse. If, on the one hand, the sole causal factors were psychological, there would be no real scope for Keynes's 'inversion' or his principle of effective demand. His theory would not really depart from standard theory. If, on the other hand, institutions as such were the key driver, there would be the risk of advocating institutional determinism.

The essentialist perspective proposed here, instead, introduces a third term into the picture as a way out of this impasse. It shows that Keynes actually manages to reconcile the two seemingly opposed notions of generality and historical specificity, without falling into the trap of either psychologism or institutional determinism. We have seen that neoclassical theory singles out self-interest as the universal force underlying the causal factors of atomistic preferences and resources. At the root of Keynes's aggregates, instead, we find the universal dimension of mutual interest, according to which agents' rationality is bounded and their decision-making relies on external reference points, such as conventions and institutions.

On these grounds, one can derive the following claims. First, it is not incongruous that the aggregates referring to human behaviour and expectations appear as the only legitimate causal factors in the *General Theory*. They allow Keynes to rule out any kind of institutional or technological determinism. In his view, institutions and technology play no causal role *per se*; they can only influence outcomes by affecting individuals' expectations and motives of behaviour.

Second, as already noted, while using psychological terms, Keynes nonetheless escapes psychologism, in a real departure from standard theory. He does so, however, without giving up the element of generality. This is possible because his aggregates reflect an abstract and general dimension, that is, the dimension referring to agents' interdependence or their mutual interest. Unlike self-interest, however, this cannot be defined in an atomistic and naturalistic fashion; it has conventional and objectivist foundations in world-3 products, such as shared mental models.

Institutions as exogenous data

The new element of generality in Keynes's approach is not inconsistent with historical specificity. The shared mental models change and give rise to historically contingent institutions. Indeed, as Denzau and North underline,

> the institutional framework of the polity and the economy...are in turn a function of the shared mental models and ideologies of the actors...systems of mental models exhibit path-dependence such that history matters, and...sub-optimal performance can persist for substantial periods of time.
>
> (1994: 27)

Moreover, it can be argued that Keynes's inversion of causal factors itself reflects historically contingent institutions, or, in other words, Keynes actually took the specific institutions of capitalism as his starting point. This claim can be understood in two different senses. The first is that macroeconomics for Keynes is an emergent layer or property, because it 'internalizes' institutions that reflect the dimension of mutual interest. In particular, in line with the bounded rationality view, agents need institutions to improve coordination, grant stability and create trust. In the logic of Keynes's model of instantaneous equilibrium, institutions must thus appear as exogenous data, because the mutual interest dimension cannot be ruled out and reduced to the logic of self-interest, as implied by methodological individualism and New Institutional Economics, for example. Indeed as Denzau and North state: 'At a moment of time, the argument implies that institutions and the belief structure are critical constraints on those making choices and are, therefore, an essential ingredient of model building' (1994: 27). In other words, this means that from the standpoint of Keynes's macroeconomics, markets are a secondary rather than a primary institution. For example, they can only exist if there is enough trust to back trade (for a similar view, see for example Rifkin 2000).

In the light of these remarks, it also appears that Keynes's macro appears to be consistent with its methodological foundations (i.e. bounded rationality), while most neoclassical macro models are not. This is because the latter often take institutions as a given, in contrast with the methodological individualist guidelines they, in principle, should endorse. They can thus be regarded at best as 'pragmatic' models.

Keynes's macro and the institutions of the modern economy

The other sense in which Keynes's macro reflects historically contingent institutions is that, as noted by Hodgson (2001) himself in discussing an important contribution by Victoria Chick, the principle of effective demand (with the asymmetric link between the investment and the saving it involves) makes sense only with respect to the institutions of the modern economy:

> [S]ome post-Keynesians have stressed the importance of history and specific economic institutions, so that the rhetoric of general theorising has been implicitly undermined. For example, Victoria Chick (1986) has shown that standard assumptions of monetary theory are specific to the financial institutions involved. As these institutions evolve through time, different theoretical principles can pertain. In particular, the nature of money itself changes, from precious metal to bank deposits, to data in computer memories. Chick argued that because of the institutional realities of pre-industrial capitalism, saving necessarily preceded investment. Subsequently, as soon as banks were able to create credit, saving no longer had to precede investment, as the banking system evolved it enhanced the capacity for the banks to create credit.

Hence, by the 1920s and the time of Keynes, banking institutions and the credit system had evolved to the point that investment could and would precede saving. This was the quite specific historic period to which the allegedly General Theory applied. Subsequently, as Chick pointed out in her paper financial institutions have developed further, with massive global speculation in a variety of financial assets. This may mean that Keynesian analyses and remedies can to some extent become obsolete.

(Hodgson 2001: 223–4, emphasis mine)

Once again, in our view it is wrong to regard the link between Keynes's concepts and the institutions of the modern economy, such as well-developed capital and labour markets, as implying a loss of generality. This would be true only if one adopted Hodgson's extensive definition of generality. As already noted, what matters for Keynes, instead, is to affirm his generality within the more limited context of the modern economy. From this standpoint, this quote shows precisely why he actually succeeds in this enterprise. Indeed, as Hodgson aptly points out, the link between saving and investment postulated by neoclassical theory (where the former precedes the latter) reflects an old economy, such as that of the nineteenth century, when peasants or small producers were still the main protagonists. Thus, neoclassical theory is completely amiss in seeking to universalize, or generalize to all times and places, conclusions that were legitimate only in that outmoded context. On the contrary, the main contention in this book is that, since the NE accelerates but does not change the basic features of the modern economy, Keynes's theory is not obsolete and still holds in the context of the NE.

Yet another criticism of the *General Theory* also merits consideration, namely that the book does not include much institutional detail. Strictly speaking, this is true. Remarks like the following thus seem to be well taken:

Keynes was concerned to examine the nature of the wage bargain, and the relation between real wages and money wages. But the institutions of the labour market and employment are not discussed in any depth. In this respect, Keynes attempted the impossible to draw quite specific conclusions from a theory that purported to be general.

(Hodgson 2001: 223)

It is important, however, not to assess this feature of the *General Theory* from the standpoint of the historian or of descriptive accuracy but in the light of Keynes's goals and the internal logic of his theory. Not only does he try to establish a theory valid in principle for slightly different institutional contexts (e.g. for all the economies that match the broad definition of 'modern economy' given earlier), but his principle of effective demand also implies that some markets have causal priority over others. Thus, it is not surprising that his book devotes much more attention to financial markets than to the labour market. While the former influence investment and the level of income, the latter plays a less important role (i.e. it determines the elasticity of employment to income, not the level of income itself). To support the key argument of his book about the role of aggregate demand, it is actually enough for Keynes to suggest, as he does, that there is a money wage bargain (and thus trade unions) and that this does not determine the real wage and employment. Moreover, as we shall see, while Keynes does not account for changes in institutional settings, his distinction between primary and secondary givens provides a method of dealing with the effects of such changes.

Keynes versus standard dynamic approaches

The last point concerning Keynes's approach we would like to mention has to do with its implications for dynamic analysis and stability. This, too, is a rather controversial issue. Once again, we start by referring to Hodgson's critique of the *General Theory*. In his view, one of the reasons why Keynes tries to build a general theory is that he neglects the lessons of the historical school:

> If Keynes had been aware of the vast historical school literature, which had tried to develop economics in full awareness that economies 'are not homogenous through time', then he would have been less likely to attempt an entirely general theory.
>
> (Hodgson 2001: 223)

Once again, we disagree. Also in this case, the main problem lies with Hodgson's definition of general theory. He regards it as an all-encompassing model seeking to account for all circumstances, including the future evolution of the economy, and therefore also 'long-run' phenomena, such as accumulation and growth. In our view, it is a mistake to apply this definition to Keynes. He did not attempt to build a general theory in this sense. As already noted, he was concerned with generality in the sense of 'light theory'. While he actually did provide a more general account of the causal mechanisms (coordination and self-interest) that govern the economy, he did not furnish an exhaustive long-run perspective of the economy as a whole. In the spirit of 'light theory', Keynes's theory had a limited scope, both in terms of historical periods (it applies only to modern capitalism) and analysis (it is not a comprehensive dynamic model, but focuses only on the causal factors at play at a given point in time). Indeed, it was precisely because Keynes was aware that economies 'are not homogenous through time' and therefore cannot be assumed to be stable on a priori grounds that he was critical of econometrics and resisted the temptation to build the kind of growth models that have become so popular in later macroeconomics. While not ruling out formal tools altogether, 'without which ... we shall be lost in the wood' (Keynes 1936: 297), he was certainly aware of their limitations, in particular, when they seek to 'provide a machine, a method of blind manipulation, which will furnish an infallible answer ... ' (ibid.).

Keynes and stability

However, it is equally wrong to believe that Keynes simply neglected long-run phenomena or concluded that structural phenomena, such as market forms or changes in technology or population, simply do not matter because in the 'long run we are all dead'. As Asimakopulos puts it: 'Keynes' vision and interest went much beyond the short period of the formal model, and at many places in the *General Theory* there is reference to changes occurring over time' (1991: 121). In particular, there is no doubting that his work suggests a perspective on global stability of capitalism in the long run. In particular, it rules out a priori assumptions about the stability of the economy. While certainly believing that capitalist economies in general are quite unstable, in the sense that there are no inherent mechanisms such as flexible relative prices that ensure that stability will prevail as in neoclassical theory, at the same time Keynes stresses that there are also no a priori reasons for catastrophic outcomes, that is, for the systematic dominance of negative effects. He made some assertions concerning the stability of actual economies by drawing on experience rather than on a priori considerations:

> It is an outstanding characteristic of the economic system in which we live that, while it is subject to severe fluctuations in respect of output and employment, it is not violently unstable. Indeed it seems capable of remaining in a chronic condition of sub-normal activity for a considerable period without any marked tendency either towards recovery or towards complete collapse. Moreover, experience indicates that full, or even approximately full, employment is of rare and short-lived occurrence.
>
> (Keynes 1936: 249–50)

Whether an actual economy is more or less stable can only be established *ex post*, on the grounds of experience, for actual instability is often held in check by appropriate policy and institutional changes. In other words, for the *General Theory*, stability is not an inherent property of the market economy (seen as the simple interaction of atomistic individuals); it is a property of the socio-economic system as a whole, once institutions are taken into account. As we shall see in greater detail in Chapter 18 this perspective is naturally associated with an endogenous view of business cycles due, for example, to shared 'errors' (e.g. pessimism/optimism, speculation based on a combination of 'popular' theories and mass psychology).

Keynes's informal dynamic method

The *General Theory* also contains insights on how dynamic analysis should be carried out. While ruling out dynamic formal modelling, Keynes did devise – in line with the 'light theory' approach – an informal, constructive method for dealing with long-run phenomena, based on the distinction between primary and secondary data. Although he only provided a sketch, and not a complete analysis, he emphasized that for this purpose we need to take into account the changes that occur in both types of data and the possible feedback taking place between them. In this way Keynes distinguished his approach from methods of mathematical analysis that provide definitive conclusions by assuming 'strict independence between the factors involved' (ibid.: 297), an independence which does not exist in the real-world historical context in which Keynes tried to place his theory.

It must be noted that this issue once again reveals the generality of Keynes's theory, primarily stemming from his theory of behaviour. One of the key implications of the fact that agents rely on changeable conventions and shared mental models is that the standard concept of given, static preferences is not applicable. It can be argued that the 'parameters' concerning aggregate demand underlying Keynes's equilibrium are malleable, that is, they are likely to take on different values according to the changing context. For example, it is possible to regard technological progress or increases in population as giving rise to changes in the marginal efficiency of capital or in the propensity to consume. Strictly speaking, neoclassical theory can also accommodate changes in the basic data, that is, preferences and physical data. However, these are bound to change only according to the rules of comparative statics, according to which comparison is made between two states of equilibrium when just one parameter changes under the *ceteris paribus* condition. Thus, for example, according to the theory, technological change will increase productivity but will not change consumers' preferences over goods. Indeed this kind of endogenous change in preference is ruled out in principle because of the assumption of stability. Thus, the true dynamic picture required for carrying out stability analysis cannot be developed.

The fact that parameters can change endogenously is what allows Keynesian theory to account for cycles and duality in general. Only these endogenous changes can explain why a given shock sometimes induces stability and at other times does not, as shown by computer simulations. It should be clear that we do not mean that in the absence of such changes it is impossible to talk about business cycles. We do have standard theories of these phenomena. However, since such theories rely on the assumption that the system is intrinsically stable, these phenomena can only occur because of external or *ad hoc* factors that determine temporary deviations from long-run equilibria or low levels of accumulation of productive factors, such as errors in expectations, confusion, institutional rigidities and the like. Paradoxically, the only way we can derive neoclassical conclusions concerning stability in a 'natural' rather than an *ad hoc* fashion is to rely on Keynes's framework. Indeed, its generality lies in that it is able to specify the general conditions that grant macroeconomic stability (e.g. certain values of the parameters of his functions or certain institutional mechanism or reforms granting a high level of aggregate demand).[1]

Another point confirming the high degree of generality that Keynes achieves, thanks to the malleability of the parameters underlying his notion of instantaneous equilibrium, is that his theory is able to account for both dynamic and structural instability. One of Keynes's major contributions is to rule out stability as an a priori assumption and to treat it as an empirical question. His theory shows that parameter instability makes it impossible to guarantee that a real-world economy spontaneously converges towards the full employment equilibrium as envisioned by neoclassicism. However, he does not stop at hypothesizing what would seem to correspond to dynamic instability or disequilibrium from the standpoint of neoclassical theory. He also suggests that the economy may reach a resting point, and that this point may be unsatisfactory but dynamically stable. In other words, Keynes holds that while the system may not return to full employment, it is nonetheless kept from catastrophe by a number of stabilizing mechanisms, such as given money wages, taxation or deposit insurance. Keynes's insights concerning instability will be treated at greater length in Chapter 18. We now turn to closer examination of Keynes's outline of dynamic analysis.

First of all, Keynes focuses on the interaction among the primary or independent variables. Once having recognized that simple formal methods are inappropriate for this complex object of analysis, he suggests that his formal analysis combined with experience can be useful to extend his theory to the long run. As Asimakopulos puts it:

> Keynes recognizes that allowance must be made for the interactions among the independent variables of his analysis . . . the complexity of these interactions means that the analysis of changes over time cannot be adequately handled by mathematical equations. Keynes goes beyond the short period when he combines his formal analysis with experience of the operations of actual economies that provide some indication of the nature and extent of likely changes in his independent variables. The time paths for employment and output that are deduced from this extension of this theory are 'illustrative' rather than 'determinate'. They show what would happen if particular patterns of interaction occurred. They provide the analyst with an indication of likely outcomes, but the actual time paths of the dependent variables depend on the circumstance surrounding the initiating changes.
>
> (Asimakopulos 1991: 136–7)

Second, Keynes argues that primary or independent variables may also be influenced by secondary factors and dependent variables (see e.g. Keynes 1936: 247). Thus, for example, structural changes or wage changes may play a role by influencing the agents' expectations underlying aggregate demand. Once again, there is no doubting that taking these indirect influences into account is relatively difficult for Keynes and is bound to make analysis relatively indeterminate. In particular, he points out that long-term expectations, unlike expectations considered in standard theory, cannot be modelled from past data. For example, after noting that 'the factors, which we have taken as given, influence our independent variables, but do not completely determine them' (ibid.: 245–6), he states that 'the schedule of the marginal efficiency of capital depends partly on the existing quantity of equipment which is one of the given factors, but partly on the state of long-term expectations which cannot be inferred from the given factors' (ibid.: 246). This is the ultimate reason why Keynes does not consider the 'long-run' to be the proper object of scientific analysis. In particular, he does not view long-run equilibrium as a pole of attraction for current values or for investment decisions (see e.g. Asimakopulos 1991: 134–5). From a strictly theoretical viewpoint, only relatively modest claims concerning the future – such as historical generalizations or the construction of various (more or less plausible) scenarios, devoid of causal significance – are possible.

Stability and the instantaneous equilibrium model

It is important to note, however, that while it is theoretically impossible to achieve precise or determinate conclusions about the size of effects induced by shocks or changes in basic data, models focusing on instantaneous equilibrium, such as those under consideration here, can still provide a useful contribution to stability analysis. This lies in their ability to highlight the direction of the expected effects, given that instantaneous equilibrium serves as a benchmark for the analysis of changes occurring in the long run. Since the concepts of equilibrium underlying the neoclassical and Keynesian theories are quite different, we can expect them also to give rise to different views of stability and instability factors. They can be expected to furnish different assessments of the likely impact of shocks and changes in dimensions of structural complexity on the economy.

Perhaps even more to the point, it seems plausible to suggest that what creates instability according to neoclassical theory may prove to be stabilizing according to Keynes and vice versa. For example, while neoclassicals regard rigid money wages as a cause of unemployment because of their emphasis on full price flexibility as the norm, Keynes considers it as a factor granting stability. This is one of the key implications of the analysis of the effects of changing money wages in chapter 19 of the *General Theory*, which is the only place where Keynes actually tries to analyse in some detail the interdependence between changes occurring in the economy and the determinants of equilibrium.

Two remarks are in order here. First, these different views of stability arise from different approaches to essence. From Keynes's standpoint, the emphasis placed by neoclassical theory on rigidities and imperfections as factors of instability is rather misleading; it gives a poor account of instability based on an abstract or ideal view of markets dominated solely by agents' self-interest. Keynes's maintains that behind the veil of imperfections lie neglected elements reflecting mutual interest, such as trust and institutions, and that these are intrinsic or 'essential' to the working of a market economy. For example, a structure of wage differentials, contracts written in monetary terms or firms' expectations concerning future demand all depend upon a certain degree of price stability. In Keynes's view, if the money wage were truly flexible, as asserted by standard theory in line with the idea of a 'pure' market system, instability might well increase rather than decrease. Downward wage flexibility together with price deflation would disrupt those essential elements; in particular, they could undermine expectations, make debtors poorer and cause social unrest and workers' resistance.

Second, it is important to keep in mind that Keynes's approach does not give rise to definitive conclusions, even regarding simple qualitative analysis focusing on the likely direction of expected changes. For example, while he rejects money wage cuts as a solution for unemployment, Keynes's conclusion is

> based on a balance of considerations, none of which can be made precise, and the assessment of which requires judgement and experience. This is the nature of economic analysis when it attempts to deal with changes occurring over historical time in actual economies.
>
> (Asimakopulos 1991: 127)

Beyond Keynes

It must be noted once again, however, that Keynes's analysis is not without limitations. In our view, his modernist approach is subject to criticism for not clearly specifying the limits of theories and thus their domain of validity; it would benefit from amendments along the lines of the neo-modern perspective. Despite having defined an alternative benchmark for stability analysis, Keynes was unsuccessful in providing a convincing bridge between his theory of instantaneous equilibrium and long-run analysis. To some extent, his failure to do so made his approach vulnerable to the widespread although thoroughly mistaken view that it applies only to the short run.

The main problem is that, although he stressed malleable parameters and drew up a general methodology for dealing with changes in structural factors, Keynes was not clear about the status of the 'long run'. His criticism of the a priori stability view, econometric modelling and predictive aims of neoclassical theory make it plain that he considered the long run unsuitable as the object of 'hard science' pursued along these lines. As already noted, he rejected the logic of long-run equilibrium and the search for universal laws on the grounds of unique formulas or models attempting to derive actual time series behaviour. However, he failed to observe that the 'long-run' is not completely beyond the reach of science. Although he briefly commented on the likely evolution of actual economy, on secular trends and so on (e.g. in the final chapter of the *General Theory*), he did not seem to consider the dynamics of capitalist evolution as subject to 'light theorising', namely as something having a quite different scientific status with respect to instantaneous equilibrium but that can still be accounted for by using an 'ordered method of thinking'.

Admittedly, his distinction between primary and secondary factors represents a crucial step towards a dynamic approach along these lines. However his strategy of dealing with complex evolution was hampered by two limitations. First, he actually failed to complete the job; he considered only a few interactions and left out many others. Strictly speaking, Keynes was fully aware of the complexity of the actual course of events. Not only did he make the above distinction, but he also hinted at a scheme of full interaction between independent and dependent variables that could make the examination of any actual problem 'more manageable' (Keynes 1936: 249). However, apart from a few scattered remarks, he did not implement such a scheme in his analysis.

Second, once having recognized that his model could only serve as a starting point or guide for the study of trends in employment over time, he emphasized that further analysis 'depends on our practical intuition ... which can take account of a more detailed complex of facts that can be treated on general principles' (ibid.). While there is no doubting that intuition is necessary for any good economist, it is hardly enough for addressing the analysis of long-run phenomena. In particular, Keynes provided neither plausible scenarios nor historical analysis to accompany theory and intuition in a full analysis of stability. While he recognized that stability depends on how structural changes affect the parameters of aggregate demand (e.g. it is only if this is high enough and/or is managed appropriately that global stability may prevail), Keynes failed to trace these effects systematically over a long period of time. While convincingly arguing that stability is an empirical issue, he did not himself accomplish this formidable 'empirical' task and thus failed to integrate his instantaneous equilibrium model into a long-run perspective. The principle of effective demand thus remained confined to instantaneous equilibrium. In this sense, our neo-modern perspective takes Keynes as a starting point, and not as a final solution, in the attempt to achieve such integration in the analysis of the NE.

Our Keynesian perspective therefore needs to go beyond Keynes. We hold that Keynesian theory has the potential to provide a full account of stability. For this purpose, we need to generalize Keynes's insights on the interaction between primary and secondary data, by taking into account the greatest number of interactions possible. Moreover, we must build the bridge between Keynes's instantaneous equilibrium model and long-run analysis by deriving the changes in the basic data from the recent history of capitalism. In this way, we regard aggregate demand as the terminal of impulses induced by a number of organically related elements reflecting the main structural trends or empirical laws of the NE. This is not a new strategy in the Keynesian literature. For example, it underlies the so-called 'transformational growth theory' which actually provides a historically based account of the evolution of demand (see e.g. Argyrous 2002; Nell 2002).

We also recognize that despite the generality of Keynes's instantaneous equilibrium model, the scenario concerning the stability of the NE that can be derived from it is not exhaustive. A truly general analysis must also take into account the insights into this issue that can be derived from a simple neoclassical macro model, which captures the real forces of self-interest and competition in a more abstract fashion. While this model is contained as a particular case within the Keynesian model, we believe it is useful in representing it more directly.

The reason is simple. Our purpose is to fill the gap between formal long-run models and informal or pragmatic scenario-building practices. We must show that a coherent global stability analysis can be obtained by putting together the various pieces of this giant puzzle. As already noted, our meta-model is based on the assumption that the two basic macroeconomic theories considered here can be thought of as complementary up to a point, for together they highlight the essential mechanisms involved. There is no doubting that neoclassical theory has a comparative advantage in representing the analytical implications of 'self-interest' as if it were acting in isolation, just as Keynesian theory has an advantage in representing the outcome of the other major force, that is, mutual interest. It can be argued that there is a sort of 'division of labour' between the two approaches. While the neoclassical model is more useful in highlighting the physiology of capitalism, Keynes's model is especially useful in pointing out its pathologies.[2]

Part IV

A preliminary account of stability of the New Economy

In Part IV of this book, we carry out the first two steps of our stability analysis. In the first step, we justify our use of Calvino's labels (multiplicity, rapidity, lightness, precision and visibility) to develop a broad definition of the NE that manages to capture its complexity as well as to single out sources of structural instability neglected by standard theory. The labels, by themselves, do not imply specific causal links between the key variables considered. The posing of causal links – which is the proper task of theory – is taken up in the second step, when we begin analysing the stability of the NE with reference to the various labels. Strictly speaking, we shall be conducting what can be considered a *prima facie* account of stability that takes stock of the various causal mechanisms emphasized by several commentators of the NE, whether or not these mechanisms are explicitly derived from macro models. This is a useful task that scenario builders often carry out; rather than engaging in theoretical debate, they usually try to investigate the impact of actual causal mechanisms triggered by some phenomena of interest, such as globalization or technological progress, by listing the positive and the negative effects (for an example of this approach see the *Economist* 28–9–2002). This step of our stability analysis thus transcends individual paradigms. In other words, we do not start from a theoretical framework and cling to the conclusions that consistently derive from it. We pose the question not of theoretical consistency, but of which factors make for stability or instability when discussing the effects of the phenomena captured by our labels. Our intention is to develop a kind of map or meta-model that incorporates insights obtained from a variety of different sources, including macroeconomic theories, concerning the effects of the NE. This meta-model can then be used to draw conclusions about stability in an *ex post* fashion, that is, after considering the relative strength of contrasting forces or tendencies in the real-world economy. This task will be carried out in Part V in the light of theoretical paradigms that allow the weighing of stability and instability factors and the definition of prevailing trends or the most likely scenarios.

10 A broad definition of the New Economy

The first step of our stability analysis concerns the definition of the NE and a description of its main features. Perhaps it is more accurate to say that we are seeking a 'vision' of the NE. As noted by Schumpeter, a vision helps to single out the set of phenomena we wish to investigate, and acquire intuitively a preliminary notion of how they hang together (see e.g. 1954: 41–2).

This description, or vision, must capture the full complexity of the NE and single out most of the likely sources of structural instability. In the light of our previous remarks, it should be clear that the elaboration of such a description cannot be carried out by relying exclusively on the methods of standard theory. This is because standard theory takes both dynamic and structural stability for granted and regards the NE as merely a technology breakthrough to be dealt with through the use of simple production functions involving a number of restrictive implications (technological determinism, atomism, institutions that remain in the background, neglect of qualitative change, focus on long-run equilibrium, etc.). The formal tools of standard analysis, in addition to the empirical evidence it considers, are bound to lead to a flawed depiction of instability factors. For example, standard analysis implies that all instability can be attributed either to imperfections in the working of markets, such as rigidities and lags in the adjustment of prices and institutions, or to the lack of productive factors.

In order to study the stability of the NE without assuming stability as a postulate, it is necessary to reject these reductionist assumptions. We therefore need to develop an alternative interpretation of the NE. In our view, the NE is characterized by the following features, which we refer to as the 'objective' dimension of qualitative change: (1) it is the product of a number of closely interrelated key factors, including globalization, weightlessness and technology; (2) it implies growing mutual influences between institutions/culture and economic factors; (3) it also implies a growing interaction between micro and macro features; (4) it consists of a number of irreversible trends that distinguish it from past stages of capitalism.

In what follows, we shall see that these features allow us to identify a few major sources of 'subjective' qualitative change and instability. In particular, our analysis shows that the instability of the NE appears to arise from significant changes in agents' behaviour due to their changing perceptions of a few key dimensions, such as those of space, time, market and value.

In what follows, we shall outline a description of the main features of the NE that is consistent with our approach. It is arrived at through the use of the five broad categories or labels first suggested by the Italian post-modern writer, Italo Calvino, in his Norton Lectures at Harvard University, to characterize the last century in general. They are: 'multiplicity', 'rapidity', 'lightness', 'precision' and 'visibility'. Besides avoiding excessive fragmentation in listing many heterogeneous facts, the advantage of this classification is that it is in line with the broad definition of the NE pursued in this book.

The NE as consisting of a number of key factors

As already noted, standard theory regards the NE essentially as a technology breakthrough. Gordon (2002: 49), for example, defines it as 'the post-1995 acceleration in the rate of technical change in information technology (ICT) together with the development of the Internet'.[1] In our view, however, this definition is inadequate in capturing the complexity of the NE. While ICT undoubtedly plays a central role in the NE, other factors, such as finance, globalization and certain policy stances, also seem to be involved.

Another aspect of the complexity of the NE is the blurring of the traditional boundaries between economics and culture. This is happening to such an extent that we tend to subscribe to a maximalist interpretation of the scope of the current transformation: the NE is producing not just an E-conomy but also an E-society and an E-polity as well as a genuinely new E-culture. Thinking along these lines, Castells (1996), for example, argues that we are witnessing the development of an 'informational mode' that is transforming production, experience and power, and that is giving rise to a society fundamentally based upon networks of information exchange (see also Cohen *et al.* 2000). Consequently, in principle, a proper account of the NE calls for an interdisciplinary perspective.

One way of developing such a perspective is by exploring analogies between the definition of the NE and other broad 'sociological' or 'philosophical' definitions of modern society advanced in the literature over the past thirty years. Definitions of information society, post-modern society and post-industrial or post-Fordist society all seek to deal with perceived changes in society with respect to some past period taken as a benchmark (see e.g. Kumar 1995). In principle, the 'post-modern' concept is much more complex than the others. It can be seen not only as an historical phase (the last phase of capitalism) but also as an existential state or condition, a style and a critique of modernism, taken as the culture of modern society (see e.g. Cullemberg *et al.* 2001: 5 and Chapter 4). In general, these concepts all emphasize a number of key aspects. Following the interpretation of post-modernism as the last phase of capitalism, Jameson (1992), for example, focuses on characteristics such as mass commodification, globalization and new technologies (see Kumar 1995).

The two aforementioned considerations (namely, the plurality of key factors constituting the NE and the blurring between economic and political cultural spheres taking place) help us in our search for the sources of instability. Intuitively, instability seems more likely to occur when not one, but a number of key factors are considered, and when the focus is not only on the economy but also on its relations with society at large.

Moreover, these considerations also provide a *prima facie* justification for using Calvino's labels to identify and classify the main features of the NE. In line with our broad perspective, these labels refer to several features of a complex reality, and characterize not just the economy, but also the twentieth century in general.

Interrelations among economic factors

The criticism laid against standard macroeconomics in the previous section must be clarified. We are not claiming that standard theory neglects the existence of other factors beyond ICT, such as globalization or finance; in fact, these are sometimes even regarded as the key features of the NE within standard approaches. What we object to, instead, are two distinct features in the way these factors are handled in standard macroeconomics. The first is that they are each dealt with separately, relying on the *ceteris paribus* clause.

The second is that, even when they are recognized, the relationships between several factors are dealt with in a reductionist fashion, that is, they are considered only in so far as they are affected by ICT. For example, Gordon (2002: 4) stresses that the new technologies are responsible not just for productivity gains, but also for the stock exchange boom and income distribution effects (i.e. growing inequality). In other words, these interpretations appear to fall into the trap of technological determinism, according to which a number of economic phenomena, including macro outcomes, are causally related to technological change.

These two features of standard theory, which are clearly involved in the use of production functions and the performance of growth accounting exercises, are subject to serious limitations. It is increasingly observed that causal links and interactions are not predetermined in the NE and that they have become much more complex. Phenomena can be imputed to multiple causes, and the key causal factors are often interrelated.

It is important to note, however, that these limitations have not gone unnoticed by perceptive standard theorists. In the general field of macroeconomics, Blanchard and Fischer (1989) admit, for example, that the causes, even of trends in macroeconomic time series (and unemployment), are complex, and they acknowledge the inadequacy of monocausal theories of the business cycle.[2] As for the analysis of the NE, Baily (2001), for example, rejects techno-deterministic accounts of the growth process and lends support to a broad definition of the NE that will encompass a wide set of factors. He makes the case that the role of ICT in relative economic performance should not be overemphasized. In particular, ICT is not the only reason for the lack of convergence between the US and other countries. Preventing a more complete convergence, instead, is the interaction between ICT and other factors. These include barriers to the process of creative destruction, and even more importantly, a lower level of competitive intensity in

Europe and Japan (Baily 2001: 223). Moreover, in another contribution, Baily points out that the causality issue is one of the reasons why the growth accounting approach may be misleading in thinking about productivity rise. For example, once having noted the correlation between the rise in productivity and investment, Baily argues that correlation determines neither the existence nor the direction of causality. In addition to the growth accounting story, that is, the surge in ICT causing the productivity surge, an over-investment story involving the reverse causality is also possible. This amounts to suggesting that when profitability was high in the mid-1990s, the stock exchange boom led to the creation of an investment bubble that burst when companies realized they had overinvested in ICT (Baily 2002: 7–8).

In our view, insights concerning the causality issue and the role of ICT need to be generalized for stability analysis to be carried out. We give particular weight to two issues: first, the NE is based on a set of relatively autonomous key factors, that is, not necessarily causally related with each other; second, these factors may all be related in various ways, that is, we do not assume a predominant, one-way causal relation.[3] General interaction of this kind is likely to account for important sources of instability. It can be argued, for example, that the stronger interaction between globalization, finance and ICT occurring in the NE is likely to lead to important changes in agents' behaviour, such as in their perception of 'space', because of the drastic reduction of distances and various other barriers (transaction costs, psychological barriers, legal barriers, etc.) which these phenomena involve. Once we allow for this effect, we should be able to identify new indicators of instability, such as the faster transmission of financial and real shocks from one country to another and the greater volatility of financial markets.

The formidable task in developing our stability analysis is in overcoming the limitations of standard methods and managing to consider the entire gamut of interactions, both at the descriptive and analytical level. In general, standard theorists usually limit themselves to making a few critical remarks before resorting to familiar methods, such as growth accounting exercises, to get precise 'results'. It is a long-standing habit to combine criticism or insight on how proper analysis should be carried out, on the one hand, with reliance on standard analytic tools for want of better alternatives (due to tractability problems, for example), on the other. The challenge is in overcoming this 'split personality' and verifying whether the insights into the need for capturing interaction can actually be developed into a coherent new methodology following the lines of the neo-modern perspective.

In what follows, we make a few moves in this direction. In the first descriptive stage of our analysis, we try to capture interactions while refraining from rigid specification of causal links. At this stage, it would be a mistake to assume any particular causal link, for example, between finance and technology. Moreover, we must allow key factors to vary independently of one another. For these purposes, the use of broad categories such as Calvino's proves very useful. Indeed, these labels help sustain a very general description of the NE, as they allow interactions at the descriptive level to be accounted for in a relatively loose way, that is, without assuming any causal links. For example, we cannot simply make recourse to the 'technological change' label because that would imply emphasis on one particular causal relation, that is, from innovation to finance. The 'rapidity' label, instead, is more general and, in principle at least, allows the causation link to go in both directions.

Similar considerations apply to the other labels. Instead of using the label 'globalization', it seems preferable to rely on the 'multiplicity' label, as this does not imply that globalization is the cause and say, technology, the effect – or the other way round. Again, instead of using the label of 'finance', which seems to assume that finance comes before technology, we use the 'lightness' label instead. In addition, our labels perform another important task. They can also be regarded as involving 'horizontal' simplification, that is, they are devices that allow the grouping of heterogeneous and unrelated elements. For example, the 'lightness' label covers the case of production using less raw material as well as finance having greater weight.

The overlap between the economic and socio-institutional spheres

As already noted, standard theory regards the NE essentially as a technology breakthrough. Due to its reliance on the use of production functions and the performance of growth accounting exercises, this theory is bound to regard technological change essentially as an exogenous shock or residual. This means that no assumption is made about the affect of institutions on the innovation process; this is treated as purely exogenous. The fact that the environment, the institutional context, is taken as given is not surprising in view of the fact that neoclassical theory is based on a mechanistic view, according to which it is possible to think in terms of atomistic relations, that is, in terms of relatively isolated sub-sets of the complex socio-economic system. In line with the universalistic claims made by this theory, this amounts to assuming that it makes sense to isolate pure market forces, given that they tend to perform the task of allocation no matter what kind of shocks or institutional context are at work in the economy.[4] For example, despite the huge institutional differences among countries, competition is assumed to bring about similar outcomes, such as the uniformity of prices across countries implied by the law of one price or the purchasing power parity theorem.

This feature of standard theory is also subject to serious limitations. In particular, as many commentators suggest, the NE is characterized by an increasing overlap between economic and the socio-institutional spheres. This is true to such an extent that one is tempted to think of them as mutual catalysts, or at the very least, to emphasize their growing complementarities. One implication of this increasing mutual influence (with causal links going in both ways) is that institutions no longer act as simple external constraints; rather, they 'interfere' with the spontaneous working of the market mechanism and perform roles which are inconsistent with the standard model; for example, they may affect the allocation of resources. It follows that it is becoming increasingly difficult to isolate the 'natural' features of economic systems and to justify the universalistic claims of standard theory. It can be argued, for example, that the role played by natural endowments and geographical location, which receives great emphasis in standard theories of international trade, is less relevant in the NE than in the past. The wealth of nations and the international division of labour increasingly depend upon non-natural, institutionally created resources, such as human capital or technology.

It is important to underline that this reciprocal influence between institutions and the economy is at least partly recognized by standard analyses of the NE. It is not just a matter of recognizing the need for new regulations (concerning issues such as privacy and intellectual property rights), connected to the introduction of the Internet (see e.g. Cohen *et al.* 2000). Nor is it simply a matter of stressing the impossibility of ignoring the consequences of changing external constraints, such as exchange-rate regimes, the degree of capital mobility and methods of conducting monetary policy emphasized by political economy approaches.[5] What we are referring to, instead, are the analyses of the sources of the ICT revolution carried out by various authors. Gordon, for example, focuses on the permanent institutional sources of US advantage, such as its large domestic market and other sources (e.g. education, government funded Military and Civilian research, capital markets with their emphasis on equity finance, venture capital and pension funds, language and immigration) that would exist even if the productivity rise were to disappear (2002: 28–40).

But this is not all. Some contributions assert that institutions lie at the root of key developments in modern capitalism and that in a certain sense they are its generative functions. This crucial point is made clear, for example, by DeLong and Summers (2001) when comparing the recent NE with the far-reaching economic transformations of the second industrial revolution driven by electrification and other late nineteenth-century general-purpose technologies. These authors suggest that although these technologies contributed to the diffusion of mass production, large industrial enterprises, industrial labour unions, and the social welfare state, increasingly rapid sustained increases in median living standards and the middle-class society, nonetheless, for these crucial changes to occur, a number of 'fundamental' institutions of modern capitalism were required:

> [Y]ou needed more than improvements in production technology...in the US the economic transformation rested on legal and institutional and political changes
>
> 1   limited liability
> 2   the stock market
> 3   investment banking
> 4   the continentwide market
> 5   the existence of an antitrust policy.
>
> (DeLong and Summers 2001: 40)

In our view, these insights are helpful for our stability analysis in two respects. First, they suggest the proper way of viewing the NE. De Long and Summers stress that a set of fundamental institutions underlies what we have labelled as the 'modern economy', that is, twentieth century capitalism. Now we argue that the same is true for the NE. It must be noted that we do not regard this as merely a formal analogy. We are not simply suggesting that the position of DeLong and Summers is consistent with the argument presented earlier that institutions can play the same generating role for complex, systemic patterns as mathematics does for the SFA patterns, and that we should look at the NE in the same way as they do for the modern economy. We believe, instead, that the analogy is even more resonant: the NE actually rests on the same set of core institutions as the modern economy. In our view, the point is that the NE is not fundamentally different from the modern economy; as we attempt to demonstrate in the following chapters, it merely accelerates some of its key features.

Thinking along these lines, what we actually propose to do is to generalize DeLong and Summers' insights to all of the features of the NE and to look for the fundamental institutions that generate them. We thus stress the following points: (a) the development of globalization is due to institutional factors, such as trade agreements, exchange rate regimes and the factors that account for different models of capitalism; (b) legal and institutional changes, such as deregulation following the end of the Gold Standard, limited liability, the stock market and investment banking, largely account for the increasing role of financial assets in the modern economy; (c) technological revolutions are favoured by such factors as the rise of trade unions, deregulation, limited liability and the development of financial markets and finally, (d) the rise of independent central banks and statistics institutes allows governments to monitor and control the growing complexity of social and economic systems.

DeLong and Summers' insights also prove helpful reasoning another way: they suggest a way of identifying new sources of instability. For example, in view of the generating role of institutions and its strong 'non-natural' characteristics the NE is likely to change another dimension of agents' behaviour, such as their notion of 'markets'. It is becoming increasingly clear that 'pure' or 'unfettered' markets are not sufficient to grant growth. Poor countries lacking adequate social, cultural and/or institutional backgrounds have no chance of ever catching up. In this sense, the NE may tend to produce even greater divergences across countries than past stages of development.

Moreover, another factor of instability that comes to mind is the 'regulatory lag'. Society develops social norms to address very real and concrete problems, but it then retains these norms and institutions well after they have served their useful purpose. In other words, instability may occur because the economy is burdened by old rules. This problem may be aggravated in the swift NE, which involves more rapid transformations than previous stages of development. It is important to note, however, that it is not so easy to say which rules are obsolete. There is a real danger of confusing rules or institutions that grant stability with those that have become a burden. For example, are trade unions a source of stability or instability? Do they stimulate technological change and productivity growth or do they impair full adjustment of the labour market? The answer to such questions depends upon the kind of benchmark or theory adopted. For the time being, we simply suggest that these institutions should be included in the description and analysis of the NE in order to overcome the limits of the standard model.

For the moment, it remains unclear as to how this task can be accomplished. Once again, it should be noted that standard theorists rarely go beyond making some critical remarks, and then they usually fall back on familiar methods, such as growth accounting and long-run analyses, which rule out any mutual influence between the various spheres of society. The emphasis on the role of power and institutions is certainly recognized by a number of approaches, such as those stressing the 'techno-economic paradigm' concept and the 'long-wave' view. We have already noted some limitations of these approaches in Chapter 3, such as the danger of endorsing technological determinism. In our view, the best way to remedy the weaknesses of the standard approach is to shift the focus away from concepts directly relating to technological revolutions to more 'neutral' or 'general' (i.e. not purely economic) concepts, such as Calvino's labels.

While reflecting the increasing overlap between economic and socio-institutional spheres that occurs in the NE, these concepts do not imply a precise specification of causal links between technological change and the socio-institutional spheres. For example, we consider the term 'rapidity' useful for summarizing the systemic relationship between innovations, corporate organization and the socio-institutional setting. Moreover, we should generalize the systemic analysis to all key features of the NE. For example, by using the term 'multiplicity' rather than 'globalisation', we reject the simple casual link running from globalization to 'necessary' changes in institutional features – which, in particular, leads in many cases to a negative regard for the welfare state in various countries (e.g. because it is costly and reduces competitiveness). Our label captures the sense of globalization not just as pure economic competition; it also captures the sense of the institutional setting that underlies it, without posing a rigid causal link between the two. In a similar fashion, 'lightness' accounts for the link between deregulation and the development of financial innovation, while 'precision' accounts for the link between central banks and the need for more precise data concerning the workings of the economy.

Micro–macro features

As already noted, a significant number of commentators regard the NE as a technological shift whose principal effects are likely to be micro or structural rather than macroeconomic.[6] The major structural transformation is not seen as having too strong an impact on key aggregate indicators, such as income and productivity growth rates. In particular, as pointed out by Delong and Summers (2001: 14), for example, it has proven difficult to link structural changes in the economy to changes in the business cycle. It can be argued that the reason this link is difficult to establish is that the scope of standard macro analytic tools and definitions is rather narrow. For example, Lucas' definition of the business cycle tightly circumscribes the object of analysis to make the application of the equilibrium method possible. He focuses on just a few 'co-movements' that can be discerned among the aggregate time series, such as output movements across sectors, the pro-cyclical behaviour of prices, short-term interest rates, monetary aggregates and velocity (see e.g. Lucas 1981; Vercelli 1991: 132–3). However, the possibility for linking macro and micro or structural adjustment is also clearly impaired by the use of purely aggregative tools, such as production functions and growth accounting analysis in empirical debates about productivity or income behaviour through time.

Many analysts recognize that the qualitative changes implied by the NE, such as the greater weight of services and intangibles in the GDP, have created severe problems for standard macroeconomics. Specific limitations to the growth accounting framework in dealing with intangibles are clearly emphasized by Baily (2002: 7–8), for example. Among the key points he mentions is that the intangible capital is treated as current expense. This leads to the understatement of the effective corporate capital as well as the misstatement of the sources of productivity. Moreover, in contrast with the simple macroeconomic arithmetics of growth accounting, Baily argues that productivity improvements come not just from ICT (or capital or labour intensification) but from a variety of other sources as well. These include microeconomic factors, such as competitive pressure, organizational improvements, big-box stores, the shift to higher-value goods associated with the growth of high-income consumers and the impact of globalization (Baily 2002: 11, 16). He also points out that one need not look at productivity data directly to understand structural changes; other indicators, such as real wages and employment, stock market values and the inflow of foreign capital (ibid.: 12–13) would also serve the purpose.

We can draw on these remarks in developing our analysis of the NE. First, we must consider the various sources of qualitative change, following Baily's insight into the plurality of causes of productivity change. Second, it can be argued that all the factors of qualitative change which remain hidden behind the aggregates or in the residual of the growth accounting framework actually represent important sources of instability. For example, in the NE, knowledge is a commodity, and ideas, concepts and images (rather than things) are the basic ingredients of value. This generates another key 'subjective' dimension of qualitative change, namely the agents' perception of 'value'. Consequently, it is difficult to price goods and services produced in the NE, due to the increased value assigned to information. Personal and governmental debt tends to increase, and intangibles call for different criteria for measurement and valuation in firms' accounting than do ordinary physical goods. This all has adverse effects on the stability of stock markets.

Third, we suggest that these structural factors be included in our description of the NE, combining micro and macro analysis as much as possible in order to overcome the limits of the standard model. This is clearly an arduous task. Once again, Calvino's labels seem more useful than standard theory for this purpose. They allow 'vertical' simplification, that is, they allow description and inclusion of a number of relevant micro–macro features under the same label, without implying any reductionist attempts to single out causal mechanisms running from one to other (which will instead be taken up in the theoretical analysis in Part V). To cite just one instance of the kind of analysis related to these labels: our 'lightness' concept refers both to the sectoral shift towards the production of intangible goods and the macroeconomic impact of this shift on stock exchange evaluation.

Acceleration of certain key trends

According to most analysts, the NE does not change macroeconomic 'laws'. It shows broadly the same regularities as other periods: the productivity rise is significant but not exceptional (e.g. Gordon 2000, 2002), there is no increase in GDP volatility (e.g. Blanchard and Simon 2001), and the business cycle has not disappeared and shows the same qualitative features as previous cycles. Once again, the most likely explanation for these claims is that the scope of standard macro analytic tools and definitions is rather narrow. In general, neoclassical theory focuses on 'laws' conceived as 'event regularities', that is, stable patterns among data series identified with the aid of econometric techniques, such as the link between money and prices in Friedman's version of the quantity theory of money (see e.g. Lawson 1997, 2003; Dow 2002: 138). Another striking example is provided by Lucas' definition of the business cycle. As already noted, this is quite restrictive compared to the meaning in common use because it must be consistent with the application of the equilibrium method implying the stability of key parameters. The descriptive capacities of equilibrium models are limited to recurrent phenomena that present a high degree of quantitative regularity (see Vercelli 1991: 141). In other words, the use of equilibrium methods involves rather strong assumptions, such as the stability of probability distributions through time. It is not surprising, therefore, that the main qualitative features of the economic time series which Lucas calls the business cycle concern only a few 'co-movements' among series, that is, the invariable regularities that can be found in the available data and that are common to all decentralized market economies. It is with respect to the qualitative behaviour of such co-movements that Lucas can conclude that business cycles are all alike (ibid.: 132–3). According to him and to NCM in general, the NE is no exception to this rule.

Once again, however, standard theory appears to be weaker in the face of the NE. The point is that the NE is characterized by another important dimension of qualitative change, namely the acceleration of certain phenomena, such as technological change or globalization. This acceleration is likely to make macro regularities break down more often than in the past, thus reducing the scope for establishing macroeconomic laws in the NE and for making successful predictions.

These features of the NE have been touched on by many analysts. To begin with, the NE is often associated with the acceleration of some key phenomena. Greenspan (1999), for example, regards the NE as 'a perceptible *quickening* in the pace at which technological innovations are applied', while Gordon actually defines it as '*acceleration* in the rate of technical change in information technology' (2002: 4, emphasis mine). As for the impact of the NE on the cycle, some suggest that the recent downturn in 2001 is quite different from those of the past forty years. While the latter occurred mainly because of restrictive policies to curb inflation, the 2001 recession instead is more like pre-Keynesian cycles, characterized by swings in private investment due to faltering business confidence (e.g. Baily 2002). Moreover, in the current debate over the state of the world economy, a growing number of economists have suggested that important qualitative changes underlie the current sluggish growth of most market economies. It is important to 'look beyond the data' because key countries such as the US have managed to keep satisfactory growth rates mainly because of drastic swings in fiscal policy stance (i.e. the budget deficit due to deficit military spending).

Moreover, the NE is starting to have an impact on standard methodology and policy-making as well. One could, for example, interpret Sims' inductive approach (i.e. without theoretical priors) in econometrics as a response to problems of structural instability of the parameters (Dow 2002: 89).[7] Similarly, one can regard the central banks' widespread rejection of monetary targeting based on the regularities of the quantity theory and its replacement with inflation targeting as a defensive policy move in the face of repeated instances of parameter instability and predictive failures.

Now our suggestion is to generalize these remarks as much as possible. First of all, in line with our broad definition of the NE, we underline that it is not just technological change that tends to accelerate but all other features (globalization, the role of finance and the role of the state in the economy) as well. These tendencies can be more precisely regarded as 'dynamic empirical laws'. They are 'laws' in that they are not individual events, such as a stock market crash or a productivity rise but show some universal property, a recognizable simplified pattern underlying the web of unique events. They are 'dynamic' because, in contrast with recurrent events, they express the rate of change, the irreversible character of certain phenomena. But they are also 'empirical' because they are not a priori, although they can be readily ascertained almost at a glance without using techniques. Similar types of laws have recently become popular in describing some features of the NE. Among these, we can mention Moore's law, Gilder's law and Metcalfe's law which relate to specific issues, such as the tendency of computer power to double every eighteen months, the tendency of bandwidth to grow at least three times faster than computer power and the fact that the usefulness of a network equals the square of the number of users. The kind of empirical laws we have in mind hold more generally, as they refer to a broader range of issues.

Second, these remarks represent another step forward in our search for the sources of instability. Due to the acceleration of key phenomena, the NE is likely to lead to another important 'subjective' dimension of qualitative change: the agents' perception of 'time'. This can be noted in the reduction of agents' planning horizons both in consumption and investment, the increasing role of confidence indexes (more unstable expectations due more and faster information), the reduction in the savings ratio, the greater differentiation of consumer goods and the growing size of advertising budgets in firms' total costs. In particular, the quickening of technological change does not only affect production and cause a productivity rise as held by standard theory; it also affects the behaviour of consumers and investors. Moreover, if we also take into account the other accelerating trends, we can argue that their combined effect is the generation of cumulative processes, with potentially negative implications for global stability.

The challenge we now face is determining how to include these accelerating trends in our description and analysis of the NE. Our approach is intended to be a first step in this direction. Once again, we believe that the use of broad categories, such as Calvino's, is very useful for the purpose of capturing both qualitative dimensions of dynamic analysis, that is, recurrent phenomena and irreversible trends. They are general enough to allow temporal simplification. By this we mean overcoming the contrast between the two dimensions and making it possible to integrate static and dynamic features and concepts that are defined in relation with time, such as stocks and flows.

On the one hand, by allowing an extremely general description of all the characteristics of the NE, they also capture recurrent events, such as the changes that are induced in the system with a new type of (general-purpose) technology underlined, for example, by 'techno-economic paradigm' concept. In other words, every new technology affects the system in the same way, that is, by affecting the methods of organizing production, distribution, skills profile of the labour force, type of raw material and inducing a similar sequence of events (e.g. over-investment, productivity rise, stock market boom, falling prices, firms going bust, etc.). 'Rapidity' captures these recurrent events. On the other hand, however, Calvino's labels also allow comparison with previous stages of growth, thus capturing irreversibility and history. 'Rapidity' and 'lightness' are not just features of the NE but go back at least to the beginning of the twentieth century. This allows us to conclude that the present NE involves more highly developed or faster financial markets and so on.

The five empirical laws of the NE

We are now in the position of providing a summary of our definition of the NE, based on the use of Calvino's labels in order to 'look beyond the data' and gain a better understanding of the qualitative behaviour of the economy. As the foregoing analysis shows, our key labels are complex bundles of factors reflecting a number of properties which are inconsistent with standard methods, such as the increasing overlap between various economic factors, that between institutions and the economy, the integration between micro and macro perspectives and the integration of historical irreversible trends with qualitative regularities. In essence, though, when viewed under these labels, the NE appears to be characterized by five major trends or empirical laws: that is, by the acceleration of globalization, technological change, the weight of the service sector and financial markets in the economy, the attempt to achieve 'precision' and the role of government in the economy. In the following chapters, we shall assess the implications of these empirical laws for the stability of the economy.

11 Multiplicity

As already noted, the 'multiplicity' label groups together the various phenomena or stylized facts linked to globalization in the age of ICT. Given the rather complex links between ICT and globalization, use of the label seems apt. The notion of globalization clearly goes beyond the mere freedom of exchange. It implies, for example, an increase in the number of actors and competitors involved as well as a diminution of the barriers to the cross-national flow of products, factors, values and ideas, not just lower tariffs.[1] As a result, it also stimulates technological progress. In turn, ICT is a key factor in the creation of a global society (see e.g. Talalay, *et al.* 1997: 1; Audretsch 2000: 64). In what follows, we shall focus mainly on the interaction between globalization and ICT. However, we will make reference to globalization only for descriptive purposes; in other words, we do not assume a one-way causal relationship between the two. Indeed it is more accurate to regard them as 'twin forces' (e.g. Audretsch 2000: 65) of mutual influence, whose interaction gives rise to a number of phenomena of interest.

It should be clear that globalization is not a new phenomenon. According to some economic historians, in many respects the degree of global integration before the First World War even exceeded that of the late 1990s (see e.g. DeMartino 2000: 2; Kaplinsky 2001: 60–1).[2] More in general, at the root of globalization we can find those legal and institutional changes, such as liberalization of markets, anti-monopolistic laws, trade agreements and exchange rate regimes, which allowed the 'creation' of transcontinental and intercontinental markets in past decades (see DeDunning 2000: 11; Long and Summers 2001: 40).

It seems difficult to deny, however, that the NE implies some kind of acceleration of this phenomenon. Indeed the current stage of globalization is characterized by a stronger propensity of various economies towards international openness, as well as greater mobility of resources (e.g. capital, labour, money) and integration of real and financial markets than in the past. For instance, growth in trade since the Second World War has far exceeded growth in economic output;[3] another example is the recent spectacular growth of cross-border financial flows: gross foreign assets have risen to about 50 per cent of world GDP (up from 20 in 1900–14) (see e.g. Basu and Taylor 1999: 47; DeMartino 2000: 2; Dunning 2000: 11).[4]

It is almost beyond doubt that this acceleration of globalization creates both 'winners' and 'losers'. But economists differ as to which side deserves greater emphasis. Some regard globalization as having mainly positive effects on the stability of the world economy, because it helps unify markets and fosters greater integration between the key participants. Others believe that, overall, the new globalization tends to create a more unstable world economy. For example, it can be seen to undermine the autonomous decision-making of individuals and national economies alike and to encourage the fragmentation of economic and social reality. In what follows, we shall not evaluate these stability claims, nor shall we ask why some effects are bound to prevail over others. This is what we are going to do in Part V in the light of the basic theoretical frameworks. Instead, our purpose here is simply to take stock of the various stability and instability factors, placing the emphasis on signs of acceleration or differences between recent trends and those of past decades.

A new division of labour

Globalization in the age of ICT may reduce cyclical instability for a number of reasons. For example, it brings about changes in the division of labour between nations – or what Audretsch (2000: 64) called 'spatial revolution in terms of the geography of production' – which seem beneficial for all countries in terms of production, aggregate demand and employment. In advanced economies, globalization is accelerating the process of creative destruction, that is, the progressive crowding-out of production which is more vulnerable to international competition from emerging low-cost economies and their substitution with new production in more advanced sectors of the economy (i.e. the more knowledge-intensive asset-augmenting activities) with potential positive net effects in terms of reduction of unemployment rates (e.g. Audretsch 2000: 65). On the other hand, thanks to international trade, emerging economies may sustain higher levels of aggregate demand in the world economy as they are now able to advance beyond the first stage of economic development – based on raw materials and low labour costs – and participate as competitors over the whole range of goods and services.

This change in the division of labour is also gaining impetus from the new technologies (see e.g. Audretsch 2000: 64; Dunning 2000: 9–10).[5] Not only does ICT reinforce positive external effects by helping the R&D effort of one firm spillover and affect the stock of knowledge available to all firms both at the national and international levels (see e.g. Audretsch 2000: 66; Stiroh 2000), but it also makes production more easily transferable from one country to another. In particular, by improving communications and reducing communication costs, ICT enables firms to implement an 'outsourcing' strategy across borders. This represents a new, highly flexible and adaptable 'cross-national production system' which both permits and results from an increasingly fine division of labour between firms and nations alike (see Cohen *et al.* 2000; DeMartino 2000: 12–13; Dunning 2000).[6]

Market unification

Another reason why the recent form of globalization may reduce cyclical instability is that some key factors, such as liberalization of international trade and investment and ICT, improve the efficiency of markets and the functioning of the price mechanism. In particular, the Internet is playing a significant role in bringing about changes that may dampen fluctuations and grant swift adjustments of economies to external shocks. By creating a tightly woven tapestry of national economies and societies around the world, the Internet has made commodity, time and space ultimately traversable as never before. By making more information available faster and cheaper, lowering transaction costs and reducing barriers to capital flows, the Internet has eliminated previous constraints of time and geographical location in buying and selling,[7] facilitated comparison pricing, cut out the middlemen between firms and customers, reduced barriers to entry and therefore generated more contestable markets (see e.g. Blinder 2000; Comor 2000: 107; Dunning 2000: 14; the *Economist* 1–4–2000; Cullemberg *et al.* 2001: 8).[8]

Finally, the current stage of globalization may reduce cyclical volatility by acting as a safety valve for large industrialized countries. Not only does it reduce their dependence on domestic demand and enlarge the supply of raw materials, but it also contributes to keeping their inflation down, despite high domestic aggregate demand, by favouring a higher penetration of imports from low-cost producers (see e.g. Zarnowitz 1999; the *Economist* 28–9–2002: 10).

Strictly speaking, as noted by Blanchard (2003: 169), the competitive pressure induced by globalization does not imply the disappearance of the unemployment–inflation relation, although it may actually reduce unemployment for at least two reasons: first, greater competition reduces monopoly power and mark-ups; second, de-location of production favours firms in collective bargaining.

Negative externality effects

Although globalization in the age of ICT may reduce cyclical instability, it can also bring about increased vulnerability. This may happen mainly because it generates two forces working in opposition to one another. On the one hand, by inducing growing interdependence, global factors tend to undermine the decisional autonomy of individuals and national economies alike; on the other, they create new structural conditions that induce fragmentation of economic and social reality. Let us start with individuals. It is not difficult to see that, thanks to the combined effect and ICT, they have to process an increasing quantity of information even more rapidly and to take more variables into account in their decision-making process than in the past. The result is a growing interdependence between individuals, with potentially negative effects on the stability of the economy. Why? It can be argued that in order to act in the new global context, individuals are compelled to simplify their decision-making process. One way to achieve this is by relying more and more on conventional practice. For example, they refer to compendiary 'general' information about the behaviour of large aggregates or the economy as a whole, instead of looking for detailed 'specific' information concerning particular events. This practice is potentially destabilizing, because it leads individual agents to act and form expectations in a very similar fashion and thus tends to amplify their reactions to any change in the news. In particular, as Brock and Colander point out, the more tightly interconnected relevant actors' expectations are, 'the more likely is a "surprise" burst of expectations revision that may be hard to reverse as well as effects that would be hard to forecast with conventional tools' (2000: 88).

One instance is the formation of a highly volatile aggregate, such as 'business confidence', which can serve as an important channel through which recession can spread from country to country. Another instance is herd behaviour on the stock exchange, often leading to unmotivated waves of optimism or pessimism and, therefore, to what Zarnowitz (1999: 70) calls 'shared errors' in private financial investment decisions. It should be clear that if globalization accelerates, as in the NE, this source of instability becomes more serious because of the higher correlation between markets and the increasing numbers of investors and traders involved.

Fragmentation of structural conditions

It would be wrong to conclude, however, that globalization simply generates greater homogeneity in individual behaviour. In the age of ICT, it is also likely to contribute to the creation of a rising heterogeneity or fragmentation of structural conditions, especially in the US and other major economies, which makes use of generalized abstractions, such as 'the consumer', 'the firm' or aggregate concepts, appear increasingly less realistic. As noted by Pryor (2000: 65–6), for example, the population in these countries is becoming increasingly heterogeneous according to such criteria as age, family structure, ethnicity, income, wealth and occupation. Similarly, production units are becoming more heterogeneous in size, type of production and location. In particular, export specialization goods – produced by networks of firms often clustered in a few subnational regions, known as 'industrial districts', due to the fact that knowledge spillovers are spatially restricted – have recently increased in major developed countries (see e.g. Storper 2000: 48–9).[9] Indeed,

> an irony of globalization is that even as the relevant geographic market for most goods and services becomes increasingly global, the increased importance of innovative activity in the leading developed countries has triggered a resurgence in the importance of local regions as a key source of comparative advantage.
>
> (Audretsch 2000: 77)

This aspect of the NE also has significant implications for macroeconomic stability, especially in mature economies. If it is true that globalization in the age of ICT is likely to favour the expansion of firms in the more specialized sectors of the economy, this expansion is not without possible negative consequences, especially on the employment levels in these economies. On the one hand, the loss of jobs in more traditional or mature sectors may be severe because they are relatively labour intensive. On the other, 'districts' may not be as labour intensive and the firms composing them generally fail to grow beyond a certain size. Moreover, it is erroneous to regard particular districts as necessarily permanent or long-lasting drivers of national income. While it is true that 'such clusters are capable of technological learning and the resulting ongoing product differentiation continuously renews their competitive advantages, outrunning their imitators' (Storper 2000: 49), it is also true that the knowledge embedded in such products or services is only 'temporarily unique' (ibid.). On these grounds, it can thus be argued that, although technological learning makes immediate imitation and diffusion rather difficult, the combined effect of ICT and globalization is to reduce the period of the competitive advantage exploitable by firms and thus favour the shrinking of manufacturing industry in advanced countries.[10]

Reduced autonomy of national economies

Similar remarks apply to national economies as well. In general, it is true that globalization also reduces the decisional autonomy of a country, whose economic conditions (interest rates, fiscal regimes, regulations for environment protection or anti-monopolistic laws or consumer protection) cannot diverge too much from those prevailing in other countries. Exposure to world markets sets a limit to deviant behaviour of governments and public institutions of a country (see e.g. Dunford 2000: 166; Kitson and Michie 2000: 13; Turner 2001). The adoption of structural policies producing higher costs to firms (even if they could be justified by positive long-run effects) could push them to move to different countries where there are fewer limitations and constraints. Similarly, powerful investors in global financial markets may 'hijack monetary policy' (DeMartino 2000: 17) Indeed, the adoption of an expansionary monetary policy to stimulate growth may be

> sabotaged by a flight of assets in the domestic currency as investors pursue the higher rates of return that are available abroad. This may depress the value of the nation's currency, raise inflation and (in the short run) lead to a deterioration in its balance of trade ...
>
> (ibid.)

In addition, by increasing the degree of international openness and, thus, the interdependence of various economies, globalization also increases their exposure to external shocks. This means, for example, that a reduction in the level of economic activity or the effects of financial crises in any one of them can be transmitted more easily to the others and, thus, tend to be amplified – with obvious negative effects on global stability.[11]

Although such instability problems are not new, many researchers suggest that the recent acceleration of the globalization process is likely to exacerbate them. In principle, globalization can help stabilize economies if they are at different stages of the cycle. However, this is only true up to a point, beyond which the very forces of global integration are likely to synchronize economic cycles more closely, with the result that downturns in different countries are more likely to reinforce one another. In other words, the acceleration of global economic integration in the NE also means that business cycles are becoming more closely correlated over time so that, for example, 'a demand shock in one country will have wider inter-national effects than in the past' (the *Economist* 28–9–2002: 31). Moreover, in the NE, financial markets are becoming a more important channel for transmitting shocks across borders. Indeed, one can observe a closer correlation between the stock markets in the US and Europe than in the past because of the formation of truly global equity markets following the increase of cross-border trading and the rise of a large number of more global firms.

Instability due to the plurality of models

It would be wrong, however, to draw the conclusion that modern societies are sim-ply converging to a unique model of economic and social organization. As pointed out by Dunning, the extent, form and pace of globalization is not uni-formly spread across the planet, nor across different value-added activities (2000: 13). On the one hand, the way the NE takes shape in each country even seems to defy the view that there is something like a 'national economy' as a distinct and homogenous entity. While this notion was appropriate for a relatively closed-economy world, it seems to be less realistic now. As noted, for example, by Jameson (1992) contemporaneous social reality is organized in a 'cellular' way, that is, it is characterized by heterogeneity, difference and fragmentation (see also Kumar 1995: ch. 6). It can be classified and analysed in various and overlapping ways, but defies simple aggregation.

On the other hand, in so far as the term 'national economy' is still acceptable, one can see that a number of different types of national systems continue to exist in the NE. Indeed 'globalization does not eliminate national systems of production but creates a system in which an increasingly global market coexists with enduring national foundations of distinctive economic growth and corporate strategies' (Rennstich 2002: 164). It is clear, for example, that while the US, France, Germany and Japan are all rich capitalist market economies, each has distinct patterns of corporate governance, labour relations and social welfare as well as a peculiar cultural background (see e.g. Cohen *et al.* 2000; Viskovatoff 2000).[12]

Now it can be argued that in a context of free international markets this variety of national arrangements, or models, is a source of global instability. For example, it tends to create tensions within each national system between those who defend a particular national model and others who advocate the adoption of foreign models that seem more attractive in some historical period, in other words, what we can call the 'leading nation model'. This tension is not new; it has been around for quite some time, although the leading model has changed in the course of time in relation to the various stages of economic growth and macroeconomic performance of individual countries. In just a few decades, for example, we have witnessed the popularity of a number of different leading models, such as the British, the Swedish, the Japanese, the German and the American model (see Kitson and Michie 2000: 18–19; Boyer 2004).

It seems likely that the recent wave of globalization exacerbates this source of instability. Given the strict link between the success of the NE and the US, it leads many to believe that, as remarked by Stiglitz (2002b), the American model based on deregulation and free markets as key mechanisms for prosperity and welfare is the only possible 'right' model and needs to be exported throughout the world. It is such an export strategy that is creating additional instability, especially because it underestimates the peculiarity of the US model which makes it difficult to imitate.

Let us, for example, focus on the trend to accelerate liberalization, which many countries have pursued in the 1990s to match this model. As several economists point out, it is the fact that such accelerated liberalization has been excessive or too rapid or implemented in countries with inadequate institutional backgrounds that is responsible for the recent growing destabilizing volatility of international financial markets and the very negative macroeconomic performance of several countries, especially in Asia and Latin America in the late 1990s (see e.g. DeMartino 2000: 8–9; Davidson 2002: 482, 490; the *Economist* 28–9–2002; Stiglitz 2002a,b).

Problems in the governance of the world economy

The NE also aggravates instability associated to the governance of the world economy. It must be noted that to solve the problems mentioned in the previous section coordinated efforts on the part of all countries in the shape of some mutually agreed-upon international rules, such as those concerning a new exchange rate system, could be, in principle, very helpful.[13] It was in this spirit that the Bretton Woods agreement was signed in 1944. However, it is difficult to believe that these rules will be implemented in the foreseeable future. This has been a major problem since the end of the Bretton Woods era in 1971, although it does not mean that the world economy is likely to collapse tomorrow. The point is that, in the absence of such a system of international rules, there are mechanisms based on tacit agreement or simple political and economic power that somehow regulate the world economy.

In practice the key regulating mechanism today is represented by one country, the US, which plays the role of the engine of growth. Its currency, the dollar, is the global liquid store of value *par excellence*. These two aspects are strictly linked. As noted by Davidson (2002), for example, the world has not fallen into recession because of the US trade deficit in recent years. On the other hand, since the dollar is the key reserve currency, the US can undertake national macro policies to maintain high levels of aggregate demand internally, without fear of a balance of payment constraints (see also Viskovatoff 2000: 149).

While this mechanism appears to be an effective surrogate for spontaneous cooperation and agreed-upon rules, it does not necessarily grant stability to the world economy. First of all, it does not eliminate the possibility of international financial crises caused or exacerbated by flexible exchange rates and free capital movements. Second, as it ties the health of the world economy to the macro-economic performance of just one country and the strength of just one currency, it is, intrinsically, fragile and vulnerable.

The NE has clearly accentuated these potential sources of instability. By strengthening the correlation between financial markets and business cycles in the leading economies, it has increased the central role of the US in today's world economy. Witness to this fact is the rapid increase in net inflow of foreign capital into the US in the 1990s owing to the fact that foreigners, like US investors, believe that the NE has increased the expected future return from US corporate capital (see Baily 2001: 243). In so doing, however, the NE clearly exposes the world economy to unprecedented risks linked to possible weaknesses and imbalances of the US economy.

One weakness of the US economy has been illustrated by the analysis of the so-called 'jobless recovery', which took place mainly in 2003. As Roach (2003) emphasizes, the limited expansion of employment in the face of income growth is not merely due to higher productivity but to globalization and ICT, which involves some collateral damage. The point is that they allow outsourcing both in manufacturing and (for the first time in history) in non-tradeable services, which accounts for the shrinking of the US productive basis (with finished goods accounting for only 28.8 per cent of their GDP).

As for the imbalances of the US economy, suffice it to say that the very same phenomena that could be regarded as forming a 'virtuous circle' when viewed through the optimistic lenses of the 1990s (the US stock market boom leading to an investment boom, a rise in consumer credit and consumption, income and employment leading in turn to increase in the expected future return on capital and capital inflows and thus to further rise in share prices and so on, both in the US and abroad) could easily turn into a 'vicious circle' in a gloomy scenario implying negative spillovers on the world economy. Indeed, as many emphasize, the world economy is more vulnerable than ever before to the painful unwinding of economic and financial imbalances in the US: overvalued share prices, excess capacity, large debt, the likelihood of decreased household net worth and the resultant increase in savings as a response to the looming shadow of recession (Viskovatoff 2000; Banerji 2002; the *Economist* 28–9–2002; Godley and Izurieta 2002; Stiglitz 2002b).[14]

Lack of convergence

A further negative effect of globalization in the age of ICT is that it intensifies the instability resulting from heterogeneity between countries. Although the lack of convergence between rich and poor countries is certainly not new, there are various reasons why the NE actually tends to amplify the gap between them, rather than narrowing it. To begin, ICT accelerates cumulative processes. As pointed out by James (2001: 159), ICT is associated with a number of powerful cumulative mechanisms causing some countries to grow rapidly, while others become increasingly marginalized from the global economy.[15] In particular, as the dissemination of new knowledge is far from perfect, self-reinforcing advantages tend to accrue to the firms and countries in which the new technology originates.

One major reason for this is that in the NE the 'know how' embodied in organizational structures (such as firms and institutions) is more important than it was for past technological changes. These structures are strictly linked to national characteristics that are often very costly or impossible to transfer and imitate. Indeed, it is true that 'more than simply an endowment of knowledge inputs is required to generate innovative activity. The underlying economic and institutional structures matters, as do the microeconomic linkages across agents and firms' (Audretsch 2000: 75).

Another important factor impairing the dissemination of new knowledge is the peculiar nature of knowledge itself, which makes geographical proximity very important for its transmission. Unlike information, which can be easily codified and transmitted thanks to ICT, knowledge and especially tacit knowledge, is vague and difficult to codify, so that the marginal cost of transmitting it rises with distance. It is sufficient to note that tacit knowledge 'can only be transmitted informally, and typically demands direct and repeated contact' (Audretsch 2000: 72).

Another explanation for the lack of convergence is that the recent trend towards globalization has worsened the terms of trade for developing countries (see e.g. Stiglitz 2002a: 7). As noted earlier, in principle, globalization and free trade may have positive effects and can be promoted on the grounds of economic efficiency if all parties gain from trade. However, it should be clear that this can happen only if the terms of trade of the goods from developing countries, such as raw materials or non-oil commodities, do not get worse. Unfortunately, this has not been the case for many decades. The relative price of food and agricultural products has been declining with respect to manufactured goods worldwide. Now the NE is only aggravating this trend, because it is based on sectors that reduce the demand for raw materials. Moreover, it pushes up the relative price of new immaterial goods with respect to both standard manufactured and primary goods.

Finally, globalization in the age of ICT implies greater global inequality in income and wealth distribution. Again, these imbalances are not new. However, there is reason to believe that today they are getting worse. Although it may well be that many of the world's populations have gained from the recent acceleration of globalization of the product markets, it also appears that these benefits have not been evenly distributed. One can note growing inequality and poverty in both developed and industrialized countries. Especially troubling for the stability of the world economy is that the increasing integration of the global economy has not been associated with higher rates of economic growth. There is, in fact, a prevalence of falling real incomes (and thus falling absolute standards of living) and a more unequal income distribution, in terms of both individual incomes and intranational income distribution. Indeed as Stiglitz points out, there is 'a growing divide between the haves and the have-nots' (2002a: 5) (see also DeMartino 2000: 10–11; Kaplinsky 2001: 45–8).

12 Rapidity

Under this label we shall group the above-mentioned stylized facts concerning the effects of technological change in the age of ICT. The label is fitting, for one of the main characteristics of the NE is, in fact, to effect such change more rapidly than in the past. Before going into detail, two points need to be made: first, as already noted, one of the reasons we use the label 'rapidity' is that it does not refer merely to purely economic and/or technological factors. In particular, we do not subscribe to a deterministic techno-centric vision. While technological change is obviously important, it does not play a unique causal role. Rather, it contributes to determining outcomes by interacting with other factors, such as globalization. In what follows, our choice to focus on technology was made only for the sake of simplicity.

Second, the emphasis in this section is on technological change in general. This is a departure from other approaches that narrowly regard the NE as consisting of the effects of ICT alone. In our view, ICT is not the sole factor in what happens in the NE (productivity gains, for example); there are a number of other independent technological improvements that interact with it. As Blinder puts it:

> Even today there are other important sources of technological improvement. Biotech, for example, looks now to be starting to deliver on its promise. And even old-line industries like steel making, automobile assembly, and textiles have registered notable technological gains in the last 10–15 years (aided, of course, by computers). Important as it is, ICT is not the whole technology show.

> (2000: 3)

In what follows, we have found it convenient to make reference to ICT, but this broader perspective concerning the scope of the NE needs to be borne in mind.

What we have been experiencing in recent years is clearly not the first major technological revolution in contemporary history. As emphasized by Schumpeter long ago and by many economists in modern times, the capitalist system is inherently dynamic and its history is characterized by discontinuous waves of technological revolutions. This has been especially true since the beginning of the twentieth century, which was marked by a number of crucial legal and institutional changes such as the rise of the trade unions, deregulation, limited liability and the development of financial markets (see e.g. DeLong and Summers 2001: 40). Even the improvement in information technology generated by ICT, which is almost universally regarded as unique to this recent NE, is not a novel fact in and of itself.[1] However, the NE undoubtedly leads to an acceleration in the rate of technological progress. This can be seen, for example, in indicators of the increased importance of innovative activity, such as the recent unprecedented jump in the number of patent applications in the US (see e.g. Audretsch 2000: 66),[2] or in Moore's law, according to which transistors on a silicon chip – and thus the power of a chip – double every eighteen months (see e.g. Cohen *et al.* 2000; Gordon 2002: 50–1).

Most economists do not deny that this trend towards acceleration in technology, like globalization, has dual effects, that is, it entails 'losers and winners'. For example, it implies the production of new goods and the replacement of old ones. Some, however, predict that it will bring about mainly positive effects on the stability of the world economy by improving the supply side of the economy and by increasing the system's ability to react swiftly to changes. Others point out that more rapid technological change might render the system generally more vulnerable through its effects on the demand side. We shall not be discussing the theoretical foundations of either claim in this chapter, for as we have already noted, theoretical frameworks will be dealt with in Part V. Instead, what we propose to do here is to take stock of the various stability and instability factors, placing the emphasis on signs of acceleration and the differences between recent trends and those of past decades.

Productivity growth

Many commentators believe that technological change in the age of ICT may reduce instability primarily because of its positive effects on the supply side of the economy. Baily, for example, notes that the NE gave rise to an increase in the rate of productivity growth in the second half of the 1990s. This has led to a significant virtuous cycle, especially in the US economy, in terms of 'faster GDP growth, lower inflation, lower unemployment, faster real wage growth, a strong stock market, inflow of capital, budget surpluses, and improved living standards' (Baily 2001: 256).[3] In particular, by boosting productivity, ICT has generated a permanent increase in the level of potential output and a lower rate of inflation. Or, as some say, it has lifted the economy's safe speed limit before inflation starts to rise (see e.g. Blinder 2000; the *Economist* 1–4–2000; Krugman 2000; Baily 2001: 238), bearing positive consequences also for the rate of unemployment and the trade-off between inflation and unemployment. As Blanchard points out, although there is no evidence of a systematic positive relation between productivity growth and unemployment, it can be argued that the natural rate of unemployment in the US has diminished since the advent of NE in the 1990s (Blanchard 2003: 169).

Strictly speaking, this scenario is not unusual. A productivity increase *per se* is nothing new. Indeed, the evidence suggests that the impact of computers and the Internet is nothing extraordinary in comparison with other general purpose technologies like the telegraph, steam engine and electric motor, all of which engendered significant productivity improvements by facilitating substantial restructuring of the whole economy and the development of complementary innovations. It is telling that despite the advances in and proliferation of computers in the 1970s and 1980s, economists have been waiting for years to see the wonders of computing show up as results in national productivity.[4] As noted, for example, by Atkinson and Court (2000), growth in per capita GDP, productivity and wages since the 1980s have lagged behind growth rates in the 1960s and early 1970s (see also Mueller 2001: 2–3). While job growth was stronger in the 1980s and 1990s than in the 1960s and 1970s, productivity and per capita GDP grew about half as fast. Acceleration in the growth of productivity has occurred only very recently (see e.g. Blinder 2000; Krugman 2000; Gordon 2002).[5,6] Moreover, part of this growth is not permanent but stems from the processes of corporate 'downsizing' or reorganization taking place as part of normal cycles.

Nonetheless, it is still possible to argue that ICT improves stability due to its relative advantages over other general-purpose technologies. One advantage is that it involves higher *potential* increases in productivity. As pointed out by Cohen, DeLong and Zysman, the current technological revolution is creating the most all-purpose tools ever – tools for thought – thus allowing a more rapid transformation of the whole of society. They observe, for example, that 'the capabilities created to process and distribute digital data multiply the scale and speed with which thought and information can be applied. And thought and information can be applied to almost everything, almost everywhere' (2000: 4).[7]

Second, thanks to the extraordinary build-out of the communications networks linking computers, the ICT has emerged faster and has spread more rapidly and widely throughout the economy than previous technological revolutions.[8]

Third, another difference from the past is that, in the NE, a wider share of the rise in productivity is accounted for by technological progress, as measured by the standard growth accounting framework, where it appears as total factor productivity growth residual. The evidence shows that while capital accumulation was the dominant force behind the growth in capital services in the US in the period 1958–98, the contribution of capital quality for the most recent period has increased its influence (e.g. Jorgenson and Stiroh 2000; Stiroh 2000: 38–40; DeLong and Summers 2001: 12).

Fourth, another advantage of the NE over other technological revolutions is that productivity improvements derive from a variety of relatively new sources. Among the drivers of productivity acceleration not only do we find new technology but also other factors, such as the greater competitive pressure induced by globalization, organizational improvements, big-box stores and a shift to higher value goods associated with the growth of high-income consumers (see e.g. Baily 2002: 11, 16).

Acceleration of positive feedbacks

The NE may further contribute to stability, and to price stability in particular, by accelerating and generalizing to the economy as a whole the positive feedback that occurs in those sectors of the economy more or less directly involved in the technological innovation. As noted, for example, by DeLong and Summers (2001: 30–1), while the old economy was characterised by negative feedback (rising demand involves higher prices, more production and less demand), the NE involves positive feedback, instead, thanks to the smooth behaviour of demand. Rapid technological progress leads to rapidly falling prices of ICT products. If demand for these products is sufficiently price elastic (as it is likely to be, given that ICT is a general-purpose technology), there will be increasing demand, leading to greater efficiency and higher returns, lower prices and still higher demand. This, in turn, will lead to rapidly growing expenditure shares, a rising share of income attributable to the ICT capital stock and the growing economic salience (i.e. a contribution to productivity growth) of this technology (Oliner and Sichel 2000; DeLong and Summers 2001: 24–5).[9]

Additionally, a number of economists believe that the stabilizing effects of this model can be further increased by two other characteristics of the NE. One is the reduced volatility, especially of aggregate consumption, which has recently been observed (e.g. Blanchard and Simon 2001: 159). The other is that network effects in the NE – that is, the value of a network to each user is proportional to the number of people on that network – become more pervasive (see e.g. Shapiro and Varian 1998).

Greater flexibility of the goods market

Another reason why ICT may increase stability is that it is capable of inducing greater flexibility in the supply side of the economy than other general-purpose technologies. According to many economists, the faster transmission of information and greater rapidity of decisions that is favoured by the new technology leads to increased market flexibility, allowing the economy to cope with shocks more effectively; it explains, for example, why recessions often last longer in Europe, where markets are more rigid than in the US (see e.g. Kumar 1995: ch. 6; Castells 1996; Greenspan 2001; the *Economist* 28–9–2002).

While ICT is presumed to improve flexibility in all markets, here we shall focus primarily on the goods and labour market. Because ICT gives rise to a smoother production system, the market for goods is bound to become more flexible. This tendency has several consequences. First of all, as many suggest, the huge reduction in information transmission costs made possible by the new technologies implies a higher opportunity cost for the use of hierarchy in place of the market in the sphere of production. The NE thus provokes a decline in the rigid and hierarchical Fordist organization in favour of more flexible web-like organizations that allow firms to adjust output more rapidly to changes in sales (see e.g. Rifkin 2000: ch. 2; Brynjolfsson and Hitt 2002: 26).[10] In practice, this means that ICT favours smaller firms and less vertical integration and a decrease in the average size of firms. This tendency has moved some commentators to speak of the 'vanishing hand' of the NE as opposed to the 'visible hand' of old managerial capitalism (see e.g. Langlois 2001). Indeed, as the evidence shows, ICT investment is higher in organizations that are decentralized and have a greater investment in human capital (e.g. Brynjolfsson and Hitt 2002: 35).

It should be clear, however, that the trend towards sectoral disaggregation does not necessarily mean that all markets are populated by small, atomistic, firms alone. It is frequently noted that some mechanisms in the NE favour market concentration and even the formation of monopolies. The ICT industry, for example, typically exhibits increasing returns to scale as a result of low marginal costs and externality or network effects. Firms in this industry have high initial investment and marketing costs but low distribution costs (e.g. Shapiro and Varian 1998; Quah 1999; Atkinson and Court 2000; Rifkin 2000: 129). On the other hand, there are also those who emphasize that monopolistic positions are not permanent, given that one of the major implications of rapid technological change is to reduce the power of existing firms by allowing the introduction of new technologies (see e.g. Teece and Coleman 1998).

Yet rather than simply generating stronger 'anarchy' or more competition between firms, the NE also exerts pressure in the opposite direction. One important effect of ICT is that it requires the growing synchronization or coordination ('co-specialisation' or 'coo-petition') between firms for the efficient working of markets. In general, the intellectual capital required is rarely the property of a single firm: 'for a firm to increase or deploy its own knowledge effectively, it may have to complement this knowledge with that of other firms, and more often than not, by way of some kind of collaborative agreement' (Dunning 2000: 10). For example, firms need to cooperate in the definition of technical standards, that is, the creation of a network of compatible technologies (e.g. Varian 1998: 12–13).[11]

Second, ICT is a time and space-shrinking technology that facilitates firms' decisions in several ways. For example, it allows improved inventory control, thus reducing the inventory-driven component of business cycles (see e.g. Arena and Feustré 2001: 3–5; DeLong and Summers 2001: 14; the *Economist* 28–9–2002).[12] Moreover, it shortens the life cycle of products, accelerates the launch of new products, and hastens improvements in the intangible aspects of existing products, such as convenience, timeliness, quality and variety. Also, while it is true, as suggested by Gordon (2002: 66–71), that unlike the great inventions of the late nineteenth century, ICT does not really create truly new products or activities but rather reduces the cost of performing old activities, it is also true that it allows continuous progress in product differentiation. New, and often more expensive, versions of the same goods are produced in ever shorter periods of time. Indeed, the increasing ratio of high-value to low-value goods can be taken as an indicator of rapidity.

Greater flexibility in the labour market

The NE tends to increase flexibility and deregulation in the labour market. One place this can be seen is in the decline of unionization, as measured in terms of the numbers of trade union members as a proportion of the labour force, and another is in the proliferation of part-time and temporary jobs. Higher labour flexibility is generally regarded by economists as increasing stability. First of all, it is one of the factors involved in the reduction of unemployment rates (see e.g. Blanchard 2003: 169). Second, it favours higher elasticity of employment, that is, the translation of income growth into employment growth. As noted by Baily (2001: 234), in the NE, a given pressure of demand in the economy is associated with a lower structural unemployment rate or Non Accelerating Inflation Rate of Unemployment (NAIRU).

Third, higher flexibility makes the labour market more efficient. The decline in unionization, together with the increase in competitive intensity due to globaliza-tion, has made it harder for workers to garner wage increases (see e.g. Katz and Krueger 1999). As a result, while wages in the past were influenced more by equity considerations and institutional conditions, in the NE they have become more market-determined phenomena. Over the past fifteen years, structural change in Europe and the US has resulted in an increased need for skilled labour devoted to the creation, processing and interpretation of information (see e.g. Pryor 2000: 65–6). The lower demand for non-qualified workers than for qualified workers is reflected in a wider wage distribution, showing that workers get their marginal productivity (see e.g. the *Economist* 21–10–2000; Baily 2001: 237–8; Blanchard 2003: 278–81).

More rapid obsolescence

Rapidity may also render the economy more unstable and vulnerable to shocks because of a number of factors undermining the virtuous cycle described in the last sections. One important factor to consider is that faster technological change and the time-shrinking nature of ICT imply that knowledge can spread more quickly than ever before, leading to both negative and positive effects. It has been pointed out, for example, that in the NE '... many kinds of knowledge (and par-ticularly those which can be imitated) become obsolete quite speedily' (Dunning 2000: 10). Faster obsolescence likely makes it more difficult for investors to assess the potential returns of investment owing to the greater difficulties of anticipating and smoothly matching the growth of market demand. What appears to be a promising project today may be made obsolete by some other innovation tomorrow (see e.g. Freeman and Perez 1988: 43). For this reason, herd behaviour among investors is likely to intensify. In other words, firms are more likely to carry out an investment simply to follow competitors that share particular optimistic expecta-tions on future economic conditions and by so doing give more easy rise to such phenomena as over-investment in one period and excess capacity and slower investment in future periods (see e.g. Rennstich 2002: 163). One can see, for example, that a rather severe crisis of over-supply has now emerged in the chip and computer industry. But it also accounts for the decreased importance of other factors determining investment, such as changes in borrowing costs. This in turn has negative implications for stability because, for example, ordinary monetary policy measures are less capable of checking investment during booms or reviving it during depressions.

Problems due to the nature of contemporary knowledge

The nature of contemporary knowledge, too, raises instability problems. First of all, the NE calls for a large amount of intellectual capital and thus runs the risk of facing increasing skilled labour shortages. Second, the fact that the intellectual capital needed in the NE is rarely the property of only one firm, forcing firms not just to compete but also to form cooperative arrangements, also creates new potential for danger. In particular, it may take some time before firms learn how to cooperate with their competitors and 'coordination problems' are likely to arise, possibly exacerbating investment volatility. Third, contemporary knowledge makes 'lumpiness' a more relevant issue for investors than before. Indeed, this knowledge can be highly expensive: '...the cost of the next generation of microchips or new drugs frequently runs into billions of dollars' (Dunning 2000: 10). And finally, the propensity to invest may also be weakened by the fact that the outcome of much investment in augmenting knowledge, for example, through R&D, is highly uncertain.

Technological unemployment

A third possible negative consequence that rapidity has on stability is unemployment. Although more rapid technological change does not necessarily cause unemployment, as Blanchard (2003: 268–77) emphasizes, such a fear is not completely unjustified, especially when the new technologies are considered in the context of the new international division of labour favoured by globaliztion. While the main effect of technological change is higher productivity and the process of creative destruction, adjustment can take time and is accompanied by the inevitable loss of jobs and a decline in relative wages for many workers.

Product differentiation

A fourth source of instability induced by rapidity is related to product differentiation. Indeed, as already noted, rapid technological change in the NE implies a continuous flood of new or differentiated products with a shorter life cycle. In particular, consumer goods often tend to be more expensive than older, mass-produced goods. While ICT has drastically reduced the cost of numerous objects such as computers and cell telephones and made them available to the general public with obvious welfare gains, 'versioning' may entail increasing costs. More generally speaking, it is not true that the new technology lowers all production costs. For example, while ICT implies lower costs in collecting information, it also entails higher costs in selecting which information is useful among the mass of data available.

However, the price dimension of product differentiation is not all that matters for stability. New versions of the same goods are also increasingly superfluous. In other words, they are linked to subtle aspects, such as status and identity, rather than to 'objective' needs. For this reason, it makes sense for producers to distinguish between different types of consumers according to lifestyles, such as *achievers*, *emulators*, *sustainers* and *belongers* (see e.g. Rifkin 2000: ch. 8), which entail quite different consumption patterns and motivations. This characteristic of consumer goods has some clear destabilizing consequences. In particular, it explains why firms tend to adopt ever more aggressive marketing strategies and pervasive advertizing in order to induce various types of consumers to revise their consumption patterns. It also explains why aggregate consumption in the NE turns out to be more fragile on structural grounds and dependent upon such volatile factors as the 'general state of confidence'. It is clear, for example, that when global uncertainty prevails (as it did after September 11, 2001) consumers may not hesitate to postpone spending on those superfluous goods, which absorb a growing share of their budget.

Greater heterogeneity in structural conditions of the household

The last negative effect of rapidity we will mention stems from the creation not just of greater product differentiation but also of greater heterogeneity in structural conditions and agents' behaviour. As just noted, rather than thinking in terms of a generic consumer, producers should distinguish consumers according to their different lifestyles. This distinction resembles the more traditional classification of households according to income bracket. Both distinctions have significant implications for the analysis of stability. There is reason to believe that composition effects tend to become more important in the NE, with adverse implications for aggregate consumption. On the one hand, following the growing weight of higher added value goods in total production, the NE is likely to favour a more rapid evolution of those lifestyles which have more volatile consumption patterns, with adverse consequences in terms of control and global predictability. On the other, ICT generates a growing wage differential between skilled and less skilled workers, which is also likely to affect aggregate consumption, in view of the fact that higher income consumers have a lower propensity to consume than lower income earners.

13 Lightness

Under the label of 'lightness' we group stylized facts that reflect the major role played by 'weightless' factors, including services, intangibles and financial assets, in the age of ICT. Here again, it is important to emphasize the complex nature of the links between these factors and ICT. For example, it can be argued that the increased expansion of financial markets is an important requirement for the development of ICT and of the high-tech industry in general. But the opposite is also true, for ICT has an undeniable role in improving the efficiency of financial markets. In this chapter, we shall point out possible interactions between financial markets and ICT and other features of the NE, without singling out particular causal relations, although for the purposes of description we shall focus on the weightless factors mentioned earlier.

Once again, we must note that lightness is not a new phenomenon. As Dunning writes, for example,

> over the last three centuries the main source of wealth in market economies has switched from natural assets (notably land and relatively unskilled labour) through tangible created assets (notably buildings, machinery and equipment, and finance) to intangible created assets (notably knowledge and information of all kinds).
>
> (2000: 8)

Like other features of the NE, lightness grew in relevance following implementation of the key legal and institutional changes – such as the deregulation following the demise of the Gold Standard, limited liability, the stock market and investment banking – characterizing the rise of modern capitalism (e.g. DeLong and Summers 2001: 40). One need only note the crucial role played both by the stock market and by banks in 'freeing' investment and consumption from the constraints of the quantity of resources available at a given point in time (e.g. current income or cash flow).[1] Due to the very nature of ICT, however, the NE undeniably implies a dramatic acceleration in lightness compared to the past

> it has, for example been estimated that, whereas in the 1950s 80 per cent of the value added in the US manufacturing industry represented primary or

processed foodstuffs, materials ... and 20 per cent knowledge, by 1995, these proportions had changed to 30 and 70 per cent respectively.

(Dunning 2000: 8)

Like multiplicity and rapidity, lightness too, in the opinions of many economists, tends to have predominant stabilizing effects on the economy. This is because lightness leads to the extension of market logic to new 'immaterial' areas, such as culture or entertainment, and the further expansion of financial markets and electronic money, with positive effects on global trade and employment. However, many other researchers warn that lightness brings with it the danger of instability, which may even outweigh the potential gains. For example, pricing problems related to intangible goods may cause important markets to become increasingly unstable or volatile. In this chapter, we shall focus on both the positive and negative implications of lightness, comparing the signs of acceleration or differences of recent trends with those in past decades. As in the other chapters of this part of the book, we shall limit ourselves to listing the mechanisms that appear to be at play, postponing a full theoretical discussion concerning the prevailing scenarios to Part V.

Extension of the market logic

Lightness in the age of ICT may reduce cyclical instability for a number of reasons related to the new hierarchy of goods and significant changes in the composition of production implied by the NE. Financial and intangible goods are the key drivers of the production of wealth (Eustace 2000: 5). At the macro level, the economy is dominated by certain sectors, such as financial services, middlemen and communication, with a stronger basis in the management and production of knowledge than in transactions of material and physical products. This clearly accounts for the growing contribution of services relative to goods in the GDP of most countries and the increasing weight of financial over physical assets in world trade.

At first it may seem that the shift towards 'lightness' in these sectors is nothing new. In fact it has been a relatively constant trend in dynamic economies since at least the start of the second industrial revolution. This can be seen quite clearly in the crucial shifts from agriculture to industry, and from industry to services, which many credit as having contributed to greater economic stability, especially after 1945 (see e.g. Mc Connell and Perez-Quiros 2000; Blanchard and Simon 2001: 155; DeLong and Summers 2001: 21; Turner 2001: 12; the *Economist* 28–9–2002).[2] However the NE contains a few key elements that may account for even greater stability than in past decades.

One major source of stability is that the NE boosts commodification. This refers to the tendency for the market logic to carry over to new 'immaterial' areas of contemporary life beyond standard manufacturing to include such services as science, education, environment and entertainment. Other important aspects of the NE include phenomena such as the progressive loss of autonomy of the cultural sphere from the economic one as witnessed by the growth of markets for cultural artefacts (see e.g. Rifkin 2000; Cullemberg *et al.* 2001: 7–8). In other words, it can be argued that knowledge in general is treated like any other commodity in the NE (see e.g. Soete 2002: 36–7). In principle, this move could contribute to stability because it compensates for the reduction of employment caused by the shrinking of the 'old' narrowly defined industrial sector.

Broader concept of value and capital

A second source of stability deriving from the NE is the potential for creating new 'light' industries as well as new goods and services within the old manufacturing sector. It is generally a mistake to identify lightness with 'de-industrialization' *tout court* or solely with the emergence of new industrial sectors. The new sectors are almost always inevitably light. For example, the ICT sector uses fewer raw materials than the old industries, and this has a rather obvious positive impact on stability (and sustainable growth).[3] However, it is not that old-style manufacturing has disappeared in the weightless economy but that it has been reinvented. Even in old or mature industries, managers emphasize that a new value chain has been established. The creation of value no longer occurs mainly in the physical transformation or traditional manufacturing of goods but in services (e.g. customer care and assistance and long-term customer relations), which allow higher profit margins than standard material products (see e.g. Eustace 2000: 16; Rifkin 2000: 127–8; Arena and Feustré 2001: 5). Moreover, as a result of ICT, the competitiveness of old sectors now strongly depends on intangible assets 'such as R&D and proprietary know-how, intellectual property, workforce skills, world-class supply networks and brands' (Eustace 2000: 5).

These microeconomic changes also significantly affect macroeconomic analysis and stability. They have led to an increasingly broad definition of investment and capital beyond tangible assets in the NE, in line with increasing awareness that growth is crucially dependent on such factors as knowledge and investment in human capital, R&D and public infrastructure (see e.g. Stiroh 2000: 43).[4] The greater role assigned to intangible assets accounts for a change in the notion of value. Indeed, given that knowledge is a commodity in the NE, we discover that the basic ingredients of value are no longer things, but ideas, concepts and images instead. The value of the new 'light' products, which represent an increasingly higher share of national GDP and command higher prices in many advanced economies, lies in the knowledge they incorporate and not in the stuff embodying this knowledge (see Quah 1999; Rifkin 2000). While knowledge was indeed as important an element in past economies as it is in the NE, as DeLong and Summers (2001) note 'knowledge was of how to create a useful, physically embodied good' like a barrel of oil or an ingot of iron. We are now moving instead 'to an economy in which the canonical source of value is not a barrel of oil but a gene sequence, a line of computer code, or a logo' (2001: 17). In principle, this move may also contribute to stability by compensating for the reduction of value and employment in activities more closely linked to the old way of doing business.

Faster expansion of financial markets

A third source of stability deriving from lightness is that financial assets tend to develop more quickly than other tangible created assets (see e.g. Toporowski 2000). As many have observed, the creation of more efficient and sophisticated financial markets improving the mechanisms of resource allocation have been favoured by ICT and by substantial institutional changes, such as the recent move towards deregulation (see e.g. Woodford 2001: 297).

In fact, it has often been remarked that the reduction in transaction costs granted by ICT favours broader and more liquid capital markets. In principle, this should lower the risk for financial crises and negative shocks, as reduced transaction costs contribute to more complete markets, including those for futures and contingencies (Shiller 2004). Moreover, ICT makes it possible to create ever-new forms of electronic money, thus contributing to stability by allowing further expansion of the market and globalization (ibid.).

As for deregulation, first of all it must be noted that this phenomenon is not unique to the NE. For example, it underwent significant expansion when the banking system was freed from the external constraint imposed by the Gold Standard. Today's deregulation, however, is subject to drastic acceleration. As pointed out by the *Economist*, in reference to a paper by Borio and Lowe:

> Until the 1980s growth of credit was constrained in some way. After the gold standard collapsed, this discipline had been provided by tightly regulated financial markets ... credit controls ... Since then governments have set their financial systems free. In the 1980s money supply targets helped to curb credit, but these, too, were abandoned ...
>
> (the *Economist* 28–9–2002: 29)

Borio and Lowe suggest that today's combination of a liberalized financial system, a money standard with no exogenous anchor such as gold and a monetary policy focused only on short term inflation, makes strong expansion of credit possible. This may lead to beneficial results, as it implies that: 'savings are better channelled to borrowers with profitable investment opportunities than lying idle under the mattress' (ibid.).

There are various ways in which the more efficient financial system brought about by the NE achieves this result, thus favouring greater stability. The first is by facilitating investment financing. One can cite the recent stock market boom – attributed by many authors to the increased importance of intangible capital in the information economy, leading to increased profits and the improved valuation of many large companies (see Mandel 1996; Baily 2001: 242–4, 2002: 14; Hall 2001)[5] – which allows firms to raise money cheaply on the stock exchange.

Moreover, one could mention the policy of low interest rates, which has also favoured the rise in investment in ICT. However, while obviously important, these are certainly not new phenomena. Indeed, as stressed by Gordon (2002: 28–40), highly developed capital markets, which emphasize short-run profit maximization and equity finance, have characterized the US economy for many years and are among the permanent sources of US advantage over other countries (see also Cohen *et al.* 2000).

What is peculiar to the NE, instead, is the appearance of new elements such as venture capitalists or new company practices such as changes in the prudent-man rule or the institution of stock options, which have greatly enlarged the scale of investment and alleviated the structural problem of small firms in obtaining funding for technology development.[6] In particular, a virtuous circle between ICT and new financial tools and institutions has been observed in the NE, especially in the US: 'the technological advance has made it easier for new firms to go public and raise capital. The ease of going public also encourages other financial intermediaries crucial to the creation of new firms, such as venture capitalists.' (D'Avolio *et al.* 2001: 125; see also Baily 2001: 215). Indeed, it is an extraordinary achievement of the US stock markets that firms not making money can list and raise capital to pursue their investment (see also Cohen *et al.* 2000; Banerji 2002: 13–15).

Second, another way developed financial markets favour stability is by increasing the potential influence of the wealth effect on consumption. This is due to the unprecedented capital gains in equity markets and the dramatic rise in the aggregate ratio of household net worth to income in the second half of the 1990s (see e.g. Greenspan 2001) on the one hand and the increasing number of market participants, on the other (see e.g. D'Avolio *et al.* 2001: 125).

A third means by which deregulation and other new developments in financial markets help stability is by improving the ability of consumers to smooth out their spending over time in the face of variations of income (Blanchard and Simon 2001: 163).[7] For example, Benjamin Friedman (2001: 169) credits the removal of regulation W controls on consumer financing for the decline in volatility of consumer durables purchases in the US.[8] Finally, another source of greater stability arising from the NE is the shift from bank debt to marketable debt, making the financial system more flexible and capable of reacting to exogenous shocks (Toporowski 2000; Cecchetti 2002).

Problems in the quality of goods

Now we shall turn to the potentially negative effects of lightness. Lightness may well generate forces that undermine the virtuous cycle described in the previous section. One factor of instability is represented by the central role played by the quality dimension of goods in the NE. The problem here is that differences in quality are not always reflected in the price system. Strictly speaking, this dilemma is not unique to the NE. It arises or is accentuated whenever goods cease to be relatively homogeneous and differ in objective or subjective characteristics, raising such complex issues as brand, reputation and trust. According to Stiroh, it is true in this case that 'prices may not adequately capture changes in the quality dimension... there are daunting practical difficulties if all attributes and quality characteristics could be correctly priced' (Stiroh 2000: 45).

However, there are at least two reasons causing the NE to exacerbate the pricing problem. First of all, as already noted when dealing with rapidity, new and better versions of the same goods tend to appear more often in the NE. As implied by Moore's Law, for example, we tend to develop faster computers in shorter intervals of time. As this change in quality is only imperfectly measured by money prices, alternative approaches, such as the hedonic price method, have been proposed in the literature to account for it (see e.g. Baily 2001: 222; OECD 2001; Gordon 2002: 50; Nordhaus 2002; Winnett 2004).

Second, for intangible goods, which are extremely characteristic of the NE, the quality dimension is even more important. As pointed out by Cohen, DeLong and Zysman (2000), ideas and 'information goods' have particular characteristics that distinguish them from ordinary goods:

> These include 1) marginal costs of reproduction and distribution that approach zero; 2) problems of transparency (in order to buy it I should know what the information or idea is; once I know it, in many cases, there is no need to buy it); and 3) non-rival possession. (If you have a hamburger, I cannot have it. But if you know something, and I learn it, you still know it. Once I know it, I no longer have an incentive to compensate you to teach me.) Together, these characteristics conspire to make market solutions problematic.
>
> (Cohen *et al.* 2000: 62)

These aspects have a clear impact on the definition of the market structure, that is, on whether the market for information goods tends to be more or less competitive. DeLong (1998) suggests that, as information assumes more of the value in goods and services produced and traded over electronic networks, markets appear increasingly less capable of pricing such items. He then argues that in an economy where the typical commodity is non-rival and not transparent, and most of the value produced is in the form of information goods, we can expect monopoly to become the rule rather than the exception in the structure of industry.

This is obviously bound to influence the general stability of the economy. For example, monopolistic markets may be more inefficient and involve higher and less flexible prices than more competitive markets (see e.g. Brynjolfsson and Smith 2000), thus potentially exerting adverse consequences on aggregate consumption as well. Moreover, the price of information goods is determined on the basis of consumers' subjective assessment concerning characteristics of the goods, rather than on the costs (see e.g. Varian 1997). Although assessment differs across consumers, externality effects cannot be ruled out. This becomes even more serious when problems of transparency concerning particular goods overlap with general confidence problems concerning the economy as a whole, thereby undermining aggregate consumption.

This potential source of instability of markets is likely to be even more significant in at least two cases. The first is when quality depends more closely upon trust and interpersonal relations, as is the case in the markets for labour or credit or financial assets. While trust can be taken for granted in the case of ordinary physical goods, as there is an institutionalized or standardized market, this is not true for at least certain types of labour skills or credit contracts. In these cases, trust rests on more fragile conventions, because standardization is limited. For example, it is difficult to inspect these goods or provide objective criteria for the assessment of their quality. Stability in these markets may therefore be more easily upset if the system is exposed to general shocks in confidence.

The second case is that of knowledge capital, and in particular, of the key source of new knowledge: R&D. As already noted, intangible capital is inherently different from the more traditional inputs of labour, tangible capital and land; in general its economic value is uncertain and asymmetric across agents, and its productivity is difficult to measure (e.g. Audretsch 2000: 66; Baily 2002). However, the problems for R&D are even more serious. R&D capital is fundamentally different from tangible and human capital; it appears to be non-competitive, since many producers can use the same idea simultaneously, and the returns may be hard to appropriate due to the potential production of spillovers (see e.g. Stiroh 2000: 43–4). As a result, incentives for private investment may be rather weak.

Instability due to deregulation

A second source of instability brought about by lightness is the recent wave of deregulation and financial innovation, which has revealed to be 'a two-edged sword' (the *Economist* 28–9–2002: 7; Simonazzi 2003). The potential for deregulation to create instability has been recognized since at least the first widespread US bank failures in the nineteenth century. However, there is reason to believe that its impact may be even worse in the NE, because it favours sectoral imbalances that can amplify the business cycle.

As can be seen in the recent evolution of the American economy, the new financial instruments induce households to assume too much debt during the boom. This is not to say that increased consumer credit is an invention of the NE; on the contrary, it was one of the pillars of mass production following the First World War. However, the decline in recent years in national private-sector net savings in the US is unprecedented. Indeed it is fair to say that although swings in credit growth and asset prices have always played a part in business cycles, 'their role seems to have increased of late' (the *Economist* 28–9–2002: 29). This has been clearly pointed out by Godley and Izurieta (2002), who emphasize that the main engine of growth during the so-called 'Goldilocks' period was 'an exceptionally rapid, credit-financed expansion of private expenditure that stimulated and was stimulated by the huge boom in asset prices' (ibid.: 41). In their view, this type of engine of growth, which is based on a highly elastic credit creation, is quite fragile and bound to make a deep recession more likely.[9] In particular, slow growth will follow if the savings rate rises back to its long-term norm and the stock market collapses, inducing a negative wealth effect on consumption.

But the recent wave of deregulation and financial innovation may also negatively affect the behaviour of firms. Not only does it generate excessive credit creation, resulting in firms overborrowing like households, but it may also induce other distortions that undermine investment stability. Stiglitz (2002b, 2003) points out, for example, that excessive deregulation of financial markets in the NE has stimulated declining accounting standards and companies' avidity, as shown by the recent scandals at US energy companies and telecoms groups. In particular, he stresses that the stock options and other financial innovations make budget assessments more difficult and tend to stimulate fraudulent practices, such as bogus revenues and inflated accounts, which mislead small shareholders and shake financial investors' confidence (see also the *Financial Times* 18–5–2002). Moreover, the diffusion of stock options, along with tax cuts for higher income brackets in various countries, also undermines stability because of its adverse income distribution effects.

Erratic behaviour of financial markets

A third source of instability in the NE induced by lightness is the erratic behaviour of financial markets. These seem to be dominated by speculation and proceed in a series of alternating periods of 'irrational exuberance' – where share price increases are not driven by 'fundamentals' but by fads (see e.g. Shiller 2000) – and periods dominated by overpessimism. That speculation may play a key role in financial markets is, of course, nothing new. Indeed, one characteristic of stock markets has always been the formation of bubbles implying a growing distance of actual values from presumed 'correct' values or 'fundamentals'. But once again, the NE is not simply a repetition of the past resulting from the dramatic acceleration of 'lightness' in recent years. Although it is true that the current NE, like other previous 'New Economies', will survive stock market crashes, it is also true that the formation of bubbles and the inefficiency of financial markets more generally are likely to increase. This has obvious adverse consequences in terms of resource allocation, as already revealed by the phenomena of over-investment and excess capacity in the ICT industry. A number of factors account for this overall tendency.

First of all, the volatility of financial markets has sharply increased over the last few years (see e.g. Zarnowitz 1999: 72–4; the *Economist* 28–9–2002). Second, the difficulty in assigning value to intangible assets makes the relationship between actual share values and 'fundamentals' more difficult to establish than in past bubbles. This claim is not contradicted by the fact that ICT implies great advances in terms of access and diffusion of information. More information does not necessarily imply greater stability or efficiency of markets; it may simply allow an improvement in arbitrage, which is unlikely 'to be effective in undoing share price bubbles' (D'Avolio *et al.* 2001: 152). The point is that

> [A]rbitrage works effectively in making sure that derivative prices are close to their theoretical values or that two bonds with nearly identical cash flows have nearly identical prices. There is no theoretical reason to think that arbitrage will work to bring prices of volatile individual securities with highly uncertain fundamental values close to fundamentals ... Arbitrage deals with local rather than global inefficiencies.
>
> (ibid.: 152)

The existence of global inefficiencies can be seen not only in the debates on the productivity paradox and the misstatement of the true sources of productivity but also in the critique of conventional accounting practices. As noted by Crockett (2001), for example, the NE implies that these practices 'are not such a good guide to the real underlying situations' (ibid.: 184). In particular, attempts to focus on actual profits when assessing the value of ICT companies are misguided. In order to make sense of the larger relative weight of intellectual capital in the economy and satisfy the expectations for higher returns raised by the NE, many commentators call for a new series of creative valuation metrics. In fact, alternative criteria for valuing new assets (especially start-ups in high-tech industry) have been proposed by analysts in the financial press during the latest stock market boom. For example, in contrast with standard practices, they emphasize revenues rather than past profits (see e.g. Rifkin 2000: 70–5; *Financial Times* 18–5–2002).[10]

One upshot of the adoption of alternative criteria for assessing future corporate prosperity is further instability of the stock market. In particular, it increases uncertainty by stimulating the spread of opinions among professional traders. During the boom, it is impossible to judge the accuracy of any particular view, be it, for example, Hall's view attributing the stock market's rise to improved fundamentals or Shiller's irrational exuberance thesis. As Baily notes in reference to Hall's view, only *ex post* will it be possible to say whether it is really justified:

> [t]he obvious issue with this view of the rise in market valuation is that the proof or refutation of this idea is out there in the future. One can tell an internally plausible story about the rise in the corporate market valuations, based on the accumulation of intangible capital that will pay off in higher returns, and, presumably, greater productivity growth in the future ... but the real question is unanswerable so far: Will the future stream of profits justify the greatly increased valuations?
>
> (2001: 243)

A third factor which accounts for the greater instability of the stock market in the NE is the dominance of a short-run logic in both the financial community and in corporate strategy. To be sure, the seeds of this kind of logic were already being sown in financial markets upon introduction of the principle of limited liability and the separation between management and ownership. Until recently, however, while speculation and short-term logic prevailed among traders on the market, corporate strategies focused more on maximizing long-term performance, perhaps reflecting the conservative accounting practices held to by the primarily permanent owners of businesses. Instead, the NE implies an acceleration in the adoption of short-termism, even within corporate strategy.

As pointed out by D'Avolio *et al.* (2001), significant changes can be seen in the business models of publicly traded companies in the NE. In particular, due to incentives like stock options they have more of a focus on current stock prices:

> Most managers prefer a high current stock price. A high current stock price makes it cheaper to pay employees with equity, to raise funds through share

issues and to make acquisitions. It also makes managers stock options more valuable. For a number of reasons the need to maintain a high equity price bas been growing with technology-induced changes in financial markets.

(ibid.: 133)

These trends however are bound to create instability. One need only note, for example, that they 'combine to create strong incentives for firms to distort the information they produce to the investor community' (ibid.: 132).

14 Precision

Under the label of precision we group those stylized facts referring to attempts at improving a number of activities, such as measurement, data collection, formalization and prediction, made on the grounds of ICT.[1] In particular, we shall focus on how ICT provides external impetus to change in economics (e.g. Dow 2002: 6). As with other features of the NE, this is not a new phenomenon. It goes back, at least, to the nineteenth century, when the positivist ideal that social theory should be capable of replicating the success of natural science began to be affirmed. Then, at the beginning of the twentieth century, the search for precision went hand in hand with the development of macroeconomics as an autonomous discipline, based on relatively simple mathematical models. Both these transformations were made possible by legal and institutional changes, such as the rise of independent central banks and statistics institutes linked to governments' need to control the growing complexity of social and economic systems. It is beyond doubt, however, owing to the very nature of ICT, that the NE implies a dramatic acceleration in the quest for precision compared to the past. One need only think of the Internet's potential for satisfying all kinds of information needs, or to the fact that ICT facilitates the use of ever more sophisticated forecasting techniques. Moreover, recent trends in economic theory call for the construction of less ambitious but more rigorous paradigms, or models, than available in the past.

In the opinion of most economists, precision has prevailing positive effects on the stability of the economy. For example, having more detailed information about smaller parts of the system, in principle, makes it easier to understand and control it. However, there are others who point out that efforts to 'make it precise' may actually increase instability, because they still fail to capture some of the most elusive and complex features of the NE, such as intangibles, thus giving a false sense of improvement. In what follows, we shall focus on both effects, placing the emphasis on the signs of acceleration or differences of recent trends as compared with past decades.

More data and better measurement techniques

The tendency to achieve more precision in the NE than in the past can be seen in a number of significant phenomena that may reduce instability. First of all, the

NE stimulates the search for greater quantitative information about events. It should be clear that this is not a recent phenomenon; it has been pursued in a systematic fashion since at least the nineteenth century. There is no doubting, however, that it has undergone a sharp acceleration in recent times, because ICT expands the scope for data collection and analysis (see e.g. Dow 2002: 6), including those aspects of economic life that involve complex quality changes. One instance is the adoption of the hedonic price indexes for dealing with quality changes of ICT products (see e.g. Baily 2001: 222; OECD 2001; Gordon 2002: 50). In principle, it is clear that greater quantitative information increases stability because it tends to reduce the grey area of phenomena which are not adequately understood and controlled, thus allowing improvements in the decisions made by agents and in policy intervention. As noted, for example, by Stiroh (2000: 41), the attempt to measure inputs properly and the extension of the definition of investment beyond tangible assets (i.e. to include investment in human capital, R&D and public infrastructure) have led to advances in understanding productivity growth.

A more important role of 'formalist' values in economics

A second phenomenon induced by the NE is that a large part of economics has moved significantly in the direction of mathematization. Not only do we see the rapid growth of specialized branches of economics using advanced mathematical tools, but there is also a more general tendency to regard the development of an adequate formalization as the standard of presentation for all types of economic analysis. Once again, this is not new. One could observe that this tendency has been quite well established since the 1920s when the general equilibrium model and various types of macroeconomic models became increasingly popular. It is true, however, that the NE implies a sharp acceleration of the move towards formalization; in particular, 'formalist' values tend to acquire an excessive importance in economics (see e.g. Backhouse 1997; Lawson 1997: 4, 2003: 3–4; Dow 2002: 10). It must be noted that this acceleration concerns not just the quantity but also the type of models that are used by economists, reflecting a major change in the nature of the discipline. This change clearly appears in today's use of the term 'economic theory' itself: this ceases to mean a body of propositions about the world and has come to mean a set of mathematical theorems (see Backhouse 1997: 208; Lawson 2003). For example, as noted by Fisher, in practice, theorists tend to concentrate on exemplifying theory, that is, simple models stripped down to the bare essentials in order to illustrate specific theoretical points, for reasons of mathematical tractability (see Backhouse 1997: 20–1).[2]

This attitude concerning formalization is justified by the fact that economics has failed to exhibit the empirical progress that was once expected. As pointed out by Backhouse, for example, such a failure is due to 'the continually changing nature of the economic world' (ibid.: 207) that makes it harder for a consensus to emerge. Indeed, 'continual change ... has caused economists to retreat into theory. The reason is that they want to produce general, if not universal theories, which militates against applied work...' (ibid.). Strictly speaking, reference to data is still regarded as being important but only to illustrate the theory derived in a purely deductive fashion on the grounds of strong restrictions.[3] In particular, the idea that theories need to be tested, or that theory choice should depend, at least in the last resort, on empirical evidence has been abandoned (ibid.: 182). In other words, theorists' major concern today is for theoretical progress, the achievement of heuristic progress, in terms of precision, internal consistency, greater conceptual clarity and analytical innovations (Blaug 1994, 2000; Backhouse 1997: 100–3).[4]

It is possible to interpret this 'formalist' move as having beneficial effects on the economy. First of all, it might promote stability as it induces people to believe that, due to the relative neglect of empirical evidence it involves, the fundamental principles of economics, including stability, are somehow 'virtually beyond question'. (Backhouse 1997: 182). Second, theoretical progress may generate greater stability by inducing economists to believe that the application of mathematical techniques has definitely transformed economics into a cumulative discipline (Backhouse 1997: 3–4; Blanchard 2000). If the last, more formalized macro model is better than the previous ones, it is legitimate to expect, for example, that it can improve policy-making and represent a better benchmark for agents' expectations.

Attempt to improve forecasting

A further expression of the tendency towards precision in the NE is the improvement of the forecasting techniques to help decision-making and policy intervention. Focus on forecasting is, of course, nothing new. Ever since the nineteenth century, the predominant view among economists has been that the adoption of better measurement systems and more sophisticated analytical techniques in economics, as in physics, is justified in the end by the need to improve predictive performance. It is difficult to deny, however, that the NE stimulates the drive towards more accurate prediction than in the past because of the challenges arising from a more complex economic environment. One can note, for example, that several attempts have been made to reduce forecasting errors in macroeconomics in the last decades. While in the 1960s and the 1970s, econometricians tried to limit such error by constructing vast multi-equation macro models, a pluralistic strategy based on the concerted use of a range of small models, as complementary lines of enquiry, has more recently emerged in the policy-making literature (see e.g. Dow 2002: 30–1).[5]

However, this is not all. It is important to note that the use of more sophisticated statistical or econometric techniques today is not taken for granted but is subject to vast critical scrutiny. While in past decades it was firmly believed that the steady application of these techniques would eventually produce precise quantitative laws and solid foundations for predictive exercises, in the NE doubt concerning the usefulness or the actual achievements of these techniques has begun to emerge due to widespread predictive failures induced by the greater variability of parameters and uncertainty. Indeed, some commentators are aware that the NE *per se* does not improve the predictive performance of econometrics. As noted, for example, by Backhouse: 'despite the immense effort, undreamed-of increasing computing power, and the development of vastly more sophisticated statistical techniques, econometrics has failed to produce the quantitative laws that many economists, at one time, believed it would' (Backhouse 1997: 136).

In particular, ICT does not compensate for the lack of foresight concerning cyclical downturns, as shown by the recent recession. As noted by Baily: 'ICT has not improved our capacity to see the economic future. Downturns are intrinsically hard to call and the consensus forecast rarely catches them. In this downturn they were pretty wide off the mark' (Baily 2001: 250; see also Krugman 2001; Banerji 2002: 21).[6]

These developments explain why many practitioners have recently started to modify their views concerning the best way to produce predictions. Instead of trying to obtain precise parameter estimates on the grounds of sophisticated econometric models, they call for the adoption of other methods, such as reliance on pragmatic, informal, empirical work aimed at describing broad stylized facts or regularities that theory can explain (see e.g. Backhouse 1997: 176), calibration methods[7] or even the tracing of simple scenarios based on different assumptions about the values of the key magnitudes to prepare people for what, conceivably, could be in store.[8]

It should be clear that while all these methods taken together do not guarantee predictive success (they are indeed quite likely to miss the 'true' or 'objective' target), they still imply some improvement in forecasting that might contribute to increasing stability in the NE. First of all, by increasing the number and variety of claims about the future, these methods make the formation of forecasters' consensus view more robust. Second, this view affects reality itself by influencing agents' expectations (not unlike the observer in quantum physics influences the object of analysis with his measurement tools). Indeed, forecasters' consensus view plays the role of benchmark for market expectations; it is part of the market process. ICT may increase stability in that it favours a faster convergence of individuals' expectations to the benchmark, for agents in the NE tend to acquire ever more information in order to deal with complexity.

Measurement problems

Now we must focus on the potential negative effects of efforts to obtain more precise measurement, modelling and forecasting techniques in the NE. This attempt, too, may create stability problems. While seemingly paradoxical, this claim can be supported by strong arguments. Let us start by focusing on the search for greater and more precise quantitative information.

First of all, this search may exercise a negative influence on agents' behaviour. As noted by Viskovatoff (2000: 145), for example, the advent of the availability of large amounts of data has led to an important shift in the way managers make decisions: they actually rely on management by numbers. Investment decisions are based on quantitative decision rules that use measures, such as expected profitability or return on investment (ROI), and abstract from the specific qualitative features of a contemplated investment project. These rules may create excessive risk aversion, focus on short-run profitability and bias against introducing innovative products; in general, the positive aspects of investment will be less apparent in a quantitative description.

Second, more precise quantitative information may also cause greater instability if it is not accompanied by a parallel revision of measurement methods and indicators. The point is that the NE has become increasingly difficult to measure using conventional methods. Many key phenomena, such as intangibles, still defy proper measurement. For example, there are major problems with measuring human capital (see e.g. the *Economist* 28–9–2004), quality change and true output growth (see e.g. Brynjolfsson and Hitt 2002: 37, 41–2). The productivity gains associated with ICT tend to be underestimated because traditional growth accounting techniques focus on the relatively observable aspects of output, like prices and quantities, while neglecting the intangible benefits of improved quality, new products, customer service and speed. Moreover, good measures of productivity growth are next to impossible to achieve in non-market sectors such as education, health and general government as well as in finance and transportation (Cohen *et al.* 2000; Baily 2001: 222).[9]

These considerations imply that a more accurate application of existing methods may well produce more information, but will also increasingly miss the target. As noted by Eustace: 'our economic and business measurement systems... are tracking – with ever increasing efficiency – a smaller and smaller proportion of the real economy' (2000: 6). The continual application of standard methods may thus increase instability, because it generates a distorted picture of the economy and a false sense of improvement which may well lead to the underestimation of new phenomena and the adoption of wrong policy stances.

Modelling problems

There is reason to believe, too, that the current formalist turn in economics may generate instability. This may happen especially if it widens the gap between theoretical and empirical progress (see e.g. Blaug 1994, 2000; Backhouse 1997), that is to say, if the new models which are assumed to represent advances in terms of greater conceptual clarity and analytical innovation fail to contribute to progress in terms of a deeper grasp of the inner triggers of economic behaviour and the workings of the economic system in the age of the NE. This gap is bound to have destabilizing consequences, mainly because it generates a false impression of knowledge, leading agents and policy-makers who are deeply influenced by theory to be overconfident about its practical implications. In particular, focusing on the modelling of various small parts of the economy, taken in isolation, gives the impression that one knows, or can take for granted, the relevant causal links, the correct distinction between exogenous and endogenous variables, and so on, when in fact this is not the case. As already noted, in the NE there is a growing uncertainty over causal links, which means that the distinction between exogenous and endogenous variables cannot be made once and for all. To take just one example, we certainly have better models today to account for expectations formation and technological progress than past generations have had. Indeed, these models may capture some endogenous aspects, such as forms of learning linked with production. However, it would be wrong to believe that they necessarily imply an improvement in explanatory terms or that they open the way to better policy conduct; expectations or technological progress, for example, also depend upon historical, institutional or cultural factors which cannot be fully endogenized.

Forecasting problems

As noted in the previous section, a number of commentators are aware that better technology and more information in the NE do not necessarily compensate for lack of foresight and may fail to grant an improvement in predictive performance. This is why they stress the limits of econometrics and call for alternative methods (such as calibration and scenarios) of forecasting.[10] While attempts to obtain precision may help stability in that they make the consensus view more robust, they may also create instability if it is forgotten that this consensus view is not objectively true (i.e. it quite likely fails to capture the true parameters of the economy) but merely constitutes a conventional representation capable of lulling agents' anxiety. Two points should be noted here. The first is that, in general, conventions are intrinsically fragile constructions and may easily break down or cause unjustified fluctuations in public opinion if they do not rest on more solid grounds such as, for example, theorists' ability to achieve true empirical progress in terms of improved analysis of real causal mechanisms and identification of the most plausible future outcomes. Second, better and more timely information in the NE may increase overconfidence as it creates a false impression of knowledge when in fact it only provides faster convergence to the conventional view. Overconfidence in the NE is likely to be more dangerous than in past decades because of the increased probability that the consensus view is wide off the mark. For example, let us take forecasts concerning income growth. In this regard, quite frankly, many recognize that: 'forecasting the rate of economic growth is always hazardous, but it is more hazardous now than usual' (DeLong and Summers 2001: 12).[11]

As noted, for example by Baily (2001), the point is that, although uncertainty should be no worse than has been the case historically (downturn is not unusual and cyclical volatility lower), longer run uncertainty about growth prospects (for the next 5 or 10 years) is increased. In particular, he suggests that uncertainties year by year that used to be partially offsetting (e.g. in the 1960s, when uncertainty about the short run did not lead to exploding uncertainty over the longer term, because potential income was fairly predictable) have become cumulative, owing to the greater unpredictability of potential income. Indeed, he points out that today we face 'unusual uncertainty' especially as concerns the productivity trend 'which makes potential income harder to predict than we thought' (Baily 2001: 253). It should be clear that the greater unpredictability of potential income has negative consequences for policy-making and stability. Monetary policy, for example, is largely based on estimates of the size of the output gap, that is, the gap between actual income and potential income. Given large measurement errors concerning the size of this gap, 'a monetary policy that tries hard to smooth the cycle could easily increase output volatility' (the *Economist*, 28–9–2002).

15 Visibility

Under this label we shall group various phenomena, or stylized facts, that relate to policy-making in the NE. This label is justified because policy is the 'visible' hand of institutions at work in the economy that counteracts the effects of the 'invisible' hand of market mechanisms. It is important to note that our visibility label is broad enough to include microeconomic policies such as deregulation and privatization, rule-based macroeconomic policies and more pragmatic policies. There are complex links between policies and other features of the NE. On the one hand, for example, appropriate policy moves stimulate globalization and technological change. On the other, the latter also constrain policy in various ways. In this chapter, we shall take into account some of these interactions, without posing rigid causal links.

As with the other features of the NE, visibility is not a new phenomenon. It has been a structural characteristic of capitalism ever since the final decades of the nineteenth century, when governments became aware of the need to take responsibility for managing the economy (see e.g. DeLong and Summers 2001). Although it is characterized by continual shifts of emphasis from one type of policy to the other, such as the shift from Keynesian demand policies of the 1960s to the restoration of supply-side free market policy in later decades, visibility, as a whole, has never disappeared. In this chapter we make two claims about it. The first is that visibility, overall, in the NE undergoes a significant acceleration with respect to the past. Despite the crises of national governments due to the rise of institutions and activities not linked to territory or operating in cyberspace (see e.g. Rifkin 2000), the need for policies in the NE, including active macroeconomic policies, has been growing, notwithstanding popular views claiming the opposite. In particular, liberalization and privatization, moves that for many signify the heart of the NE, do not imply the end or the reduction of public intervention in the economy, at either the micro or the macro level. There is, instead, a shift from one type of policy to the other. As noted for example by Audretsch:

> The downsizing of federal agencies charged with regulation of business in the USA and Great Britain has been interpreted by many scholars as the eclipse of government intervention. But to interpret deregulation, privatisation, and the increasing irrelevance of competition policies as the end of government

intervention in business ignores an important shift in the locus and target of policy. The last decade has seen the emergence of a broad spectrum of enabling policies initiatives that fall outside the jurisdiction of traditional regulatory agencies.

(2000: 77–8)

Before going into detail about these enabling policies, we suggest that what Audretsch claims in the cited passage is true for policy in general, including macroeconomic policy. Our second claim is that the NE certainly does not imply the end of traditional demand policies and the universal adoption of tight, simple rules; rather, policy rules more often need to be integrated with pragmatic policy moves. On the one hand, governments commit themselves, in principle, to strict rules, such as balanced budgets, derived from what they consider to be a solid theoretical framework. On the other, however, they are often forced, in practice, to break those very rules and to adopt more pragmatic stances to face the challenges posed by a global and complex environment characterized by more frequent shocks. They are actually able to do so because ICT provides more information, making it easier to implement 'fine-tuning'.

Like other features of the NE, visibility affects stability. The most common view is that the current combination of theoretically based rules and actual pragmatic policy moves, which represent visibility today, is regarded as having mainly positive effects on the stability of the economy. Swifter fine-tuning, more timely 'piece-meal' intervention and more flexible interpretation of rules all seem, to many, capable of granting the creation of a stable long-term economic environment (in terms of low inflation and high levels of unemployment). On the other hand, however, there is also reason to believe that the current combination of rules and pragmatism is also likely to increase instability. In particular, one could note that there is a growing potential gap between the official rules adopted and the elusive, complex nature of the NE, which sometimes gives rise to systemic failures, for example, those due to fast global financial markets which dominate slow production processes. This is a gap which pragmatism no longer seems able to bridge. In what follows, we shall focus on both these effects, placing the emphasis on the signs of acceleration or differences of recent trends as compared with past decades.

Monetary policy rules

The tendency to maintain precise policy rules is a crucial part of government strategy in the NE to grant macroeconomic stability. Let us start from monetary policy. That this policy is based on rules is certainly not a new phenomenon. Indeed, as monetary history shows, the control of money has often been pursued by following some system of rules, such as the Gold Standard, the Bretton Woods system of fixed exchange rates or monetary targeting. In particular, the adoption of rules has characterized the behaviour of independent central banks ever since their foundation at the beginning of the twentieth century.[1] However, what is relatively recent is the specific rule which characterizes the NE, namely inflation targeting.

It can be argued that this evolution of rules is guided by the attempt to reduce economic and financial instability in the face of changing economic circumstances. For example, leading to the breakdown of the Bretton Woods system was, among other factors, the growing awareness among policy-makers that the goal of full employment which was pursued by Keynesian monetary and fiscal policy in the two previous decades exposed the economy to the danger of rising inflation and market instability (see e.g. Baker 2003: 804–5). The control of inflation thus became the main policy goal and monetary policy, based on the control of the money supply, gradually became the preferred instrument to reach it (see e.g. the *Economist* 28–9–2002: 29). The main idea behind this rule, inspired by monetarism and the quantity theory of money, was that changes in the money supply controlled by central banks, in the long run, only generate inflation without influencing employment and the trend growth rate or potential income. The latter depend upon real factors such as productivity and labour supply growth, which are exogenous, that is, outside the control of central banks.

However, monetary targeting was not a lasting rule. What led, in turn, to its breakdown and the adoption of inflation targeting was instability deriving from a number of sources, such as the uncertain causal links between money and prices, the difficulty of tracking monetary aggregates in the face of financial innovation making the demand for money unstable,[2] the lack of uniformity in market expectations concerning both inflation and the conduct of monetary policy and the problem of choice of the appropriate policy instruments for pursuing short-run stabilization.

It is the attempt to solve these instability problems that lies at the heart of inflation targeting. First of all, by focusing on the end of the causal chain, that is, inflation, rather than the beginning, that is, money, this policy rule seeks to bypass the problem of the uncertain causal links between these two variables. One need only note, for example, that monetary aggregates are quite unstable in the NE (because of the faster processes of financial innovation and continuous changes in the forms of money) and that their behaviour may not be related to inflation. A rise in M3, for example, may simply reflect changes in the composition of investors' portfolio (a shift from shares to deposits) rather than willingness to spend and create inflation.

Second, this policy rule simplifies the choice as to the best policy to pursue macroeconomic stabilization. In principle, stability can be reached in various ways according to the policy goal. If the main goal is full employment, governments could rely on either fiscal policy or exchange rate policy or monetary policy. If low inflation is the main goal, monetary policy becomes the key instrument of macroeconomic stabilization, in view of the comparative advantage held by independent central banks in this matter.[3] Indeed the current conventional wisdom in the NE is that, by keeping inflation low, monetary policy is the key stabilizer at the macroeconomic level, cooling the economy off when it is running too hot (i.e. when actual income grows more than potential income) and warming it up when it is running too cold. In particular, in case of depression or when income grows too slowly to grant sufficient employment expansion, central banks can even act aggressively to restore confidence (see e.g. Baily 2001: 249, 256).[4]

This does not mean that fiscal and exchange rate policy should never be used. However, many consider these policies to be less effective short-run stabilizers in the NE than monetary policy. In Krugman's view, for example, monetary and fiscal policy are a bit like aspirin and morphine; it is better to use the former first and the latter in exceptional cases, such as when the system falls into the liquidity trap. The main reason is that monetary policy can operate much more rapidly, as shown by Greenspan's successful attempts to save the US on several occasions (1987, 1990–1, 1998) by quickly modifying interest rates. While tax cuts require time and cannot be easily reversed, interest changes instead are quickly reversible (see e.g. Krugman 2001: 38–9).[5]

Finally, inflation targeting in the NE is designed to provide an anchor to market price expectations. This point is clearly underlined by Woodford (2001). Unlike authors such as Benjamin Friedman and Mervyn King, who suggest that the central banks' power is undermined by the NE because financial innovation reduces the demand for a monetary base and develops e-money, Woodford starts by noting that in the NE monetary policy should be even more effective than in the past – that is, more able to achieve its stabilization goals – because of improved private-sector information (see e.g. Woodford 2001: 316–17).[6] One reason for this is that successful monetary policy is a matter of affecting, in a desirable way, the evolution of market expectations regarding interest rates or inflation. Clearly, if the beliefs of markets' participants are widespread and poorly informed, this is difficult. Woodford makes it clear that to influence expectations the central banks must lead the markets and resist the temptation to follow them:

> [B]ecause if the central bank delivers whatever the markets expect then there is no objective anchor for these expectations. Arbitrary changes in expectations may be self-fulfilling because the central bank validates them. This would be destabilizing for both nominal and real variables.
>
> (ibid.: 314)

It is for the purpose of leading the market that central banks need to conform to a systematic rule of behaviour, and to explain it clearly, in order to improve the private sector's understanding of the central banks' current decisions and future intentions: 'Policy should be rule-based. If the Bank does not follow a systematic rule then no amount of effort at transparency will allow the public to understand and anticipate its policy' (ibid.). Woodford then stresses that the definition of rules rests on an explicit model of the economy and thus concludes by stating that this is the only objective anchor for market expectations in the NE:

> Rule-based policy-making will necessarily mean a decision process in which an explicit model of the economy (albeit one augmented by judge-mental elements) plays a central role, both in the deliberations of a policy

committee and in explanations to the public...One can only expect the importance of models to policy deliberations to increase in the NE.

(ibid.)

Pragmatic monetary policy

Once the official policy stance is clarified, it is important to realize that it does not necessarily correspond to the actual policy pursued by central banks. As evidence shows, when dangers other than inflation materialize and give rise to market instability, central banks do not always insist on their official targets and adopt a more flexible or 'pragmatic' monetary policy; this essentially amounts to taking into account not just inflation but also growth (see e.g. the *Economist* 28–9–2002). There are two kinds of pragmatic moves. One follows from the fact that inflation targeting is not the unique determinant of the central banks' behaviour. The evidence suggests that this strategy is not applied mechanically. In practice, there are degrees of freedom that are used, especially in the face of negative events. The second type of pragmatism follows from the fact that the official rules are less strictly codified or publicized, so that central banks enjoy some further room for manoeuvre. The European Central Bank (ECB) is an instance of the first approach. Its strategy involves the specification of a clear inflation and money supply target (a certain M3 growth rate). As recent data shows, however, the ECB has often failed to raise interest rates systematically when actual inflation was higher than its 2 per cent target, or actual M3 growth was higher than its 4.5 per cent target (e.g. Talani 2004).[7]

The FED, instead, is an instance of the second type of pragmatism. Strictly speaking, the FED does rely on theoretical principles of a monetarist kind, such as the NAIRU, As noted by Baker, for example,

> it seems clear that the Federal Reserve Board came to view the NAIRU as a guide for its actions. When the unemployment rate began to fall below the range of estimates for the NAIRU in 1988, it raised interest rates.
>
> (2003: 814)

It fails, however, to specify targets for inflation, and its strategy is much broader than the ECB's. It is intended not only to pursue monetary stability but also economic stability in terms of income and employment, exchange rate and financial stability, in line with the role of the key engine of growth in the world economy played by the US. From the start, this broader perspective intuitively favours a balanced approach to money management.

It must be noted, however, that the FED's pragmatism is not always a matter of rational choice or 'formal' decisions. Sometimes, it is due to simple error. Stiglitz (2002b), for example, talks about 'lucky' errors by the FED, who made wrong estimates of GDP growth and NAIRU in the late 1990s (the actual unemployment rate went below 6 per cent but inflation did not rise) and failed to raise interest rates, thus favouring the boom (see also Baker 2003: 819).[8] At other times it is linked to the key role of economic leaders like Alan Greenspan, whose informal comments often manage to exercise 'moral suasion', that is, to persuade or reassure the markets that the FED will behave in a certain way conducive to stability and prosperity; for example, that it will intervene to face confidence crises or to avoid bankruptcies (see e.g. Banerji 2002: 16; DeLong 2003).[9] It should be clear that, owing to the key roles played by expectations, trust and rapidity of information in today's global markets, this kind of intangible aspect of monetary policy is more important than ever before.

Although both types of pragmatism end up taking growth into account (see e.g. the *Economist* 28–9–2002), the second one seems more successful in achieving stability of growth. According to many economists, recent moderation of the business cycle in the US is due to very important knowledge gained about how to conduct monetary policy more efficiently (see e.g. DeLong 1999, 2003; C. Romer 1999; Clarida *et al.* 2000; Blanchard and Simon 2001; Banerji 2002; Baker 2003; Bernanke 2004; Martin and Rowthorn 2004). In particular, the FED has managed to carry out a few key pragmatic moves in the last two decades. DeLong stresses, for example, the 'FED's greater success at maintaining its balance: at acting pre-emptively and maintaining an appropriate balance between price stability and maximum purchasing power, rather than careening from one objective to the other...' (2003), as well as 'the swift reaction of the FED to 1987, to 1998, to 2001' shocks (stock market crashes and financial panic).[10]

Fiscal policy rules

In the NE, fiscal policy is also based on the adoption of rules. In particular, the basic view is that there is no need for active fiscal policy to support aggregate demand. Governments all over the world should stick to the principles of sound finance and balance the budget at least over the cycle. Once again, it must be noted that this view is not a recent one. One need only call to mind the so-called Treasury view in Britain in the 1920s, or the fiscal straitjacket in the 1970s when the so-called Keynesian fine-tuning aimed at averting recessions went out of fashion and was replaced by anti-inflationary policies (see e.g. Baker 2003) Instead, what differentiates the NE from past stages of capitalist economies is that the balanced budget view is expressed in terms of formalized rules based on a more accurate statement of the reasons why discretionary fiscal policies are ineffective and tend to increase instability, at least in the long run. One set of reasons is quite traditional and has been discussed by economists for years. It has to do with the fact that these policies tend to generate further budget deficits that have some well-known negative effects on the economy. In particular, they may make the debt burden in many countries practically unsustainable, implying either higher taxes or inflation. Moreover, by raising interest rates, they may crowd out private investment (ibid.).

Another set of reasons for fiscal policy ineffectiveness is more closely linked to the flimsy nature of the NE. First, it can be argued that, due to the greater instability of parameters and the rapidity of decision-making it involves, the NE exacerbates the problem of getting the timing of fiscal measures right. It is for this reason that tax cut proposals, such as those recently advanced in the US, are often criticized by economists. According to Krugman (2001), for example, cutting taxes is not a good idea because these cuts require time and cannot be easily reversed. Moreover, there is a high probability that predictions concerning long-run budgets may be wrong (see also the *Economist* 28–9–2002).

Second, fiscal policy is best avoided as an instrument of stabilization because it has become redundant, at least in part. In the NE several 'automatic' stabilizers still exist, such as income tax, the emergence of unemployment compensation and, more in general, the welfare state, all of which have exercised substantial beneficial effects on the economy since their introduction, especially after the Second World War (see e.g. Baily 2001; Blanchard and Simon 2001: 135–6).

Finally, fiscal policy in the NE is less effective than in the past because of the increased openness of economies and greater international capital mobility. In a floating exchange rate regime, expansionary fiscal policies in one country either tend to attract foreign capital inflows and generate a 'strong' currency, which crowds out net exports or have the opposite effect if they badly impact investors' expectations.

For all of these reasons, it is easy to understand why many authors argue that the NE emerged at a time of extraordinary fiscal discipline. According to Baily (2001: 256) and Stiglitz (2002b), for example, fiscal discipline (i.e. Clinton's deficit cut) did not create the NE but it helped start the virtuous cycle going as it bene-fited the US economy through lower interest rates. Indeed, it is the conventional view, which also underlies the Maastricht Treaty and the stability pact in Europe, that deficit cuts by themselves allow economic recovery and growth in the NE.

The critique of the use of fiscal policy as an anti-cyclical instrument in the NE does not imply the impossibility of using it for other purposes. Indeed, the current conventional view holds that, in order to grant true economic stability, fiscal policy should be used in a long-run perspective as part of a broader set of supply-side policies seeking to influence the determinants of growth, such as investment, saving, labour supply and innovation. In other words, while it is legitimate to leave short-run stabilization to central banks, it is wise to use tax cuts as incentives for people to work more and save more, take greater risks and expand productive capacity (see e.g. Krugman 2001).[11]

Pragmatic fiscal policy

Once again, it must be noted that the official policy stance does not necessarily cor-respond to the actual policy pursued by governments. As the evidence clearly shows, the attempt to balance the budget cannot be maintained as a permanent policy rule, especially in the face of shocks. This is also true in the NE. Indeed, in the past two years, interest in a more flexible fiscal policy has revived both in the US and Europe. Faced with the greater variability of parameters and the persis-tence of pronounced business cycles, many governments have taken steps to relax tight 'official' fiscal stances and adopt expansionary measures to support demand

and output in the short run and help the economy move out of recession rapidly. One can distinguish between two types of pragmatic moves for fiscal policy, as well.

The first type can be regarded as pragmatism 'within' formal rules, and follows from the fact that adherence to fiscal rules does not uniquely determine governments' behaviour, but allows some room for manoeuvre. The second type instead is pragmatism 'outside' the rules, in the sense that while policy is still based on broad commitments to balance the budget, it is not, however, constrained by specific rules.

An instance of the first type of pragmatism is reflected in current debate concerning the European stability pact. The recent modest reform of the pact in March 2005 – allowing temporary extra-deficits (e.g. 3.5 per cent rather 3 per cent) – reveals the growing awareness by policy-makers of having reached a kind of stalemate. On the one hand, they now realize that full compliance with the original pact would be very costly in terms of short-run output in a context characterized by fundamental uncertainty and sluggish growth. On the other, they suspect that changing it substantially is not a viable political option, at least in the short run.

An instance of the second type of pragmatism can be seen in the US, where the lack of a precise formal rule with which to comply makes it is easier to adopt a flexible stance in the face of adverse conditions than in Europe. One could note, for example, that the tax cuts and military expenditure made in order to avoid recession in the US after the terrorist attacks have rapidly turned the budget from a surplus to a deficit without much discussion. Godley and Izurieta rightly describe this dramatic change in policy stance as a drastic change of view, a swift, silent total *volte-face*:

> Barely a year ago, it was widely accepted...that the US growth rate had been permanently raised, the business cycle had been abolished...fiscal policy should never be used as an instrument of policy, the budget would always be in surplus, and judicious adjustments to short-term interest rates by the Federal Reserve were all that was needed to keep non-inflationary growth permanently on track...the consensus has been downright confuted...by the course of events. But no one is saying he is sorry. There has been...no statement of what went wrong that is other than descriptive, and no sense has been conveyed that the system of ideas that might be held to underlie the previous orthodoxy has come under threat or requires modification. However, a recognition generated by *force majeure*, has emerged that a fiscal stimulus is needed immediately.
>
> (2002: 48–9)

This is not the first time that such rapid swings have occurred in the US and, more in general, that pragmatic options to support the economy have been taken. Even fervent supply-siders like Reagan have managed to increase deficits. However, these swings are even more likely to occur in the NE. In other words, if it is true that in the NE visibility accelerates in the form of more frequent reliance on pragmatic moves by fiscal authorities, this does not necessarily mean an increase in the ratio between public expenditure and GDP. It may simply mean that a more important role is played by the capability of reacting swiftly to shocks and change policy stance.

Apart from the clear difference between Europe and the US in terms of rapidity and the effectiveness of decision-making, there is one element of pragmatism which they have in common: in both cases it is much more likely to find a permanent budget deficit than a permanent budget surplus. To a varying degree (more in Europe than in the US), this reflects the existence of a large chunk of relatively stable expenditures, due to automatic stabilizers and the welfare state, which are a 'normal' part of the structure of the economy. As noted by Blanchard and Simon (2001: 135–6), for example, the stability of these expenditures, especially after the Second World War, accounts for greater overall output stability.

Rules for markets

In the NE, governments also implement structural policies aiming at the definition of rules concerning the governance of economic activity and institutions, which are designed to improve the market mechanism and the development of new technologies. Strictly speaking, according to the conventional view, this is almost all a government should do in terms of policy. Free-market policies were crucial for the rise of ICT, and there is little justification for a more active or interventionist role of the state now that the NE is well established. The point is that markets are self-adjusting and always able to grant optimal outcomes, once appropriate rules for their operation have been defined.

It must be noted that this regulatory stance, too, is not peculiar to the NE. It can be seen at other points in history when important economic transformations necessitated redefinition of the systems of governmental regulation. As already noted, the development of mass production, for example, required not only improvements in production technology but also crucial legal, institutional and political changes, such as limited liability, the stock market, investment banking, deposit insurance, modern social insurance, the continent-wide market and the existence of an antitrust policy (see DeLong and Summers 2001: 40). Indeed, on this point one can see a significant analogy between this period and the 'progressive era' of the last quarter of the nineteenth century that led to the foundation of the FED:

> Just as in the last quarter of the 19th century, which was the greatest period in US economic development, with a great number of innovations and with all kinds of new people coming into business, regulation of markets has to catch up to the new economic reality. There were a lot of benefits. We have clean water...we have the Federal Reserve System as a consequence. The same holds here that regulation needs to keep up with what we see in markets.
>
> (D'Avolio *et al.* 2001: 192)

Several types of regulatory policies in the NE resemble those that characterized earlier periods. In particular, policies assuring competitive markets and encouraging productivity growth are as essential today in granting stability in the markets as they were in the past (see e.g. Baily 2002: 19–20).

As already emphasized, what distinguishes the NE from past stages of capitalist economies is the drastic acceleration of a number of phenomena already present in previous decades. This is true for this 'governance' issue. First of all, in the NE there is a stronger wave of deregulation.[12] In general, the NE

> [s]hift(s) the policy focus away from the traditional triad of policy instruments constraining the freedom of firms to contract – regulation, competition policy or antitrust in the USA, and public ownership of business. The policy approach of constraint was sensible as long as the major issue was how to restrain footloose multinational corporations in possession of considerable market power. This is reflected by the waves of deregulation and privatisation along with the decreased emphasis on competition policy throughout the OECD.
>
> (Audretsch 2000: 77–8)

Another justification for deregulation is that the new technologies tend to undermine cases of natural monopoly for which regulation is more appropriate. In particular, while it is true that there are core products, such as software, that favour monopolistic structures because they have high fixed costs for development and extraordinarily low costs of replication and distribution as well as network externalities, rapid technological change in the NE reduces the power of existing firms as it lowers the barriers to entry and allows new technologies (thus opening up competition between technologies) (see e.g. Klein 2000).

Second, as noted by Audretsch (2000) in the above quote the NE also seems to imply fewer antitrust policies. This point is moot, however. Economists hold quite differing views on this issue. According to DeLong (1998) for example, the NE justifies, instead, more antitrust policies because creating open and competitive markets in the NE is likely to prove even more difficult than in the past, given the peculiar nature of the new markets. As shown by the Microsoft case, when the typical commodity in an economy is non-rival and not transparent, and most of the value produced is in the form of information goods

> we can expect monopoly to become the rule rather than the exception in the structure of industry.... The antitrust division of the Justice Department might become the most important branch of the government, as it tries to keep the structure of industry as competitive as possible.
>
> (DeLong 1998: 12)

Other economists (in particular those influenced by Austrian views like Levy 1998), consider antitrust an inadequate means of dealing with ICT markets since competition is dynamic and continuous innovation can undermine monopolies. To favour this outcome, they say, it would be best to abolish antitrust policy altogether. For others still, antitrust is still viable but needs to apply more loosely to high-tech sectors (see e.g. Jacobson 2001) for example, because the definition of markets and dominant positions are based on static indicators that may not apply to the NE. Moreover, traditionally, antitrust regulation is suspicious of horizontal relations among competitors; competition and inter-firm coordination are usually regarded as antithetical. However, as noted earlier, coordination can be necessary in the NE for firms to survive.

Third, the NE calls for a more accurate definition of rules concerning such thorny issues as privacy, security, and the definition of new property rights and responsibilities that are necessary for markets to function effectively.[13]

Fourth, we can regard the faster tendency towards unification of rules and markets across countries as typical of the NE. In particular, the success of the NE in the 1990s transformed the US economy into the only model of capitalism in the world that is also valid from the regulatory policy standpoint. As noted by Stiglitz (2002b), the view that deregulation and markets are the key mechanisms for prosperity has become almost a myth or a dogma.

Fifth, the NE exacerbates the need for regulating financial markets, given their exponential growth. Recent events demonstrate, for example, that the US government is going through a remarkable regulatory *tour-de-force* in response to scandals, such as bogus revenues and inflated accounts at US energy companies and telecoms groups, favoured by excessive deregulation or liberalization of financial markets in the 1990s (see e.g. *Financial Times* 18–5 2002).

Sixth, given its more dynamic nature, the NE makes policies dealing with the basic issues of labour flexibility and fairness more urgent than in past stages of development. Cohen, DeLong and Zysman stress in particular the link between flexibility and inclusion:

> As has been the case throughout industrial history, development has meant the destruction of particular jobs, professions, specialties, and the emergence of new ones. But often the people who fill the new jobs are not the people who filled the old ones. Flexibility is discomforting; it is, by definition, up setting. Institutions – and people – resist changes that are not clearly and visibly to their benefit. Flexibility must be based on inclusion. For, if the benefits are not broadly understood, broadly seen as accessible, and broadly shared, the transformation will be stunted at whatever economic price. Policy aiming at flexibility must, therefore, aim at inclusion.

(2000: 66)

Finally, the NE assigns greater weight to policies aimed at the continuing development of skills. This is not surprising in view of the peculiar nature of the knowledge society, where the returns to education and skills have risen dramatically, widening the wage and income distribution (see e.g. Baily 2002: 19–20).

Pragmatic structural policies

It must be noted that, in the case of market 'rules', the official policy stance does not always correspond to the actual policy pursued by governments. As evidence abundantly shows, governments quite often tend to play a more active role in the economy than implied by mere regulatory policy. And the NE is no exception. Even in the era of full deregulation and globalization, most governments, directly or through international organizations like the WTO, often adopt or advocate protectionist measures and/or carry out active industrial policies to protect national industries in the face of uncertainty concerning the global economy (see e.g. the *Economist* 21–10–2000) or favour the rise of new sectors or technologies. As Audretsch emphasizes,

> to interpret deregulation, privatisation, and the increasing irrelevance of competition policies as the end of government intervention in business ignores an important shift in the locus and target of policy. The last decade has seen the emergence of a broad spectrum of enabling policies.... which focus on enabling the creation and commercialisation of knowledge. Example of such policies include encouraging R&D, venture capital, and new firms start-ups.
>
> (2000: 77–8)

It should be noted that ICT itself has been created to a large extent by economic policy. This is especially true in the US where governments have managed to avoid cutting expenditures, such as military, high tech and research, in large infrastructures and universities that have positive externalities. Indeed, even in the light of changing views concerning free markets, no US government has abandoned its role of coordination and direction in developing ICT. As noted by Cohen, De Long and Zysman

> [f]or the past fifty years, US government policy has played a major role in enabling America to lead in developing information technology – and just as important – in creating the conditions for America to lead in the *use* of information technology throughout the economy. The American government largely got policy right...(concerning) public investment in science and technology and in the technological-age education of people needed to realize the benefits of the E-conomy ...
>
> (2000: 2)[14]

This is not all, however. In cases of depression or turmoil in financial markets, both national governments and international organizations (such as the IMF) generally fail to adopt or recommend simple regulatory or non-interventionist stances, such as 'waiting' for the necessary 'cleaning' of the markets that will gradually eliminate excesses or unprofitable firms. They generally step in to save the markets and restore confidence instead.

On the limits of general policy rules

We now turn to the potential negative effects of the expansion of visibility on the stability of the economy. In particular, there are reasons to believe that the two-stage policy approach, that is, the combination of the adoption of strict rules and pragmatism, is likely to increase instability.[15] First of all, we shall consider the limits of the specific policy rules analysed in the previous sections and suggest a few reasons why they may be wrong and why they may cause undesired effects at the macroeconomic level. Our main argument is that policy rules have no general validity. It is a mistake to think that low inflation, balanced budgets or deregulation alone inevitably grants stable growth and should, therefore, be pursued at all costs. In particular, efforts to control the economy through the adoption of these kinds of rules are appropriate only if markets always work, and this is simply not universally the case. Systemic failures tend to occur from time to time. In these cases, adherence to strict rules becomes part of the problem rather than its solution; it may even contribute to aggravating instability.

These points are often emphasized in the literature. As the *Economist* openly admits, for example, seeking to keep inflation low does not always grant optimal outcomes. Indeed, 'the current conventional wisdom that central banks will reduce economic and financial instability by keeping inflation low and stable is flawed. Low inflation is not a guarantee of economic stability' (the *Economist* 28–9–2002: 7). On the contrary, attempts to control inflation can easily lead to depression. As pointed out by Christina Romer (1999: 3–4), monetary policy was one of the main sources of business cycles in the four decades after the Second World War. In the post-war period many recessions were deliberately induced by monetary authorities to curb inflation (see also DeLong 1999, 2003; Friedman 2001: 169).

Similar claims concerning fiscal policy rules can also be easily found. In particular, many now recognize that a tight fiscal policy *per se* is not a guarantee of prosperity and better growth prospects. Indeed, as noted by Stiglitz (2002b), it is not true, in general, that deficit cuts allow economic recovery. It would have been wrong, for example, to follow this policy in the recent crises in Japan or Argentina and, indeed, it is not odd that most economists have advocated deficit increases to fight recession in these countries.

Finally, even establishing a set of 'universal' prescriptions for the working of markets does not *per se* grant optimal outcomes and may generate destabilizing effects. For example, deregulation or market flexibility may not represent solutions for all problems in all places, especially in developing countries. The point is that, as noted by Rifkin (2000), for example, the market is a secondary, not a primary institution. It can exist and prosper only if certain conditions, such as sufficient trust for the backing of trade, prevail. In turn, social trust and social capital are not natural givens; in particular, they depend upon a culture that generates empathy, that is, the ability to meet the minds of other people via thought or sentiment. Thus, if culture is weak, social trust is at risk, and the market cannot produce it. Trying to start or develop a business in this context may prove hopeless.[16]

Lack of a general model to guide monetary policy

Let us now focus on some more specific instability problems deriving from the adoption of such policy rules, starting with monetary policy. First of all, instability may derive from indeterminacy concerning the model used by monetary authorities to analyse inflation. One can note, for example, that in order to estimate future inflation, inflation targeting central banks use a vast number of indicators and make reference to several models of inflation,[17] which they seek to combine in a coherent strategy. Their aim is to choose the combination of models that best fits a particular context and to adopt a course of action consistent with it. Central banks could, for example, choose models that suggest a tolerance to inflation when it is caused by cost factors such as oil price increases in a depressed environment, or, instead, curb it when it is due to excess demand in a full employment context. Or, they may choose a different combination of models, implying a more mechanical application of the rule, that is, curb inflation in the same way across all contexts, without distinguishing between various causes. It is not difficult to see, in this case, that inflation targeting may easily create instability: fighting cost inflation in a depressed context is likely to make depression worse. Moreover, the central banks' behaviour may not be consistent in all contexts (i.e. a single bank may decide to apply the rule in different ways), thus generating further uncertainty in the market about their strategy.

The inflation target may be too low

Another reason why the existing monetary policy rule may fail to grant economic stability is that the central bank may set the inflation target far too low, which is likely the case of the ECB's strategy, for example (see e.g. the *Economist* 28–9–2002: 21). The problem in this case is that actual inflation is often above its official target. To combat this situation, the bank can obviously react in two ways, both of which may yield destabilizing effects. The first is to stick to its official rule and raise interest rates. It should be clear however that such passive rule-following induces an upward bias in the bank's strategy. It is always compelled to raise rates, never to reduce them, resulting in the generation of unemployment or even deflationary tendencies that sharply increase the risks of economic volatility, as shown by Japan's recent fall into the liquidity trap. The second reaction is to do nothing. However, this too is bound to exercise negative effects on stability because failing to act when missing the target undermines the bank's credibility.

Uncertainty about the potential growth rate

One further reason for possible inflation targeting failures is that monetary policy cannot be used with surgical precision. Various possible errors may undermine its functioning, such as those due to variable lags and uncertainty about the potential growth rate and the size of output gap, or the growing uncertainty common to the NE, in view of the greater variability of parameters. It should be clear that with large errors in measurement concerning the size of this gap, a monetary policy that tries hard to smoothe the cycle could easily increase output volatility (see e.g. the *Economist* 28–9–2002: 20).

Macroeconomic problems beyond inflation

Focusing on inflation as the main problem for the economy may also have undesirable effects on the stability of the NE, because it may lead the central banks to neglect other dangers, such as asset price inflation or debt and credit explosion, which derive from the existence of widespread market imperfections and other peculiar features of the weightless economy. Among the opinions which have gained influence following the end of the euphoria in financial markets one can note, for example, those summarized by the *Economist*, namely that 'low inflation does not guarantee financial stability...America's biggest bubbles developed when inflation was low' (the *Economist* 28–9–2002: 26), or that 'The Federal Reserve should have raised interest rates sooner in the late 1990s to let air out of Americas' stock market bubble and curb an unsustainable boom in investment' (the *Economist* 22–4–2002: 80) or that the current monetary policy's framework 'concentrates on inflation but places no constraint on credit growth' (the *Economist* 28–9–2002: 7).

The risk of moral hazard

In the end, paradoxically, instability may arise from the success of the central banks in achieving control of inflation and a certain stability of the global financial system. As pointed out by Banerji, there is no doubting that in recent decades 'the conduct of monetary policy has surely become skilful' (2002: 16) and more capable of influencing real events, as shown by the high reputation attained by some individuals like Alan Greenspan. However, the problem is that this has led markets to overestimate 'the inherent limits to what any central bank can do'. (ibid.) This problem is compounded in the NE by the fact that better indicators and more information, *per se*, give both policy-makers and agents a false sense of improvement and increased ability to deal with shocks and market failures. Now, there is a clear element of fragility and moral hazard involved with these mechanisms that accounts for instability in financial markets, both at the national and international level: agents are inclined to take more risks than necessary in the belief that the central bank will step in to avoid the worst.

Crowd-in effects may be weak

Let us now focus on some more specific instability problems deriving from the adoption of fiscal policy rules in the NE. First of all, a tight fiscal policy rule might lead to greater instability because the crowding-in effect may not be significant. It is true that the attempt to balance the budget may have beneficial effects on the economy because it lowers interest rates. There is no guarantee, however, that the reduced deficit may actually generate the desired fall in interest rates. As noted, for example, by Baker with regard to the experience of the Clinton administration

> [d]eficit reduction, through a combination of tax increases and spending cuts, became the main fiscal focus of the Clinton administration. The basic position was straightforward. The administration hoped that lower deficits would lead to lower interest rates, which would in turn stimulate housing construction and investment. In principle, lower interest rates should also reduce the value of the dollar, as wealth holders seek higher returns in other currencies. This would also increase net exports in the United States, as a lower dollar makes US goods cheaper...and makes imports more expensive....(However there was only)...a limited drop in interest rates...the impact on investment and housing was not as large as many had hoped.
>
> (2003: 807–89)

Moreover, if the interest rate fall is substantial, there is no guarantee that private investment will rise sufficiently to compensate for the reduced expenditure or the tax increase, especially in a depressed context. Indeed, as the recent Japanese experience shows, the liquidity trap is something more than a textbook ideal type.

Instability due to expenditure cuts

Further instability may arise when deficit reduction is achieved through cuts that hit certain kinds of expenditures having special value. In general, the implementation of strict quantitative rules may imply the neglect of qualitative issues. For example, it may lead to neglect of the fact that growth in the NE calls not so much for an absolute drop in public expenditure but a significant shift of emphasis from certain types of expenditure to others, especially to those having greater externalities and/or delivering goods that the market is unable to provide. In particular, we refer to all those expenditures encouraging R&D, venture capital and new start-ups and, therefore above all, public investment in science and technology and in the technological-age education of people.

It should be clear, however, that it would be mistaken to regard other types of expenditures not included in these priorities as being necessarily 'unproductive' and therefore to be cut. The welfare system, for example, represents not just a burden but an achievement for Western societies; it can be seen as providing an important public good, such as social cohesion, which is certainly not irrelevant for growth itself. It can be argued that generalized cuts to this sector, which have already been implemented in various countries, make up one of the factors likely to increase instability. It goes hand in hand, for example, with the increasing disparity of income and wealth observed in the last twenty years in industrialized countries, and especially in the US (see e.g. Galbraith 1997; Rifkin 2000; Krugman 2001).

Moreover, the attempt to reduce deficits through cuts may also severely undermine future growth (especially in developing countries) if it affects those expenditures broadly concerning 'culture' that play a crucial role in building intangible goods, such as social trust or social capital, and which enable the full development of a market system (see e.g. Rifkin 2000).

Instability due to tax cuts

Another reason for which tight fiscal policy rule might lead to greater instability is associated to the attempt to meet the balanced budget requirement, not through lower expenditure but through lower taxes, that is through the so-called supply-side policy. The problem is that the effects of tax cuts on the supply side and long-run growth are highly uncertain. As noted by Krugman (2001), for example, there is no evidence that the effects of the cuts carried out by Ronald Reagan in 1981 were significant. On the other hand, during the Clinton administration there was a boom on the supply side and an increase in the productive capacity, despite the fact that Clinton actually raised taxes (see e.g. Baker 2003: 806). The fact that governments quite likely tend to overestimate the positive incentive effects of tax cuts on long-run growth is not without negative consequences for macroeconomic stability. First, as shown by the Reagan experience, if the tax cuts fail to lead to strong growth, huge budget deficits quite inevitably follow, with negative consequences on interest rates and investment as well as on those public expenditures that are likely to be cut to reduce the resulting deficit. Second, the cuts tend to generate adverse income distribution effects. As shown by recent US experience, for example, lower taxes mean tax cuts, especially for higher income brackets (see e.g. Galbaith 2004).

The limits of setting rules for markets

Let us now focus on some specific instability problems deriving from the adoption of rules for markets in the NE. We place particular emphasis on two points: labour market flexibility and deregulation of financial markets.[18] First of all, efforts to increase labour market flexibility might not always have the kind of beneficial effects on the economy often hoped for. In particular, this flexibility is not a precondition for granting full employment. As pointed out by Cohen *et al.*, quite the opposite seems true. Full employment is a condition for flexibility, not the other way round:

> Nothing makes flexibility easier than full employment. If employees know they could get a roughly equivalent job quickly should their current job disappear or become intolerable, they are much more prepared to accept the risks and pursue the benefits of change. Our economy's ability to sustain full-employment rests on correct macro-economic policy by our government. Specific policies such as pension and health insurance portability (meaning that such social protections are maintained when jobs change) greatly reinforce the positive impact of a full employment environment.
>
> (2000: 66)

Although the pursuit of increased flexibility may be a positive aim, it follows that instability may occur if it is forgotten that flexibility in and of itself does not guarantee increased employment. The point is that there are other determinants of full employment. Moreover, higher labour flexibility may also generate instability, because it is usually associated with lower productivity.

Second, as with market flexibility, liberalization of capital markets at both the national and international level may not be the panacea that free market ideologues have proclaimed (see e.g. Davidson 2002: 477, 491). As already noted, markets do not work in the same way everywhere but are affected by many specific institutional and cultural factors which determine their degree of effectiveness. This accounts for the coexistence of the several models of capitalism we can observe today. Taken together, these remarks lead us to conclude that pressuring every country in the world to conform rapidly to a unique set of market rules (e.g. those which govern the US economy) may prove to have serious destabilizing consequences. As noted by Stiglitz (2002a), for example, the IMF and other international institutions were wrong in pushing for the liberalization of capital markets in developing countries in Asia and Latin America. Indeed, the dramatic crises faced by these countries (reflected in balance of payment problems, capital flights, exchange rate instability, slower growth and higher unemployment) were not simply due to crony capitalism and lack of transparent practices but to the fact that this liberalization process was too rapid.

It would also be misguided, however, to believe that liberalization or deregulation processes always work in advanced economies, for widespread market failures generally impair the working of free markets. As Stiglitz (2002a,b) emphasizes, deregulated financial markets in the NE have generated declining accounting standards and paved the way for serious fraudulent practices. Moreover, dropping the distinction between commercial and investment banking and pushing for rapid deregulation processes in sectors like energy and telecoms quite likely account for destabilizing phenomena, such as irrational exuberance on the stock market and enormous misallocation of resources.

On the limits of pragmatic policy

Having noted some of the negative implications of policy rules, we now consider the limits of the pragmatic moves carried out by governments faced with critical situations. It seems plausible to argue that pragmatism, too, has limited validity. It turns out to be more of a defence or survival strategy than an effective remedy. Pragmatism may be an effective remedy when systemic failures are relatively rare; but it loses its efficacy when these failures occur more frequently, as in the NE. Insisting on pragmatism in this context may have further negative implications for stability, because it does not force critical evaluation of the rules themselves, thus increasing the costs stemming from misguided official policy orientation. At least three types of problems undermine pragmatic moves in the NE.

First, these moves may not be of the required scope. Due to the more frequent systemic failures it involves, the NE calls for relatively wide swings in policy stance.

These swings are quite difficult to achieve when policy is constrained by rigid rules. As pointed out by Arestis and Sawyer (2003: 30–1), for example, the relaxation of tight fiscal stance that has been recently implemented in Europe is too limited to lead quickly to real recovery.

Second, pragmatic moves may be too slow. In the NE, where swift financial markets dominate slow production processes, pragmatism may fail simply because appropriate policy responses may take too long to materialize when policy-makers are constrained by policy rules which cannot be readily dismissed. Thus, for example, if policy rules focus on inflation, central banks may only realize that deflation is the real problem after a dangerous delay. Moreover, while the NE implies faster convergence to equilibrium, equilibrium can be either good or bad. Slow policy-making may condemn a country or region to stagnation for a long period of time. This has recently been the case in Japan or Europe, where the governments have recently agreed to reform the stability pact only after a long and harrowing decision-making process.

Third, pragmatic moves may lack credibility. In the NE, where expectations and confidence are more influential than in the past and where policy-makers must adopt a clear strategy to maintain credibility, pragmatism may fail because it creates tension between two alternative views (the official and the more flexible, pragmatic one) and thus causes confusion in the markets.

In the end, pragmatic moves are idiosyncratic because, almost by definition, they are based more on the intuition of a few great leaders or policy-makers than on good models providing an 'objective' understanding of why things may go wrong or why systemic failures occur. In the context of the NE, where these failures are becoming more and more serious and frequent, it is clear that this strategy is no longer enough.

Part V

The New Economy and macroeconomic theories

In Part V of this book, we carry out the last step of our strategy for deriving a plausible broad account of stability. This consists in drawing a comparison between the alternative scenarios of the NE proposed by the two basic paradigms, that is, New Classical and Keynesian macroeconomics. In addition to suggesting the specific causal mechanisms of the 'NE map' reconstructed in the previous chapters, these paradigms provide opposing global interpretations, or scenarios, in which some tendencies indicated by the map are bound to prevail over others. The aim of our comparison is to try to overcome the one-sidedness of each account of the NE. This does not imply, however, a refusal to assess their relative plausibility. We shall try to show that the claim in Part III, that there are a priori reasons for considering the Keynesian approach as more general than its neoclassical counterpart, is also justifiable in the light of their interpretation of the NE.

16 New Classical Macroeconomics and the New Economy

An overview

In this chapter, we discuss the stability of the NE in the light of a broadly defined neoclassical macro theory, by reconstructing the most likely scenario or tendencies that can be derived from it. In line with the view that this model is narrow or limited rather than simply false or wrong, we show that it does capture a certain number of intersections on our map, or matrix. In particular, it assigns a lot of weight to those mechanisms we have labelled as 'positive'. The 'negative' mechanisms giving rise to instability, while not necessarily ruled out, are regarded as being weaker or temporary phenomena in the working of a market economy.

In what follows, we shall demonstrate these claims by focusing on the analytical apparatus of NCM, which provides the most refined version of neoclassical theory. Proponents of this approach maintain that the NE is more stable than the old economy. Indeed, we can take NCM as the best representation of those interpretations that emphasize the future of the NE as a linear development of current technical potentialities.

In order to analyse this claim, it is convenient to separate it into two parts. This means, according to NCM, that the following two statements are true: (a) the NE does not violate the stability postulate. Thus, it confirms the general laws of economics, that is, those broad qualitative mechanisms that are at play in all market economies. NCM theorists, therefore, concur with those who suggest that despite the occurrence of 'disturbing' phenomena, such as network effects and path-dependence, information economics does not really change the basic laws of economics (e.g. Liebowitz and Margolis 1999); (b) the NE provides an additional contribution to stability, because it implies that markets are more efficient. In particular, the NE approaches the perfect competition model as it brings about an improvement in the functioning of the price mechanism, the reduction of the role of the state and an improved monetary policy transmission mechanism in view of the more efficient use of information allowed by ICT (see the *Economist* 1–4–2000). Indeed, the advent of ICT is one of the key factors that accounts for the rise of NCM itself. 'It is, of course, no accident that rational expectations have thrived in the age of information technology. The existence of powerful computers and software has enabled us to simulate models in which the agents are using information efficiently' (Minford 1997: 110).

The NE and the 'deep' parameters

Further understanding of the NCM interpretation of the NE can be achieved by relating the distinction just made between the two parts of its overall stability claim to yet another distinction: that between different 'levels of reality' that underlies the equilibrium approach to the analysis of economic fluctuations developed by prominent NCM theorists such as Lucas. Indeed, as Vercelli points out, it is important to realize that for Lucas

> Economic reality...can be divided into two levels: that of phenomena, characterized by erratic movements (disequilibria, in this particular sense) and by structural instability of parameters; and a deeper and more basic level (one is temped to say an 'essential' level) – characterized by the parameters of general economic equilibrium, which are considered structurally stable.
>
> (1991: 137–8)

On these grounds, the task of Lucas' equilibrium method becomes clear: it is meant 'to bring macroeconomic phenomena, with all their apparent disequilibria – erratic movements and episodes of instability – within the scope of the essential level' (ibid.: 138).

The NCM manages to achieve this result by regarding fluctuations in the levels of potential income, natural rate and inflation as agents' equilibrium response to shocks. Fluctuations are inevitable because of information errors or imperfections of some kind. The NCM approach considers the economy to be in continuous market equilibrium. However, for the sake of simplicity, we can distinguish between a 'normal' state of the economy with no shocks or errors (which we refer to as the systematic part) and another state characterized by the occurrence of some kind of shocks and errors (which we regard as the non-systematic part). This distinction proves relevant for our analysis of the NE. It can be argued that, according to NCM, the NE does not affect the systematic part so much as the non-systematic part of the economy. In particular, it reduces the role of information imperfections which makes the key assumption underlying NCM models – that of a continuous market clearing equilibrium – even more plausible.

The 'normal' working of the economy

Let us start by analysing the 'normal' working of the economy implied by NCM, and by neoclassical theory in general. The first point to note is that the macro-economic picture being focused on here (described implicitly or explicitly in many textbooks) can be seen as a simplified representation of a full-blown general equilibrium state, where the 'essential' forces of self-interest and competition bring about optimal outcomes. In other words, the so-called deep parameters (i.e. preferences, technology and endowments of productive factors) determine the system of relative prices that will make agents' plans consistent on all markets.

In order to understand the core of neoclassical macroeconomics, a convenient starting point is the following equation: $Y \rightarrow C + I$.

This reflects the view that supply (production or income, Y) creates its own demand $(C + I)$, in line with Say's Law. In other words, the equilibrium level of income is determined by the supply conditions. The standard model implies that certain economic mechanisms, such as price flexibility in all markets, guarantee that actual income always equals potential income, that is, that which can be produced by employing all available productive factors. Therefore, these supply factors pose a constraint on actual income growth because they determine potential income.

Neoclassical theorists thus place the emphasis on long-period analysis, on the determinants of capital accumulation and labour force growth. As shown by most macroeconomics textbooks, the standard production functions can be used to summarize the main factors at work (see e.g. Mankiw 2001, 2003; Blanchard 2003).

$$Y = Af(L, K, H, N)$$

where A = state of technology. This can be defined in a narrow sense as the blue-print of techniques and goods that could be produced or in a broad sense as encompassing other factors, such as the degree of market competition and 'perfection', norms and the political climate.[1] L = labour; K = physical capital; H = human capital; N = natural resources, which can also be stated in productivity terms by assuming constant returns to scale: $p = Af(1, K/L, H/L, N/L)$ where p = productivity and K, H, N, per worker.

In the flow chart below we have indicated the main features of this analytical framework, assuming a constant labour supply and lack of technological change.[2] One of the key points this diagram highlights is the interaction between production, capital and savings (S). In particular, the diagram shows that potential income is determined by supply factors. It can be calculated as the product of three factors: productivity (p), number of workers (L) and the price level (P). Productivity depends on a number of factors, such as the state of technology and the size of resources, which are taken as exogenous, that is, unaccounted for by the model. L is determined on the labour market, where the forces of demand and supply (L_d, L_s) are equilibrated by the real wage (W/P). P is determined by the money supply (M), in line with the quantity theory of money, according to which money is neutral and does not modify real variables.

Potential income is then either consumed or saved, and savings (S) is simply reinvested (I). In turn, this implies other key assumptions, such as that capital markets are efficient – with the rate of interest (r) equilibrating savings and investment – and that, in view of the scarcity of resources, increasing the production of capital goods (investment) requires growth in savings and a reduction in the production of consumer goods.

Figure 16.1 also reveals that this analytical apparatus implies a very high level of aggregation; in principle, there is no problem of singling out or specifying other components of aggregate demand beyond consumption and investment.

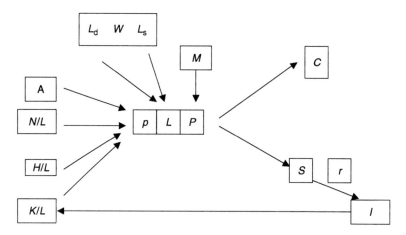

Figure 16.1 The neoclassical macro model.

The point is that relative prices (including exchange rates) will automatically generate the right amounts of it. In the case where relative prices are not enough, absolute price changes will stimulate demand through, for example, the Pigou effect or the Keynes effect. This analytical apparatus implies, therefore, that competitiveness issues, distribution effects and structural unbalances are not relevant at the macroeconomic level. On the one hand, price flexibility and competition will favour the appearance of new sectors and the disappearance of mature ones; more in general, they will rule out quantity adjustments and spillover effects. On the other hand, neoclassical analysis rests on the assumption of the representative agent, ruling out any distinction between different types of agents.

Economic fluctuations

In NCM, Figure 16.1 described in the previous section also forms the basis for studying the dynamic behaviour of the economy, both in the short run (i.e. analysis of fluctuations) and the long run (i.e. analysis of accumulation and growth). Before dealing with these issues, two aspects of the kind of 'dynamic' analysis allowed by the NCM must be clarified. First, from this perspective – where the equilibrium described by the model coincides with the 'objective' equilibrium in the real world – the exact procedure by which equilibrium is reached has no scientific importance. Any other equilibrium would only be transitory, as it would imply the existence of overlooked opportunities that would eventually be discovered and exploited by agents (see e.g. Dow 2002: 94). Second, the analysis of change is conducted on the grounds of something like standard comparative statics analysis. As we shall see in the next section, the NCM somehow departs from the latter as it adopts a different notion of equilibrium; in essence, however, the meaning is the same. If we suppose, for example, that changes in the parameters occur, the NCM model indicates the characteristics of the new equilibrium that follows. The stability assumption grants that this equilibrium will be reached and can be compared with the previous one.

However, the stability assumption and comparative statics exercises do not completely resolve the problem. There is also the issue of how to justify or explain fluctuations, the rapid swings in employment, output and prices that characterize real-world economies. It is here that the contribution of NCM proves itself more useful than standard neoclassical analysis. While the latter typically relies on *ad hoc* or disequilibrium factors to explain these movements, Lucas and others reject this view, assuming that the theory that explains the 'normal' state of the economy or long-run equilibrium growth can also be used to explain short-run fluctuations of output and employment.

There is no doubting that extending the theory in this way is a formidable task calling for considerable technical ingenuity. For example, the only way to resolve the striking contradiction between the ordinary static general equilibrium and the dynamic empirical economic cycle would be through a redefinition of the very concepts of equilibrium and business cycles themselves. This is what Lucas actually achieves in his contributions.

On the one hand, as Vercelli points out (1991: 70), Lucas is aware that the application of scientific method based on equilibrium analysis calls for the identification of elements of regularity in economic behaviour. The concept of stochastic equilibrium he proposes implies that regularity can be detected only in situations of risk when the stochastic processes analysed are stationary and agents know the systematic features of the processes. Strictly speaking, this means that the concept of equilibrium does not apply at the level of actual phenomena but at a higher level of abstraction, that is, a stationary stochastic process, of which observed phenomena constitute just one possible realization.

On the other hand, as already noted, Lucas' definition of the business cycle is much narrower than the meaning of the term in current general and technical use. To be consistent with equilibrium, it is limited to recurrent phenomena that present a high degree of quantitative regularity, such as the 'co-movements' discernible among the aggregate time series in all major countries (e.g. output movements across sectors, pro-cyclical behaviour of prices, short-run interest rates, monetary aggregates and velocity; see Vercelli 1991: 129, 132–3, 141). One major implication of this narrow definition is that NCM analysis, and in particular its key concept of rational expectations, applies only to recurrent events and to situations of risk. It should be clear that Lucas thus ends up excluding many factors from his object of analysis. He rules out complicating factors such as path-dependence (or hysteresis) and indeterminacy (multiple equilibria), in addition to 'normal' aspects that cannot be defined as invariable regularities or do not show consistent cyclical behaviour. The latter include international aspects which depend upon the degree of openness of the economy, real wages and even data on productivity and income distribution (ibid.: 134).

Let us now turn to a more detailed examination of the actual achievements of the Lucas project in bringing erratic movements and episodes of instability within the scope of the essential level of analysis. First, cyclical fluctuations are seen as equilibrium movements in the sense that, throughout the cycle, agents optimize and markets clear in line with the assumption that production is always at its natural level.[3] In particular, the business cycle appears as the optimal adaptation of a representative agent to unpredictable fluctuations in the general price level induced by erratic exogenous single shocks (see e.g. Vercelli 1991: 164–5; Louça 2003: 796–9).

Second, NCM theorists differ on the nature of the shock emphasized. For example, while Lucas stresses erratic monetary policies as the typical shock, the so-called Real Business Cycle (RBC) theory instead underlines real shocks driven by technological innovations (see e.g. Kydland and Prescott 1982, for comments see e.g. Vercelli 1991: 164–5; Blanchard 2003; Louça 2003: 796–9).

Third, a proper theory of business cycles must also demonstrate that these shocks are able to induce fluctuations, without introducing assumptions that contradict the rationality postulate. The only way to do so is to assume the existence of some kind of errors or information imperfections that generate temporary price rigidities. In NCM models, agents optimize and form rational expectations in a perfectly competitive economy working with fully flexible prices and wages; however, they do not possess perfect information. For this reason, whenever shocks occur, they are bound to misperceive phenomena. In NCM models, for example, agents often become temporarily confused between monetary and real signals, leading them to 'overreact' in such a way as to generate cyclical fluctuations (e.g. Louça 2003: 796–9).

To make this point clear, it is sufficient to assume that both kinds of shocks make working and producing more attractive in the current period than under the conditions expected to prevail in the future; thus, in both cases, employment and income rise in the current period. Insofar as the supply shock is due to technological change, if it is seen as permanent and as signalling higher productivity for the future, new investment projects are initiated to exploit the favourable contingency. These projects will increase income and employment until they are completed, spreading the effects of this shock forward into the future. They also carry within them the seeds of a future downturn, both because they increase the capital stock and because workers will be less willing to supply labour in future periods (see Vercelli 1991: 165).

We are now in a position to understand the ultimate goal of Lucas's research programme to construct macroeconomics entirely on the grounds of general equilibrium theory. Once both 'normal' states of the economy and fluctuations are accounted for on the grounds of the same theoretical apparatus, economists are in a position to predict how the economy will react to changes in economic policy. This is because the 'deep' parameters of general equilibrium are structural and, in contrast with the parameters of Keynesian models, do not vary according to changes in economic policy (ibid.).

A general view of the NE

The claim that the NE is more stable than the old economy can now be translated in terms of NCM as follows: the NE does not affect the 'normal' picture, that is, the causal links between key variables in Figure 16.1, but influences the factors that play a role in fluctuations. In particular, it implies a 'smoothing out' of business cycles and, thus, a faster convergence to the normal state. In our terms, the NE has more to do with reducing frictions, such as errors and misperceptions, than with the essential level of the deep parameters concerning the basic laws of economics deriving from the key forces of self-interest and competition.

Therefore, although it accepts that new technologies contribute to stability, the NCM does not go so far as to adopt the extreme view put forward by the 'New Economic Paradigm' in the early years of euphoria suggesting that the laws of the old economy are no longer valid and that the business cycle is simply dead (e.g. Kelly 1998). According to NCM theorists, the crux of the matter is that, while ICT certainly improves information, it does not actually make it perfect. What the NE does, instead, is to rule out (or reduce) those types of information imperfections or asymmetries that have justified the long adjustment lags for wages and prices, emphasized especially by New Keynesian economists. The NE, therefore, makes the key assumption that the system is always in market clearing equilibrium much more plausible and reduces the scope for alternative approaches to macroeconomics.

In what follows, we shall see that the number of intersections captured by the NCM stance is limited, resulting in a rather one-sided account. While it captures the most obvious 'positive' factors that make for an improvement of the efficiency of the market mechanism in the NE, it is bound to miss many of the 'negative' implications of the NE. The fact that the NCM considers business cycles to occur because of *ad hoc* errors or inessential mechanisms affecting the supply side shows that it cannot capture duality in a systematic way. While NCM manages to account for some observable cyclical co-movements on the grounds of some *ad hoc* story, its methodological and analytical apparatus actually impairs its ability to capture the truly significant sources of instability, especially those that hit the demand side.

Some of the general limits of the explanatory power of NCM are the following. First, although it does deal with the key issues captured by our five labels from Calvino, the NCM analyses them separately. Reliance on the production function implies that the factors that influence output are independent. The analysis of globalization or technological change or financial innovation is dealt with in separate models based on *ceteris paribus* assumptions; if, on the other hand, some links between these factors are emphasized, the analysis does not escape the limits of technological determinism. Moreover, economic cycles, as we have seen, are considered to be the product of a single monetary policy or technology shock. In this way, however, the NCM fails to appreciate the sources of endogenous instability deriving from the interplay of a number of factors.

Second, despite making clear reference to institutions, the NCM places the emphasis on deep parameters, implying the primacy of the market over institutions; in methodological terms, this means that no explanation is acceptable unless all the relevant factors (including institutions) are accounted for in terms of first principles. However, this suggests that NCM cannot fully capture the systematic influence exercised by institutions on market outcomes and, thus, is bound to neglect some sources of instability related to this aspect.

Third, notwithstanding its clear reference to business cycles, their definition in terms of a few co-movements among aggregates, together with reliance on the representative agent device, inevitably leads NCM to overlook some dimensions of structural changes that are also significant for stability. Finally, in its attempt to encompass the dimension of time in the analysis, NCM's emphasis on recurrent events impairs its ability to grasp the acceleration of certain trends, one of the main sources of instability in the NE.

17 New Classical Macroeconomics and the key features of the New Economy

We shall now seek to draw more specific conclusions about the NCM interpretation of the NE by focusing on the various labels set out in previous chapters. It is important to note that for each of these, we shall not simply consider the destabilizing factors as being irrelevant, as we should in principle, because of the stability assumption made by NCM. Leaving this assumption aside (or trying to see behind it), it is interesting to consider in more explicit terms why NCM does not actually consider these factors as instability problems. Two different types of answers can be provided here. The first (of a methodological kind) is that NCM models simply cannot capture these factors. The second (more analytical) is that the logic of NCM suggests clear reasons for which these negative factors cannot prevail over the positive ones. What we can learn from this type of analysis is that the assumption of stability is just shorthand for a more complex analysis that is often, simply, taken for granted.

Multiplicity

In what follows, we shall try to evaluate the stability claims concerning the effects of globalization in the age of ICT in the light of NCM's basic theoretical framework. We will try to show why, for NCM, some effects are bound to prevail over others. NCM models certainly account for the positive effects on the stability of the world economy induced by globalization.

First of all, the increasing international competition and the higher degree of unification of markets brought about by globalization are factors fostering productivity, which are captured by the term A in the production function previously described.

Second, the NCM also naturally captures the improvement in the efficiency of markets and the functioning of the price mechanism due to the diffusion of ICT and the liberalization of international trade and investment. For example, it reduces information errors and trade barriers that in real-world economies impair the tendency to establish standard neoclassical results, such as the law of one price and the purchasing power parity theory. This effect is further strengthened by the discipline imposed by global financial markets.

Third, NCM also accounts for the positive effects on the natural unemployment rate subsequent to the reduction of monopoly power and mark-ups and the weakening power of trade unions induced by greater competition and de-location of production. The point is that the natural rate is not a fixed magnitude but can change through time.

Now let us turn to the analysis of what we have described as potentially negative or destabilizing factors in our discussion of multiplicity. We shall see that, in terms of the NCM perspective, these factors do not actually generate instability, either because NCM models cannot capture them, and/or because there are reasons for which these negative factors cannot prevail over the positive ones.

The first factor is the growing interdependence of individuals in the NE. This can be seen in phenomena such as agents' reliance on a narrow number of general indicators and herd behaviour or shared errors that give rise to waves of optimism and pessimism on financial markets. It is not difficult to see why these phenomena are ruled out by NCM. Indeed, they are quite simply inconsistent with NCM models, which are based on atomistic preferences and the representative agent device. Strictly speaking, although this device implies homogeneity of expectations (i.e. that all agents' expectations are alike), in line with this effect of globalization, atomism rules out the possibility that agents influence each other. This is not all, however. The NCM claim that these phenomena do not represent a source of instability also follows from the ultimate meaning of the rational expectations hypothesis, according to which, while such forms of behaviour and errors can well occur, they are not systematic, in view of the fact that people's expectations are influenced by market fundamentals as summarized in the 'true model' of the economy.

The second negative factor is the growing distance between 'winners' and 'losers' both within individual countries (e.g. the expansion of firms into new sectors and the decline of others) and in the world economy (e.g. the gap between rich and poor countries). More in general, this can also be seen in the fragmentation of structural conditions induced by globalization. Strictly speaking, in principle, in addition to competitiveness issues, NCM cannot capture composition and cumulative effects either, because of its aggregative framework and reliance on representative agent models. Moreover, at the analytical level, it relies on theories of international trade, such as Ricardo's comparative advantage principle, according to which these outcomes are not supposed to happen, as specialization should work to the benefit of all (Storper 2000: 44; Kaplinsky 2001: 50; Davidson 2002: 478–9)

However, NCM has recently made an effort to rationalize empirical findings, such as the lack of convergence between rich and poor countries (Lucas 2002; Mankiw 2003: 221), which call into question these principles and, in particular, seem to undermine old neoclassical growth theory, according to which, for example, capital should flow to underdeveloped countries where, in principle, there is higher marginal productivity of capital. As emphasized by endogenous growth theory, also developed by NCM theorists such as Lucas and Barro, it is possible to account for these 'anomalous' findings by adopting a broader concept of capital than the standard one (see e.g. Fine 2003; Mankiw 2003: 222). What proves crucial in the NE is not just physical capital, but also human capital, public expenditure and knowledge. In particular, these latter three should be taken as a type of capital good, one which exhibits increasing returns because of the increasing pace of scientific and technological innovation. When these extensions are considered, the marginal productivity of capital in poor countries does not result high, due to a lack of qualified labour force and inefficient government, while in rich countries it is not low even if capital is abundant.

On the grounds of this reconciliation between empirical evidence and neoclassical theory, one can see why negative phenomena, such as the lack of convergence, do not actually represent a source of instability for NCM. Its basic argument should be that in the aggregate, either at the national or the world economy level, they do not really matter, because full employment is the rule granted by flexible relative prices. Indeed, once the broader concept of capital is considered, and the necessary institutional adjustments made (such as those defying corruption or inefficiencies in the public sector), it is still the price system that provides the proper incentives for resource allocation. The structure of market prices will automatically reflect any kind of heterogeneity (including that in capital endowments among countries) and will stimulate those adjustments capable of benefiting all participants to trade.

The third negative factor is that globalization also increases individual countries' exposure to various kinds of external shocks (financial and/or real, with possible interactions). From the methodological point of view, NCM models are unlikely to capture this effect because of atomism and the *ceteris paribus* clause, according to which phenomena are to be dealt with separately. Thus, for example, globalization, technological change and financial innovation should not be studied as interdependent phenomena. On the other hand, NCM theorists are also bound to stress that faster transmission of shocks is not a real problem since ICT and greater competition imply more efficient markets and flexible prices which reduce the scope for quantity adjustments.

The fourth negative factor is the continual existence in the NE of different types of national systems, each with its own distinct pattern of corporate governance, labour relations and social welfare, as well as a peculiar cultural background. In principle, there is no doubting that NCM models are inconsistent with this plurality of models. The point is that, while allowing for the existence of institutions, these models rule out any direct influence on market outcomes and deep parameters. The latter remain the primary explanatory factors in terms of which all relevant phenomena should be accounted. Moreover, NCM's neglect of institutional detail is also justified by its narrow search for universal laws of business cycles, such as the identification of co-movements among aggregates that are similar in all developed countries.

The fifth negative factor is the problem of governance of the world economy, which the international community seeks to resolve not by relying on spontaneous cooperation and agreed upon rules but by allowing the US to play a predominant role on the world scene. Once again, reliance on the deep parameters explains why NCM cannot accommodate the role of power as a mechanism capable of influencing market outcomes or even of leading to the 'creation' of markets, as occurred in past decades with globalization. Moreover, the *ceteris paribus* clause involving separate analysis of various factors, such as technology change and financial markets, globalization and policies, impairs the full-blown analysis of the US case. At the analytical level, this claim is also justified by the fact that NCM favours universal, flexible exchange rates as a solution to governance problems, and deals with the possibility of either real or financial crises (such as that potentially hitting the US) as due to single external shocks, rather than to interdependent internal factors.

Rapidity

Let us now assess NCM's claims concerning the effects of technological change on stability. NCM certainly accounts for all the improvements ICT brings about in the supply side of the economy. First, it captures the increase in the rate of productivity growth and the virtuous cycle it has triggered, especially in the US economy. As already noted, the RBC theory – which explains both long-run equilibrium growth and short-run fluctuations of output and employment in terms of standard neoclassical theory – emphasizes that a favourable technology shock, like ICT, increases the current productivity of both labour and capital, which leads to an increase in production, lower unemployment and prices, and an increase in consumer welfare.

Second, NCM also captures the fact that in the NE a wider share of the rise in productivity is accounted for by technological progress. Due to its reliance on production functions, it can perform growth accounting exercises to measure it. Third, NCM naturally emphasizes the faster transmission of information and greater rapidity of decisions, favoured by the new technology, which make all markets more flexible and efficient and allow the economy to cope with shocks more effectively. In terms of our discussion above, for NCM, ICT reduces the friction, or 'noise', and pushes the economy closer, or faster, to its 'normal' working described in Figure 16.1. One major example is the labour market, where, thanks to deregulation and the decline of unionization favoured by ICT, wages have become more market-determined phenomena, wage differentials appear to reflect marginal productivity theory and lower actual unemployment can be interpreted as a permanent reduction in the natural rate of unemployment. Another example concerns the goods market, where ICT allows for better inventory control that will diminish the inventory-driven component of business cycles.

Fourth, the NCM manages to consider the positive feedback that occurs in the NE thanks to the smooth behaviour of demand, that is, the fact that ICT has drastically lowered the cost of items such as computers and cell telephones and made them available to the general public, with obvious welfare gains and further stimulus to production. Not only does NCM emphasize relative price flexibility to adjust demand and supply in particular sectors, it also accepts, as do most macroeconomists, a broader inverse relation between aggregate demand and the price level, thanks to the working of various mechanisms, such as the real-balance effect and Keynes's effect. Moreover, the NCM also accounts for another aspect of a well-behaved demand side, that is, the reduced volatility of aggregate consumption. Its models may regard this effect as a sign that ICT improves the process of formation of expectations, including consumers' ability to estimate permanent income and make choices in an intertemporal perspective.

We may now turn to the analysis of what we have described as potentially negative or destabilizing factors in our discussion of rapidity. Once again, we shall see that, in terms of the perspective of NCM, these factors do not actually generate instability, either because they cannot be captured by NCM models, and/or because there are reasons why these negative factors cannot prevail over the positive ones.

The first negative outcome of the recent accelerating trend in technology is that it tends to generate both 'losers and winners'. The process of creative destruction may, for example, generate technological unemployment. Now it is clear that this effect is not captured by the NCM, in view of its aggregative framework and reliance on the device of representative agents, which rules out composition effects. In more analytical terms, the NCM is also bound to play down this effect on the grounds that the NE gives rise to a swifter adjustment of markets, which justifies the key assumption of continuous market clearing.

Second, the NCM also fails to capture the tendency towards market concentration and even the formation of monopolies in certain high-tech industries due to increasing returns to scale, low marginal costs and externality or network effects. The point is that NCM relies on the assumption of perfect competition. It must be noted, however, that for NCM theorists these phenomena do not pose serious instability problems, especially if one interprets competition in dynamic terms, that is, as a process. From this perspective, for example, monopolistic positions are only transitory, because rapid technological change tends to reduce the power of existing firms by allowing the introduction of new technologies.

Third, it is clearly difficult for NCM to cope with another important aspect of NE, that is, the requirement of a growing synchronization or coordination between firms due to the nature of contemporary knowledge (e.g. the fact that intellectual capital is rarely the property of only one firm). Once again, NCM's reliance on an aggregative framework, based on a representative firm, rules out the analysis of firms' interrelations at the industry or inter-industry levels. At the analytical level, this aspect certainly represents a further element of departure from the neoclassical model in which cooperation is seen as incompatible with competition and thus as a source of inefficiency. However, one possible defence for the position of the NCM is that this does not really matter at the aggregate level where competition is, by far, the most significant and systematic force that is actually made stronger by the NE.

A fourth negative factor that NCM fails to detect is the faster obsolescence of knowledge because of faster technological change and the time-shrinking nature of ICT. This phenomenon may generate anomalies in investors' behaviour, causing difficulties in expectations formation concerning future returns, herd behaviour, over-investment and interest inelasticity, which contrast with the presumed stability of deep parameters. For NCM, this aspect of rapidity is not an actual source of instability because it is likely to stimulate imitation and competition between investors and thus generate the appropriate amount of investment.

There are a number of other effects of rapidity that NCM cannot capture, such as greater product differentiation and greater heterogeneity in structural conditions and agents' behaviour. In particular, the emphasis on consumer confidence, the distinction between different types of consumers' lifestyles, income brackets and the consideration of growing wage differentials are overlooked by NCM models because of their emphasis on deep parameters and aggregate structure, all of which imply the systematic neglect of composition effects. At the analytical level, NCM theorists do not regard these factors as creating dangers for stability on the demand side. In a sense, phenomena such as these are the evidence that markets work and provide the right incentive for agents to spend their income (e.g. product differentiation increases consumers' choice) or produce their effort (growing wage differentials reflect the difference between skilled and less-skilled workers). Now, so long as markets work, and prices are flexible, these factors, at the most, can only generate sectoral problems rather than aggregate demand failures.

Lightness

Let us now assess the claims of NCM concerning the effects of lightness on stability. There is no doubting that NCM accounts for the improvements that this brings about in the economy. First, it captures the extension of the market logic to new non-material goods going beyond standard manufacturing. NCM, like all macroeconomic theories, does not deal with these factors explicitly, but lumps them together in aggregates such as national income, which appear in the Figure 16.1 earlier. The fact that this extension of the market improves stability – for example, by offsetting the reduction of employment caused by the shrinking of the 'old', narrowly defined, industrial sector – is implicitly accounted for by the NCM through its emphasis on the smooth working of the system of relative prices, which is the mechanism that allows this positive outcome. New goods, for example, typically command higher relative prices (with respect to old goods) that stimulate capital inflows and the expansion of production into new sectors.

NCM captures this extension of the market logic in more explicit terms at the input level, that is, by broadening the definition of investment and capital beyond tangible assets, as shown, for example, by the human capital label, H, in the production function in the Figure 16.1. Moreover, this broader perspective underlies the endogenous growth models, reflecting the growing awareness that growth crucially depends on such factors as knowledge and investment in human capital, R&D and public infrastructure (see e.g. Lucas 1989; Barro 1990). In particular, this extension of the concept of capital to public investment in R&D is motivated by the recognition that the incentive for private investment in this type of capital may be weak (the marginal productivity of capital may be low and/or decreasing).

This is because it appears to be non-competitive (many producers can use the same idea simultaneously and the returns may be hard to appropriate due to potential production of spillovers) (see e.g. Stiroh 2000: 43–4).

Second, NCM manages to consider the faster development of financial markets in the NE favoured by ICT and institutional changes such as deregulation. It is one of the factors strengthening the causal links between variables represented in Figure 16.1. Following the general equilibrium perspective underlying their approach, NCM theorists hold that the creation of more efficient, liquid and sophisticated financial markets (e.g. futures and contingencies markets) – allowed by the new technologies and lower transaction costs – imply a reduction of potential market imperfections. For example, they help agents hedging against risk, reduce the impact of shocks, and rule out those types of market imperfections, such as liquidity constraints or credit rationing which, in the view of New Keynesians, undermine the inter-temporal plans of consumers and investors. Indeed, the NE offers greater opportunities for consumers to smooth out their spending over time, in the face of variations of income, in line with the Fisherian theories of consumption, such as the Life Cycle or the Permanent Income Hypothesis, which are emphasized in NCM literature.

Let us focus, now, on what we consider the 'negative' factors of lightness. In terms of NCM, however, these factors do not actually generate instability, either because its models cannot capture them, and/or because they are held in check by key mechanisms at play in a market economy. The first negative product of lightness is the greater significance of the quality dimension of goods in the NE which, because of various problems of pricing, non-competitive market structure, externality and information imperfections (all of which are emphasized by the New Keynesians), may impair the working of markets. Now clearly the NCM cannot capture this aspect, as it relies on the perfect competition assumption implying, among other things, homogeneous goods and perfect information about their characteristics. Moreover, its reliance on representative agent models rules out the consideration of such factors as asymmetric information or trust issues. However, it can be argued that, from the perspective of NCM, the heterogeneity of goods does not matter so much at the aggregate level so long as relative prices – which for NCM theorists constitute the best, although not perfect, signal at agents' disposal to make choices – are set free to equilibrate markets. In principle the NE, by improving information, should reduce rather than worsen the impact of these problems.

Second, the NCM fails to capture some negative aspects of deregulation and financial innovation, such as sectoral imbalances (e.g. households and firms assuming too much debt, over-investment, declining accounting standards and excessive diffusion of stock options), all of which may negatively hit the demand side (e.g. through income distribution effects). Once again, this is due to NCM's reliance on representative agent models, impairing the analysis of sectoral problems. However, the fact that agents assume more debt is also true for NCM and is not necessarily a sign of instability. It is a sign, instead, that the NE rules out credit rationing or liquidity constraints, which are instead emphasized by the

New Keynesians. On the other hand, even if it is true that phenomena such as firms going bust, scandals due to excessive debt and over-optimism occur in the NE, NCM theorists are bound to stress that they are not endogenous instability problems generated by some basic flaws of the market mechanism. In particular, they are not considered due to deregulation, *per se*, or to errors of the private sector but as induced mainly by erratic monetary policy moves which have mis-led the market by injecting too much money in the economy or by failing to keep market interest rate in line with the natural rate. This means that the unwinding of these imbalances is a long and painful process that the market, itself, is able to accomplish.

Third, the NCM finds it difficult to cope with the erratic behaviour of finan-cial markets that seem to be dominated by speculation or 'irrational exuberance' and that give rise to bubbles, implying a growing distance of actual values from presumed 'correct' values or 'fundamentals' (i.e. those based on the present value of expected dividends). There is no doubting that NCM theorists lack the tools to capture irrational or conventional behaviour, given their emphasis on agents' strong rationality. It is also true, however, that they do not consider financial markets as a true font of instability. On the contrary, financial markets are regarded as quite efficient markets. The stock market, for example, acts as a trust-worthy barometer of the economy and is ultimately capable of translating the productivity of capital into rising equity prices. Thus, from the perspective of the so-called efficient market model, the stock market boom that characterized the NE was not a bubble at all, but a reflection of changes in fundamentals. As pointed out, for instance, by Hall (2000), the boom was due to the increased importance of intangible capital in the information economy. Corporate invest-ment and, hence, profits had been substantially underestimated in the 1990s because the acquisition of intangible capital had not been measured.[1] In other words, according to NCM, the existence of new forms of capital is not a source of valuation problems to the stock market. Rather, ICT is seen as increasing the stability and efficiency of this market by allowing an improvement in information processing that helps agents to carry out arbitrage, which brings prices of volatile individual securities, with highly uncertain fundamental values, close to funda-mentals. From this perspective, even the increased volatility of financial markets in recent times is not a sign of inefficiency. It reflects, instead, the intensified role of forward-looking behaviour and expectations that dominate financial markets in the NE, making them more reactive to any change in information about those variables, such as dividends and interest rates, upon which the fundamental values of share prices depend.

Precision

Let us now assess the claims made by the NCM about the effects of precision on stability, which reflect the improvements that precision brings about in the economy. First, the NCM has much to contribute to the search for greater quantitative infor-mation about events. It can be argued that its models provide a conceptualization of economic phenomena that in some way tends to further understanding and allow improvement in measurement and indicators. One instance is the broadening of the definition of investment and capital beyond tangible assets, leading to advances in understanding and measuring productivity growth. Another instance is the introduction of rational expectations theory in macroeconomics, which has helped economists to understand the role of expectations and devise better theories and indicators concerning agents' forward-looking behaviour.

Second, the NCM has contributed significantly to the increasing mathematization of economics. This has contributed especially to the clarification of the nature and role of economic models. As Lucas points out, for NCM, theories are not hypotheses about the real world, but tools. Theorists should not aim at providing 'realistic' or descriptive models, but should devise an explicit set of instructions for building imitation economies, artificial systems that replicate how the real economic system reacts to a certain combination of shocks. Indeed, 'progress in economic thinking means getting better and better abstract, analogue models not better verbal observations about the world' (Lucas 1981: 276; see also Vercelli 1991: 141; Dow 2002: 98). It is clear that this goal can only be achieved by using ever more sophisticated techniques. This does not mean, however, that NCM economic models are descriptively false. At the root of all theorizing in macroeconomics, as in general equilibrium theory, one can always find the deep parameters that are meant to capture the essence of economic behaviour. In the eyes of theorists like Lucas, this makes the various analytical formulations of NCM the expression of a unique, 'true' model of the economy that contributes to stability by providing an objective anchor to agents' expectations.

Third, one of the aims of NCM is clearly that of improving forecasting techniques to assist in decision-making and policy intervention. Strictly speaking, widespread predictive failures have led many econometricians to change their views concerning the best way to produce predictions, or even to seriously question the ability of econometrics to produce precise quantitative laws, despite increasing computing power and the development of vastly more sophisticated statistical techniques. Nonetheless, as Backhouse (1997: 180–1) points out, many do not regard the failure of predictions as necessarily being a problem for standard theory. There are those, such as Rosenberg, who suggest that neoclassical theory is not an empirical science; on the contrary, its approach to modelling individual behaviour proves to be inconsistent with its desire to improve predictive power. While neoclassicals are committed to modelling behaviour in terms of expectations and preferences, these cannot be identified in isolation of other expectations and preferences. They are immeasurable. Notwithstanding these observations, however, neoclassical theory is still relevant, and is justified by its normative role (it shows that the market mechanism produces order, which is preferable to central planning) (see also Backhouse 1997: 107–8).

Still, in our view, these remarks are not enough to contradict the claim that the NCM project intrinsically strives toward predictive power. This is the implication of the well-known 'Lucas' critique'. In particular, it is because his equilibrium models rely on the deep parameters that Lucas hopes they can help achieve better predictive performance concerning the impact of alternative economic policies with respect to their Keynesian 'disequilibrium' counterparts. He notes, for example, that 'an equilibrium model is, by definition, constructed so as to predict how agents with stable tastes and technology will choose to respond to a new situation', while 'any disequilibrium model...will be of no use in predicting the consequences of non-trivial policy changes' (Lucas 1981: 220–1).

We now turn to analysis of the 'negative' factors of precision. Once again, we conclude that NCM does not consider these factors among the sources of instability. This is either because its models cannot capture them, and/or because there are mechanisms in the market economy that ensure they cannot prevail over the 'positive' ones.

First of all, the NCM cannot capture the fact that the search for greater quantitative information may exercise a negative influence on agents' behaviour. The assumption of stable parameters impairs consideration of changes in agents' qualitative behaviour, in particular because of their reliance on 'management by numbers', implying excessive risk aversion, focus on short-run profitability and bias against introducing innovative products. However, for NCM, this aspect of complexity may be kept at bay if one considers that the relevant information needed for agents to act in a decentralized market economy is still relatively limited and can be summarized by prices. The fact that the new technologies allow agents to be more informed about prices is not a drawback but an advantage that helps reduce the information imperfections and asymmetries that account for economic fluctuations.

Second, NCM also risks generating a distorted picture of the economy, derived from the use of conventional methods to analyse key NE phenomena that still defy proper measurement (e.g. intangibles). Indeed, the familiar tools NCM relies upon, such as aggregate production functions, actually imply that these factors can be properly measured.[2] For theorists like Lucas, however, this representation problem does not exist and is not a threat to stability. Economic models must be abstract and may not have precise empirical counterparts. What matters is that they are able to mimic the behaviour of real-world systems. The key prerequisite for doing so is their internal consistency; namely, they must rely on the deep parameters only and do without the whole range of 'disequilibrium' factors.

Third, the NCM is unable to cope with the widening gap between theoretical and empirical progress, or in other words, the fact that theoretical progress alone may be misleading for agents and generate their unjustified overconfidence in the practical implications of theory. Clearly, the NCM is one of the main elements responsible for this rising gap. NCM models are undoubtedly more refined than the macroeconomic models of a few decades ago, but it is not so clear that they have actually achieved better explanatory or predictive performance. Once again, for Lucas and other NCM theorists, this is a moot point. The fact that progress has been made in modelling the behaviour of economic systems (in particular, the business cycles) so that economists have at their disposal a more refined version of the true model of the economy also guarantees empirical progress, because agents' expectations are ultimately based upon such a model.

In the end, NCM cannot address instability problems related to the lack of satisfactory predictive performances of its models stemming from cumulative uncertainty in the NE. NCM cannot capture this cumulative uncertainty because its equilibrium method applies only to stationary stochastic processes, or stable probability distributions (implying that uncertainties year by year are offsetting), and deals with economic change by performing exercises of stochastic comparative statics, based on comparison of the properties of different stationary stochastic processes. While perceiving the problem, NCM theorists generally remain committed to their fundamental approach. They still seem unwilling to relinquish any of their key assumptions in order to get a better statistical fit; rather, they seek to intervene on the testing side by softening econometric methods, as shown by the emphasis on calibration.

For NCM, however, this indeterminacy problem does not actually create instability. The point is that there is no genuine competition among models in trying to win the prediction contest. In fact, there really is no contest, because NCM models are the 'only game in town', as they provide the best, true understanding of the systematic part of the economic process. Predictive failures may be due to some noise or stochastic disturbance that is left unaccounted for by such models, or caused, also, by the fact that agents may not be fully aware of this superiority. There is nothing wrong with this lag as agents normally take some time to single out the best products in any market because of search costs, for example, or information problems. Here, however, the NE makes a positive contribution in speeding up, or facilitating, this learning process.

Visibility: general remarks

Now we shall turn to the claims of NCM concerning the effects of visibility on stability. In general, NCM captures the tendency of governments to stick to precise policy rules in order to grant macroeconomic stability. Strictly speaking, this policy stance is not just an implication of the NCM interpretation of the NE. It follows, instead, from the belief that the system is always in equilibrium, and that income is always at its potential or natural level. This amounts to taking general equilibrium theory as an accurate description of actual economic systems and drawing from it normative conclusions concerning the most desirable type of policies to implement in various real-world contexts (see e.g. Hahn 1982). From the outset, this standpoint sets clear limitations as to what policy can achieve, and gives rise to precise policy rules.

There is reason to believe, however, that NCM considers the policy rules in the NE to be even more stringent. As already noted, one key point of its interpretation is that the NE, while improving information, does not make it perfect; it cannot eliminate a certain degree of uncertainty concerning the true functioning of the economy, as shown by the persistent measurement problems of key concepts, such as the output gap and the Phillips Curve. In particular, because of its growing complexity, the NE cannot reduce the chronic indeterminacy of the effects of policies. In this context, NCM theorists argue, traditional Keynesian policies should not be pursued at all, as they could make things worse and increase uncertainty. In other words, the most general policy conclusion they draw is that the NE further reduces government scope for stabilizing the economy through active or discretionary demand policies, (see e.g. Blanchard 2003: 514–25).

Strictly speaking, NCM held that this scope was very limited even before the NE. For example, at the end of the 1960s, the original Phillips Curve allowing the trade-off between wage increases and unemployment rate started to be called into question by monetarists, who stressed the tendency of the economy to go back to full employment equilibrium pushed by inflationary expectations. The introduction of rational expectations made this kind of equilibrium an even more important attractor with obvious policy implications. Indeed, if the economy is always in equilibrium, with actual income always at its potential or natural level, the short-run trade-off between wage increases and unemployment rate quite simply disappears, and no improvement can be obtained by implementing a systematic stabilization policy. In principle, if agents' expectations are rational, only unanticipated changes in this policy might have some effects. However, even these limited effects may, to some extent, vanish in the NE as this improves agents' ability to anticipate the effects of policy changes. According to the NCM theorists, this occurs not only because agents are more capable of processing information thanks to ICT, but also because they operate in a context dominated by forward-looking financial markets that are increasingly concerned with the sustainability of stabilization policies. They may react badly, for example, if they imply excessive deficits or debt (see e.g. Winkler 2004).

More specific policy implications can be derived from consideration of the fluctuations in the natural levels of income induced by shocks. It can be argued that, insofar as the business cycle is induced by real shocks as implied by the RBC model, the best response is to leave the market process free to accomplish its purging role. A policy designed to stabilize the economy would be undesirable, in that it would induce inefficiencies. Indeed, as noted by Winkler (2004), smoothing of the cycle could be detrimental to innovation and growth, as it contributes to delaying the necessary structural adjustments or to the prolonging of structural macro imbalances.

On the contrary, if the business cycle, or any malfunction of the market in general, is induced by monetary shocks giving rise to inflation, efficiency gains are possible through policies that stabilize the money supply. As Lucas puts it: 'Insofar as fluctuations are induced by gratuitous monetary instability, serving no social purpose, then increased monetary stability promises to reduce aggregate, real variability and increase welfare' (1981: 234).

Monetary policy

Let us now turn to more specific types of policies that are accounted for by NCM. First of all, NCM is, at least partly, consistent with the inflation targeting rule (ITR). Strictly speaking, ITR involves dropping several tenets of monetarism and the quantity theory of money. In particular, as it focuses on the end of the causal chain, that is, inflation, rather than the beginning, that is, money, ITR implies that the quantity of money plays no unique causal role in the analysis of inflation. It is no longer exogenous but endogenous; it adjusts to the price level as determined by other factors. As shown, for example, by the strategy followed by the European Central Bank (ECB),[3] for ITR, information concerning cost factors (such as oil prices and wage settlements or productivity) matter in the assessment of inflationary tendencies. Moreover, ITR allows discretion in reaction to changed economic conditions. In contrast with Friedman's k-percent regime, where the central bank has no hand in manipulating interest rates, according to ITR, the ECB sets interest rates and may, thus, even engage in the fine-tuning of aggregate demand.

However, NCM is consistent with ITR for other reasons. One reason is that it involves the primacy of monetary policy as a key tool with which to pursue macroeconomic stabilization in view of its potential advantages in terms of accountability and transparency. Another reason is that ITR supports the view that price stability is conducive to growth and employment; indeed as Winkler notes,

> maintaining price stability is an essential precondition for efficient allocation of resources, sustainable growth and employment creation in the longer run. In firmly pursuing price stability with a medium-term perspective, monetary policy, at the same time, makes its best contribution to the stabilisation of output and employment in the shorter run.
>
> (2004: 178)

In particular, price stability over the medium term can contribute to cyclical output smoothing through stabilization of expectations, confidence and promotion of investment, via stable long-run interest rates. In the end, so long as ITR rests on an explicit model of the economy and provides an anchor to market price expectations, NCM theorists regard it as being consistent with their emphasis on rational expectations and the true model of the economy.

Second, NCM also captures, to some extent, pragmatic monetary policy, that is, the fact that central banks do not always insist on their official targets (especially when the system is hit by supply shocks) and adopt a more flexible monetary policy, which essentially amounts to taking not just inflation, but also growth, into account (see e.g. the *Economist* 28–9–2002). This stance is obviously inconsistent with NCM, which rules out discretionary policy. Indeed, if governments accept precise rules in theory but fail to stick to them in practice, markets will be misled and some forms of Keynesian discretion will be restored. This will lead to many negative consequences, such as the loss of credibility, that NCM regards as the essential ingredient for the success of policies in line with rational expectations and Lucas' critique. This negative assessment is bound to become stronger in the NE, as the NE implies faster convergence to equilibrium.

However, one can still suggest that the inconsistency between pragmatism and NCM is not absolute, but only a question of degree. Strictly speaking, what really counts in the end for the NCM is that, for example, even the rather flexible and pragmatic FED does rely on theoretical principles of a monetarist kind, such as the NAIRU, even if it does not always stick to it in practice. Keynesian principles only appear in disguise, that is, not as 'high' theory but as a kind of common sense procedure for guiding everyday conduct within the grand strategy set by NCM. In other words, the NCM wins the theoretical battle and remains the only game in town, even despite temporary lapses, which can always be accommodated as being due to the unavoidable gap between theory and monetary policy.

Fiscal and structural policy

NCM accounts for the tight fiscal policy rules adopted by many governments in the NE. The key point that underlies NCM is that there is no trade-off between stability (i.e. balanced budgets) and growth. Indeed a credible commitment to sound public finance is a prerequisite for both successful cyclical stabilization and longer-term growth, as it promotes confidence and investment.

In the NCM literature, many arguments have been made for adopting a framework for sound and sustainable public finance, such as the need to limit risk premia, avoid passing tax burden on to future generations, and the time inconsistency problem that could arise if a single authority pursues multiple objectives in a discretionary manner. Not all of these arguments are new nor have they been put forward by NCM alone. Typical of NCM, however, is that it considers the main problem not to be the deficit *per se*, but government spending. As noted by Baker, for leading NCM theorists, such as 'Robert Barro and Martin Feldstein... the deficit does not directly crowd out investment to any significant extent; the more serious concern is that the actual commitment of resources in the form of government spending will crowd out investment.' (2003: 807). This claim can be justified on the grounds of the so-called Ricardian equivalence view, according to which when the government's budget constraint is taken into account, neither deficit nor debt have effects on economic activity, and the method of government financing of public expenditure is neutral. In particular, households recognize deficits as being the equivalent of future taxes. When they see higher deficits, households discount future taxes and save more in the current period. In this way, deficit does not lead to interest rate increases or harm capital accumulation.

Of course, this does not mean that deficit reduction is irrelevant. For the NCM, it is much preferable that it occurs through spending cuts than through tax increases. As Baker emphasizes, whereas NCM economists 'would have been satisfied to see large-scale deficit reduction if it took the form of cuts in spending, they viewed deficit reduction based on tax increases as having little economic merit' (ibid.). This claim is justified by the fact that higher taxes may distort economic incentives and may, therefore, alter the behaviour underlying the determinants of growth, such as investment, saving, labour supply and innovation. Indeed, tax increases 'would discourage work and saving, promote tax evasion and, therefore, lead to little net increase in revenue' (ibid.).

Moreover, NCM can also accommodate some forms of pragmatic fiscal policy. While, in principle, by ruling out discretionary moves, NCM may still justify the occurrence of deficits due to a sudden increase in public expenditure in exceptional circumstances; one example is when governments face war or terrorist attacks, as in the recent experience of the US.

In the end, NCM also accounts for structural policies aimed at the definition of rules designed to improve the market mechanism and the development of new technologies. The NCM favours policies that assure competitive markets and boost productivity growth, such as deregulation, privatization and policies aimed at setting rules of the game for competitors. This policy stance clearly follows from its reliance on the standard general equilibrium model and the assumption of perfect markets as the norm for assessing real-world markets. In this view, structural reforms are necessary in order to favour the positive impact of the NE on the working of markets, reduce the imperfections or rigidities which may, for example, generate too high a level of the natural rate of unemployment, or slow down the adjustment to shocks.

The predominant free-market orientation of NCM does not imply a complete neglect of a more active role for governments in the economy than is implied by mere regulatory policy. As already noted, the endogenous growth models, for example, accommodate the role played by certain forms of public expenditure, such as military high-tech and research in large infrastructures and universities, that have positive externalities.

NCM and instability due to visibility

We can turn now to the analysis of the 'negative' factors of visibility. Once again, we will see that, for NCM, these factors do not actually generate instability, because either its models cannot capture them or because there are market mechanisms that ensure that they cannot prevail over the 'positive' ones.

First, NCM cannot accommodate the fact that in order to face uncertainty due to sectoral crises and global competition national governments or international organizations adopt or advocate protectionist measures: active industrial policies to protect national industries, favour the rise of new sectors, or simply save unprofitable firms from bankruptcy. Clearly, this is explained by the fact that NCM relies on an aggregative framework and a representative firm device, both of which imply the neglect of competitiveness issues. At the analytical level, NCM does not consider the lack of industrial policy to be destabilizing; on the contrary, as the markets alone can perform the required adjustments, these policies represent undue interference in the delicate resource allocation mechanisms, potentially weakening private entrepreneurship and, in the end, generating undesired outcomes such as moral hazard.

Second, the NCM cannot capture the instability that may derive from indeterminacy concerning the model used by central banks to assess inflation. This problem arises since ITR is consistent with a vast number of indicators and models of inflation, which may lead central banks to behave in different ways in different contexts (e.g. a context of moderate inflation, or of stagflation due to cost increases is one thing; a context characterized by high inflation and buoyant demand is quite another). This is not captured by NCM, as it cannot distinguish between different types of inflation or different contexts. Due to its reliance on quantity theory and full employment equilibrium, it inevitably affirms that inflation is always a monetary phenomenon and an evil, as such (whatever its level), as it distorts the market signals (i.e. relative prices) which guide agents' decisions. Making a distinction between different contexts amounts to accepting discretionary views with all their negative implications. However, for NCM, this kind of confusion between models of inflation and contexts is not really worrying so long as central banks remain formally committed to seeing the control of inflation as their true priority, leading them automatically to focus on the NCM model as the key source of inspiration.

Third, NCM cannot capture the problem that a focus on inflation as the main problem for the economy may lead central banks to neglect other dangers, such as unemployment, asset price inflation, debt and credit explosion. Once again, the NCM assumption of continuous market clearing rules out the possibility that unemployment can occur because of a lack of aggregate demand. If severe unemployment exists, it is due to structural problems that keep the natural rate high. Reducing it cannot be the goal of central banks, but of national governments, which have the power to carry out structural reforms. Moreover, the other phenomena that are typical of a bubble economy are not endogenous or caused by errors of the private sector. Ultimately, they are due to the faulty conduct of central banks that have adopted an unduly expansionary monetary policy. Thus, the kind of automatic control of the money supply suggested by monetarism may be, in the end, the best way to contrast all the major sources of imbalances. However, once these occur there is no need to neglect the self-adjusting nature of the economy, that is, the best policy is simply to let the market alone do the dirty job of cleaning the waters.

Fourth, the NCM cannot capture the instability that is due to tight fiscal policy implemented by cutting certain types of public expenditure that have special value for growth, such as R&D, education and the welfare system. While it is true that NCM contributes to endogenous growth models stressing the positive role of public expenditure, these models retain certain characteristics of general equilibrium theory and neoclassical analysis, in general, that still imply a mechanistic view of development and growth. In particular, these models retain the view that markets 'come first', and have priority over institutions, culture or social capital, in line with the tendency to seek general laws of the economy. In general, the vision of the economy held by NCM is that markets can contribute to the development of society better than governments, so that these expenditure cuts cannot really have dramatic consequences. On the contrary, such cuts might limit government failures and the instability deriving from discretionary fiscal policy.

Fifth, the NCM cannot accommodate instability problems arising from attempts to balance budgets through lower taxes, such as adverse income distribution effects. As already noted, NCM relies on the representative agent device, which does not allow consideration of these effects. In general, it is wrong to believe that they could generate true instability. The point is that cutting taxes has both positive short-run and allocative effects (e.g. providing the incentive to work harder) that, in principle, outweigh these effects.

Sixth, NCM cannot accommodate the negative consequences of increased labour market flexibility, such as lower productivity. It regards flexibility as a key precondition for full employment, in line with the general equilibrium benchmark. It is true that, as implied by marginal productivity theory, so long as greater flexibility induces employment rises, lower productivity follows from the more extensive application of labour to given capacity. However, for NCM this is not a true instability problem as, in general, one can expect perfect markets to produce the appropriate incentives for continual technological change and productivity growth.

Finally, NCM is also unable to capture instability problems that are due to capital market liberalization, such as the crises faced by developing countries, or declining accounting standards in more advanced economies. As already noted, this follows from its reliance on general equilibrium theory, according to which flexibility and liberalization of markets are necessary for optimal outcomes. Moreover, NCM is unable to accommodate the pluralism of models and the possibility that markets can work differently in different places, as it relies on the ideal type of perfect competitive markets and focuses on universal laws of economics. Once again, for NCM there are reasons for not considering such problems as being a real source of instability. The point is that only free markets (once the appropriate rules have been devised for their functioning) have the power to cure them. While the adjustment may be painful, the benefits will, in the end, certainly accrue.

18 Keynesian theory and the New Economy

An overview

In this chapter, we discuss the main lines of interpretation of the NE provided by the broadly defined Keynesian view defined in Part III. We hold that the Keynesian model proves to be more general than its NCM counterpart, because it captures a greater number of intersections of our matrix. Unlike NCM, it places both 'positive' and 'negative' mechanisms on the same footing, rejecting the view that positive mechanisms are permanent while negative ones are weaker or temporary. The ultimate implication of this model is that we can make no a priori assumption about the stability of the economy. Following the insights of the *General Theory*, the Keynesian model presented here suggests that capitalist economies, in general, are quite unstable; in particular, there are no inherent mechanisms, such as flexible relative prices, which ensure that stability will prevail, as in the NCM. However, at the same time, there are also no a priori reasons for catastrophic outcomes, that is, for the systematic dominance of negative effects. Whether an actual economy is, more or less, stable can only be established ex post, on the grounds of empirical analysis. The point is that actual instability is often held in check by policy and institutional changes. In other words, for the Keynesian model, as for the *General Theory*, stability is not an inherent property of the market economy (seen as the simple interaction of atomistic individuals); it is a property of the socio-economic system as a whole, once account is taken of institutions and visibility.

From the standpoint of our Keynesian perspective, the NE confirms the basic insights of the *General Theory*. There are reasons to believe that it tends to be more unstable than the old economy, unless appropriate policies and/or institutional changes are implemented. While allowing progress and growth, the features of the NE may also bring about further instability. Indeed, the NE confirms the general characteristic of capitalism: it can develop and prosper only by becoming more unstable. If the system does not collapse in the end, it is only because of the more active counteracting role of policy.

The NE and Keynes's broader notion of essence

To get a better understanding of the Keynesian view of the NE, one has to bear in mind Keynes's concept of equilibrium and his analysis of the 'normal working' of the economy. Strictly speaking, Keynes does not reject the distinction between different levels of reality that underlie the NCM, namely that of phenomena characterized by erratic movements or disequilibria, and a deeper and more basic 'essential' level characterized by stability and equilibrium. However, as noted in Chapter 8, he manages to define the notion of 'essence' in broader terms than neoclassical approaches.

In particular, Keynes does not call into question the distinction between an invariant essence of economic behaviour and its more contingent characteristics altogether, but shifts the boundary between the two. In his view, an element of invariance and rationality also exists in conventional or herd behaviour, which neoclassicals simply regard as irrational. Indeed, his contribution is to suggest that a new determinant of agents' behaviour, namely their 'mutual interest', must be considered along with self-interest and competition, which are emphasized by neoclassical theory. It is important to note that the dimension of mutual interest has a dual nature: on the one hand, it reflects an invariable or stable characteristic of agents' behaviour, that of seeking coordination with other agents. On the other, it can be embodied in forms (e.g. various types of conventions) and products (e.g. historical contingent institutions or theories), which change according to time and place.

Keynes's notion of equilibrium thus departs from that of NCM because it involves different parameters. The factors that play a causal role in one framework become a secondary given in the other. While NCM stresses the causal role of deep parameters, defined in terms of natural or exogenous factors, such as technology, physical resources and atomistic preferences, Keynes emphasizes, instead, the casual significance of aggregates, such as the propensities of consumption, investment and liquidity preference, which crucially depend upon agents' interdependence and institutions. This alternative notion of equilibrium represents a new benchmark for assessing stability.

Based on his notion of equilibrium, Keynes, like Lucas, tries to bring macro phenomena within the scope of the essential level. He tries to account not just for the 'normal' state of the economy but also for fluctuations in the level of income on the grounds of agents' rational behaviour. The main difference, with respect to NCM, is that he considers fluctuations not simply a result of external shocks but also of endogenous factors, such as agents' 'rational mistakes' – that is, agents acting on 'false', but rationally argued, beliefs – that are intrinsic to the market mechanism and not induced by external shocks.

This distinction between the normal state of the economy and fluctuations is also relevant for the Keynesian view of the NE. According to the Keynesian view, like NCM, the NE does not so much affect the normal or systematic part of the economy, as summarized in the *General Theory*. In other words, Keynesian macroeconomic analysis, based on the principle of effective demand, continues to hold in the NE. The most important impact of the NE, instead, is on the endogenous causes of fluctuations; it implies, in principle, more frequent shifts from one state of equilibrium to the other, unless counteracted by some form of state intervention.

The 'normal' working of the economy

In order to make these points clear, let us first focus on the 'normal' working of the economy implied by Keynesian theory.[1] Once again, we start from the following equation: $Y = C + I$. This time, however, we pose the reverse causal link: $C + I \rightarrow Y$. This reflects the view that Keynes rejects Say's Law and regards the equilibrium level of income, as determined by demand conditions, in line with the principle of effective demand. According to Keynes, there are no economic mechanisms, such as price flexibility in all markets, which grant that actual income always equals potential income. The system may well find equilibrium, even in the presence of high unemployment rates, so long as firms' plans, as summarized in their short-run expectations, are satisfied. Keynesians, therefore, logically start their analysis by placing the emphasis on the determinants of these expectations.

The scheme below illustrates the main features of this analytical framework. First of all, it shows that actual income is determined by the demand factors. Here too, as in Figure 16.1, we see that income can be derived as the product of three factors: productivity (p), number of workers (L) and the price level (P). Productivity in instantaneous equilibrium can be taken as given, but with the passage of time, it is influenced by the forces of demand. L is not determined on the labour market, but by the forces of demand listed on the left-hand side, consumption (C), investment (I), exports (X) and public expenditure (G), while the money supply (M), together with liquidity preference (LP), exerts its influence through the interest rate (i) and investment. P is also influenced by productivity and the given money wage (W) determined by the bargaining between workers and employers.

Second, Figure 18.1 shows that investment (I) determines saving (S) through the multiplier (represented by the interaction between consumption and income) and income changes. In particular, an increase in the propensity to save does not increase savings and investment, but only lowers income. Third, the rate of interest is not a real variable, determined by factors such as thrift and productivity on the capital market, but is a monetary variable. In the end, this figure does not show any significant element of retroaction from the price changes to aggregate demand. The point is that, while for Keynesians prices are flexible and adjustment

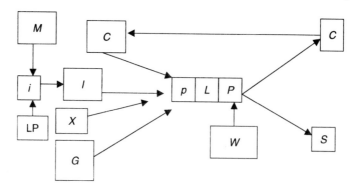

Figure 18.1 The Keynesian macro model.

mechanisms such as the Pigou and the Keynes effects may in principle take place, these mechanisms cannot be regarded as being really effective; in particular, deflation may fail to bring about a shift towards a better state of equilibrium as it may impact firms' expectations rather badly.

A broad view of economic fluctuations

In Keynes's theory, the 'normal' picture described in the previous section also serves as the basis for studying the dynamic behaviour of the economy, both in the short run (i.e. analysis of fluctuations) and in the long run (i.e. analysis of accumulation and growth). Indeed, as noted by Chick, to Keynes the business cycle was not a temporary aberration but 'an integral part of economic experience, something to be understood in the same frame of reference that, to his satisfaction, explained employment and output generally' (Chick 1983: 285; see also Jarsulic 1997: 372–3). In particular, his instantaneous equilibrium model is the basis for understanding fluctuations and growth.

Despite the limitations of Keynes's dynamic analysis underlined in Part III, the *General Theory* does shed light on a number of qualitative features of business cycles in real-world economies. The first is that Keynes's definition of the business cycle is broader than Lucas's. In his sketch of a theory of the cycle, Keynes, like Lucas, does try to provide reasons for its regularity and for the appearance of a crisis, the sudden replacement of an upward movement by a sharp downward tendency (see e.g. Chick 1983: 286; Asimakopulos 1991: 132; Jarsulic 1997: 373; Tvede 2001). However, the fact that his approach is divorced from the long-run equilibrium logic and the search for universal laws, on the grounds of unique formulas or models attempting to reflect actual time series behaviour, explains why, for example, it is not limited to recurrent phenomena that present a high degree of quantitative regularity, such as the 'co-movements' that can be discerned among the aggregate time series in all major countries.

In principle, Keynes accounts for complicating factors, such as path-dependence and indeterminacy (multiple equilibria), as well as for more 'normal' aspects which cannot be defined as invariable regularities or do not show consistent cyclical behaviour. In particular, as Chick points out (1983: 287–8), he considers both the physical facts of the production line, that are important for the regularity of cycles (such as those linked to the characteristics of the various types of capital involved in the process, the time needed to eliminate excess productive capacity and excess stocks of commodities) and the psychological aspects, that are especially important in the crisis and may be less regular (such as the waves of optimism and pessimism underlying agents' expectations). More in general, Keynes's analysis is consistent with our broad irreversible empirical laws that transcend cyclical fluctuations and have to do with long-run trends of actual economies.

The endogenous nature of business cycles

A second feature of Keynes's view of the business cycle is that this appears as endogenous rather than due to erratic exogenous single shocks. Keynes regards the cycle as the outcome of fluctuations in aggregate demand, mainly due to investment decisions. In particular, as these must be made without knowing the future, fluctuations in firms' long-term expectations determining the marginal efficiency of capital (MEC) may be large enough to broadly account for cyclical regularities (see e.g. Chick 1986: 288–9; Asimakopulos 1991: 132; Vercelli 1991: 164–5; Jarsulic 1997: 371; Tvede 2001; Louçã 2003: 796–9). There is no doubt that this is a peculiarity of Keynes. As noted by Chick, in contrast with the prevailing monetary theory of business cycles that emphasized the crisis in terms of the rate of interest and regarded a low interest as being sufficient for recovery, for Keynes, the collapse of the MEC is the key, and even low rates may be unable to revive investment in the face of pessimistic expectations (see Chick 1983: 288).

In addition, while the MEC does play a crucial role in determining fluctuations, these are also complicated and aggravated by associated changes in other independent variables. Keynes's explanation of the cycle rests, for example, on the awareness of the key interdependence between financial and real sectors of the economy as reflected in the interaction between firms' expectations and speculation on the stock exchange. Indeed, in certain passages of the *General Theory*, he even goes so far as to refer simultaneously to both the demand for equities and for capital goods. In particular, in his description of a downturn, it is not clear whether it is the collapse of stock exchange or the MEC that really causes the trouble. The most plausible explanation, however, is the one already emphasized: the collapse in the MEC is the key, while the financial side transforms it into a sharp crisis (see Chick 1983: 288–9). It must be noted that in the debate concerning business cycles developed after the *General Theory*, several authors have elaborated on Keynes's account by introducing other sources of endogenous instability, such as the possibility of financial implosion due to the increased burden of debt, as emphasized by Fisher and Minsky or of bank failures.

'Global' versus 'local' imperfections

A further key feature of Keynes's account of fluctuations is that it does not necessarily imply agents' irrationality. Indeed, Keynes manages to provide an endogenous explanation of business cycles mainly because he adopts a broader concept of rationality. In his view, due to insufficient knowledge, rationality certainly does not correspond to the logic of atomistic choice. In making their decisions, agents also rely on conventional representations of reality or on theories that are the product of 'mutual interest'. This means that even when agents endorse theories that turn out to be *ex post* 'erroneous' (i.e. contradicted by actual outcomes) they are not violating the canons of rationality, so long as such theories are shared by a sufficient number of people. For example, as already noted, fluctuations in the MEC are due to waves of optimism and pessimism. Now, it can be argued that while these are based, to some extent, on general features of human nature (e.g. psychology) they also reflect objective factors, such as theories concerning the market potentials of new technologies, which become so diffuse as to create the waves. Indeed, it is the fact that nobody knows the true 'fundamental' returns accruing in the external sphere of production that ultimately justifies the fact that agents (including entrepreneurs) refer to alternative valuation criteria which are intrinsic to the market and deprived of absolute foundations (and thus difficult to distinguish on a priori grounds). As Keynes noted, 'the entrepreneurs, who are directly responsible (for new investment), will find it financially advantageous, and often unavoidable, to fall in with the ideas of the market, even though they themselves are better instructed' (Keynes 1936: 315).

We believe that special emphasis needs be placed on these 'shared errors'. Not only do they play a crucial role in Keynes's approach to fluctuations (and in others, such as Zarnowitz's), but they also represent a crucial line of demarcation between two alternative conceptions of macroeconomics and, in particular, two alternative approaches to the 'imperfections' issue. To clarify what we mean by this, we suggest labelling shared errors as 'global' imperfections (or inefficiencies, in the terminology used by D'avolio *et al.*, see Chapter 13 earlier), in order to distinguish them from the other type of imperfections emphasized by most economists, especially New Keynesians, which can be instead regarded as 'local' imperfections.

In order to show the difference made to macroeconomics by emphasizing one or the other type of imperfection, let us refer to just one popular type of local imperfection, namely asymmetric information, underlying many New Keynesian models. This imperfection generates phenomena, such as adverse selection and moral hazard, that may account for price rigidities and inefficient outcomes in various markets. On the credit market, for example, these phenomena explain why the market rate is not set by banks at the market clearing level and credit rationing may occur (see e.g. Stiglitz 1987).

One important feature of the models embodying asymmetric information is that they deal with adverse selection and moral hazard in *ceteris paribus* fashion, that is, they take the rest of agents' behaviour as conforming to the assumptions of standard economic theory, such as the strong assumption of rationality and stable preferences, and focus on just one market in isolation. This means that a typical New Keynesian model is, for many reasons, just like a standard model. It, too, singles out an 'optimal solution'. Its peculiarity consists in stressing just one basic reason (i.e. a particular type of imperfection) that accounts for the departure from the standard result. A model of credit rationing, for example, identifies an 'optimal' rate that corresponds to the natural rate of interest in standard theory, equilibrating saving and investment, and then shows why this rate is not achieved in the market. In other words, local imperfections have to do with the attempts to derive Keynesian results, such as unemployment, by underlining specific reasons why the markets that compose the neoclassical sequence may not work efficiently.

Now it is not difficult to see that this approach contradicts the *General Theory* and our Keynesian model. The crucial point is that the effective demand problems emphasized by Keynes are not rooted in local imperfections and 'wrong prices'. Several key points should be made on this.

First, such problems do not originate from the working of individual markets, but from market spillovers. For example, what occurs on the labour market depends on the goods market; thus a 'wrong' real wage cannot be responsible for unemployment. Moreover, income equilibrates saving and investment and replaces the natural rate as the key adjustment mechanism on the capital market.

Second, the Keynesian logic rules out the concept of 'wrong prices' because it rejects the existence of norms of 'right' prices, such as the natural interest rate and equilibrium real wage. These prices make sense only if one adopts the Walrasian model as an ideal state, or 'external' reference point or benchmark, to assess actual economies. It is only in this case that piecemeal deviations from such an ideal state due to various kinds of local imperfections can be meaningfully discussed. Keynesian analysis, instead, is built around an alternative benchmark. It is not external but 'internal' to the working of actual markets, and is consistent with a different notion of norm. What is a normal price cannot be defined in *ex ante* terms but only in *ex post* terms; it is the price that agents themselves, including policy-makers, regard as normal (or as an equilibrium price) in a given context, in the light of current expectations and market theories. Strictly speaking, this does not mean that actual, normal prices may not be 'wrong' in the sense, for example, of not being consistent with full employment or some desired growth path. Since there is a plurality of theories that at any moment shape agents' expectations it is, of course, possible that 'bad theories' (i.e. shared errors), push actual prices to levels that do not favour full employment. This is, indeed, one of the reasons why we speak of 'global imperfections'. It is possible in the Keynesian logic, for example, to argue that the money interest rate is too high to stimulate a sufficient level of investment. However, this assessment does not derive from comparison with an external benchmark, such as the natural rate, but from consideration of an internal benchmark, such as whether the levels of actual income and investment are satisfactory or not in relation to some policy goal.

In other words, by stressing the difference between internal and external benchmarks, we are underlining once again the unbridgeable gap between the two basic notions of equilibrium. While the logic of Walrasian equilibrium is intrinsically *ex ante*, as it relies on atomistic behaviour defined by the axioms of rationality, Keynesian equilibrium, instead, is dominated by an *ex post* logic, because it relies on aggregates ultimately depending upon the products of agents' interactions, such as market theories, which cannot be defined on a priori grounds.

Third, according to the Keynesian logic, the lack of effective demand and unemployment are not generally caused by relative prices rigidities. In our Keynesian theory, prices are generally flexible but they may still fail to grant the tendency to full employment. Moreover, even when tending to be somewhat sticky as money wages, their full flexibility is not an antidote against unemployment. Indeed, as already noted for Keynes, if money wage or the price level fell it would be even worse for the economy, as a whole. There is no doubting that one major implication of his theory – popularized by the emphasis on animal spirits – is that if the system does not reach full employment, it is not because of price rigidities but because of autonomous effective demand problems, that is, due to factors unrelated to price changes. This is where global imperfections obviously come in. Indeed, their key role is not only to push actual prices, for instance, of financial assets or interest rates, to 'wrong levels' but also to justify these kinds of autonomous fluctuations in key variables. For example, investment may fluctuate for reasons quite unrelated to interest rate and credit availability. Even if rates are low and credit abundant, investors may overreact to shocks or news concerning, for example, the discovery of new technologies, and follow expectations that have been influenced by some bad theory, thus leading them to overoptimistic estimates of the market potential of such technologies and, ultimately, over-investment.

Business cycles and institutional changes

The last feature of Keynes's analysis concerns the introduction of institutional changes to modify the cycle. In the *General Theory*, Keynes makes some assertions concerning the stability of actual economies by drawing on experience rather than on a priori considerations. He argues, for example, that experience shows that they are not violently unstable:

> It is an outstanding characteristic of the economic system in which we live that, while it is subject to severe fluctuations in respect of output and employment, it is not violently unstable. Indeed it seems capable of remaining in a chronic condition of sub-normal activity for a considerable period without any marked tendency either towards recovery or towards complete collapse. Moreover, experience indicates that full, or even approximately full, employment is of rare and short-lived occurrence.
>
> (Keynes 1936: 249–50)

Keynes suggests that this moderate instability is due to a number of factors that characterize actual economies, such as low values of the multiplier and the propensity to consume due to established levels of consumption, moderate changes in investment due to rising short-period supply prices of capital goods in response to an increase in prospective yield or to a fall in interest rate, and stability of prices due to moderate changes in marginal costs, and so on (see also Asimakopulos 1991: 128–9). However, for Keynes, this state of affairs is certainly not optimal; it can be described as unemployment equilibrium.

At the root of his work lies the idea that it is possible to moderate the cycle in such as way as to make full employment a more permanent condition. In view of the lack of self-adjusting properties of market economies, this aim can only be achieved by policy. He advocates not just stabilization or discretionary policy but also more structural policies (e.g. income distribution to sustain consumption) and institutional changes (e.g. the Bretton Woods system to sustain international trade) capable of granting steady demand. Indeed, as pointed out by Jarsulic, Keynes's point 'is that market economies are never stable and that aggregate demand can fail, then an institutional structure to limit the effects of instability and sustain demand becomes crucial' (1997: 390).

Since the Second World War, these insights have been further developed by several Keynesian economists (e.g. Marglin and Schor 1990) in the face of major changes in the business cycle. The need for institutional coherence and stability as necessary to maintaining high levels of aggregate demand has been reinforced, especially by the experience of the so-called 'Golden Age' in the period from 1945 to 1973, which was characterized by long expansions and short contractions, reduced variability of investment, anomalous increases in GDP and productivity growth rates. The 'Golden Age' period is distinguished by key institutional factors, such as a stable international financial and trade regime, the expansion of state spending relative to GDP providing a stable source of demand, the commitment to use monetary and fiscal policy to maintain full employment and the proportional growth of real wages and productivity, which sustained consumer demand and helped to stabilize prices and investment (see Cornwall 1997: 394–5; Jarsulic 1997: 385–8). Now, as Jarsulic points out, there is a link between the dissolution of this institutional context and the increased fluctuations of investment, and the decline in productivity and growth during the 1970s and 1980s:

> The 'Golden Age' ended as each of these institutional constants dissolved in the 1970s. The fixed exchange rate system of Bretton Woods was abandoned, the world financial markets were allowed to become quite volatile. The ascent of monetarist policies...signalled an attack on aspects of the state sector spending, and an unwillingness to use fiscal and monetary policy in the pursuit of employment targets...
>
> (Jarsulic 1997: 389)

The analysis of long-run trends

As for the analysis of growth and accumulation, in Part III we have already seen the main reasons why Keynes did not provide a formal account similar to modern growth theory, and remained highly sceptical of the first contemporary dynamic developments, such as Harrod's. Once again, however, we emphasize that Keynes's analysis is not completely irrelevant to the study of long-run trends. The key point is that, following our 'essentialist' interpretation of the key parameters of his model, these do not 'disappear' in the long run to leave the stage for neoclassical deep parameters but continue to play a role also in the analysis of stability and growth. The plausibility of this interpretation is strengthened by the fact that Keynes, himself, provided a first sketch of dynamic analysis by making the distinction between primary, or causal, factors and secondary factors.

In order to extend the analysis beyond the short run, using Keynes's model, all we need to do is to shift the focus from the independent variables (or primary or causal factors) to the secondary factors (such as the size and quality of productive factors, technology, population and the structure of markets) as prime movers. In the analysis of instantaneous equilibrium, which provides a starting point for the analysis of the business cycle, it is legitimate to focus on the interaction among his key independent variables and take the secondary factors as given. In the analysis of long-run trends, we consider how changes in the dependent variables (income) and the secondary factors affect the primary factors underlying aggregate demand. This kind of analysis is possible because Keynes's parameters can change endogenously and thus, in principle, account for cycles and duality in general.

Keynes himself provides one major instance of this type of analysis when he discusses the effects of money wage changes. The logic of his model is that

> a favourable impact on employment will only occur if the reduction in money wages produces suitable changes in the determinants of the equilibrium position. The examination by Keynes of the effects of falling money-wage rates, in response to unemployment, thus involves him in a dynamic analysis that attempts to trace the possible changes in other factors that are set off by declining money-wage rates.
>
> (Asimakopulos 1991: 125)

As is well-known, Keynes draws quite a negative conclusion on the effectiveness of money wage cuts as a cure for unemployment (e.g. because of adverse income distribution effects and expectations). However, these are not definitive but

> based on a balance of considerations, none of which can be made precise, and the assessment of which requires judgement and experience. This is the nature of economic analysis when it attempts to deal with changes occurring over historical time in actual economies.
>
> (ibid.: 127)

Now, it can be argued that this kind of analysis can be generalized and used to derive a Keynesian interpretation of the NE. In what follows, then, we shall regard the components of aggregate demand as terminals of all the impulses generated by the factors summarized by our labels.

A general view of the NE

Let us now focus on the Keynesian interpretation of the NE. From the Keynesian standpoint, this should, in principle, influence the factors that play a role in fluctuations rather than change the normal workings of the economy. In particular, when seen through Keynesian lenses, the NE appears to be dynamically stable. It implies a faster transition to the equilibrium state, as it reduces certain types of friction, or imperfections, which we can call 'local' imperfections, mainly due to transmission of information. Strictly speaking, for Keynesians, as for Lucas, the economy should be seen as constantly in equilibrium. What's more, following the Keynesian logic as presented in this chapter, the NE also increases other types of imperfections, the 'global' ones, linked to the fundamental opacity and complexity of the economy. These increase structural instability and the likelihood that equilibrium positions are not optimal.

This Keynesian account of the NE is, of course, controversial because there are many Keynesian interpretations. It is important to be aware of the reasons why it differs from others. In particular, our assessment implies a departure from the views held by authors of the neoclassical synthesis or Old Keynesians, such as Samuelson and Solow, as well as New Keynesians, such as Blanchard, DeLong, Mankiw, Romer and Stiglitz. In general, they do not seem to be convinced that the NE really has a significant impact on macroeconomics. Their verdict on stability is mixed. Few of them would deny that the NE brings about an improvement in the functioning of the price mechanism, as the result of a more efficient use of information. However, they all believe that this improvement is not enough to undermine their basic macroeconomic stance, according to which 'local' market imperfections – such as, price rigidities, information asymmetries, contracts and institutional constraints preventing fast adjustments on the labour markets, credit and liquidity constraints – explain why the economy may be, at least temporarily, outside neoclassical long-run equilibrium. This means that in their view the NE does not shake beliefs in the long-run stability of the economy. In other words, these authors suggest that the NE does not call into question either the existence of such imperfections or the validity of the long-run equilibrium concept (with its implicit stability assumption) as the benchmark of macroeconomics.

The theoretical background underlying these Keynesians is similar to what has been called the 'new consensus' macro paradigm (see e.g. Arestis and Sawyer 2003: 2–5) or 'core of modern macroeconomics' (e.g. Blanchard 2003) or 'pragmatic macroeconomics' (Solow 1997) and can be summarized as follows:

> 1) output and employment fluctuate in response to unexpected shocks...
> 2) fluctuations take place around a long-period value of... 'potential output'...
> 3) the economic system responds to shocks with variations in quantities and not solely in prices because of imperfections in the organisation of markets, in the transmission of information or of disincentives by economic agents against price changes... 4) neither fiscal nor monetary interventions on aggregate demand are able to alter the level of potential output... permanently, their only effect would be to raise the average level of inflation above 'core inflation'.
>
> (Tamborini 2004: 156)[2]

In most cases, Keynesians combine this core of macroeconomics with New Growth Theory to study long-run trends.

Our approach calls into question this approach. First, it holds that the NE confirms Keynes's view that we need to change benchmarks, and in particular we need to drop the long-run equilibrium and natural rate concepts. The NE involves greater instability of parameters (e.g. the collapse of agents' time horizons) leading to greater unpredictability of outcomes and an overlap between cyclical and structural phenomena. It, thus, undermines the validity of models, such as those of New Growth Theory, based on just one or two fundamental equations to assess growth or long-run stability issues. These models emphasize the supply side of the economy and neglect the demand side (see e.g. Setterfield 2002; Thirlwall 2002).

This is certainly a major weakness of these Keynesian approaches. They misleadingly reduce the validity of the principle of effective demand to the short run, in order to study cyclical phenomena, failing to regard it as an expression of a more essential level of analysis – based on the products of agents' interactions such as theories and institutions – which is relevant, also, in the study of long-run structural trends. In other words, they overlook the fact that the NE makes the old-fashioned, pragmatic distinction between Keynesian short-run and neoclassical long-run equilibria obsolete and that differences between the fundamental macroeconomic frameworks can be best expressed by thinking in terms of alternative benchmarks that are based on key parameters referring to instantaneous equilibrium.

This shortcoming makes a vast difference to the interpretation of the NE. Reliance on the neoclassical benchmark leads Old and New Keynesians to accept the view that the market economy is intrinsically stable, at least in the long run. It also causes them to miss one major implication of the *General Theory*, reflected in the principle of effective demand: namely, that stability is not an inherent property of the economy, but the product of a set of fundamental institutions. Thus, these authors would accept the NCM conclusion that, at least in the long run, the NE increases stability as it pushes towards greater deregulation, flexibility in all markets, reduction of the state spending and so on. Instead, for other Keynesians (more in tune with Keynes), this would be problematic since institutional features, such as fixed exchange rates, collective bargaining and welfare, have been devised to induce greater, not less, stability; they are not imperfections to be removed to favour growth but essential prerequisites of it. In other words, for Keynesians, the NE involves self-defeating tendencies. On the one hand, features of the NE (the patterns of growth captured by Calvino's labels) have developed because of a certain institutional framework. On the other, the NE, itself, tends to call into question that very same framework.

Second, we argue that the NE reduces the scope for the kind of imperfections emphasized by New Keynesians. For example, by improving the transmission of information, it makes the adjustment of expectations more rapid and information asymmetries less relevant; by making capital markets more efficient, it reduces the impact of liquidity constraints, and so on. More in general, it reduces the impact of factors that account for the slow adjustment of prices and markets in real-world economies, and justifies the reliance on the short-run/long-run distinction. It even reduces the scope for NCM explanations of fluctuations based on misperceptions, or confusion, between relative and absolute prices. In other words, thinking in terms of standard 'local' imperfections alone doesn't seem to leave much room for a Keynesian interpretation, based on the long-run equilibrium benchmark, and opens the way to the justification of the NCM view that the NE makes the assumption of perfect competition and continuous market equilibrium more plausible.

In our view, however, there is room for the alternative Keynesian stance presented here, stressing a new equilibrium or benchmark for economic analysis based on the products of agents' mutual interest and their interaction. In this view, the NE increases the role of other types of imperfections or errors, the 'global' imperfections, which bring about fluctuations, more frequent shifts from one state of equilibrium to the other, or prolonged states of underemployment. Among these global imperfections, we place emphasis on agents' 'shared errors' that are the endogenous factors accounting for speculation and waves of optimism and pessimism during the business cycle. In particular, in the NE, many new theories to guide agents in their market behaviour are generated and diffused at a greater speed. In a context dominated by increasing complexity and systemic uncertainty, agents find it more difficult to grasp the fundamentals so that they are bound to rely on simplified analytical tools, such as aggregate indexes or ratios, in order to make decisions. Herd behaviour is more likely to follow from such conditions, with the exacerbation of speculation and waves of optimism and pessimism.

The Keynesian model and specific features of the NE

The explanatory power of the Keynesian model can be better understood by considering its interpretation of the key features of the NE. We shall start by making a few general claims.

First of all, our Keynesian model provides a systemic analysis of features of the NE. Unlike the local imperfections approach taken by New Keynesians, which gives rise to a sequence of unconnected models that pick up just one possible mechanism operating on individual markets, the global imperfections view allows, instead, a unified representation of market interactions and the economy as a whole. This is possible because the phenomena of globalization, or technological change, can be seen as impulses hitting the same terminal: the demand side of the economy captured by the key parameters of the Keynesian model. Important advantages of this approach are twofold: it avoids falling into the trap of technological determinism (e.g. technology has no influence, *per se*, but only through expectations), and that it manages to identify the sources of endogenous instability deriving from the interplay of a number of factors.

Second, our Keynesian stance places heavy emphasis on institutions, overcoming the limits of NCM. It can be argued that NCM provides a narrow interpretation of the NE because it fails to capture the generating role of institutions, regarding them as simple rules of the game or exogenous constraint. Thanks to a broader notion of essence, the Keynesian view instead regards certain institutions as the foundation of aggregate behaviour and stability.

Third, in contrast with NCM's narrow view of business cycles, our Keynesian perspective manages to account for key dimensions of structural change, which are also significant for stability. Moreover, as it is not bound to insist on recurrent events, this approach is also consistent with the focus on the acceleration of certain trends that represent a source of instability in the NE.

Fourth is the Keynesian model itself, which captures duality, that is, both 'positive' and 'negative' effects triggered by each feature. Indeed, these appear as two sides of the same coin because of the double role of markets: while allowing tremendous growth opportunities, they also imply greater instability. In view of the expansion of markets it brings about, the NE represents the last, and most sophisticated, stage of this process. The broader conception of essence that underlies the Keynesian model allows the positive and negative mechanisms to be placed on a par. In this model the relevant demand variables influenced by the products of mutual interest are liable to induce either stability or instability. Both outcomes are equally 'rational' on a priori grounds and are endogenous, that is, they arise autonomously from agents' interaction.

In other words, it can be argued that the introduction of aggregate demand, in the long-run context, represents a step towards a conditional analysis. Keynesians do not deny, for example, that the NE may benefit the world economy, but point out that no rosy scenario should be taken for granted. Factors such as globalization or technology do not affect outcomes directly, as in the NCM model, but only through the determinants of aggregate demand, that is, the products of mutual interest, such as the institutional set-up and theories influencing agents. It is highly possible that negative effects may also be generated through this route. It can be argued, for example, that if globalization leads to complete deregulation, rather than a context of agreed rules, it is bound to generate autarchy or trade wars. The Keynesian model suggests that the net result of these tendencies cannot be determined on a priori grounds. Strictly speaking, however, following the view that capitalism can create progress only by becoming more vulnerable, then, in principle, greater instability is bound to prevail for the non-policy features of the NE. Visibility is therefore necessary for keeping the system stable. However, policy-makers themselves may fail to do the job, so in the end, whether global stability will occur is not a matter of assumption but only of *ex post*, empirical analysis.

What we can learn from the Keynesian approach is that the analysis of stability is more complex and roundabout than standard theory would have it. However, as Keynes argued, what is important is not to provide infallible answers, but to devise a method of orderly thinking that is capable of providing valuable insights for policy-makers.

19 Keynesian theory and multiplicity

In the next five chapters, we draw more specific conclusions about our Keynesian interpretation of the NE by focusing on the various labels and pointing out how it differs from the NCM account. In what follows, we shall evaluate the stability claims concerning globalization. We shall attempt to show why our Keynesian model allows us to conclude that its negative effects are bound to prevail over its positive ones. The model does not deny that the liberalization of international trade and investment, together with the diffusion of ICT, brings about effects that are, in principle, beneficial for all those countries that take part in international trade. These range from an increase in international competition, a higher degree of unification of markets, an improvement in the efficiency of markets and the functioning of the price mechanism, to a reduction in information errors and trade barriers as well as in monopoly power and mark-ups.

However, the logic of the Keynesian model is that this favourable scenario should not be taken for granted, as neoclassicals tend to do following their deterministic stance, but can only happen under well-specified conditions. Macroeconomic outcomes ultimately depend upon the way these factors affect the primary givens underlying aggregate demand and their determinants, such as the institutional set-up and agents' theories. Keynesians admit the possibility that globalization may have a neutral effect on these determinants, or may even change them favourably in such a way as to increase aggregate demand. Indeed, firms' MEC may well be stimulated as new investment opportunities are created by the unification and opening up of new markets, implying more potential buyers. Moreover, agents' propensity to consume may benefit from the lower prices induced by greater competition. Exports may also tend to increase, thanks to lower trade barriers and market unification.

However, from the Keynesian standpoint, globalization in the age of ICT is more likely to affect the key determinants of aggregate demand in such a way as to generate destabilizing tendencies. In particular, the Keynesian model is able to capture the sources of instability as well as to explain why they actually arise and may prevail over the positive factors.

Growing interdependence between individuals and countries

The Keynesian model naturally captures the growing interdependence between individuals and countries. Such interdependence is a major factor of instability in the NE, and is revealed by phenomena such as agents' reliance on a narrow number of general or simplified indicators, herd behaviour or shared errors on financial markets giving rise to more pronounced waves of optimism and pessimism, higher correlation of business cycles and faster transmission of financial turbulence across countries. This is not surprising from the methodological viewpoint, because the Keynesian model is not based on anything similar to the atomistic preferences and the representative agent device that we find in the standard model; from the start, it incorporates the products of the agents' mutual interest dimension and the possibility for endogenous changes in the parameters underlying the primary variables.[1] In particular, the Keynesian model is able to explain these phenomena as being the product not of psychological factors, such as irrational exuberance, but of important changes in the agents' collective perception of economic dimensions induced by globalization. One could note, for example, that the more rapid information flows across world markets allowed by ICT, together with the reduction of physical and psychological barriers, involve the diffusion of new conceptual representations of the world economy, itself, that lead agents to change their perception of time, space and value. Professional stock market traders or even ordinary people become more willing, for example, to buy foreign assets or revise their investment at shorter intervals of time, or attach a lot of weight to indicators or simple market theories to assess the value of assets simply because they are used by colleagues, or other people, in other parts of the world, which are all forms of behaviour leading to 'shared errors'.

Moreover, in contrast with the rational expectations hypothesis, Keynesians hold that such forms of behaviour and errors may be sufficiently systematic and persistent. The point is that people's expectations are influenced not just by market fundamentals, as summarized in the 'true model' of the economy but also by a plethora of models. As already noted, the Keynesian model focuses on equilibrium at a point in time and is foreign to such concepts as stochastic equilibrium, and objective and subjective probability distributions which ensure the weeding out of 'false' hypothesis and the convergence to the true model. From the standpoint of instantaneous equilibrium, all theories have some rational justification (NCM's true model is just one of them) and represent, more or less, efficient devices produced by agents' interaction to help people make decisions. On these grounds, therefore, it is not surprising that markets can get stuck in positions that increase aggregate demand failures on a global scale. The Keynesian stance suggests, for example, that 'wrong' exchange rates, which are determined mainly by speculative capital flows rather than real flows and which fail to reflect inflation differentials as predicted by the purchasing parity theorem,[2] may alter the distribution of aggregate demand and shares of world trade in such a way as to slow down the growth of the world economy (e.g. by penalizing more dynamic countries that have higher growth potential or by undermining the take-off of backward economies).

Winners and losers

The Keynesian model also accounts for a second factor of instability, that is, the growing distance between 'losers' and 'winners' both within individual countries (e.g. the expansion of the firms in new sectors and the decline of others), and in the world economy (e.g. the gap between poor and rich countries), and, in general, the fragmentation of structural conditions induced by globalization. At the methodological level, the Keynesian model is able to deal with composition and cumulative effects as well as competitiveness issues because of its reliance not on representative agents but on a population of heterogeneous agents, coordinated not just by a system of prices, but also by products of mutual interest, including institutions, theories and knowledge in general.

Thus, this model makes sense of key non-price mechanisms through which the diffusion of knowledge occurs, including imitation and organizational structures. On the one hand, due to its reliance on changeable parameters of behaviour, it accounts for the fact that one effect of changing perceptions of time and space due to globalization is to alter the timing of knowledge diffusion; for example, they accelerate the rate of imitation. On the other hand, because the Keynesian model relies on the view that institutions affect market outcomes, it also accounts for the fact that knowledge is a public good that cannot be transmitted or imitated perfectly, mainly because it is embodied in organizational structures linked to national characteristics which are often very costly or impossible to transfer and imitate.

Now, for Keynesians, the reason these mechanisms are a source of instability can be understood in light of the view expressed, in particular, by Kaldor (e.g. 1981, see also Thirlwall 2002), according to which growth is led not by factor supply and productivity, as in standard theory, but by demand (in particular, exports), as determined by international competitiveness. In this view, the supply of factors, itself, is driven by demand; mobile workers and capital are attracted by sectors and countries where demand is high. Globalization makes this process more effective by increasing the mobility of factors. In the NE, the more dynamic sectors of the economy – that is, where demand and net exports expand faster and are potentially able to make up for the loss of jobs in other sectors – are those based on ICT and for which knowledge stocks are essential.

It is clear that the difficulty of transferring knowledge and the outflow of qualified workers generates a systematic underproduction of knowledge in many poor countries, or other 'losers' in the changing division of labour. This may prevent them from catching up and getting a competitive edge in those new sectors, with negative consequences for global aggregate demand (if these countries do not take off or grow at a sufficient rate, they cannot absorb the goods produced by the more developed countries) and for the balances of payments of these countries. In particular, the external constraint for poor countries is aggravated by the unfavourable terms of trade between new goods incorporating knowledge and standard commodities and agriculture products, reflecting the well-known gap between activities subject to increasing returns and those subject to decreasing returns (see e.g. Thirlwall 2002: 2).

Governance of the world economy

The Keynesian model is also able to deal with a third negative factor induced by globalization, that is, the fact that it worsens the governance problems of the world economy. By generating stronger competition, complete deregulation and flexibility throughout all markets (including exchange rates), it induces the international community to tackle governance issues, not by relying on spontaneous cooperation and agreed rules, but by 'brute force', thereby allowing the US to play a predominant role on the world scene. Unlike the standard model that suggests an abstract idea of markets, the Keynesian approach fully recognizes the link between growth and institutional aspects and, in particular, accommodates the role of power as a mechanism capable of influencing market outcomes or even leading to the 'creation' of markets. Moreover, our Keynesian model is able to allow assessment of the complex role of a leading country (such as the US) in the world economy, because it rejects the *ceteris paribus* clause underlying standard theory, according to which markets and key phenomena must be dealt with separately. In particular, it focuses, from the start, on the mutual interactions between financial and real phenomena. It is clear, for example, that to understand the US case, globalization, technological change and financial innovation should be studied as interdependent phenomena.

Now, from the Keynesian standpoint, there are several reasons why these effects of globalization may be a source of instability. First of all, they tend to undermine the context of agreed rules, granting a sufficient growth of world trade and aggregate demand, and the development of 'multiplicity' itself. Indeed, Keynesians often stress that in past decades, and especially until the 1970s, globalization and the extension of international trade were favoured not just by legal changes tending to liberalize markets but also by trade agreements and fixed exchange rate regimes (see e.g. Jarsulic 1997; Davidson 2002). In their view, it follows that the disappearance of these 'rules' and, in particular, the complete deregulation of capital flows and the adoption of flexible exchange rate regimes on a full scale is not a panacea, as suggested by NCM advocates, but a threat to the stability of political relations among partners and to the very openness of world economies. This provokes the risk for the development of protectionist tendencies and a reduction in export opportunities for all (see e.g. Davidson 2002).[3]

Second, due to the greater integration of the economies and synchronization of business cycles in the age of ICT, globalization tends to create excessive dependence of the world economy upon engines of growth, such as the US. Whereas NCM regards flexible prices as being sufficient for granting the smooth working of the world economy, Keynesians consider engines of growth important for the growth of world trade and exports of many countries. In this context, it is clear that real or potential financial crises hitting the US expose the rest of the world economy to increasing risks.

20 Keynesian theory and rapidity

In what follows, we shall try to evaluate Keynesians' claims concerning the effects of technological change on stability. To reiterate, the Keynesian model does not deny the potential positive effects on the stability of the world economy induced by technological change such as an increase in productivity, greater flexibility on the goods and the labour market, better inventory control and the launch of new products. These factors can indeed generate a virtuous cycle in terms of higher income, and lower rates of unemployment and inflation. In contrast with the technological determinism embraced by NCM and other approaches, the Keynesian model suggests, however, that this rosy picture is just one possible outcome that can occur only under well-specified conditions. While NCM's unconditional vision of the positive impact of technological change is based on a simple, causal link from exogenous technological change to productivity and high income, Keynesian analysis emphasizes a more complex link.

In terms of Keynes's distinction between primary and secondary givens, two major claims can be made. First, technological change is a secondary given that influences income, not directly, but through its impact on the primary givens, that is, the parameters that underlie aggregate demand. Second, because it is a secondary given, technological change itself is not an ultimate independent variable, but the product of economic activity. Indeed, a certain level of aggregate demand favours innovation activity, technological change and productivity growth. The latter are, therefore, at least partly endogenous (see e.g. Kaldor 1981: 603, Setterfield 2002; Thirlwall 2002). This claim is consonant with a view, expressed by Keynesians such as Kaldor, that economic growth is always induced by aggregate demand and is not constrained by resources, such as capital and labour. Indeed, these do not determine growth, because they are mobile and never allocated optimally. In particular, capital is generated automatically as part, and in consequence, of aggregate demand growth.

In what follows, we shall consider both of these aspects, starting from the way rapidity affects the determinants of the primary givens underlying aggregate demand, such as the institutional set-up and agents' theories, both at the national level and the international level. Once again, from a Keynesian standpoint, it may well be possible that technological change affects these determinants in such a way as to increase aggregate demand. Of course, the new technologies may stimulate firms' MEC as they create new opportunities for investment. Moreover, the agents' propensity to consume may benefit from lower prices induced by technological change. Exports of advanced countries may also tend to increase, thanks to the competitive edge gained in the new sectors. However, for Keynesians, the influence of rapidity on the key determinants of aggregate demand is more likely to generate instability. In this regard, once again we shall see that the Keynesian model is able to both capture the sources of instability and explain why they actually arise and may prevail over the positive factors.

Technological change and labour market flexibility

First of all, the Keynesian model naturally captures the possibility that more rapid technological change causes unemployment through its direct effects on the labour market. In contrast with standard theory's reliance on the representative firm device and the view that the new technologies allow more flexibility and swifter market adjustment in the NE, Keynesians in principle account for composition effects and structural adjustment processes as they consider a population of heterogeneous agents. This allows them, for example, to talk about 'losers and winners' both at the national and international level. At the analytical level, the key insight of Keynesian theory is that the possibility of unemployment does not arise simply because of objective 'lags' in the adjustment process concerning the physical features of the production line. As already noted, these are an important part of the business cycle and it may well be that one key effect of the NE is to reduce them. However, they are insufficient to deal with the unemployment issue. Another important aspect of the explanation of business cycles lies in the behaviour of key variables, as reflected in the primary givens of aggregate demand. In other words, the peculiarity of Keynesian analysis of stability and growth is to stress the interaction between the objective and subjective dimensions of structural change, and to rule out a clear-cut dichotomy between structural and cyclical issues. As already noted, one important implication of this view is that the factors of technological change and market flexibility do not exercise an autonomous causal influence on macroeconomic outcomes but can only potentially affect them through the primary givens underlying aggregate demand.

On these grounds, one can see why increased flexibility on the labour market, induced by new technologies, may represent a source of instability. This view contrasts with conclusions from the deterministic approach of standard analysis, which is dominated by supply factors and which considers a more flexible labour market to be a 'panacea for all evils'; in other words, that it is sufficient, *per se*, to increase employment. In the Keynesian model, based on effective demand, this may not be the case. Greater flexibility tends to have two quite different effects. On the one hand, it increases the elasticity of employment with respect to income. For while in standard theory the labour market directly determines the equilibrium wage and the level of employment, in Keynesian theory it only determines the extent to which given income growth is translated into employment increases. In this sense, for example, one can assert that this elasticity rises in the

NE so that a given pressure of demand in the economy is associated with a lower structural unemployment rate (see e.g. Baily 2001: 234).

On the other hand, however, greater labour flexibility in the NE may lead to a lower aggregate demand and higher unemployment. This may happen if the tendency towards complete deregulation of the labour market ends up weakening some of the institutions upon which rapidity itself rests, such as trade unions. It is important to see why, from the Keynesian standpoint, this weakening can be detrimental to stability. The very existence of trade unions indicates that money wages are not fully determined by the market, and justifies the assumption of given money wages made in Keynes's theory. It would be wrong, however, to regard this as a rigidity causing unemployment, as in standard theory. This would be the case only if downward money wage flexibility (given the price level) were the key adjustment mechanism, capable of restoring the 'right', real wage rates, that is, those granting full employment. In the Modern Economy (ME) of the 1930s considered by Keynes, this mechanism, however, simply did not work. The primary reason was that unemployment was not the result of high real wages but of low levels of demand. The NE confirms the validity of this analysis. In particular, it is still true today that if money wages fell it would be even worse for firms, because it would trigger deflation and adverse expectations.

Wage flexibility: dynamic versus static analysis

It is important to note, however, that Keynesians do not suggest that wage flexibility is unimportant to firms. It is clear, for example, since they fix prices covering unit labour costs (defined as ratio between money wages and productivity, i.e. $P = W/p$), that there must be an adjusting mechanism capable of restoring the equilibrium between prices and costs, whenever they differ. Thus, in static analysis, when focusing on equilibrium at a point in time, there seems to be no alternative to downward money wage flexibility, since productivity is given. In a dynamic context, however, when productivity rises, a quite different adjustment mechanism takes place, one which is, in principle, capable of reconciling rising real wages with higher profit margins and low inflation and lower average unemployment.

This dynamic mechanism has been effectively summarized by Baily (2001) in his analysis of the NE. He starts by pointing out that prices are primarily based on labour costs, and that there is a certain inertia in nominal wage setting. Indeed, the wage inflation in any given period is largely predetermined. The key point is that 'nominal wages do not respond immediately to an acceleration of the productivity trend' (ibid.: 229) so that

> an increase in productivity growth will reduce the rate of increase of unit labour costs. Some part of this may translate into higher profit margins, but with competition, some part will also yield lower price inflation. Lower price inflation then holds down wage increases on the next round.
>
> (ibid.: 235)

It is clear that so long as nominal wages fail to rise in line with productivity in each period, both real wages and profit margins can increase, with obvious positive effects on inflation rates as well as on unemployment (higher real wages also imply higher demand). The element of flexibility underlying this dynamic mechanism concerns, therefore, the distribution of productivity gains. Indeed, this mechanism leaves room for wage bargaining and, thus, for an active role of trade unions in the economic process.

Four remarks concerning the role of this mechanism in the NE can be made. First, this dynamic mechanism, like rapidity in general, is not unique to the NE but represents the normal workings of modern capitalism. It started on a significant scale in the ME when electrification, and the other general-purpose technologies that characterized the second industrial revolution, made mass production, large industrial enterprises and industrial labour unions possible. However, it is also true that the NE implies an acceleration of the dynamic process. Indeed, by keeping inflation low, the NE makes it clear, once and for all, that the crucial way wage flexibility is achieved in advanced economies is not through a money wage downward flexibility, in the face of constant prices, but through relative nominal wage stickiness in the face of productivity gains.

This has also been true for other stages of modern capitalism ever since the First World War. However, these were often characterized by 'disturbing' factors generating, for example, high price inflation, and inducing people to think, instead, that the key problem is the adjustment of money wages to price inflation and, thus, the distribution of a given level of income between wages and profits. In other words, the NE makes it clear that what really matters for firms and workers alike is the dynamic problem of distributing a growing income rather than the static problem of distributing a given level of income.

Second, this dynamic perspective does not necessarily contradict the claim that the labour market in the NE is more flexible and deregulated. In particular, deregulation and flexibility do not mean that nominal wages have become flexible in both directions, like the price of fish or vegetables. As pointed out, for example, by Katz and Krueger (1999), a decline in unionization and the increase in competitive intensity have made it harder for workers to push for wage *increases* in line with productivity gains.

However, flexibility is a matter of degree. In particular, it is true that the NE has the potential for producing an excessive weakening of trade union power due to the combined effect of technological change, greater international competition and delocation of production. The Keynesian perspective suggests that, while a completely rigid labour market should certainly be ruled out on efficiency grounds, pushing flexibility beyond a certain point, towards a pure competitive market ideal, represents an element of instability. It may hit aggregate demand for at least two reasons: it weakens, to some extent, the stimulus to investment and innovation, and the large productivity gains that have occurred. Second, it favours a more inequitable income distribution, with a fall in the relative share of wages on national income.

Third, the analysis of this dynamic mechanism reveals one of the points where the differences between the two basic macro paradigms are most evident: namely, the role of institutions in economic theory. For standard theory, markets are self-regulating, and institutions are exogenous constraints needed only to guarantee their optimal functioning. A long tradition in neoclassical theory, for example, has regarded rapidity (i.e. technological progress and productivity) as exogenous, and considered trade unions a likely cause of market failure or imperfection that undermines the adjustment process on the labour market, based on full price flexibility. Unfortunately, in this way, however, the positive dynamic link between the two factors, which underlies both the ME and the NE, is completely neglected. To put it more plainly, technological progress is generated by a set of complementary institutions, including the national system of innovation and trade unions.

For Keynesians, instead, institutions generate the path that influences the development of markets and agents' behaviour. Trade unions are part of the generative process of rapidity, and the dynamic adjustment mechanism becomes of crucial significance. Keynes's instantaneous equilibrium model captures it by making the assumption of given money wages. However, at the same time, one should also refrain from regarding Keynesian analysis as 'institutional determinist', in the sense that, for good or bad, institutions determine everything. For example, a central feature of this analysis is that innovation (R&D and directions of research) and productivity, while certainly favoured by the set of complementary institutions, are also partly endogenous to the economic sphere, as they depend upon expected profits and level of activity (see e.g. Blanchard 2003).

Fourth, another significant implication of this analysis is that the Keynesian framework is consistent with the existence in the NE of a plurality of models of capitalism, each with its own distinct pattern of corporate governance, labour relations and social welfare, as well as a peculiar cultural background. In contrast with standard theory, it does not single out just one 'right' type of capitalism fitting the ideal of perfect competition and does not justify the orthodox claim that both technological change and globalization inevitably push all developed countries to conform to a 'leading model' of capitalism, such as the US, which is closer to that ideal. First of all, it is not clear where the boundary between good and bad flexibility lies. Second, as shown by the case of the US, potentially superior economic performance by the leading country may be due not just to better institutions, but to other factors that keep aggregate demand high.

The nature of contemporary knowledge

The Keynesian model is also able to capture instability factors that have to do with the direct impact of faster technological change on aggregate demand. The first factor is linked to the nature of contemporary knowledge. ICT is a time-shrinking technology that induces, for example, a faster obsolescence of knowledge. At the methodological level, the Keynesian approach can account for it because, in contrast with NCM's deep parameters, it rests on malleable parameters and can therefore explain agents' changing behaviour.

At a more analytical level, this phenomenon proves to be a source of instability in that it may generate further anomalies in investors' behaviour, which are factors likely to generate wider fluctuations in the MEC and income, in line with

Keynes's account of business cycles. In particular, the characteristics of knowledge in the NE may exacerbate investment volatility by influencing certain endogenous factors of investment in plants and equipment. These are known almost inevitably to cause some fluctuations, such as postponability, competitive pressures to expand capacity, the uneven development in the relative growth rate and capital intensity of various sectors of the economy, lumpiness (i.e. indivisibilities in many large investments) and the accelerator principle.[1]

On the one hand, the accelerator effect may be weakened because of the greater difficulty of forecasting demand in the NE, due to the more volatile nature of much consumption expenditure. On the other hand, factors such as 'lumpiness' and uncertainty concerning the outcome of much investment in augmenting knowledge, for example, by R&D, tend to make investment more independent a variable, more interest inelastic, and subject to changes in investors' long-term expectations. These expectations are more likely to lead to herd behaviour and 'shared errors', such as over-investment and excess capacity, than in the past, because they are artificial, that is, not grounded in adequate knowledge and a true model of the economy (see also Shackle 1967; Freeman and Perez 1988: 39–43). The greater complexity of the NE and the time-shrinking nature of ICT seem to reduce the basis for making reliable estimates about future events, such as the impact of new technologies on the economy.

This point has been noted, for example, by economists such as Baily and Summers who emphasize the peculiarity of the last cycle compared to those of the recent past. It conforms more to the so-called investment boom and bust model, according to which cycles are induced by big swings in investment expenditure due to factors such as optimism and pessimism, rather than to those emphasized by standard theory (which basically assumes the existence of one basic type of business cycle). As the *Economist* puts it

> [m]ost economists...are assessing the current downturn as if, in key respects, this were a business cycle like any of the other nine that America has experienced since 1945. One observer...thinks not. Larry Summers...has recently argued that America's current cycle is fundamentally different from its post war predecessors – though not because it is 'new'. He argues that it has more in common with economic cycles as they worked before the Second World War – or even with... Japan's during the late 1980's.
>
> (the *Economist* 10–3–2001: 73)

Additionally, as noted in our account of rapidity, another feature of contemporary knowledge is the fact that intellectual capital is rarely the property of only one firm, thereby creating a need for growing coordination between firms. Keynesian analysis captures this because it does not rely on the standard assumption of atomistic representative firms and deep parameters but on a number of heterogeneous firms that need to be coordinated by products of mutual interest dimension, such as knowledge. Unlike the neoclassical model, which sees cooperation as being incompatible with competition and a source of inefficiency, in Keynesian theory, in principle, these two dimensions must coexist. According to this theory, instability may also occur in this case because, given that knowledge is a public good, the returns are difficult to appropriate and so there may not be enough incentives for private enterprise and investment.

Greater heterogeneity in structural conditions and agents' behaviour

The Keynesian model is also able to deal with another set of instability factors linked to the greater heterogeneity in structural conditions and agents' behaviour, following the diffusion of product differentiation and market concentration in certain high-tech industries (due to increasing returns to scale, low marginal costs and externality effects) allowed by rapidity. We refer, in particular, to the distinction between different types of consumer lifestyles, income brackets or the consideration of growing wage differentials that raise the relevant composition effects. This is possible because, in contrast with NCM, the Keynesian approach does not rely on perfect competition and representative agents, and allows for agents' heterogeneity. However, this does not mean that it relies on imperfect competition, either.

This is one of the points where it is important to make a distinction between the *General Theory* and later Keynesians. For Keynes, there is no direct link between market forms and macroeconomic outcomes as can instead be found in the modern micro-foundations literature.[2] There is no link, for example, between the price rigidity that derives from models of imperfect competition and price stability in macroeconomics, as they are determined by entirely different sets of factors. In his view, agents' heterogeneity, in general, is only an empirical or descriptive assumption. In actual economies one can find, for example, a whole spectrum of market forms depending on the sector and type of good. In his macroeconomic scheme, these forms are not irrelevant, but are one of those secondary givens that can influence outcomes only through the primary givens of aggregate demand.

From this standpoint, it can be argued that product differentiation has a macroeconomic impact, because it affects the changeable parameters of consumers and investors. The fact that new goods, or new versions of the same goods, appear at an increasing pace on the market may create macroeconomic instability because it makes consumption more volatile by changing consumers' perception of time. In particular, it shortens their planning horizon and makes them more uncertain and dependent upon such collective entities as the state of confidence. For this reason, it compels firms to adopt ever more aggressive marketing strategies.

However, product differentiation also affects the nature of investment and exports. It implies, for example, that a higher portion of firms' budgets needs to be allocated to marketing and advertising expenditures, thus increasing the overall fragility of investment.

Finally, Keynesian analysis also accounts for composition effects deriving from rapidity, such as the distinction between different types of consumers, or the growing inequality in income distribution. These, too, may have negative implications for macro stability, as they are likely to affect aggregate consumption (e.g. higher income consumers have a lower propensity to consume than lower income earners).

21 Keynesian theory and lightness

In this chapter, we assess the effects of lightness on stability from the point of view of the Keynesian model. As in previous chapters, we shall be examining the implication of the model that indicates that the negative effects, in this case of lightness, are bound to prevail over the positive ones. Here, as before, the Keynesian model does not deny that lightness can potentially have positive effects on stability, such as greater expansion in output due to the appearance of new sectors other than standard manufacturing, or increased consumption and investment financing due to the accelerated development of financial markets. Rather, it denies that these positive effects inevitably come about and unconditionally prevail. Macroeconomic outcomes, instead, ultimately depend on how lightness affects the primary givens underlying aggregate demand and their key determinants, such as the institutional set-up and agents' theories.

Strictly speaking, for Keynesians, lightness may well have either a neutral or even a positive impact on these determinants. Indeed, firms' MEC may be stimulated as new opportunities for investment are created in new 'immaterial' sectors, and the agents' propensity to consume may benefit from higher capital gains deriving from the higher number of shareholders than in the past. Exports of leading countries producing the new goods may also increase.

However, the Keynesian logic reveals that lightness is more likely to affect the key determinants of aggregate demand in such a way as to generate destabilizing tendencies. Once again, the Keynesian model is able to both capture the sources of instability and explain why they actually arise and may prevail over the positive factors.

The quality issue

The first source of instability generated by lightness that the Keynesian logic accounts for is the increased role of the quality dimension of goods in the NE. This can be seen in several key factors, such as the larger share of light goods in the composition of output, the broader concept of capital, the greater weight of financial over real assets, the greater role of intangibles and the quality characteristics of goods. This is not surprising from a methodological standpoint, given that the Keynesian model does not rely on certain key features of standard theory, such as atomistic preferences, representative agent devices or the perfect competition assumption that, for example, implies homogeneity of goods.

However, as already noted, this does not necessarily mean that it relies on the modern theories of imperfect competition, either. These theories underlie the New Keynesian approach, which deals with the quality issue in terms of 'local imperfections', such as problems of pricing, externality and information imperfections (e.g. asymmetric information). The Keynesian model presented here suggests, instead, that 'global imperfections' play a key role. This distinction is important because it can be argued that the NE, while reducing the scope for local imperfections, increases the scope for global ones. One can note, for example, that by improving the transmission of information, the NE makes information asymmetries less relevant. By making capital markets more efficient, it reduces the impact of liquidity constraints, and so on. On the other hand, the NE is also more likely to generate 'shared errors' leading to the anomalous behaviour of the key variables of aggregate demand, which in turn could create various forms of global instability.

On these grounds, it is now possible to clarify how the Keynesian model deals with issues of quality. In the *General Theory*, they are considered among the key factors that justify the inversion of parameters characterizing the principle of effective demand with respect to standard theory, resulting in a new sequence in which aggregate demand variables, rather than the endowments of productive factors, play a causal role. For instance, Keynes affirmed that financial markets play a prominent role in promoting growth. In his scheme, the autonomy of investment from saving is due to its dependence upon 'light' factors (e.g. expectations and theories) and institutions, such as the stock market and banks. It can be argued that the increased role of quality factors in the NE further justifies this inversion in parameters.

Quality factors are also likely to exercise a strong influence on the dynamics of the economy by affecting the primary givens of aggregate demand, that is, the agents' perceptions of some of the key dimensions, such as value and markets. This can lead to several important outcomes. First of all, the peculiar nature of knowledge, coupled with its greater role in the NE, may generate instability by changing the agents' perception of the market. Agents no longer see the market as a self-contained entity or as the space of private enterprise, but as increasingly linked to the institutional and cultural spheres. This is especially relevant for private investment in the NE, which can be undermined by a number of factors. These include the difficulty in appropriating returns due to the public good nature of knowledge; its dependence upon institutionally determined R&D, which makes for an intrinsic overlap between public and private investment; and the difficulty in understanding the strong link between cultural factors and economic ones, especially for those firms wishing to invest in developing countries.[1] Neoclassical theory captures these factors by simply expanding the concept of capital in production functions. An example is endogenous growth theory. Our Keynesian model, instead, sees these factors as a sign of growing autonomy of investment from savings, its driving role in the sequence of variables, and its greater independence from changes in the market interest rate.

Second, the same light factors that account for weak investment in the NE may also generate further instability by undermining exports of advanced countries (e.g. large parts of Europe) that were relatively strong in traditional manufacturing activities. In particular, exports may not grow enough to offset the reduction in employment caused by the shrinking of the 'old', narrowly defined, industrial sector induced by globalization and a more competitive environment. These composition issues are insignificant for NCM, since the smooth working of the price mechanism is assumed to grant full employment both at the national and international level. However, according to the Keynesian concept of export-led growth, à la Kaldor, this is just not so.

Third, the ever-growing importance of intangible goods and the influence of qualitative features of normal goods in the NE may create instability by influencing the agents' perception of value. Transparency has become an issue of great concern, and there is a call for greater control of the conventional assessment both of firms' accounting and everyday consumption activities. This means, for instance, that firms and investors are forced to rely on specialist or institutional advice for assessing the quality of companies' accounts. Similarly, consumers are more dependent upon collective entities and independent bodies to supply quality certification, trust and reputation. These factors tend to make financial asset prices and aggregate consumption more volatile and vulnerable to global confidence shocks.

Deregulation and financial innovation

The second source of instability generated by lightness that the Keynesian logic manages to accommodate is the negative effects of deregulation and financial innovation (see e.g. Simonazzi 2003). Examples of such effects include sectoral imbalances (e.g. households and firms take on too much debt), over-investment, declining accounting standards and excessive diffusion of stock options. Again, from the methodological standpoint, this is possible because the Keynesian model does not adopt a representative agent device, which impairs the analysis of sectoral problems, but relies on a heterogeneous population of agents (including, for example, both good and bad firms). Moreover, thanks to the simultaneous consideration of a number of sectors and interdependent phenomena, this model does not consider these negative factors to be the product of policy errors but as the result of endogenous sources of instability. In the end, unlike the standard model that suggests an abstract idea of markets, the Keynesian approach fully recognizes the link between growth and institutional aspects and, in particular, accommodates the role of institutions as mechanisms capable of influencing market outcomes or even leading to the 'creation' of markets.

These effects of deregulation may be a source of instability from the Keynesian standpoint for several reasons. First of all, phenomena such as agents' over-borrowing, firms going bankrupt, scandals due to excessive debt and over-optimism are a sign of endogenous instability for an important number of Keynesians. Following the insights of authors such as Minsky and his financial instability hypothesis (e.g. Minsky 1982), many Keynesians suggest that these phenomena are generated not by policy errors, as NCM would have it, but by some basic flaws of the market mechanism. For example, they may stem from agents' shared errors due to their changing perception of value and default risk induced by lightness (see also Dow 2002: 30).[2] When combined with the shortening of agents' horizons, induced by globalization and ICT, this accounts for the fact that the creation of more efficient, liquid and sophisticated financial markets in the NE has not led people to improve their inter-temporal plans, as supposed by NCM. Instead, they may simply underestimate the default-risks and go into debt without much concern for future prospects. Once again, it is important not to see this as purely psychological phenomena. Such risks belong to the category of shared errors that are significantly favoured by objective factors, too, such as the diffusion of theories (e.g. that the NE implies the end of the business cycle, or that the central banks will step in to prevent or cure major financial crises), or the central banks' low interest rate policy.

The endogenous nature of these phenomena makes them even riskier for macroeconomic stability. It is clear, for example, that they are not isolated but can be found in various sectors of the economy, raising composition issues whose impact on the economy as a whole is potentially serious. For example, when analysing the various imbalances characterizing the US economy over the last few years (government deficit, current account deficit and private deficit) as a set of interdependent phenomena, it is quite clear that they are no longer easily sustainable[3] and pose a threat to the stability of aggregate demand, both at the domestic and international levels. In particular, as noted by Godley and Izurieta (2002: 39–43), slow growth will follow if the savings rate climbs back to its long-term norm.

Second, the negative phenomena just described tend to undermine the context of rules that grant sufficient growth of aggregate demand and the development of 'lightness' itself. Indeed, Keynesians emphasize that the enormous expansion of financial markets in the past few decades was favoured not just by liberalization moves and the elimination of barriers across countries, but also by new rules and institutions granting the correct behaviour, and the quality of players, on such markets (see e.g. Stiglitz 2003). In their view, without such 'rules', markets could not work because of possible crises in confidence as a reaction to fraudulent practices. It is clear that, so long as it favours complete deregulation of financial markets, the NE has the potential to generate unprecedented confidence shocks that could call into question, or even reverse, the trend towards the continuous expansion of markets, and precipitate obvious negative consequences for aggregate demand.

Erratic behaviour of financial markets

Finally, the Keynesian model naturally captures a third source of instability linked to lightness: the erratic behaviour of financial markets, where speculation dominates and gives rise to waves of optimism and pessimism. As already noted, this is because the Keynesian model does not rely on the assumption of atomistic rationality and stable preferences. Instead, from the start, it incorporates the products of the dimension of agents' mutual interest and allows the possibility of endogenous changes in the parameters underlying the primary variables.[4] This means that the Keynesian model regards these phenomena as being the product not so much of psychological factors, such as irrational exuberance, but of important changes in the agents' collective perception of the dimensions of time, space and value, induced by the various features of the NE, including lightness. While these phenomena have also characterized other periods of capitalism, they tend to accelerate in the NE, and are therefore more likely to generate 'shared errors'. In particular, due to the existence of intangible capital, which is giving rise to new valuation problems, the NE implies both a greater number of competing hypotheses, or models, of stock markets, and a higher rate of updating of agents' models. This accounts for growing anomalies in financial markets and concomitant possible negative implications for effective demand.

In order to understand these implications, it is important to realize to what extent this view is different from the standard theories. Unlike the 'efficient markets view' of NCM, according to which current share prices correctly incorporate all relevant information about the fundamentals described by the only true model of the economy, the Keynesian view, emphasized here, instead implies that the stock market is inefficient. This must be understood in two different, although related, senses.

First of all, by 'inefficient' stock market we mean that the 'true' fundamentals cannot be known or ascertained on a priori grounds, and that there is no mechanism that grants convergence of actual share prices to their true fundamental value. For this reason, our Keynesian standpoint also differs from the so-called 'behavioural finance' approach (e.g. Shiller 2000), which is the most frequent rival of standard finance theory and provides an explanation for the impressive number of financial crises in recent years. The key point is that this approach regards the market as being inefficient and subject to waves of irrational exuberance: 'behavioural finance…attempts to find psychological explanation for otherwise mystifying movements in the stock market. The current bear market seems to vindicate behaviouralists who argue that there has been a huge stock market bubble' (the *Economist* 22–3–2001: 111).

In other words, the behavioural finance approach suggests that it is possible to define shares' 'true' fundamental values, based on the present value of expected dividends and expressed in the form of observed patterns, such as a certain 'normal' value of the price–earning ratio over a number of years, and the extent to which their actual prices deviate from them. They can either be undervalued or overvalued (e.g. the case of a company's share whose fundamental value is zero), when their value is not justified by important news concerning dividends or interest rates but by fads (e.g. when people simply believe that future yields are based on past yields).

In general, our view is that no model or simple theory should be given privileged status, or is better than any of the others in an absolute sense as a guide to traders' behaviour. All the competing models should be treated on a par as tentative rationalizations of past and future events; there is no way to distinguish *ex ante* the 'correct' from the 'false' hypotheses, or the rational from the irrational moves. Thus, for example, it was not at all clear at the time for traders that ICT and dot.coms were a bubble. It is only *ex post* that we can say that this was the case. As suggested by the 'rational bubble' approach, many *rational* arguments, or more or less plausible explanations, for the boom were provided:

> Given the link between stock market behaviour and the ICT sector with the birth and subsequent bust of the dot.com bubble, it is perhaps understandable that irrational exuberance is now being offered as a reason for the telecommunication crisis. However, the idea is potentially misleading since it characterizes as illogical what may be complex, but logical, reactions to uncertainty. Acquisition access, the payment of licence fees that are too high, viewed *ex-post*, and unrealistic business models have all been preferred as example of irrational exuberance...However, such firm behaviour, even when *ex post* misguided, need not be irrational.
>
> (Cooper and Madden 2004, quoted in
> Western 2004: 90)

In other words, even the dot.com bubble possesses 'a significant degree of rationality, that is, economic agents acted rationally in response to the information set that confronted them *at the time*' (ibid., emphasis in original.). This clearly does not imply that the boom years were rational – *ex post*, as suggested by NCM, according to which the market boom in the NE was not a bubble at all but reflected some changed fundamentals.

Taken together, these considerations indicate that the stock market is inefficient because there is no privileged standpoint *ex ante*; what justifies the success of one particular model on the market, at a given moment in time, is simply the conventional or inter-subjective agreement among the members of the financial community itself. It is clear that this conventional basis is not built on solid ground; it is subject to sudden changes, in line with varying times and places.

The second sense in which the stock market is inefficient is that it is not a simple mirror, or trusty barometer, of the economy. In particular, whereas the NCM sequence regards productivity as being exogenous and the stock market as translating changes in the productivity of capital into equity prices, the Keynesian view holds that the role of the stock market is more complex. As noted earlier, in the *General Theory* there is no one-way relationship, but an interaction, or even an overlap, between the two variables. On the one hand, there is no exogenously given real productivity; this is largely an endogenous variable also influenced by equity prices themselves. On the other, equity prices do not reflect real productivity in a passive and linear way. Indeed the stock market is not a mirror but a driver of growth. It is based on two autonomous 'engines' that may push actual share prices quite a distance from real profitability or fundamental values: the increasing proportion of stocks of financial wealth relative to income flows that allows fast global financial markets to dominate slow production processes, and the large number of theories used by traders.

It is important to note that this overlap helps justify the parameter inversion in Keynes's sequence with respect to standard theory. Indeed, it is the stock exchange together with the banking system that has been able to generate lightness, that is, to free investment from its strict link with the flow of savings, as is the case in a barter economy. In other words, as Keynes understood, ever since the development of mature financial institutions in the modern economy, investment is indeed an autonomous variable that opens the sequence of variables, as we foresee in our model (see e.g. Chick 1983; Nell 2002). Clearly, the more sophisticated the markets, the greater the financing opportunities for investment. However, once again, the Keynesian view suggests that, in the NE, this is paid at a cost of greater instability. An increasingly important role is being played by conventional assessments of asset prices (reflected in the existence of a larger number of models) and changes in agents' perception of time and value (implying a higher rate of updating of these models) on the stock market. Consequently, more volatile asset prices can be expected, with negative implications, especially for investment, in view of the overlap between asset prices and firms' MEC.

22 Keynesian theory and precision

Let us now assess the claims about the effects of precision on stability that can be made from the Keynesian standpoint, which as we shall see, once again defends the conclusion that negative effects prevail over positive ones. The Keynesian approach does not deny that precision in the form of greater quantitative information about events, increasing mathematization of economics and better forecasting techniques can grant stability by helping decision-making and policy intervention. Indeed, Keynes himself was a driving force behind the development of national accounting. However, the logic of the Keynesian approach does not allow these achievements to be taken for granted. Unlike NCM, it suggests that improved decision-making and policy can occur only if precision positively affects the determinants of aggregate demand, on which macroeconomic outcomes ultimately depend.

According to Keynesians, one cannot simply rule out the possibility that precision might have a neutral effect on these determinants or might even modify them in such a way as to increase aggregate demand. Agents' expectations may well be influenced by greater quantitative knowledge about market conditions or more sophisticated forecasting techniques that might help reduce uncertainty, or by better models allowing them to single out the truly important causal factors. However, it seems more likely that precision may affect the key determinants of aggregate demand in such a way as to generate destabilizing tendencies. Once again, it can be seen that the Keynesian model is able to capture the sources of instability as well as to explain why they actually arise and may prevail over the positive factors.

Management by numbers

The Keynesian model naturally captures the first factor of instability, which is the negative influence on agents' behaviour exercised by the search for greater quantitative information and by 'management by numbers', in the form of excessive risk aversion, focus on short-run profitability and bias against introducing innovative products. This is possible because, unlike its NCM counterpart, the Keynesian model does not rely on the assumption of stable parameters, but allows for changes in agents' qualitative behaviour due to their changing perception of key economic dimensions. In particular, management by numbers favours the shortening of the agents' time horizon. This may prove to be destabilizing from the Keynesian standpoint particularly in that it undermines investment. It makes it more difficult, for example, to carry out investment projects with longer expected 'lifespans'. Moreover, greater quantitative information *per se*, if not accompanied by a parallel improvement in elaboration or interpretation techniques, may be destabilizing because it increases complexity and causes people to rely on oversimplified conceptual schemes in order to make decisions. This is more likely to generate herd behaviour in all markets, as well as more pronounced fluctuations.

The Keynesian stance presented here implies a constructive proposal for counteracting this source of instability by increasing the power of handling the growing amount of data. In contrast with current trends in economics, which favour piecemeal modelling of individual aspects or markets, it provides a general framework for arranging the entire range of information about the economy as a whole and for determining a hierarchy among the indicators. For example, it stresses the importance of classifying variables in relation to their influence on aggregate demand, following the distinction between primary and secondary variables.

Conventional methods and indicators

The Keynesian model also accounts for the apparent instability arising from the use of conventional methods in the representation of NE phenomena, such as intangibles, which still defy proper measurement. Whereas NCM relies on stable preferences and perfect competition, resulting in having to abstract from differences between different types of goods, the Keynesian approach captures the objective dimensions of structural change, such as lightness, and tries to see what impact they make on agents' key propensities. Unlike NCM, this approach does not regard prices as coalescing all the relevant information and as being sufficient devices for the coordination of agents' behaviour. Agents' propensities or expectations are also influenced and coordinated by theories and indicators. In this regard, Keynesians believe that there is no one unique model of the economy that singles out relevant indicators and coordinates agents' expectations, but that there is a plurality of representations, with no necessary convergence to the 'true' one. People may therefore act on the grounds of 'false' or misleading representations (e.g. those that assume that nothing is changed in the structure of the NE) that lead them to make 'shared errors', giving rise to otherwise 'unjustified' changes in consumption and investment decisions.

Once again, the Keynesian stance provides a constructive proposal. For example, it identifies a new type of indicator capable of capturing the trends of the NE and changes in agents' propensities of time, space, value and market. The new foundations of Keynesian methodology allow this constructive move. The basic concepts of neoclassical macro theory, such as that of the atomistic individual, are not operational. They do not naturally refer to aggregates, so proxies must be found, as in the case of natural income or expected income (e.g. they are represented by averages of observed values). Instead, Keynesian theory relies on aggregates that are much closer to the surface and are fully operational, as shown by the crucial role played by the *General Theory* in the development of national accounting.

The widening gap between theoretical and empirical progress

In the third place, the Keynesian model is able to cope with the widening gap between theoretical and empirical progress, that is, the fact that theoretical progress alone may be misleading for agents and generate their unjustified overconfidence in the practical implications of theory. Again, this is possible because Keynesians allow for the influence of a plurality of models on agents' propensities and expectations, including of course those of NCM, which are mainly responsible for this gap. The reason why this is a source of instability is that agents (and especially governments) in many cases actually believe in the NCM models so that they may act in such a way as to neglect effective demand problems and overemphasize the stability and self-adjusting nature of the economy. Moreover, the reaction to the gap in the NE is destabilizing because it induces economists to retreat into even more self-contained, though internally consistent, conceptual frameworks, which are likely to capture ever-smaller bits of reality, thus furthering the gap itself.

The Keynesian standpoint presented in this book suggests a constructive move to break this vicious circle and close the gap. This move consists first of all in clarifying the reasons for which such a gap arises. The key point seems to be that the deep parameters stressed by NCM are not a good foundation for studying the complexity of the economy as a whole. They lead to consideration of crucial phenomena as irrelevant or as friction and, therefore, capture only a relatively small part of real-world economies.

The next and crucial step is to indicate an alternative modelling strategy. The key suggestion that can be made here is that such a strategy must be based on a broader notion of essence, according to which those factors dismissed as irrelevant by NCM are included among the key factors. In practice, this means singling out the parameters underlying aggregate demand as the new set of primary or causal variables.

Predictive failures

The Keynesian model also manages to address instability problems deriving from the lack of satisfactory predictive performances of macroeconometric models in the NE. As already noted, Keynesian analysis can accomplish this task because, in contrast with NCM, it is aware of parameter instability, which undermines the applicability of the concept of stochastic equilibrium and the validity of econometric exercises.

Strictly speaking, it is true that a certain degree of stability is achieved by the fact that a certain consensus view among forecasters (to which NCM itself contributes) may grant a sufficient anchor to agents' expectations. However, it is also true that this consensus is intrinsically fragile, as all conventions and repeated predictive failures may actually turn out to be destabilizing. The main reason for this, according to Keynesians, is that in the context of the NE, they induce people to respond in ways that ultimately worsen decision-making and policy-making problems, with negative consequences for aggregate demand.

To make this point clear, it is important to bear in mind that in addition to helping agents and institutions make decisions in the face of complex social and economic environment, a key aspect of precision in the NE is that it fuels unjustified expectations concerning the scope of economics and social science in general. In other words, it fosters the illusion that the increasing power of computers makes it possible to achieve the ideal of ever-greater forecasting ability. Strictly speaking, it can be argued that the attempt to pursue this ideal may even be self-defeating in the end. On the one hand, it induces people to try to obtain ever better forecasts. On the other, since the goal is unattainable, as shown by repeated failures, it fosters the search for increasingly complex but narrow models or sophisticated techniques and improved indicators. However, the production of new tools and indicators *per se* increases complexity even more and thus undermines the ultimate aim of precision: to assist policy-making.

The Keynesian model suggests a way out of this vicious circle. As a growing number of scholars have convincingly argued in recent times (see e.g. Lawson 1997, 2003), the first step is to point out that the predictive ideal is misleading and has forced economics into a blind alley. It unduly narrows down the object of scientific analysis to those few aspects of business cycles which can be predicted.

The second step is to set a different goal. The Keynesian view is extremely constructive from this point of view. While rejecting the predictive ideal, it still implies, for example, that the government can act and intervene; it implies a presumption that policy effects will not be reversed or undermined by agents' behaviour. On what grounds does it stand? From the experience of the last seventy years, it seems that to maintain a viable Keynesian policy stance, models of instantaneous equilibrium, such as that underlying the *General Theory*, are not sufficient. Policy must be based not on prediction but on the ability to consider scenarios describing the most likely patterns of change in the medium or long run. In other words, the key point is not to establish invariable parameters, as in NCM models, but to be able to say something about their evolution. In this regard, considering Keynesian parameters as purely phenomenic and changeable with policy, as Lucas does, is a mistake. While the parameters do change, they change systematically, for they rely on the recognizable products of mutual interest.

23 Keynesian theory and visibility

In this chapter, we assess the Keynesian claims concerning the effects of visibility on stability. In particular, we shall try to show why, according to the Keynesian model presented here, the combination of strict policy rules and old-style pragmatism which prevails in Western economies today may turn out to be destabilizing and may, therefore, worsen rather than remedy the growing potential instability of the private sector. This model suggests that, if it is to play a stabilizing role, policy must not simply be more pragmatic but must be more openly discretionary and based on a well-informed understanding of the NE.

Growth as a condition for stability

One general feature of our Keynesian stance is to call into question the link between policy rules and growth posed by NCM. This does not mean that governments should pose no limits to detrimental phenomena, such as deficits and inflation. The question is how best to achieve stability and growth. The logic of the Keynesian model is to reject the standard view according to which strict policy rules granting stability in terms of financial consolidation and very low inflation are the universal condition for growth. From the Keynesian standpoint, the opposite is true: growth is a condition for stability (see e.g. Bibow 2002b, 2003). As already noted, policy rules *per se* have no general validity and may fail to deliver the goods; indeed pursuing them at all costs is even likely to generate destabilizing tendencies. The Keynesian standpoint justifies these claims. It is because they exercise a negative influence on aggregate demand that such negative outcomes may occur. This does not mean that stability, that is the goals of balanced budgets and low inflation, should not be sought at all but that they are better achieved in *ex post* rather than *ex ante* fashion, that is, as the result, rather than a condition, of growth.

The intrinsic limits of pragmatism

Another aspect of our Keynesian model is that it emphasizes the intrinsic limits of old pragmatism in the NE. Strictly speaking, it certainly does not deny that pragmatism is quite useful in tempering the rigour of strict policy rules. To a large extent, Keynesians are certainly pragmatic policy-makers. However, in the NE, the old-fashioned pragmatism – based on a combination of *ex ante* acceptance of orthodox theoretical principles and *ex post* Keynesian increases in public expenditure or interest rate cuts to remedy the actual flaws of the market economy – is no longer as successful as it used to be for at least two reasons. First, adjustment processes to new equilibrium positions in the NE, whether good or bad, are faster than before. Therefore, there is less time for observation and *ex post*, passive intervention. Second, the widespread adoption of formal policy rules in the NE makes pragmatism quite destabilizing because it undermines people's confidence. The point is simple. As the European experience with the stability pact shows, governments tend to place more emphasis on commitment to such formal rules. Policy-making becomes a matter of signing treaties or even constitutions. People therefore find it difficult to understand why government themselves do not strictly adhere such rules in the first place.

A new discretionary policy stance

To remedy the flaws arising from the combination of rules and pragmatism, the Keynesian model suggests that policy-makers wishing to stabilize the economy need to adopt a more active stance that is based on an accurate analysis of the NE. In other words, a proper Keynesian policy view should not be confused with pragmatism, or with *ex post* remedies. It is a more theoretically oriented discretionary stance, based on different principles from those of standard theory and policy rules.

One major point is that demand policies can be implemented without adherence to precise rules. In contrast with the determinist and universalist claims of NCM models, the crucial implication of the principle of effective demand is that it incorporates a temporal dimension consistent with the path-dependence view and the insights of complexity theory. As noted by Brock and Colander (2000: 81), the path-dependence conception implies that even solutions to problems have a temporal dimension: the best policy will change over time; solutions are temporary and changing.

Moreover, policy proposals should be scenario based. This means, for example, that they should take the form of qualifications, rather than statements; or that multiple policy results should be expected from a specific policy; or that there should be increasing concern for occurrence of abrupt changes. What is more, in our view, it also means specifying the policy targets following the logic of 'thresholds'. For example, inflation and budget deficits are not evils as such. They can be acceptable or even positive so long as they are moderate and remain within a certain threshold; they become detrimental beyond that point. On this view, one of the tasks of economic theory is to determine the relevant thresholds, bearing in mind that these, too, may change over the course of time.

To be more specific, let us consider the definition of macroeconomic stability as applied to Europe today. In contrast with what is generally inferred from standard theory, in our view, stability does not necessarily imply a zero deficit and 2 per cent inflation as prescribed by the current European Monetary Union policy rules. Critics of this policy framework are not necessarily in favour of unlimited deficit and ever-increasing inflation. In line with the threshold logic, they could argue that within limits, perhaps 3 or 4 per cent, both inflation and budget deficits are positive for the economy and can be sustained indefinitely; they become pathological phenomena only when these limits have been exceeded (see e.g. Arestis and Sawyer 2003).[1] In this view, it is clear above all that concerns about the sustainability of public deficit and debt seem to lose some of their relevance. Indeed, there is no compelling reason for which public debt must be fixed at zero or at any other specific value.

Strictly speaking, this policy stance is not simply an implication of the Keynesian interpretation of the NE. It follows instead from Keynes' belief that the system is not always in full employment equilibrium, and that income does not tend to its potential or natural level. This belief implies the rejection of general equilibrium theory as the proper basis for drawing normative conclusions. It indicates the need for adopting an alternative benchmark based on the normal or positive role of stability factors – in particular institutions, such as trade unions, central banks, trade agreements or fixed exchange rates – that were introduced in the past as correctives to market economies and whose elimination could worsen rather than improve the situation.

For Keynesians, there is reason to believe, however, that the NE makes orthodox policy rules even less appropriate, and increases governments' scope to stabilize the economy through active or discretionary demand policies. As already noted, the NE increases endogenous instability due to global imperfections or agents' 'shared errors' and the likelihood of exogenous shocks, which undermine aggregate demand and bring about either more frequent shifts from one state of equilibrium to the other or prolonged states of underemployment. In particular, in the NE, output and unemployment show even less of a tendency to reach their natural rate level than ever before. This concept proves only to have *ex post* value (it is obtained as the average of actual values), rather than the real attractor for actual economies. One can note, for example, that the price level in the NE fails to adjust aggregate demand and supply at the full employment level; inflation tends to remain relatively low and stable both in economies characterized by low underemployment rates and in those plagued by high rates. As pointed out by Blanchard (2003), this means that sometimes the economy can get stuck for relatively long periods of time, as shown by the recent cases of Japan and many European countries. Although macroeconomists were confident of having learned a lesson following the Great Depression that would permit macro policy to avoid another major depression, Blanchard concludes that today 'we can hardly be sure' (2003: 483).

Monetary policy

More specific policy conclusions follow from this general view. Let us start from the current combination of rules and pragmatism in the field of monetary policy.

There is no doubting that ITR is at least partly consistent with the Keynesian model. In contrast with old monetary rules, ITR involves dropping several tenets of monetarism and the quantity theory of money. It stresses the role of interest rate setting rather than money supply targeting, the balanced analysis of multiple factors of inflation instead of the exclusive emphasis on money and the view of the transmission mechanism as complex and uncertain rather than mechanistic.

However, the Keynesian model also explains why this policy rule may also create instability by undermining aggregate demand. From the demand standpoint, ITR is certainly positive if it encourages central banks to behave in a more conditional or discretionary manner than the automatic pilot strategy advocated by Friedman, that is, to behave differently in different contexts. It would also be positive if it helped them realize that moderate inflation is not a pathology or that inflation due to cost increases in a depressed context is quite different from inflation due to strong demand, so trying to curb it is likely to make depression worse. However, ITR may be negative if its balanced approach to the causes of inflation does not lead central banks to call into question the view that inflation is an evil as such, that price stability is an essential precondition for growth and constitutes their only possible goal. This view is bound to create confusion in the markets and cause conflict within the strategy of the central bank itself. While recognition of the plurality of inflation sources is coherent with the Keynesian model, insistence on price stability as the exclusive goal of monetary policy, instead, implies that markets work smoothly and that there demand problems do not arise from other sources.

This conclusion is firmly rejected by Keynesian analysis of the NE. According to this analysis, there are two reasons for which monetary policy should not be unduly concerned with inflation. First, inflation is not the most important danger in the NE. For a number of reasons, such as greater competition due to globalization, productivity increases, less intensive use of raw materials and reduced wage pressure, the NE generates low inflation or even deflationary tendencies, even in the face of demand pressures. This means that inflation that is temporarily higher than expected should not be a matter of concern, as it could be the result of exceptional circumstances, such as oil shocks or exchange rate depreciation.

Second, there are other important factors, in the NE, such as the greater volatility of output and exchange rates, asset price inflation, debt and credit explosion, which can potentially undermine aggregate demand and which should therefore be more openly addressed by monetary policy. Indeed, while it is true that this policy has improved stability and counteracted growing endogenous instability since the Second World War, it will only continue to do so in the NE if it addresses this broader range of issues.

In addition, the Keynesian model also captures pragmatic monetary policy to some extent. For example, it can accommodate the fact that central banks do not always insist on their official targets (especially when the system is hit by supply shocks) and that they adopt a more flexible monetary policy, which essentially amounts to taking not just inflation but also growth into account. However, there is also a degree of inconsistency between such pragmatic moves and the

Keynesian model. This derives from the fact that Keynesian principles tend to come into the central banks' strategy only in disguise, that is, not as 'high' theory but as a kind of common sense framework for guiding everyday conduct within the grand strategy set by NCM. For example, even the rather flexible and pragmatic FED relies on theoretical principles of a monetarist kind, such as the NAIRU, even if it does not always stick to them in practice.

From the Keynesian standpoint, this is not a positive tactic, because it undermines the effectiveness of the policy moves required for supporting aggregate demand in the context of the NE. Indeed, only letting Keynesian thinking in through the backdoor or through the informal comments of insightful leaders accounts for the several flaws of purely pragmatic strategies, such as the slow adoption or insufficient scope of required changes in the face of the systemic failures, shared errors and confidence crises that the fragile NE is most likely to generate. Clearly, if central banks start to think in terms of NAIRU and automatic adjustment processes, such failures can only be recognized and contrasted after some dangerous delay.

Fiscal policy

Let us now focus on the current combination of rules and pragmatism in the field of fiscal policy. Strictly speaking, the Keynesian model, while supporting the idea that public deficits are relatively normal, does not imply that such deficits and the resulting stock of debt should permanently increase. However, this model rejects the kind of tight fiscal policy rules adopted by many governments in the NE, especially in Europe. In particular, the Keynesian model suggests that these rules may create instability by undermining aggregate demand. From the demand standpoint, there are several reasons why these rules may be counterproductive.

First of all, the causality argument. According to our Keynesian model, a commitment to sound public finance is not a pre-requisite for both successful cyclical stabilization and longer-term growth as implied by the neoclassical model. The main cause of instability in the NE is not excessive public expenditure or deficit. On the contrary, as clearly shown by European experience with the stability pact, governments tend to run deficits because of the insufficient economic growth resulting from a combination of endogenous mechanisms and external shocks which keep aggregate demand low. In this context, insisting on tight fiscal rules may prove to be a self-defeating tactic. Expenditure cuts imply lower growth, lower taxes and ever-higher deficits (see e.g. Arestis and Sawyer 2003; Blanchard 2003; Stiglitz 2003; Heipertz and Verdun 2004; Togati 2004). This is the most important reason why fiscal policy should be aimed at balancing budgets in indirect ways, that is, by favouring growth rather than by seeking to cut public expenditure.

Second, tight fiscal policy tends to create instability and reduce growth, especially when it is carried out by cutting certain strategic types of public expenditure, such as R&D, education and the welfare system. According to the Keynesian model, these expenditure cuts are likely to generate low demand, because they are unlikely to be compensated for by growth in private enterprise. The point is that they concern typical 'public goods' (producing 'stability' in a broad sense including trust, social capital and social cohesion) that, in general, tend to be insufficiently produced by the market or, rather, are the premises for its efficient functioning. This is the reason why these forms of expenditures and, in general, the so-called built-in stabilizers were gradually introduced into market economies during the last century. In this sense, by encouraging generalized expenditures cuts, the NE may prove to be self-defeating, that is, it may lead to call into question the very basis of its success.

Third, attempts to balance budgets through lower taxes and supply-side effects are likely to be unsuccessful and a source of instability because they generate adverse income distribution effects which add to those spontaneously generated by the NE features, such as rapid technological change and greater heterogeneity of society. These effects undermine aggregate demand because of the different propensities for consumption of high and low income groups of consumers.

Fourth, a tight fiscal policy rule might also lead to greater instability because the positive effects on aggregate demand expected by the advocates of such policies are insufficient. In the first place, crowding-in effects may not be significant. On the one hand, the Keynesian model suggests that there is no guarantee that the reduced deficit may actually generate the hoped-for decline in interest rates. The increased flow of savings may not influence interest rates, as it is increasingly dominated by stocks of financial assets in line with the different sequence of variables that underlies this model. On the other hand, even if the decline in the interest rate were substantial, there would be no guarantee that private investment would rise sufficiently to compensate for the reduced expenditure or the tax increase, especially in a depressed context. As already noted, the NE tends to produce a more interest-inelastic investment, through various changes in agents' perception of space, time, market and value. Moreover, people may not increase current consumption by discounting less future taxes. In other words, the NE implies that agents have a shorter planning horizon.

From the Keynesian standpoint these arguments can be reversed, implying, for example, that in the NE there is more room for more active fiscal policy. In other words, the negative effects of fiscal policy emphasized by NCM are less likely in the NE. As noted, for example, by Blanchard (2003: 559), consumers do not consider future taxes increases and react positively to tax cuts. This contradicts the Ricardian equivalence view. Indeed, evidence shows that the growing budget deficit over the last two decades has not been accompanied by an increase in private savings.

Another reason tight fiscal policies may create instability is that they tend to create a lack of aggregate demand in the world economy. From the Keynesian standpoint, the adoption of a strict policy stance in several countries (particularly in Europe) means that they prefer to rely on external demand rather than internal demand as a key driver of growth. If all major countries were to follow the same type of policy, it would lead to the risk of creating a deflationary environment, with no engines of growth. By generating more synchronized cycles and fostering competition across the world economy, the NE is likely to aggravate the situation. In particular, it tends to undermine agreed rules and the possibility for countries to coordinate their policies to keep aggregate demand high.

We now turn to how the Keynesian model accounts for pragmatic fiscal policy. The Keynesian model is consistent with the relaxation of tight fiscal stance recently implemented by governments in various parts of the world. We refer, for example, to the fact that strict application of the stability pact in Europe has been avoided in practice (e.g. Germany and France have both managed to avoid sanctions despite their excessive budget deficits) and to the drastic swing from budget surplus to deficit in the US. Clearly, these moves are justified by the policy-makers' realization – in line with Keynesian logic – that tight fiscal rules may be counterproductive for aggregate demand and income, especially during a slowdown.

However, once again such pragmatic moves are not completely consistent with the Keynesian model, for governments consider these moves as a remedy of last resort based on common sense, rather than following from a theoretical analysis of the NE. Their formal or official strategy is always based on the orthodox principles of sound finance and balanced budgets following either from NCM, which rules out all kinds of demand policies, or from 'consensus macroeconomics', which limits the validity of Keynesian policies and the possibility of deficits to the short run. From the Keynesian standpoint advanced here, this is deleterious because it undermines the effectiveness of the policy moves required for supporting aggregate demand in the context of the NE. Indeed allowing Keynesian thinking only as a kind of temporary remedy accounts for the several flaws of pragmatic strategies, such as the slow adoption or insufficient scope of required changes in the face of the systemic failures, shared errors and confidence crises that the fast and fragile NE is most likely to generate. If governments think, for example, in terms of the Maastricht criteria for sound finance or even balanced budgets over a number of years and accept the idea that either in the short run or in the long run budget deficits are not needed because of the intrinsic stability of the market economy, the problems faced in the NE cannot be dealt with successfully. Two remarks are in order here.

First, there is a real danger that the proper decisions will be taken only after long and painful conflicts between alternative views (i.e. between the official and the pragmatic one). For example, it was only after a long and harrowing decision-making process that European governments recently agreed to reform the stability pact by introducing more flexible prescriptions. Second, the fact that markets are faced with contradictory statements and policy moves (concerning tight rules and pragmatism or between short-run and long-run views) pose a risk in the NE, due to the greater role that 'shared errors' play in it. The most important policy task is to create confidence and provide a firm anchor for agents' expectations. The Keynesian model does so by putting forward a unified view of cyclical and growth processes and of short and long-run mechanisms. It finds a coherent policy expression in the 'threshold' logic, according to which, for example, budget deficits and debt are not an evil as such and can be run forever so long as they do not exceed a certain point.

Structural policies and rules for markets

Finally, let us consider the current combination of rules and pragmatism in the field of structural policy and governance. The definition of rules concerning the governance of economic activity and institutions is at least partly consistent with the Keynesian model. As already noted, since the beginning of the last century crucial legal, institutional and political changes have underlain the key patterns of growth which are captured by the *General Theory*. However, while institutions overall play a generating role for Keynesians, they do not determine aggregate outcomes uniquely. They are able to influence them by affecting the determinants of aggregate demand. It is not surprising, therefore, that the Keynesian model suggests that the definition of rules for markets (including what is regarded as deregulation) can also create instability by undermining aggregate demand. This may happen for a number of reasons.

First of all, let us focus on the labour market, starting from the causality argument. For Keynesians, labour market deregulation is not a prerequisite for both cyclical stability and long-term increase in employment and income as is implied instead by the neoclassical model. Following its rejection of the assumption of perfect markets as the norm for assessing real-world markets and the effects of structural reforms, the Keynesian model does not regard labour market rigidity as a major cause of instability in the NE. On the contrary, labour markets may also be rigid because of insufficient economic growth caused by the combination of endogenous mechanisms and external shocks that keep aggregate demand low. By reducing the level of employment, low demand also induces workers to resist changes more vigorously as they see less alternative job opportunities arising. In other words, as pointed out by Cohen *et al.* (2000), full employment is a condition for flexibility.

It follows from these remarks that, although improving flexibility may sometimes be the right choice, instability may occur unless it is remembered that this is not sufficient for increasing employment. More in general, it is important to bear in mind that, in the light of the Keynesian model, structural policies aimed at increasing factor productivity and flexibility in key markets are not a panacea as implied by deterministic models; they may well fail to improve growth prospects in the absence of a sufficient increase in aggregate demand. They are a complement, not a substitute, for demand policies.

Strictly speaking, this is true in a closed economy. In an open economy, where growth is at least to some extent export led, this argument must be qualified. In this context, there seems to be a causal link running from structural policies to growth; these policies stimulate growth, because they reduce firms' costs and improve their competitiveness, thereby increasing exports. However, this link is different from the unconditional one established by neoclassical theorists. It can be argued that exports only increase if there is sufficient aggregate demand at the international level. In this case, it is true that for individual countries choosing to rely on exports rather than internal demand as key drivers of growth, structural reforms may be seen as a substitute for demand policies. However, this is not true from the standpoint of the world economy as a whole. One implication of this view is that those who support structural reforms in individual countries, as in Europe today, for example, are not necessarily endorsing a neoclassical model, but may be advocating a kind of export-led growth, after all.

It can also be argued that, in the light of the Keynesian model, insisting on deregulation *per se* in a depressed context may even prove to be a self-defeating tactic. Keynesian authors tend to suggest, for example, that a more flexible labour market, *ceteris paribus*, lowers productivity, undermines trade unions and negatively impacts income distribution with adverse implications for aggregate demand. Policy should thus be aimed at increasing market flexibility in more indirect ways, that is, by favouring the expansion of aggregate demand.

Second, the Keynesian model explains why liberalization and deregulation of capital markets both at the national and international level may be destabilizing. It may push developing countries in Asia and Latin America to suffer serious financial crises and balance of payments deficits that ultimately call for a reduction of internal demand. However, it may also generate declining accounting standards and fraudulent practices that undermine aggregate demand in most developed countries by exacerbating stock market volatility and distorting investment prospects.

Let us now turn to pragmatic structural policy. The Keynesian model obviously captures the fact that governments quite often tend to play a more active role in the economy than implied by mere regulatory policy, such as protectionist measures, active industrial policies or attempts to save unprofitable firms from bankruptcy. In Keynesian thinking, this is not surprising, since the state is assumed to play a positive role in resource allocation and adjustment processes that are not totally left to the market. This can happen in a number of ways, from the national system of innovation to various kinds of industrial policy then promote the competitiveness of national firms.

However, there is also a degree of inconsistency between such pragmatic moves and the Keynesian model. Once again, the point is that Keynesian principles influence governments' strategy only in disguise. Calling into question the view that markets are always the most efficient allocation mechanisms is usually carried out in two ways. First, it is seen not as a matter of 'high' theory, but as a matter of common sense strategies or tactics for political survival, for example, in the face of strong lobbying either from financial or industrial groups acting in the name of a presumed 'national' interest standpoint or from trade unions.

Second, it may be justified at the theoretical level by the view that markets are imperfect, and structural reforms are needed to make them conform to the perfect competition ideal. Both approaches are misleading from the Keynesian standpoint, as they undermine the effectiveness of the policy moves required in the context of the NE. Above all, they imply that there is no recognition of the fact that there is no clear-cut dichotomy between structural and cyclical aspects, and that a structural dimension is linked to aggregate demand as well. This can be interpreted in two ways. First, the level of aggregate demand also has inevitable consequences on the structural aspects of the economy, such as the level of structural or frictional unemployment. This is the position taken within the hysteresis view (see e.g. Blanchard 2003). Second, structural policies themselves may influence aggregate demand. One can note, for example, that the degree of trust or confidence – necessary for markets to prosper and a major determinant of the key drivers of Keynesian theory, such as the propensities to consume, invest and hold money – is not a mere psychological attitude. It can be influenced by the 'quality' of institutions, which can be improved by appropriate structural policies.

Conclusion

The neo-modern perspective and the building of scenarios

In this book, we propose a new methodology for the assessment of the macroeconomic stability of the NE in an effort to compensate for the lack of satisfactory coverage offered by standard theory. The shortcomings of standard theory are well exemplified by the gap between descriptions of the NE and the theoretical approaches seeking to account for it. Whereas many descriptive analyses or scenarios regard the NE as a complex phenomenon involving the interaction of several key variables, including ICT, globalization and the increasing significance of intangibles and financial markets, standard theory depicts the NE instead as essentially a technological shift giving rise to strong productivity gains. Although other factors are not necessarily ignored, typical macroeconomic analysis of the NE is cast in terms of production functions; economists are thus led to consider the explanatory variables of productivity increases as being mutually independent and/or unrelated to institutional factors. In any case, standard neo-classical theory is not alone in its inability to furnish a satisfactory account of the stability issue. In its standard version, Keynesian theory also fails on this score, for it is often seen to apply only to short-run cyclical issues or to rely on simplified, formalistic approaches to long-run growth that fail to detect the myriad interactions taking place among the key factors.

In order to advance the study of stability, we reject these reductionist views. Strictly speaking, we do not drop the use of current macro theories altogether. We recognize that the NE is but an acceleration of certain trends, such as globalization and rapid technological change, that have characterized the Modern Economy since the 1920s; current macroeconomic theories are thus not completely ineffectual in dealing with it. However, significant aspects of these theories need to be called into question if the study of stability is to be made feasible.

For this purpose, we have put forward what we refer to as the 'neo-modern' perspective. We suggest that dealing with the dynamic behaviour of economic systems – and in particular with stability, intended in the broad sense as encompassing both growth and fluctuations – requires a balanced combination of empirical analysis and 'light theory'. In other words, the role of current macroeconomic theories should be relatively modest and it should be limited, in particular, to highlighting the causal factors that underlie states of instantaneous equilibrium. These factors do not disappear in long-run analysis but merely represent tendencies that may not be actualized because of disturbing factors or countervailing causal mechanisms. This means that there are no grounds for assuming, for example, that the predictions of standard theory, such as those of the quantity theory of money, can be backed by empirical evidence. Nor is there any reason to assume, more generally, that stability will always prevail in real economic systems, as is implied instead by the long-run equilibrium or natural rate concepts underlying growth models and much of current macroeconomics.

In practice, the neo-modern perspective suggests that all that economists can do when addressing long-run issues is to analyse stability in an *ex post* fashion, that is, to assess and compare the stabilizing and destabilizing factors that occur in actual economies. The best way to accomplish this task is to build scenarios, seeking to capture the most significant interrelations between key economic and institutional factors. This is what many researchers are already doing, after all. However, most scenarios in the current literature lack an explicit theoretical background, whereas we claim that advancement of knowledge about stability requires more 'formal' scenarios of the NE, that is, full-blown analyses of the interactions between key phenomena and institutions explicitly relying on existing macroeconomic paradigms.

This perspective has led us to develop a three-step modelling strategy. In the first step, we single out a new type of empirical evidence that characterizes the NE. In particular, we use Calvino's labels ('multiplicity', 'rapidity', 'lightness', 'precision' and 'visibility'), to define the NE in terms of five broad empirical laws addressing the acceleration of globalization, technological change, the weight of services and financial markets in total production, the collection of data and measurement techniques and a certain policy stance.

In the second step, we develop a *prima facie* account of stability by drawing a map that takes stock of the various causal mechanisms accounting for both the stability and instability tendencies related to each of the five labels.

In the last step, we build two alternative scenarios assessing global stability on the grounds of a unifying perspective derived from the two basic macroeconomic paradigms, that is, NCM and Keynesian theory, implying different interpretations of instantaneous equilibrium. Two key premises underlie this last step. The first is that it makes sense to consider only these two paradigms; in this book we try to justify this move in terms of fundamental issues, such as the 'essential' mechanisms they focus upon. The second premise is that by comparing these two scenarios it is possible to obtain a more balanced account of global stability.

The generality of the Keynesian scenario

One of the key results of this comparative analysis is that the Keynesian account of stability proves to be more general than that of NCM, and manages to capture a greater number of intersections on our map of stability mechanisms. As noted earlier in the book, this is ultimately due to Keynes's broad notion of essence, according to which a new dimension of agents' behaviour, namely agents' interdependence or mutual interest, should be added to the others considered by neoclassical theory, that is, self-interest and competition. This accounts for the fact that the principle of effective demand, which is one of the clearest expressions of this new dimension (as testified by the paradox of saving or the multiplier which only make sense if the interaction of many agents is considered), is valid not just in the study of cyclical phenomena but also of long-run structural trends.

The advantage of the principle of effective demand is that it is deeply 'conditional', following Keynes's distinction between causal factors and secondary givens and their possible interaction. In particular, this means that, unlike NCM and other 'deterministic' approaches (including neo-Schumpeterian views), changes in the secondary givens or what we refer to as 'objective' dimensions of structural complexity, for example, technological change or changes in market structures, have no causal role *per se*; they do not influence the economy directly but through the propensities which underlie aggregate demand. In view of the fact that this influence is not certain on a priori grounds, the Keynesian model in principle allows one to account for 'duality', that is, for the possibility that the structural changes might not only have simple beneficial effects but also negative ones.

In particular, this duality is rooted in three characteristics of the Keynesian analysis of capitalist dynamics. First, markets play a double role: on the one hand, they allow tremendous growth opportunities; on the other, however, they also imply instability. Paradoxically, it is because markets work that they need to be held in check. The NE represents the latest and most sophisticated stage of this process. By implying a further extension of the market logic as the combined product of its key features, it also inevitably exposes the system to greater instability.

Second, the broader conception of essence that underlies the Keynesian model allows us to place both the positive and negative mechanisms on a par, both from the methodological and analytical points of view. This is possible because the same products of mutual interest shaping the key parameters of this model, such as theories, are liable to induce either stability or instability. Both outcomes are equally 'rational' on a priori grounds and are endogenous, that is, they arise autonomously from the agents' interaction.

Third, the counteracting role of 'visibility' is itself not guaranteed. While it may be true that endogenous mechanisms of the private sector are bound to generate more instability, it is not so obvious that policy-makers are smart enough to keep it at bay. Visibility itself may be a source of instability.

For these reasons, the Keynesian model accounts for the broadest range of outcomes, including those that can be derived by thinking along NCM lines. Indeed, while NCM regards itself as the only universal model of the economy, our analysis suggests, instead, that it covers just one possible outcome that occurs only under well-specified conditions, namely those in which the structural changes do not affect the basic parameters underlying aggregate demand. This is one way of restating Keynes's claim about the generality of his approach, which encompasses the Classical one as a particular case. One of the main results of the analysis carried out in this book is to demonstrate the validity of this claim beyond the static realm in which it was originally conceived.

The generality of the Keynesian contribution emerges in several aspects of the analysis of the NE. We shall make this clear by considering the way in which the two basic paradigms deal with the dynamic and structural stability of the NE and its main features.

The dynamic stability of the NE

One of the major conclusions of the previous analysis is that, according to both paradigms, the NE should be seen as dynamically stable, that is, as being in constant equilibrium or capable, at least, of making a faster transition to the equilibrium state. The point is that the interaction between ICT, globalization and the expansion of financial markets reduces the impact of 'local' frictions due to the imperfect transmission of information (e.g. slow adjustment of expectations, some types of asymmetric information, confusion between absolute and relative price changes and liquidity constraints). However, behind this shared conclusion the two paradigms tell quite different stories.

NCM emphasizes that the NE increases stability, because it reduces the role of rigidities and imperfections that imply a departure from the 'normal' state of optimal equilibrium described by the deep parameters of Walrasian theory (that which can be regarded as the 'systematic' part of the economy where there are no shocks or errors). In other words, it reduces the size of fluctuations and strengthens the normative role of the neoclassical notion of equilibrium.

One of the major reasons that our Keynesian account of dynamic stability is more general than that of NCM is that it considers two types of imperfections. In particular, it stresses that the NE does not just reduce 'local' imperfections but also tends to increase the 'global' imperfections, namely imperfections of an 'endogenous' kind. These include imperfections linked to the fundamental opacity and complexity of the economy and reflecting the intangible products of agents' interaction, such as lack of social capital, trust or confidence and 'shared errors' due to erroneous theories, which influence expectations on financial markets and the key propensities of consumption and investment. Such imperfections are so important in the NE (due to its growing dependence upon intangible aspects) that the private sector is likely to become more unstable, in the sense that aggregate demand may be systematically low and the system could get stuck in sub-optimal equilibrium positions, unless appropriate counteracting policies are implemented. In other words, in line with the view that the market system is intrinsically unstable, our Keynesian stance holds that, although equilibrium may be reached faster in the NE than in past stages of development, it may be highly unsatisfactory in the absence of adequate policy moves, especially of those supporting aggregate demand.

The structural stability of the NE

The generality of Keynes's contribution also emerges in the assessment of the structural stability of the NE, for once again, it accounts for a greater range of possible events. While NCM is constrained by its reliance on the deep parameters to regard the NE as being structurally stable, our Keynesian model suggests instead that it is likely to involve structural instability as well. Here too, while NCM is bound to focus on just one outcome, the Keynesian model is able to account for a broader range of possibilities. The point is that, unlike the deep parameters of NCM, the key functions of the Keynesian model are changeable. Indeed, it is because it regards agents' expectations as mutually affecting each other endogenously – that is, as being dependent upon the key products of mutual interest – that the Keynesian model manages to consider the occurrence of 'global' imperfections, such as waves of optimism and pessimism, which are instead ruled out by the neoclassicals, or regarded as mere psychological or irrational moves. Such imperfections explain why the NE is not only more likely to get stuck in sub-optimal states of equilibrium, but also to shift from one negative equilibrium to another.

In this book, we have introduced a preliminary detailed analysis of some of the key aspects of structural instability, although much work remains to be done. In particular, the Keynesian distinction between primary and secondary factors has led us to underline that the 'objective' dimensions of structural complexity in the NE (i.e. secondary givens) determine changes in the 'subjective' dimensions of qualitative change, such as agents' perceptions of space, time, market and value that underlie Keynes's key aggregate functions (primary givens). In our analysis, we have discussed a number of these changes, emphasizing that they represent potential new sources of instability that are often neglected by official statistics. In principle, they need to be captured by a new set of indicators if stability analysis is to improve. Our analysis allows some tentative progress in this direction.

One key change in agents' perceptions concerns the dimension of 'time'. In particular, the NE induces a shortening of both consumers' and investors' horizons. Among the new indicators that could capture this change we can mention the reduction in the savings ratio, together with the increasing velocity of circulation of money and its dematerialization (due to increasing pressure to spend and less concern for long-term needs), the greater differentiation of consumer goods and the growing size of advertising budgets in firms' total costs (due to the quickening of technological change and the firms' need to induce consumers to buy) and the increasing role of confidence indexes (more unstable expectations due to the fact that agents now face larger and faster information flows).

Second, a change also occurs in the agents' perception of the 'market' in the NE. In this regard, we are led to focus on broad indicators concerning the existence of adequate cultural background and social capital, which are important, for example, for assessing the potential diffusion of innovations and developing countries' 'catching-up'.

Moreover, the NE also brings about a change in the agents' perception of 'value'. Some of the new potential indicators could include the tendency to increase the size of personal and governmental debt, which is favoured by structural characteristics of the NE, such as low interest rates (also due to low inflation and more skilful monetary policy), the need to counter shocks and the range of different criteria for measurement and valuation of intangibles in firms' accounting practices.

Macroeconomic theories and the features of the NE

The generality of Keynes's contribution concerning the analysis of stability is also revealed by analysis of the individual features of the NE. It can be argued that, unlike NCM, the Keynesian model captures the essence of the phenomena that we have described through the use of Calvino's labels. The key point revolves around the role of institutions, intended as the products of agents' interaction. Our labels stress the fundamental interrelation between economic phenomena and institutions, or what we have defined as the generating role of institutions. 'Multiplicity' is not just globalization, but also the set of trade agreements that have made it possible. Similarly, 'rapidity' is not just technological change but also the set of complementary institutions known as the 'national system of innovation' and trade unions which stimulate it. 'Lightness' is not just the growing weight of intangibles or services and the financial sector, it is also the context of rules granting, for example, the fair behaviour and the quality of the players on such markets. 'Precision' refers not to just better measurement techniques, but also to institutional factors, such as central banks and statistics institutes devoted to the control of social and economic systems.

On these grounds, it appears that NCM provides a narrow interpretation of the NE, because it fails to capture this generating role of institutions – that is, the fact that in the real-world institutions also influence agents' behaviour and stimulate growth – in line with its narrow view of essence that rules out the autonomous role played by the products of agents' interactions. It thus regards the two terms of growth and institutions as either separate or even as linked in the opposite way, that is, with growth driving institutional change.

On the one hand, in view of its emphasis on the exogenous deep parameters, NCM considers the expansion of the market process as a linear, self-regulating autonomous process which can only be impaired by an excess of 'regulation'. On the other, its macro models tend to regard institutions as simple rules of the game or as exogenous constraints necessary for the optimal functioning of a universal type of market driven by exogenous forces, such as preferences and technology, which institutions do not influence.

Moreover, we have seen, in line with the principle of methodological individualism, that neoclassical theory even advocates that institutions themselves should be reduced to the first principles of economics and thus explained in terms of the deep parameters. This means that neoclassical theory is able to capture only one side of the phenomena captured by our labels: namely, the quantitative expansion of markets and the increase in resource endowments.

Take 'lightness', for example. Neoclassical theory does not disregard the creation of banks and the rise of the stock exchange in the past centuries or the further expansion of financial markets in the NE. However, not all these developments are seen as influencing agents' qualitative behaviour, in view of the assumption of structural stability. The capital market is assumed to behave in the same way as in the past and in the same way as any other ordinary market. In particular, neoclassical theory continues to postulate the same link between savings and investment (according to which the former precedes the latter and the rate of interest balances the two flows) which was plausible in the economy of the nineteenth century, when peasants or small producers were still the main characters involved.

Two main implications follow from these remarks. The first is that, by missing the organic link between institutions and our patterns of growth, NCM quite mistakenly seeks to universalize, or generalize to all times and places, conclusions that were legitimate only in that outmoded context. Second, this theory cannot regard the NE as changing the basic laws of economics in any way. Growth and fluctuations in the NE follow basically the same patterns as previous stages of development. In other words, the NE confirms its basic view that all business cycles are alike.

Thanks to his broader notion of essence, Keynes's view instead captures the generating role of institutions. It thus regards institutional change as driving growth. Indeed, the development of markets is not impaired but is stimulated by institutional factors; as already noted, stability is not an inherent property of the economy but the product of a set of fundamental institutions. Thus, there is no room for autonomous deep parameters: agents' propensities and technologies are malleable and can be influenced by institutional factors. This view thus allows for the possibility that in economics, unlike in physics, theories can change in relation to new historical and institutional patterns.

Take 'lightness' once again. Keynes's theory, and in particular its principle of effective demand, reflects the fact that the rise of banks and the stock exchange made a change in the analysis of the saving–investment relationship plausible as early as the 1920s. Thinking along these lines, we suggest that the economist's task is to assess the validity of models in relation to a changing context. In this regard, one of the key conclusions of this book is that the recent NE not only broadly confirms the basic lines of Keynesian thinking, it also makes it even more stringent, given the greater range of financing opportunities for investment, the increasing predominance of stocks over flows and, more in general, of fast financial markets over slow production processes.

Policy implications

The generality of Keynes's analysis of stability of the NE finds an obvious counterpart in terms of policy conclusions. To make this point clear, let us start by recalling the policy guidelines of NCM. Due to its reliance on the stability assumption, NCM is led to make rather drastic policy suggestions. First, it endorses strict macroeconomic policy rules granting stability in terms of financial consolidation and very low inflation. As the NE is bound to make the private sector even more stable than in the past, the introduction of such rules to tie policy-makers' hands appears to be the universal condition for growth. Indeed the NE should induce all countries to rule out any discretionary macroeconomic policy, in order to 'let markets work'.

Second, NCM advocates the implementation of structural reforms involving greater deregulation and flexibility in all markets in order to push their economies closer to the perfect competition model. In particular, exogenous factors or institutional rigidities, such as fixed exchange rates, collective bargaining and the welfare state implying high taxes, need be removed. Otherwise, instability in terms of high levels of natural rates of unemployment, unsatisfactory accumulation of productive factors or sluggish growth will inevitably follow. In other words, in line with the view that the market economy is intrinsically stable, instability can only derive from exogenous factors (including the lack of adequate policy moves for removing obstacles) that impair the working of markets, that is, full price flexibility.

Third, NCM also recommends 'positive' policy moves, including the use of fiscal policy to favour the accumulation of productive factors such as fiscal incentives to saving, investment in physical and human capital and R&D.

The notions of equilibrium underlying the Keynesian and NCM model are quite different. Therefore, it is not surprising that their normative conclusions are quite different, too. The policy guidelines deriving from the Keynesian model can be regarded as being more general than those of NCM because they concern both the aggregate demand and supply side of the economy. In particular, while NCM rules out any active demand policy and focuses on supply-side policy, the Keynesian view is more balanced and considers both types of policy as being useful. On the one hand, it holds that demand policies have both a cyclical and a structural dimension, in view of the fact that demand plays a causal role in both short-run and long-run analysis (i.e. it determines the level of activity). On the other, the Keynesian stance also suggests that standard structural supply-side policies play a complementary role, as they influence outcomes by affecting the causal factors of aggregate demand. Strictly speaking, this means not that they are irrelevant but that their beneficial effects on the economy can no longer be taken for granted. To show more precisely the policy implications of our Keynesian approach, three points need to be made.

First, following its conclusion concerning the increasing instability of the private sector in the NE, the Keynesian standpoint suggests that strict macroeconomic policy rules *per se* have no general validity and may not furnish a solution; indeed pursuing them at all costs is even likely to generate further destabilizing tendencies. This does not mean that stability, in terms of balanced budgets and low inflation, should not be pursued at all, but that it is better achieved in *ex post* rather than *ex ante* fashion, that is, as the result, rather than a condition, of growth.

In other words, Keynesians suggest that there is room in the NE for advocating active discretionary macro policy to counter the increasing instability of the private sector.

Second, the Keynesian model holds that standard policies favouring the accumulation of productive factors, including policies for increasing innovation, R&D and the formation of human capital, should not be expected to exercise a mechanical effect on growth in the NE. In the Keynesian analysis, productive factors do not play a causal role; they are secondary givens that affect outcomes only through the causal factors, such as the propensity to invest. This is not just an aggregate, but a complex variable that reflects a bundle of factors shaping 'entrepreneurship' in particular contexts. These include psychological moves, theories and expectations as well as factors that affect the rate of innovation and competitiveness in various sectors and areas (e.g. districts). Indeed, in contrast with NCM and standard aggregate models, the Keynesian logic is consistent with disaggregated approaches focusing on particular sectors because it holds no a priori view of stability and does not regard relative prices as allocating resources efficiently at the microeconomic level. Thus, for example, policy can also be implemented at the micro level to favour the competitiveness of particular sectors.

In the end, according to the Keynesian model, removing institutional features such as fixed exchange rates, collective bargaining and welfare may well undermine stability. For in the age of the NE, these features do not represent imperfections that impair growth but are actually the essential prerequisites for growth, in that they produce key public (or mutual interest) intangible goods, such as trust, reduced uncertainty and social cohesion.

Notes

Introduction

1 Gordon (2002), for example, defines it 'as the post-1995 acceleration in the rate of technical change in information technology together with the development of the Internet' (p. 49). Only a few economists deny the existence of the NE *tout court*. For example, Leibowitz and Margolis (1999) argue that the NE does not exist because the markets work, have always worked and will always work.

2 He points out, for example, that the economy changes only slowly: much employment and output today is similar to what it was in the early 1990s. Moreover, the business cycle is still alive and the current recession, which involves large swings in inventory and investment, resembles old-style recessions (see Baily 2002: 18).

3 These authors note, for example, that

> [t]he term 'E-conomy' points at the fact that today's economic transformation is driven by the development and diffusion of modern electronics-based information technology. The term emphasizes that the ongoing shift is a change in structure, and not primarily a macroeconomic or cyclical phenomenon. The E-conomy is a structural shift, bringing transformation and disruption. But the economic transformation is not about soft landings, smooth growth, permanently rising stock prices, government surpluses, and low rates of interest and inflation. It is about structural transformation and developments that carry disruption and change.
>
> (Cohen *et al.* 2000: 3)

For a similar view, see also DeLong and Summers (2001). Those who suggest that the NE has no major macroeconomic effects base their view on two main arguments: (1) the business cycle has survived; (2) those important changes in the business cycle that do take place may well be driven by forces independent of the rise of the E-conomy. Christina Romer (1999), for example, argues that the real change in the business cycle is more likely to be due to the rise of independent central banks.

4 This view is especially emphasized by Dornbusch (1999).

5 This point is underlined by Mandel (1997) who holds that 'with high tech having grown so big, the economy is now vulnerable to a high-tech slowdown in a way that was never true before'.

6 In a similar vein, see also the contributions by Banerij (2002), the *Economist* (28–9–2002), Stiglitz (2002a, 2003: ch. 8), Godley and Izurieta (2002).

7 In this vein, Beck (1992) characterizes modern society not only as 'new' or 'post-industrial' but also as a 'high risk' society.

8 The American version of Calvino's lectures uses slightly different terms for two of the five labels: 'rapidità' is translated as 'quickness' and 'esattezza' as 'exactitude'. However, we believe that the terms 'rapidity' and 'precision' are more appropriate choices for the purposes of this book.

1 Equilibrium without structural change

1 In his theory of the business cycle, for example, Lucas focuses on invariable regularities and seeks a unified explanation of the business cycle grounded in general laws governing market economies, rather than in political or institutional characteristics specific to particular countries or periods (see Lucas 1981; also Vercelli 1991: 132–2).

2 In Solow's model, the diminishing marginal productivity of capital rules out the possibility of sustaining growth through the continual accumulation of capital. This accounts for one of the most famous results of this model, that is, that 'changes in the propensity to save (and hence of accumulation, since Solow considers saving to be identical to investment) cannot affect the long-run growth rate' (Setterfield 2002: 3).

3 As shown by Sonnenschein (1972), for example, 'there are basic features of market economies (such as complementarity among goods) that are inconsistent with the stability of equilibrium' (Vercelli 1997: 290).

4 In this sense, the rational expectations hypothesis is the product of the principle of fixed and immutable structure. Since market process is of no importance, it is simpler to assume that we can rapidly converge on the postulated equilibrium (see Prasch 2000a: 218).

5 Among those who have made such rapid shifts is the *Economist*, which has published two very different surveys, one in 2000 (see the *Economist* 1–4–2000) stressing that the NE meant that the perfect competition model can almost be realized and another one in 2002 (see the *Economist* 28–9–2002) admitting instead that Internet economics has proved 'a bit of a disappointment'.

6 Sargent is one of several prominent theorists who have taken great pains to represent uncertainty and learning in terms of the rationality axioms. See Sent (1998: ch. 5), Dow (2002: 85).

2 Instability and dynamic equilibrium

1 Keynes expressed his reservations on the use of past data for the purpose of testing such theories by posing two questions: 'Is it assumed that the future is a determinate function of past statistics? What place is left for expectations and the stare of confidence relating to the future?' (Keynes 1973: 287). As noted by Asimakopulos, Keynes denies the 'ergodic assumption', which implies the belief in long-run equilibrium independent of initial conditions (see 1991: 131; also Davidson 1982–3).

2 According to Kalecki, 'Current investment is a determinant of current profits while current profits, through their influence on the expectations of the profitability of investment, are determinants of current investment decisions, and thus of future investment expectations' (Asimakopulos 1991: 134).

3 'Equilibrium theory will be concerned not only with what size, but also with what rate of growth of certain magnitudes is consistent with the surrounding circumstances' (Harrod 1937: 86).

4 As noted by Fine, Harrod argued that even if the steady state of balanced growth path which equals the two rates is reached 'it is liable to be unstable as optimistic (pessimistic) expectations will prove to be more than self-sustaining sending the economy into explosive growth (decay)' (Fine 2003: 204).

5 For a survey of the debate on the Harrod model see King (2002: 59–78).

6 As Vercelli states, it is 'only in the early 1970s that non-linear dynamics fully emerged from underground, attracting the attention of many scholars in different disciplines, under such imaginative labels as "catastrophe theory," "theory of chaos," "theory of fractals," "complex dynamics" ' (1997: 288).

7 Dependence on initial conditions implies for example that 'any error about the initial state of the dynamic system will cumulate as an attempt is made to forecast the trajectory of the dynamical system' (Jarsulic 1997: 381).

8 As noted by Vercelli (1997: 292) an attractor should not be confused with the stable equilibrium of standard beliefs; it turns out to be a much more complex concept.

9 See Aghion and Howitt (1998) for a summary of various NGT models.

10 Apart from the fact that the general notions underlying NGT find their roots in theories such as Kaldor's technical progress function, the emphasis on increasing returns can be traced back to Adam Smith, Alwyn Young and Arrow (see e.g. Thirwall 2002: 33).

11 In particular, in Romer's model, three elements, that is, the existence of decreasing returns in the production of new knowledge at the firm level, externalities associated with new knowledge and the increasing returns in the production of output 'ensure that a competitive equilibrium will exist, even in the presence of externalities' (Ruttan 2001: 25).

12 Tvede (2001: 165) provides a useful synthetic definition of these phenomena:

> *Positive feedback loops*: Vicious circles in which a given event stimulates another, which in turn stimulates the first. Mill and Marshall suggested that people accelerate spending when they see prices going up.
>
> *Echoes*: Clusters of investment in durable capital goods or in consumer goods.
>
> *Cascade-reactions*: Chain reactions with a built-in amplifier effect. This is a typical phenomena in theories of mass psychology, where sentiments in one section spread by means of 'social contamination'.
>
> *Lags*: Phenomena in which an action or event appearing now has an effect that surfaces later in time. Cobwebs and accelerations are examples of such phenomena, as are many under-consumption and over-investment theories.
>
> *Disinhibitors*: Phenomena in which potential negative feedback processes are temporarily blocked by positive feedback processes. Many psychological theories incorporating tendencies towards conventional behaviour can be described as such.

As Tvede repeatedly emphasizes, the sheer number of feedback phenomena discovered poses a challenge to economists:

> [T]here (is) something frightening about the rapidly rising number of theories and rules which (seem) plausible. Given the complexity of combined dynamics, how could anybody ever be able to develop a clear picture of the overall behaviour – let alone be able to forecast it?
>
> (ibid.: 166)

13 In the statistical work associated with NGT

> it is reasonably recognised that several variables will affect endogenous growth, not least differences in saving rates and the host of economic and social factors that have been deployed in NGT. Consequently, the regression is augmented by any number and combination of variables – a hundred or more – from R&D expenditure to levels of democracy and trust or indeed any variable that might be deemed to affect economic performance.
>
> (Fine 2003: 211)

3 Structural change without equilibrium

1 As pointed out, for example, by Preston, the TEP approach

> avoids the hard technological determinist claims concerning a shift to a distinctively new socio-economic order, such as those advanced in various third wave and information society theories ... whilst marking the contemporary as a moment of long-wave crisis and restructuring alongside the potential new opportunities afforded by the advances in ICTs, the neo-Schumpeterian approach remains relatively open as to the course and direction of future developments.
>
> (2001: 41)

There is perhaps some leeway for making a distinction between the 'reasoned history approach' and the TEP view here. After having noted that their approach is similar to the conceptions held by historians and economists such as Veblen Mokyr, Von Tunzelmann Galbraith and Perez who have all stressed the link between technological change and organizational change as well as political and institutional change, Freeman and Louçà point out that

> their approach differs from most of them in two respects. First, it attaches greater importance to science and to general culture.... Second, it does not attempt to assign primacy in causal relationships to any of the five theories at the level of analysis, whereas most other theories assign primacy to technology or to the economy or to both. It emphasizes the relative autonomy of each of the five spheres ...
>
> (2001: 124–5)

2 Keynes is praised for stressing the implausibility of structural constancy not just for fifty or one hundred years but for even shorter periods of time:

> Keynes' discussion with Tinbergen was motivated by his opposition to correlations established for ten years. This presumption of causal stability, the exact same causes acting in exactly the same fashion in such different periods, furthermore added to the requirement of endogeneity, i.e. the same causes explaining the whole time process are not compatible with real history.
>
> (Freeman and Louçà 2001: 116)

4 The crisis in economic theory and the neo-modern perspective

1 See for example Dow (2001: 61) and Cullemberg *et al.* (2001: 21–2).
2 However, this cultural movement also influenced the hard sciences including physics, as testified by the development of the theory of relativity and quantum theory, which called into question the canons of Newtonian mechanics.
3 The tendency to break with history reflects a broader cultural move. As Klamer notes

> Commitment to the new called for a liberation from tradition, the future and not the past, should eliminate the present (cf. the avant-garde, the shock of the new.... Modernists seek to overcome historical and cultural barriers in the search for universal truth, peace, a better world, or all three.
>
> (1995: 320)

4 Post-modernism can be seen as historical phase, existential state or condition, style and critique; Cullemberg, Amariglio and Ruccio (2001: 4). Among its most influential proponents, we find French authors such as Derrida, Lyotard, Baudrillard, and American authors, such as Jameson. The features of post-modernism are also summarized by Kumar (1995); Backhouse (1997: chs 3 and 4); Cullemberg *et al.* (2001), Preston (2001: ch. 5).
5 Dow (2001) develops her analysis of the relationship between modernism and post-modernism in dialectical terms.
6 That post-modernism is able to capture duality (both stability and instability) can be seen, for example, in Derrida's deconstructionist approach, that puts forward a textual reading

> in which the play of words and signs within a text, presumed to produce stable and intelligible meanings, is shown on the contrary to precisely undo such stability and significance ... deconstruction ... (shows) inability of any sentence or text to stand for singular meanings and, hence, to eliminate contradiction, ambiguity, multiplicity ...
>
> (Cullemberg *et al.* 2001: 16)

7 The world of science is developing along the lines of chaos and uncertainty, rather than in accordance with a view of the unified structure of nature.

8 In particular, as Cullemberg *et al.* note

> [f]or some critics it is wrong to include such elements as indeterminacy, the critique of representation and the decentred subject within the confines of post-Modernism because these themes emerged within 'high Modernism' of their own field of work and study. In this view, post-Modernism may be said to be a strengthening rather than a weakening of certain crucial components of Modernism, a moment in the continuous development of Modernism.
>
> (2001: 23)

9 Dow (2002: 125), for example, stresses that this turn has occurred in geography (see e.g. Minca 2001).

10 In general, this means that a post-modern perspective accepts pluralism and a multi-faceted society. It can be argued that, from this perspective, all traditions can be seen as having some foundation. But this pluralism is not organized or unified on the grounds of precise principles: fragmentation prevails.

11 Economics, for example, was typically regarded as being based on utility.

12 As noted by Preston, for Jameson

> the interrelationship of cultural and the economic realms must not be viewed as separate or a one-way street. Rather it must be conceived as a process involving continuous reciprocal interaction and feedback loops. He suggests that postmodernism may well lead to a completely new perspective on subjectivity as well as on that of the object. Jameson proposes that post-modernism is a situation where the modernisation process is complete, 'nature is gone for good' and culture has become a veritable 'second nature'.
>
> (2001: 92)

13 Once having recognized the need to take into account such factors as incomplete markets and imperfect competition to explain actual fluctuations, Blanchard and Fischer stress the difficulty to build a unified approach and a model encompassing all the major insights: '[W]e believe that waiting for a model based on first principles before being willing to analyse current events and give policy advice is a harmful utopia .... Thus we see no alternative to using shortcuts' (Blanchard and Fischer 1989: 28).

14 MCloskey (1986) argues against any notion of rules (see also Dow 2002: 121). On post-modernism as an inadequate basis for science, see Backhouse (1997); Lawson (1997, 2003); Hodgson (2001); and King (2002).

5 Complexity theory

1 Among these, one could mention the Brussels School approach, the Stuttgart School approach, the ecological approach, the macroecology approach (see e.g. Brock and Colander 2000: 73), as well as Luhmann's system theory (Viskovatoff 2000: 139). As noted by Prasch (2000a: 216), apart from heterodox schools, SFA is the latest challenge to general equilibrium emerging from within the citadel, after game theory, chaos theory and the discussion of rhetoric.

2 According to Wible, there are strong links, for example, between the SFA conception of the economy as an emergent, self-organizing evolutionary process and Hayek's notion of spontaneous order (e.g. Wible 2000: 22).

3 Louça stresses that biological and physical analogies are useful, but limited, as tools for creative thought. In particular, they may be subject to the obliquity error, because the logical relation of causality cannot be translated from biology or physics into economics (see e.g. Louça 1997: 66). A general vision is one thing, but a precise causal

mechanism is quite another. Thus, we cannot go beyond a certain point in drawing analogies or construct models implying certain causal mechanisms. See also Comim (2000: 160). On the role of metaphors in general, see also Dow (2002).

4 In a similar vein, Colander (2000a: 3) stresses that complexity focuses on emergent properties. In particular, he argues that the laws of complex systems are statistical probability laws. They refer to large groups of actors and are not reducible to laws of individual actors. Complexity thus allows that some aspects of reality can emerge from chance and the law of large numbers. The whole can be deterministic, even though the individual components are chaotic and indeterministic.

5 As noted by Holland (1995), new mathematical tools, such as those based on combinatorial analysis and population-level stochastic processes, need to be developed if complexity is to be captured. See also Comim (2000: 158–9).

6 Indeed, because there is pluralism of levels in the SFA vision of complexity, computer simulation of aggregate economic events does not make narrow predictions about outcomes for specific individuals, thus escaping the strong reductionism bent of neoclassical theory which would reduce all economic phenomena to the level of an optimizing individual (see Wible 2000: 24).

7 Scaling laws are a way of representing patterns in the sizes and durations of the chain reactions; these are distributed according to a power law (such as Pareto's Law of income distribution). See Brock (2000: 30).

8 As emphasized by Prasch, the secondary role of prediction in complexity theory follows from the fact that 'the structure and the exact qualities of the emergent order are not known to anyone in advance, and is not presumed to be globally stable anyway' (2000a: 216).

9 As already noted, instability undermines predictability. Although many try to understand the scaling laws underlying financial markets (especially chain reactions) in order to predict when an 'avalanche' will occur, what 'size' it will be, and how 'long' it will last, and so on, overall there seems to be a lack of exploitable patterns or out-of-sample predictability (see e.g. Brock 2000: 31–3).

10 See also Comim (2000: 160). On the role of metaphors in general, see also Dow (2002). Viskovatoff (2000: 136) is sceptical about the ability of SFA to produce a research programme more successful than neoclassical economics. The SFA either relaxes the rationality assumption (but without bringing it closer to the rationality of actual human beings) or is based upon physicalist metaphors which are no better than the original neoclassical metaphor of preferences as a potential function.

6 Our approach to stability: structural change and instantaneous equilibrium

1 This stance also underlies other approaches. Institutionalists, for example, also 'do not attempt to build a single, general model...' (Hodgson 1998: 166). Institutional economics resembles biology rather than physics. Evolutionary biology 'has a few laws or general principles by which origin and development can be explained' (ibid.), while in physics, 'there are repeated attempts to formulate the general theory of all material phenomena, the so-called "theory of everything"'. (ibid.)

2 A tendency is defined as the

> broad movement or trend that is apparent in some phenomenon when viewed over time and/or space. It captures a change or development in something that is in evidence after abstracting from features regarded as non-systematic, short-run, local and so on.
>
> (Lawson 1998: 493)

The definition given by John Stuart Mill for 'empirical laws' has been summarized as follows: 'As Mill recognized one can find regularities in complicated phenomena... which Mill called "empirical laws"' (Hausman 2001: 294), which are a valuable part of science because they constitute data which theories should explain and because they may be of use' (ibid.).

3 Moreover, as noted by Hollingsworth (2000: 603), 'at the macro level, it is institutions that provide a cognitive framework whereby individuals can cope with their reality'.

4 'Essentialist scientific realism is a specific form of scientific realism which holds that scientific theories either reveal or approximate to the truth about the hidden essence of the actual world. In this connection the epistemic acceptance of an economic theory is based on its explanatory power' (Boylan and O'Gorman 1995: 125). In this book, we cannot deal at length with stimulating discussions concerning the varieties of realist views. For references see Boylan and O'Gorman (1995: ch. 4) and Lawson (1997, 2003).

7 The neoclassical macro model

1 Mill's view has recently been restated as a contribution to economic methodology, especially by Tony Lawson from his perspective as 'critical realist'. Several implications of this methodological perspective are particularly useful here. For example, it views the economy as 'open' and determined by a number of tendencies at play, so that

> there is no sense in which the outcome, prior to its realization, was inevitable. In the open economy, any actual situations will be the result of many different things that are going on... To obtain a comprehensive and indeed practical understanding of the situation, tendency statements must be interpreted... as expressing a mechanism that is in play.
>
> (Lawson 1998: 495)

2 Strictly speaking, there are crucial differences between standard neoclassical macroeconomics and Menger's view; however, for our purposes, such differences are not significant.

3 This interpretation is also supported by Cullemberg, Amarglio and Ruccio, who actually criticize Friedman's 'as if' method as a form of essentialism. In their view, Friedman's approach

> still implies that it is possible to discern transdiscursive truth via a method of ascertaining regularities through scientific observation. Such observation 'reads' essences (in the form of abstractions) in the myriad perceptions that are picked over for what is necessary or useful in testing the proposition and what is not.
>
> (2001: 26)

4 According to McCloskey, for example, the rational economic man metaphor is designed to capture the essence of economic behaviour (see Dow 2002: 117). For an essentialist interpretation of neoclassical theory see also DeMartino (2000: 32–4, ch. 1) and Gerrard (2002). The latter, for example, holds that 'the axiomatic approach in mainstream economics can be viewed as dealing with deep structures and mechanisms' (2002: 118–19).

8 Keynes's macro model

1 On these grounds, one can see why the complexity view may not be so relevant for macroeconomics. The point is that the complexity view's most important input is institutional design, while it has far less to add to policy debates once the institutions are shaped. However, macro models typically focus on equilibrium at a specific point in time based on given institutions.

2 For a critique of Davidson, see also King (2004).

3 'The classical theory is not general, in part because it assumes price flexibility, excludes radical uncertainty and underestimates the role of money as a store of value and means of dealing with an uncertain future' (Hodgson 2001: 220).

4 As noted by Vercelli, Lucas's equilibrium method

> is meant to bring macroeconomic phenomena, with all their apparent disequilibria – erratic movements and episodes of instability – within the scope of the essential level. By contrast the Keynesian models, from this point of view, stop at the level of phenomena and so fail to transcend the 'appearances' of things.
>
> (1991: 138)

5 Strictly speaking, Keynes's independent variables are not the same as our causal variables, although there is a large overlap between the two. In particular, he includes the given money wage among the independent variables, while we consider it preferable to regard it as a secondary variable. The point is that it affects the level of activity only indirectly through the money supply (in wage terms) and the level of aggregate demand (e.g. by influencing expectations).

6 As noted by several authors, Keynes's stance can be described as involving the concept of 'situated rationality', which is a more general concept than that underlying standard theory (Lawson 1997: 187–8; Dow 2002: 144–5). It concerns practical reason suited to the situation, such as the conventional techniques to get by as a basis for action. Rationality is understood more broadly than merely applying reason to certain knowledge.

7 Keynes, like Marshall, referred to agents in their ordinary business life where both aspects of conduct are inevitably considered together. His reference to maximization was not in contrast with this view. It is only with the axiomatic revolution of the 1930s that the two aspects of self-interest and mutual interest were sharply separated, with the axioms of rationality clearly involving reference only to atomistic, self-interested behaviour. It is therefore impossible today to use the maximization terminology without accepting this logic of separation.

8 For a map of agents' motives of behaviour and coordination mechanisms, see Hollingsworth (2000: 606–7).

9 Some key differences between Keynes and the 'Classics'

1 This aspect of Keynes's contribution also finds a counterpart in Einstein's theory of relativity. His views concerning the malleability of parameters, the fact that agents are in principle capable of behaving differently in different contexts and that standard theory has a specific realm of validity, all find more than an echo in Einstein. For example, Einstein makes a distinction between different contexts where different theories apply. He shows that the standard Newtonian model is not a truly universal model as it applies only at 'low speeds'; it breaks down instead at 'high speeds', as indicated by the occurrence of several anomalies. Relativity theory is called for to solve the latter. According to this analogy, one could argue that the 'low speeds' context is where neoclassical theory applies. It corresponds to a number of cases when it is legitimate to assume stability and the *ceteris paribus* condition, such as the standard partial equilibrium analysis of a certain market which does not require any analysis of interdependence, or the case when individual agents' expectations can be taken as given. Mistakes are made when generalizations from these cases are made in order to deal with the 'high speeds' context, where interdependencies can no longer be ignored and 'anomalies' occur in the shape of qualitative changes in behaviour. Keynes's contribution is called for at this stage. For a detailed analysis of this analogy see Togati (1998, 2001).

2 Once again, it must be noted that this perspective is not completely new. In some respects it underlies the research programme advocated by Vercelli (1991) who stresses, for example, the complementarity between the two approaches of Keynes and Schumpeter, as they focus respectively on the pathological and physiological aspects of capitalism. Unlike Vercelli, however, we do not seek to build a formal model of instability, but an informal scenario.

10 A broad definition of the New Economy

1 In a similar vein, Greenspan (1999) regards the NE as 'a perceptible quickening in the pace at which technological innovations are applied'.

2 'The reader should remember the major correlations and conclude that no simple monocausal theory can easily explain them' (Blanchard and Fischer 1989: 20; see also Backhouse 1997: 197).

3 We thus distance ourselves from the Techo-Economic Paradigm approach on this issue. As already noted (see Chapter 3), the latter criticizes the standard interpretation of the NE for taking the new technology as an isolated phenomenon (e.g. Rennstich 2002: 150) and stresses that the new technology gives rise to a new paradigm characterized by a number of related economic factors, such as a certain type of raw material, labour force structure, consumption pattern, corporate organization, industrial and financial structure and public investment (see e.g. Freeman and Perez 1988: 59). However, this concept appears to involve a degree of technological determinism, as it places technological change at the centre of the NE. In our view, instead, centrality in not justified. It is not clear on a priori grounds, for example, whether technological change comes first and financial innovation follows or the other way round. Moreover, major financial crises and economic recessions may develop because of the influence of other factors quite unrelated to innovations and technological change.

4 In his theory of the business cycle, Lucas focuses on invariable regularities and seeks a unified explanation of the business cycle grounded in general laws governing market economies, rather than in political or institutional characteristics specific to particular countries or periods (see Lucas 1981; also Vercelli 1991: 132–2).

5 As Obstfeld and Taylor (1998) state in their political economy interpretation:

> For over 100 years policy makers have wrestled with three basic macro challenges; macro policy trilemma (fixed exchange rates to avoid instability, free capital mobility to ensure efficient allocation and permit smoothing and activist monetary policy to address domestic policy goals; the three are mutually inconsistent; only two of three are attainable (trade off). Any naïve attempt to approach macrohistorical data without some knowledge of these institutional events and the broad contours of change in the global capital market, could lead to major misinterpretations.
>
> (quoted in Basu and Taylor 1999: 63)

6 As Cohen *et al.* put it: '[T]he economic transformation is not about soft landings, smooth growth, permanently rising stock prices, government surpluses, and low rates of interest and inflation. It is about structural transformation and developments that carry disruption and change' (2000: 2).

7 In particular, Sims developed time-series analysis using vector autoregression (VAR) as a way of identifying relationships from the data themselves, rather than from deductive theory (the so-called Cowles's approach). Sims rejected the latter mainly because of the impossibility of testing the full structure of theories for a number of reasons (for example, supply and demand could be interdependent). Sims' approach is one way of drawing generalized descriptions from the data. However, because the data analysis deliberately avoids referring to theory structure, the kind of descriptive information it provides relates to theories only at the reduced-form level (see Dow 2002: 89). In our terms, Sims' approach can be regarded as an instance of 'light theory'. Another 'defensive' strategy carried out by econometricians is calibration (see Backhouse 1997: 179–82).

11 Multiplicity

1 'Globalization refers to the multiplicity of linkages and interconnections between the states and societies which make up the present world system' (McGrew1992: 23, quoted in Dunning 2000: 13–14).

2 It can be argued that globalization and the rise in freedom of exchange reached their peak in the period 1890–1914. Only now, after ten years of liberalization of capital movements, is the world beginning to resemble that of a hundred years ago described by Keynes in his 1919 book, *The Economic Consequences of the Peace*.

3 For example 'between 1950 and 1994, while world manufacturing production rose to a factor of five, total world manufacturing exports grew fourteen fold' (DeMartino 2000: 12).

4 For other empirical evidence concerning this issue, see Dunning (2000: 11).

5 It is important to note that the new division of labour does not correspond in a simple manner to the distinction between high tech (in advanced countries) and low tech industries (in less-developed countries). The point is that intellectual capital is very different from other forms of capital and it also greatly affects the production of traditional goods. As Dunning points out:

> With the development of ... the microchip and the computer the distinction between 'high' and 'low' technology as proxied by the final output they produce, is becoming less and less meaningful. In their use of knowledge, parts of the textile, food-processing, retail construction, and health care industries are just as technologically advanced as the electronics, pharmaceutical, financial services and management consultancy sectors.
>
> (2000: 9–10)

6 DeMartino emphasizes the role of the trend in 'intra-firm' trade as an indicator of the increasing importance of what he calls the 'global workshop'. Intra-firm trade refers to 'the cross-border flow of components and final products between subsidiaries and branches of the same corporation'. Today 'this is the fastest-growing share of trade, having risen from about one-fifth of world trade in the early 1970s to about one-third of world trade in the early 1990s' (2000: 12–13). This kind of trade has risen particularly dramatically for the US.

7 For this reason, it is possible to talk about 'the Death of Distance' (see Audtresch 2000: 64). O'Brien (1992) even suggests that the emergence of the Internet and global financial integration is heralding 'the end of geography'.

8 The Internet application receiving the most public attention is consumer merchandizing. Companies use the Internet in an attempt to provide more efficient and effective customer service, to lower the cost of sales and marketing, and to pursue new sales opportunities. However, the biggest economic impact of the Internet is likely to come from business-to-business e-commerce, which cuts companies' costs in three ways: (a) it reduces purchasing costs; (b) it allows better supply-chain management; (c) it allows tighter inventory control (see e.g. Blinder 2000; Comor 2000: 107; the *Economist* 1–4–2000; Arena and Feustré 2001: 3–5).

9 As noted by Storper:

> These are the sectors or parts of sectors that each economy is particularly good at. Such advantages have many potential causes, among which are scale, resource-based comparative advantages or skill and institutionally embedded know-how. There is much reason to believe that the importance of the latter has generally increased, and that knowledge-based, export oriented industries are major components of the emerging, knowledge-driven system of world capitalism.
>
> (2000: 49)

10 As pointed out by Cohen *et al.* (2000), in the NE, investors face a series of often unexpected challenges from sources on the global stage; in general national innovations and developments are played out more quickly on larger stages, regional and 'global' theatres.

11 It is important to note that these effects are especially significant for developing countries (see DeMartino 2000: 17). While taking benefit from new developments, such as

rapid economic liberalization coupled with ongoing technological progress, transport and communication, these countries are also exposed to new risks. Indeed, as Dasgupta *et al.* point out,

> these developments have yielded significant benefits to developing countries ... but they have also created new risks especially with regard to private capital flows and vulnerability to sudden shocks ... [we see] evidence of contagion as crises in one country have spilled over to other countries in the same region and elsewhere because of increased trade and financial integration ... and increased volatility.
>
> (2001: 1)

12 On the cross-cultural comparison between Japan and US see, for example, Viskovatoff (2000: 148). Japan, for example, retains many features of archaic societies, such as the focus on the interaction system and on long-term relations.

13 Indeed, as Cohen *et al.* recognize, just as new rules for privacy, security, taxation and intellectual property are being built up in each country to allow the new information technology system to operate, 'new international rules, will be required to reconcile the several national arrangements.' (2000: 8).

14 As Viskovatoff (2000: 149) points out, the outstanding US performance is due to three components: (a) lack of wage increases; (b) devaluation of the dollar; (c) maintenance of aggregate demand by means of an increase in consumer and business debt relative to GDP. Viskovatoff is pessimistic about this state of affairs because, rather than having overcome its economic disadvantages, the US has adapted to it by offsetting the lowered labour productivity growth with downsizing of labour employed and by lowering labour costs and devaluation. However, in his view this strategy is not sustainable in the long run for at least three reasons: (a) labour productivity is raised by having many jobs at high wages; (b) low-wage growth aggravates the aggregate demand problem and hence necessitates increased debt; (c) if the dollar is devalued past a certain point, foreign capital will flow away from the dollar, thus impairing the financing of the US trade deficit and increasing the danger of a lack of aggregate demand at the global level. The current problems in global governance, which are actually worsened by the NE, have been around for quite a long time. The fact that they raise serious problems of instability, similar to those underlying the Great Depression of the 1930s, has already been emphasized by Freeman and Perez in their 1988 contribution (see e.g. 1988: 63).

15 In line with the views of economists such as Myrdal and Kaldor, Prasch (2000b: 182–3) underlies that positive feedback mechanisms (such as those between income increases and investment) will tend to reinforce differential growth between wealthy and poorer areas. The fact that technological progress can take on cumulative traits and that it is the result of organizational work, not just scientific or technological, has long been recognized by economists and economic historians such as Veblen and Gerschenkron. Again, what the NE does with its emphasis on human capital is to accelerate this recognized feature of the process of economic growth.

12 Rapidity

1 As Blinder puts it

> better information technology is nothing new – it has been improving for centuries. The Internet can be seen as the latest step along a path that began with the movable type, and progressed through the typewriter, the telephone, radio, television, photocopying, and fax machines, to name just a few.
>
> (2000: 3)

2 'Throughout this century, patent applications fluctuated within a band between 40.000 and 80.000 per year, by contrast, in 1995 there were over 120.000 patent applications.' (Audretsch 2000: 66). Audretsch points out that another indicator of increased innovative activity is that in recent times the demand for less skilled workers has decreased dramatically throughout the OECD, while at the same time the demand for skilled workers has exploded.

3 In a similar vein, Greenspan (1999), regards the NE as 'a perceptible quickening in the pace at which technological innovations are applied' which argues for the hypothesis that 'the recent acceleration in labour productivity is not just a cyclical phenomenon or a statistical aberration, but reflects, at least in part, a more deep-seated, still developing, shift in our economic landscape'.

4 As Blinder puts it: 'This surprising phenomenon came to be called "the computer paradox" after Robert Solow's famous 1987 quip: "We see the computer age everywhere except in the productivity statistics." ' (2000: 3)

5 Blinder stresses that these productivity gains are not unlike those of the past:

> Similar surges in productivity can also be found in 1990–1992, 1983–1986, and 1977–1978. But they all followed recessions. And they were all subsequently reversed. On the other hand, only one of these events (1983–1986) was as big as what we have witnessed recently.
>
> (2000: 3)

Despite his scepticism, Blinder however does admit that due to these productivity gains a higher sustainable rate of growth is possible and he draws the conclusion 'in that limited respect, at least, we appear to be in a "New Economy." ' (ibid.: 6).

6 Moreover, if we consider the social impact of the new technologies, there is little doubt that 'direct-dial long-distance calling and television made more real difference to our lives than the Internet and DVD' (Krugman 1997).

7 As Cohen *et al.* put it:

> Computer chips, lasers, broadband Internet, and software are the key components of the technology that drives the E-conomy. The technological explosion of the invention of the semiconductor and subsequent productivity gains in making semiconductors has produced and will produce a stunning advance in information-processing power. In rough orders of magnitude, by 2010 computers will have ten million times the processing power of computers in 1975. The market price of computing power has fallen more than ten thousand-fold in a single generation, with the result that the installed base of information processing power has increased at least million-fold since the end of the era of electro-mechanical calculators in the 1950s.
>
> (2000: 4)

8 For example,

> it took more than a century and a quarter after the invention of the steam engine in Britain before steam became the dominant source of power in nineteenth-century Britain, then the most industrialized nation in the world. Similarly it took seventy years following the initial commercialization of electricity for electric motors to replace steam as the source of power in America's factories.
>
> (ibid. 2000: 70)

9 In other words, technical change in the production of information technology assets lowers their relative price, induces massive high-tech investment and is ultimately responsible for the recent productivity revival (see Stiroh 2000: 48).

10 As Brynjolfsson and Hitt (2002: 26) point out, this transition from 'mass production' to flexible, computer-enabled, 'modern manufacturing' is driven by exogenous change in the price of ICT.

11 These concepts reflect a tension between cooperation and competition; positive feedback and network conomies make crucial cooperation among firms in order to establish the standard, but once the standard, has been reached, firms can compete to win market shares (Shapiro and Varian 1998).

12 Indeed, as noted by Blanchard and Simon (2001: 160), there has been a change in the sign of correlation between inventory and sales in the last decade with investment in inventory becoming countercyclical. They go on to stress though that this point raises a puzzle: just-in-time methods lowering the inventory–sales ratio should lead to more procyclical, not less procyclical, inventory behaviour.

13 Lightness

1 Lightness was especially favoured by limited liability when the separation between real investment and property became possible:

> Consider investment in that earlier era. Massive investments in large factories were needed to realize the economies of scale possible in serving the mammoth national market; these required that savings be gathered out of tens of thousands of pockets to provide the equity capital. But who, in the absence of the protecting shield of limited liability, would commit their savings to equity investments in huge bureaucratic enterprises over which they had no control? At the time, limited liability was viewed by many as an exorbitant new privilege for investors. Yet in retrospect we see it as necessary if the possibilities for economic organization opened up by the new technologies were to be realized.
>
> (Cohen *et al.* 2000: 58)

2 As De Long and Summers point out, from this standpoint the NE appears as a new version of an old story: 'Past "new economies," past "economic revolutions" have also seen extraordinary growth in technology, the rise to dominance of new industrial sectors .... They changed the canonical sources of value and the process of production' (2001: 18).

3 To a certain extent the accelerating tendency towards a weightless economy accounts for the rather different (i.e. much less negative) consequences of the oil shock in 2000 as compared with 1973 or 1981.

4 For data concerning R&D, patents, the proportion of the age group 15–24 engaged in higher education, and capital spending on ICT see, for example, Dunning (2000: 9).

5 There are also other explanations for the rise in the stock market that are not linked directly to ICT. Some suggest, for example, that it results from a reduction in the equity risk premium or to a greater willingness to hold risky assets (for a discussion of this topic see Baily 2001: 239; Banerji 2002: 13–15).

6 The development of venture capital has been favoured by changes in the prudent-man rule which allowed institutional money (e.g. pension funds) to enter the venture business. In a similar fashion

> the growth of compensation through stock options that reward stunning success with stunning wealth allowed founders to share a significant portion of the risk and rewards of a new company with like-minded employees. The institution of stock options meant that a cut in pay and a move across country could suddenly represent an opportunity not a failing – if the reward were a share in value of a venture start-up. And large established firms followed by seeking ways to encourage and to participate in spin-outs, start-ups, and venture funds.
>
> (Cohen *et al.* 2000: 24)

7 As the *Economist* notes,

> [f]or instance, rather than holding loans on their books, banks now bundle loans into securities and sell them on the secondary market. The resulting stream

of liquidity allowed the banking system to lend more during the boom. New financial instruments and greater competition in the mortgage market have made it easier for households to borrow.

(28–9–2002: 29)

8 Similarly, the introduction of a secondary market for mortgages and the removal of regulation Q on interest ceilings accounts for reduction of volatility in homebuilding in the US (see Friedman 2001: 169).

9 Borio and Lowe suggest that the concept of elasticity of private credit creation is useful in gauging the vulnerability of a monetary regime to financial instability. This elasticity indicates credit's potential for allowing financial imbalances to build up unchecked during a boom. The *Economist* summarizes their view as follows:

> [C]ompared with the early part of the 20th century ... the elasticity of private credit creation has increased significantly ... today's combination of liberalised financial system, a money standard with no exogenous anchor such as gold and a monetary policy focused only on short term inflation raises the risk of longer and bigger build-ups in credit. That makes asset-price and debt bubbles more likely.

(28–9–2002: 29)

10 Following the end of the speculative bubble and the disappearance of most dot.coms, this trend has started to be reversed. Many now deny that capital markets had actually discovered new truths in corporate valuations or that higher productivity would necessarily lead to higher returns (see e.g. *Financial Times* 18–5–2002).

14 Precision

1 Strictly speaking, in this chapter we use the term 'precision' in a rather broad sense. In a more restricted sense, 'precision' can be regarded as the opposite of generality. As noted, for example, by Backhouse (1997: 101), a precise theory has greater empirical content than a general one.

2 This theory has limited utility in that it cannot tell us what must happen, merely what *might* happen (see Backhouse 1997: 20–1).

3 A number of contributions taking account of developments within methodology in the 1990s detect the disillusionment with the positivist approach in methodology and a revival of interest in the deductivist approach (see e.g. Lawson 1997, 2003; Dow 2002: 105).

4 This attitude is clearly not without consequences for the content of the theory. For example, expectations are dealt with by modern economists in a very different way from those writing in the 1930s, that is, on the grounds of probability theory rather than, say, animal spirits (see e.g. Dow 2002: 10).

5 Similarly, econometricians have tried ever more refined ways to capture structural change. For example the VAR approach is more attuned to detecting structural change from the data than are the structural models which start form a presumed structural form (see e.g. Dow 2002: 46).

6 In particular, Baily suggests that it is becoming more difficult to predict potential income: 'Unfortunately, during the past twenty-five years out ability to predict the growth of potential output and to predict the long-term fiscal position of the economy has been weak' (Baily 2001: 253).

7 Calibration methods offer the promise of short cuts to simple, empirical generalizations that can be used as a basis for theorizing. See for example, Backhouse (1997: 179–82).

8 Godley and Izurieta (2002: 39–43), for example, describe both optimistic and realistic scenarios. See also Zarnowitz (1999: 79).

9 For all of these reasons, national income accounts no longer appear as satisfactory as they were (see e.g. Crocket 2001). More in general, it can be argued that the NE widens

the gap between the precision with which physical constants are measured and the precision of analogous constants in economics (on this issue see Backhouse 1997: 151).

10 Even if precise predictions are impossible, econometrics might be expected to play a key role in establishing empirical generalizations and in persuading economists to accept or reject theories. According to many critics, this has not happened. Although econometrics has played a role in the development of economics, its influence on the way economists conceive of economic phenomena has been a minor one (see Backhouse 1997: 136).

11 Similarly, Hall (2001: 172), in line with Phelps, finds it anomalous that Blanchard and Simon conclude that volatility is much lower than it used to be because recent five- and ten-year forecast errors have been huge. Blanchard and Simon focus on movements in real GDP that have too high a frequency; it would be better to observe medium-frequency movements.

15 Visibility

1 The foundation of central banks like the FED (founded in 1914) was obviously a crucial step in the evolution of the control of money and the economy. While in the pre-First War era, governments could affect the economy through the choice of monetary standards and banking regulation, only the FED was able to effect short-run movements in interest rates (see e.g. C. Romer 1999: 34).

2 Indeed, as noted by many (see e.g. Arestis and Sawyer 2002: 4–5; Kuttner and Mosser 2002), financial innovation in the NE has created a more unstable demand for money and has altered the channels through which monetary policy affects the economy.

3 As noted, for example, by C. Romer (1999), Blanchard and Simon (2001) and B. Friedman (2001), the rise of independent central banks pursuing price stability has led to the decline in inflation volatility and the dampening of the business cycle with respect to the pre-Depression era.

4 In other words, the task of policy is to manage the demand for goods and services so as to keep it more or less in line with the economy's capacity for supply. This point is well summarized by Blinder:

> If demand (measured by real GDP) falls short of capacity (which is sometimes called 'potential' GDP), the economy develops what is politely called 'slack' – and what is less delicately called unemployment. If demand exceeds supply, the economy is said to 'overheat,' leading to higher inflation. Because of this, the trend growth rate essentially sets the economy's long-run 'speed limit'.... This number is among the most important pieces of information the Fed must know (or rather, must estimate) in order to conduct monetary policy. And productivity growth is the crucial ingredient.
>
> (2000: 2)

5 Similarly, the NE undermines exchange rate policy. As noted by Godley and Izurieta (2002: 47), the point is that the exchange rate does not respond reliably to changes in interest rates. Nor do market forces cause exchange rates to move in a way that corrects imbalances in a timely fashion.

6 According to Woodford, Central Banks in the NE retain the power to control the level of overnight rates and, by so doing, regulate spending and pricing decisions in the same way as at present.

7 On the interpretation of the ECB's strategy as a pragmatic one see, for example, Issing *et al.* (2001).

8 Baker stresses that 'the late 1990s experience of low unemployment without accelerating inflation seems to directly contradict the NAIRU view, which had come to dominate the economics profession and provide the basis for monetary policy' (2003: 819).

9 DeLong underlines that confidence in the FED plays an important part in reducing the magnitude of shocks. For example, one result of confidence in the FED is the emergence of more private-sector willingness to speculate on stability.

10 As Baker puts it

> the Greenspan Fed was quite explicitly engaged in fine-tuning. It raised and lowered interest rates on the basis of its perception of the economy's current momentum. To a large extent, it appeared that its tweaking of the economy worked: the Fed was largely successful in its efforts to control the rate of economic growth over this period. At the very least, economists may acknowledge that monetary policy is more effective than most had previously believed.
>
> (2003: 820)

11 In principle, many economists agree that taxes disincentive work so that cutting taxes has a certain incentive on supply. The main differences arise concerning the quantitative dimension of the effects. Strict supply-siders believe that cutting taxes from today's level would have enormous positive effects on the supply side without causing problems for the budget; indeed taxes would actually increase. Others are much more sceptical. On this issue, see Krugman (2001).

12 In order to avoid confusion, it is important to note that 'deregulation' is quite a misleading term. In general, 'regulation' does not really disappear. Indeed, as shown by industrial history, direct regulation has proven necessary in order to create competitive markets. In the case of ICT the process is far from complete. Initiative did not originate in the Congress, or in the Executive power; it fell to the courts on anti-trust grounds, as did years of detailed oversight in implementing the decisions (see e.g. Cohen *et al.* 2000).

13 As Cohen *et al.* 2000 put it

> individual markets rest on rules ... For markets to work there must be rules about property, defining who owns what; in many cases these must get rather specific. There must also be rules about deal-making, about what in a contract can be enforced by law and about what responsibilities are expected from the parties making the deal.
>
> As tools for thought, information technology increasingly touches everything in an economy; the rules for that E-conomy will increasingly define not only how individual markets work, but also how the over-all market economy works ... The cyber world is intertwined with, not independent of, our traditional world. We will not have a cyber world free of regulation.
>
> Translating the old rules for a new era, not to mention creating totally new rules for totally new phenomena, requires real choices and decisions not just casual tinkering.
>
> (2000: 54)

14 For a similar view, see Gordon (2002: 28–40), who includes government funded Military and Civilian research among the sources of ICT revolution and US advantage. On the link between ICT and military expenditure (over 40 per cent of total expenditure on research is carried out by military organizations), see Kumar (1995).

15 As pointed out by Zarnowitz (1999), although discretionary macro policies may reduce or end cyclical instability, incorrect policies can also destabilize the economy.

16 Rifkin refers to the failure of attempts to start business and trade after the collapse of the former USSR, which had destroyed the cultural institutions constituting the so-called third sector (see Rifkin 2000: 323). Moreover, he also stresses that it is only recently that financial institutions like the World Bank have started to gain a better understanding of the link between the economy and culture. After financing (in vain) expensive projects to promote growth in developing countries in the belief that creating

a solid economy could help social development, they have now started to finance projects of social development in the belief that strong community and solid culture is a fundamental condition for economic development rather than the other way round.

17 As shown, for example, by the second pillar of the ECB's strategy for inflation targeting the money supply, information concerning cost factors, such as oil prices and wage settlements or productivity, matter in the assessment of inflationary tendencies. This means that it is consistent with many explanations for inflation.

18 These two instances do not exhaust all the potential destabilizing effects of regulatory moves. For example, antitrust policy too can have negative effects as it may impair innovation in the dynamic context of the NE where it is not easy to define unambiguously dominant positions of firms and the boundary of markets.

16 New Classical Macroeconomics and the New Economy: an overview

1 Opinions among macroeconomists differ here. New Keynesian economists like Blanchard tend to favour broader interpretations, while a narrow view is held by NCM.

2 For a similar chart, see Blanchard (2003: 220).

3 In other words, for NCM all fluctuations are changes or shifts in the natural level of production or the natural rate of unemployment, not deviations from the natural level. Technical progress is one of the major factors that determine these changes in the natural levels of income.

17 New Classical Macroeconomics and the key features of the New Economy

1 Hall points out that the valuation of many large companies, in general, bears very little relation to the amount of tangible capital held by these corporations. He stresses, for example, that in recent times there has been a dramatic rise in Tobin's q, that is, the ratio of market value of corporations to the replacement cost of their tangible capital. It was unity in the 1990s, and it nearly tripled in ten years (see also Baily 2001: 242–4, 2002: 14).

2 Strictly speaking, these problems are not new. Neoclassicals have been facing them since the introduction of expectations or the concept of 'natural' rate of unemployment in macroeconomics, which also seem to pose serious measurability problems. A number of *ad hoc* solutions have been found in applied economics, such as using an average of actual rates of unemployment as a proxy for the natural rate.

3 In Blanchard's view, the ECB behaves as a *de facto* inflation targeter. The point is that although the ECB does not formally pursue an ITR, it does pursue a monetary strategy with a clear commitment to price stability over the medium term (see also Arestis and Sawyer 2003: 7, 14).

18 Keynesian theory and the New Economy: an overview

1 In the terminology introduced by Vercelli (1991: 176), we focus here on Keynes' 'heuristic model', the logical scheme of the *General Theory*, which consists of a causal plot and a set of instructions for use which remain largely implicit.

2 Blanchard (2003) emphasizes that naturally not all agree on these propositions. Opinions differ especially as to the length of the short run, the length of time through which aggregate demand influences production. At one extreme RBC theorists stress that income is always at its natural level (so that short run is truly short), at the other extreme hysteresis theories of unemployment suggest that effects of aggregate can last for a long time, so that the 'short-run' is actually quite long.

19 Keynesian theory and multiplicity

1 Moreover, our Keynesian model does reject the *ceteris paribus* clause underlying standard theory, according to which markets and key phenomena must be dealt with separately. It focuses from the start on the mutual interactions between financial and real phenomena. Thus, for example, globalization, technological change and financial innovation should be studied as interdependent phenomena.

2 The view that the NE defies standard laws of exchange rates mainly because of the enormous size of financial flows is quite widely shared. As noted, for example, by the *Economist*:

> Two puzzles (in macroeconomics) are to do with prices and currencies: that similar goods often do not cost the same in different countries; and that there are no short-term links between fluctuations in exchange rates and measures of economic activity.
>
> (5–8–2000: 74)

3 Indeed, as pointed out by Davidson (2002: 477, 491), in Keynes's times it was already clear the liberalization of international financial flows creates a global environment in which each nation independently sees significant advantages in a policy of export-led growth even though the pursuit of these policies simultaneously by many nations 'injures all alike', that is to say, creates global stagnation and recession.

20 Keynesian theory and rapidity

1 On these aspects of investment, see Freeman and Perez 1988.

2 Sheila Dow compares New Keynesians' emphasis on credit rationing and Minsky financial instability hypothesis and suggests that they represent two alternative ways of approaching the default risk issue and the micro–macro relation: while New Keynesians try to explain macro results as arising from standard rational individual behaviour, for Minsky changes in agents' confidence are important and are best analysed directly at the macro level (see e.g. 2002: 30).

21 Keynesian theory and lightness

1 They would require, for example, growing injections of net credit and a growing inflow of foreign capital.

2 Moreover, our Keynesian model does reject the *ceteris paribus* clause underlying standard theory, according to which markets and key phenomena must be dealt with separately. It focuses from the start on the mutual interactions between financial and real phenomena. Thus, for example, globalization, technological change and financial innovation should be studied as interdependent phenomena.

3 As Western points out, however, these are historical trends and 'may shed a dim light on current trends. To the extent that stock analysts are captive to past regularities their ability to predict major turning points in stock prices is severely limited' (2004: 80).

4 On the view that share prices both reflect economic activity and influence it, see for example, Blanchard 2003.

23 Keynesian theory and visibility

1 This view is justified by evidence provided by Ghosh and Phillips (1998: 674), who stress two important nonlinearities in the inflation–growth relationship: at low inflation rates inflation and growth are positively correlated. Otherwise, there is a negative correlation (see also Arestis and Sawyer 2003: 3).

Bibliography

Aghion, Philippe and Howitt, Peter (1998) *Endogenous Growth Theory*, Cambridge, MA: The MIT Press.

Alexander, Jeffrey (1994) 'Modern Anti, Post, and Neo: How Social Theories Have Tried to Understand the "New World" of "Our Time" ', *Zeitschrift Für Sozioogie*, vol. 23, no. 3, 165–97.

Archibugi, Franco (2000) *The Associative Economy: Insights Beyond the Welfare State and into Post-Capitalism*, London: Macmillan.

Arena, Richard and Feustré, Agnes (2001) 'Markets in the "new economy": Some Elements of an Austrian Approach', contribution to the *Third conference of the Association of Historians of the Austrian Tradition in Economic Thought*, Pisa (Italy), 24–26 May.

Arestis, Philip and Sawyer, Malcolm C. (2003) 'Macroeconomic Policies of the Economic and Monetary Union: Theoretical Underpinnings and Challenges', paper presented at the *Evolutionary Association for Economic and Political Economy* conference, Maastricht.

Arestis, Philip and Sawyer, Michael C. (2002) 'Can Monetary Policy Affect the Real Economy?', *The Levy Economics Institute Working Paper*, no. 355.

Arestis, Philip, Palma, Gabriel and Sawyer, Michael C. (eds) (1997) *Markets, Employment and Economic Policy: Essays in Honour of G.C. Harcourt*, 2 vols, London: Routledge.

Argyrous, George (2002) 'Endogenous Demand in the Theory of Transformational Growth', in M. Setterfield (ed.) *The Economics of Demand-led Growth*, Cheltenham: E. Elgar.

Arthur, Brian W. (1994) *Increasing Returns and Path Dependence in the Economy*, Ann Arbor, MI: Michigan University Press.

Arthur, Brian W. (2000) 'Complexity and the Economy', in D. Colander (ed.) *The Complexity Vision and the Teaching of Economics*, Cheltenham: E. Elgar.

Arthur, Brian W., Durlauf, Stephen N. and Lane, David (eds) (1997) *The Economy as an Evolving Complex System*, SFI Studies in the Sciences of Complexity, 2 vols, Reading, MA: AddisonWesley.

Asimakopulos, Athanasios (1991) *Keynes's General Theory and Accumulation*, Cambridge: Cambridge University Press.

Atkinson, Robert D. and Court, Ranolph H. (2000) 'Nine Myths About The New Economy', http://www.neweconomyindex.org/#Table_of_Contents (accessed 20 March 2001).

Audretsch, David B. (2000) 'Knowledge, Globalization, and Regions: An Economist's Perspective', in J. Dunning (ed.) *Regions, Globalization, and the Knowledge-Based Economy*, Oxford: Oxford University Press.

Auerbach, Alan J. (2002) 'Is There a Role for Discretionary Fiscal Policy', Proceedings of a *Symposium on Rethinking Stabilisation Policy*, sponsored by the Federal Reserve Bank of Kansas City, Jackson Hole, WY, 28–31 August.

Backhouse, Roger E. (ed.) (1994) *New Directions in Economic Methodology*, London: Routledge.

Backhouse, Roger E. (1997) *Truth and Progress in Economic Knowledge*, Cheltenham: E. Elgar.

Baily, Martin N. (2001) 'Macroeconomic Implications of the New Economy', Proceedings of a *Symposium on Economic Policy for the Information Economy*, sponsored by the Federal Reserve Bank of Kansas City, Jackson Hole, WY, 30 August–1 September.

Baily, Martin N. (2002) 'The New Economy: Post-Mortem or Second Wind?', *Journal of Economic Perspectives*, vol. 16, no. 2, Spring, 3–22.

Baker, Dean (2003) 'Macro Policymaking in the New Economy', in D. Jones (ed.) *New Economy Handbook*, Amsterdam: Elsevier.

Banerji, Anirvan (2002) 'The Resurrection of Risk', *Challenge*, March–April, 7–27.

Barrel Ray, Mason, Geoffrey and O' Mahony, Mary (eds) (2000) *Productivity, Innovation and Economic Performance*, Cambridge: Cambridge University Press.

Barro, Robert J. (1990) 'Government Spending in a Simple Model of Endogenous Growth', *Journal of Political Economy*, vol. 106, no. 2, 407–43.

Basu, Susanto and Taylor, Alan M. (1999) 'Business Cycles in International Historical Perspective', *Journal of Economic Perspectives*, vol. 13, no. 2, Spring, 45–68.

Beck, Ulrich (1992) *Risk Society: Towards a New Modernity*, London: Sage.

Bernanke, Ben S. (2004) 'The Great Moderation', Meeting of the Eastern Economic Association, Washington, DC, February 20.

Bibow, Jorg (2002a) 'The Euro: Market Failure or Central Bank Failure?', *Challenge*, vol. 45, no. 3, 83–99.

Bibow, Jorg (2002b) 'The Monetary Policies of the European Central Bank and the Euro's (Mal-) Performance: A Stability Oriented Assessment', *International Review of Applied Economics*, vol. 16, no. 1, 31–50.

Bibow, Jorg (2003) 'Is Europe Doomed to Stagnation? An Analysis of the Current Crisis and Recommendations for Reforming Macroeconomic Policymaking in Euroland', *The Levy Economics Institute Working Paper*, no. 379.

Blanchard, Oliver (1998) 'Discussion to "Regional Non-adjustment and Fiscal Policy" ', *Economic Policy*, no. 26, April, 249.

Blanchard, Oliver (2000) 'What Do We Know about Macroeconomics that Fisher and Wicksell Did Not?', *NBER Working Papers*, no. 7550.

Blanchard, Oliver (2003) *Macroeconomics*, 3rd edn, Upper Saddle River, NJ: Prentice Hall.

Blanchard, Oliver and Fischer, Stanley (1989) *Lectures in Macroeconomics*, Cambridge, MA: The MIT Press.

Blanchard, Oliver and Simon, John (2001) 'The Long and Large Decline in U.S. Output Volatility', *Brookings Papers on Economic Activity*, vol. 1, 135–74.

Blaug, Mark (1994) 'Why I am not a Constructivist: Confessions of an Unrepentant Popperian', in R.E. Backhouse (ed.) *New Directions in Economic Methodology*, London: Routledge.

Blaug, Mark (2000) 'Is There Really Progress in Economics', *European Society for the History of Economic Thought*, Graz, Austria, February, mimeo.

Blinder, Alan S. (2000) 'The Internet and the New Economy', January, *Internet policy Institute*, http://www.internetpolicy.org/briefing/1_00.html (accessed 20 March 2001).

Boggio, Luciano and Seravalli, Gilberto (2003) *Lo sviluppo economico: Fatti, teorie, politiche*, Bologna: Il Mulino.

Boland, Lawrence (1982) *The Foundations of Economic Method*, London: Allen and Unwin.

Bortis, Heinrich (1996) *Institutions, Behaviour and Economic Theory. A Contribution to Classical-Keynesian Political Economy*, Cambridge: Cambridge University Press.

Boyer, Robert (1988) 'Technical Change and the Theory of "Regulation" ', in G. Dosi, C. Freeman, R. Nelson, G. Silverberg and L. Soete (eds) *Technical Change and Economic Theory*, London: Pinter.

Boyer, Robert (2004) *The Future of Economic Growth. As New Becomes Old*, Cheltenham: E. Elgar.

Boylan, Thomas A. and O'Gorman, Paschal F. (1995) *Beyond Rhetoric and Realism in Economics. Towards a Reformulation of Economic Methodology*, London: Routledge.

Bresnahan, Tim and Trajtenberg, Manuel (1996) 'General Purpose Technologies: Engines of Growth?', *Journal of Econometrics*, vol. 65, no. 1, 83–108.

Brock, William B. (2000) 'Santa Fe Scenery', in D. Colander (ed.) *The Complexity Vision and the Teaching of Economics*, Cheltenham: E. Elgar.

Brock, William B. and Colander, David (2000) 'Complexity and Policy', in D. Colander (ed.) *The Complexity Vision and the Teaching of Economics*, Cheltenham: E. Elgar.

Brown, William S. (2000) 'Market Failure in the New Economy', *Journal of Economic Issues*, vol. 34, no. 1, March, 219–27.

Brynjolfsson, Erik and Hitt, Laurin M. (2002) 'Beyond Computation: Information, Technology, Organizational Transformation and Business Performance', *Journal of Economic Perspectives*, vol. 14, no. 4, Fall, 23–48.

Brynjolfsson, Erik and Smith, Michael D. (2000) 'Frictionless Commerce? A Comparison of Internet and Conventional Retailers', *Management Science*, vol. 46, no. 4, 563–85.

Calvino, Italo (1993) *Six Memos for the Next Millenium*. The Charles Eliot Norton Lectures 1985–86, Harvard University, New York: Vintage International.

Caserta, Maurizio and Chick, Victoria (1997) 'Provisional Equilibrium and Macroeconomic Theory', in P. Arestis, G. Palma and M.C. Sawyer (eds) *Markets, Employment and Economic Policy: Essays in Honour of G.C. Harcourt*, London: Routledge, vol. II.

Castells, Manuel (1996) *The Rise of the Network Society*, Oxford: Blackwell.

Cecchetti, Stephen G. (2002) 'The New Economy and the Challenges for Macroeconomic Policy', *NBER Working Paper*, no. 8935.

Chick, Victoria (1983) *Macroeconomics after Keynes. A Reconsideration of the General Theory*, Oxford: Philip Allan.

Chick, Victoria (1986) 'The Evolution of the Banking System and the Theory of Saving, Investment and Interest', *Economies et societès, Cahiers de l'ISMEA, Serie 'Monnaie et Production'*, no. 3.

Chick, Victoria (1995) ' "Order Out of Chaos" in Economics?', in S. Dow and J. Hillard (eds) *Keynes, Knowledge and Uncertainty*, Cheltenham: E. Elgar.

Chick, Victoria (2003) 'On Open Systems', paper presented at the *Conference of the International Network for Economic Method*, Leeds, 2–3 September.

Chick, Victoria and Dow, Sheila C. (2001) 'Formalism, Logic and Reality: A Keynesian analysis', *Cambridge Journal of Economics*, vol. 25, 705–21.

Clarida, Richard, Gali, Jordi and Gertler, Mark (2000) 'Monetary Policy Rules and Macroeconomic Stability: Evidence and Some Theory', *The Quarterly Journal of Economics*, vol. 115, no. 1, 147–80.

Cohen, Stephen S., DeLong, J. Bradford and Zysman, John (2000) 'Tools for Thought: What Is New and Important About the "E-conomy" ', *BRIE Working Paper*, no. 138, http://www.j-bradforddelong.net/OpEd/virtual/technet/TfT.html (accessed 25 March 2001).

Colander, David (2000a) 'Introduction', in D. Colander (ed.) *Complexity and the History of Economic Thought*, London: Routledge.

Colander, David (2000b) 'A Thumbnail Sketch of the History of Thought From a Complexity Perspective', in D. Colander (ed.) *Complexity and the History of Economic Thought*, London: Routledge.

Colander, David (2000c) 'Introduction', in D. Colander (ed.) *The Complexity Vision and the Teaching of Economics*, Cheltenham: E. Elgar.

Colander, David (2000d) 'Complexity and the Teaching of Economics', in D. Colander (ed.) *The Complexity Vision and the Teaching of Economics*, Cheltenham: E. Elgar.

Comim, Flavio (2000) 'Marshall and the Role of Common Sense in Complex Systems', in D. Colander (ed.) *Complexity and the History of Economic Thought*, London: Routledge.

Comor, Edward (2000) 'Household Consumption on the Internet: Income, Time, and Institutional Contradictions', *Journal of Economic Issues*, vol. 34, no. 1, March, 105–16.

Cornwall, John (1997) 'Notes on the Trade Cycle and Social Philosophy in a Post-Keynesian World', in G.C. Harcourt and P.A. Riach (eds) *A 'second edition' of the General Theory*, London: Routledge, vol. I.

Crockett, Andrew D. (2001) 'General Discussion on Technology, Information Production, and Market Efficiency', Proceedings of a *Symposium on Economic Policy for the Information Economy*, sponsored by the Federal Reserve Bank of Kansas City, Jackson Hole, WY 30 August–1 September.

Crook, Ed (2000) 'The Oldest Rules Could Still Hold Good in New World of Electronic Commerce', *Financial Times*, 26 February.

Cullemberg, Stephen, Amariglio, Jack and Ruccio, David F. (2001) 'Introduction', in S. Cullemberg, J. Amariglio and D.F. Ruccio (eds) *Post-modernism, Economics and Knowledge*, London: Routledge.

Dasgupta, Dipak, Uzan, Mar and Wilson, Dominic (eds) (2001) *Capital Flows Without Crisis? Reconciling Capital Mobility and Economic Stability*, London: Routledge.

David, Paul (1991) 'Computer and Dynamo: The Modern Productivity Paradox in a Not-Too-Distant Mirror', *Technology and Productivity: The Challenge for Economic Policy*, Paris: OECD, 315–45.

Davidson, Paul (1982–3) 'Rational Expectations: A Fallacious Foundations for Studying Crucial Decision Making Processes', *Journal of Post Keynesian Economics*, vol. 5, 182–97.

Davidson, Paul (2002) 'Globalization', *Journal of Post Keynesian Economics*, vol. 24, no. 3, Spring, 475–92.

Davidson, Paul (2004) 'A Response To King's Argument For Pluralism', *Post-Autistic Economics Review*, no. 24, 15 March; 1–4, http://www.btinternet.com/~pae_news/review/issue24.htm (accessed 14 April 2004).

D'Avolio, Gene, Gildor, Efi and Shleifer, Andrei (2001) 'Technology, Information, Production and Market Efficiency', Proceedings of a *Symposium on Economic Policy for the Information Economy*, sponsored by the Federal Reserve Bank of Kansas City, Jackson Hole, WY, 30 August–1 September.

DeLong, J. Bradford (1998) 'How "New" is Today's Economy?' and http://econ161.berkeley.edu/comments/how_new.html (accessed 26 March 2001).

DeLong, J. Bradford (1999) 'Introduction to the Symposium on Business Cycles', *Journal of Economic Perspectives*, vol. 13, no. 2, Spring, 19–22.

DeLong, J. Bradford (2003) 'Thoughts on Stock and Watson', Proceedings of a *Symposium on Monetary Policy and Uncertainty: Adapting to a Changing Economy*, sponsored by the Federal Reserve Bank of Kansas City, Jackson Hole, WY, 28–30 August.

DeLong, J. Bradford and Eichengreen, Barry (2001) 'Between Meltdown and Moral Hazard, The International Monetary and Financial Policies of the Clinton Administration', *Kennedy School Conference: American Economic Policy in the 1990s*, May.

DeLong, J. Bradford and Summers, Lawrence H. (2001) 'The "New Economy": Background, Questions, and Speculations', Proceedings of a *Symposium on Economic Policy for the Information Economy*, sponsored by the Federal Reserve Bank of Kansas City, Jackson Hole, WY, 30 August–1 September.

DeMartino, George F. (2000) *Global Economy, Global Justice. Theoretical Objections and Policy Alternatives to Neoliberalism*, London: Routledge.

Denzau, Arthur T. and North, Douglass C. (1994) 'Shared Mental Models', *Kyklos*, vol. 47, no. 1, 3–31.

Dornbusch, Rudiger (1999) ' "Financial Crises": What Have We Learned from Theory and Experience?' in P. Iasar Jr., A. Razin and A.K. Rose (eds) *Summary of Panel Remarks, International Finance and Financial Crises: Essays in Honor of Robert P. Flood*, Kluwer: Academic Publishers, International Monetary Fund, 57–61.

Dosi, Giovanni, Freeman, Chris, Nelson, Richard, Silverberg, Gerald and Soete, Luc (eds) (1988) *Technical Change and Economic Theory*, London: Pinter.

Dow, Sheila (2001) 'Modernism and Postmodernism. A dialectical analysis', in S. Cullemberg, J. Amariglio and D.F. Ruccio (eds) *Post-Modernism, Economics and Knowledge*, London: Routledge.

Dow, Sheila (2002) *Economic Methodology: An Inquiry*, Oxford: Oxford University Press.

Dow, Sheila and Hillard, John (eds) (1995) *Keynes, Knowledge and Uncertainty*, Cheltenham: E. Elgar.

Dunford, Michel (2000) 'Globalization and Theories of Regulation', in R. Palan (ed.) *Global Political Economy. Contemporary Theories*, London: Routledge.

Dunning, John H. (2000) 'Regions, Globalization and the Knowledge Economy: The Issues Stated', in J.H. Dunning (ed.) *Regions, Globalization and the Knowledge-Based Economy*, Oxford: Oxford University Press.

Eatwell, John and Milgate, Murray (1983) 'Introduction', in J. Eatwell and M. Milgate (eds) *Keynes's Economics and the Theory of Value and Distribution*, London: Duckworth.

Eatwell, John and Milgate, Murray (eds) (1983) *Keynes's Economics and the Theory of Value and Distribution*, London: Duckworth.

Economist, the (2000) 'Internet Economics. A thinker's guide', 1 April.

Economist, the (2000) 'Bulls, Bears and Greenspan', 5 August.

Economist, the (2000) Anti-Liberalism Old and New', 21 October.

Economist, the (2001) 'What a peculiar cycle', 10 March.

Economist, the (2001) 'Of pimps, punters and equities', 22 March.

Economist, the (2002) 'More Bubble and Squeak', 22 April.

Economist, the (2002) 'The Unfinished Recession. A Survey of the World Economy', 28 September.

Elam, Mark (1994) 'Puzzling Out the Post-Fordist Debate: Technology, Markets and Institutions', in A. Amin (ed.) *Post-Fordism. A reader*, Oxford: Oxford University Press.

Eustace, Clark G. (2000) 'The Intangible Economy Impact and Policy Issues', *Report of the European High Level Expert Group on the Intangible Economy*, Brussels: European Commission.

Financial Times (2002) 'New Economy: Dream or Reality', 18 May.

Fine, Ben (2003) 'New Growth Theory', in Ha-Joon Chang (ed.) *Rethinking Development Economics*, London: Anthem Press.

Fitoussi, Jean P. and Creel, Jerome (2002) *How to Reform the European Central Bank*, London: Centre for European Reform.

Foster, John (2004) 'Why is Economics Not a Complex Systems Science', *International J.A. Schumpeter Society Conference*, University of Bocconi, Milan, June 9–12.

Freeman, Chris (1988) 'Introduction', in G. Dosi, C. Freeman, R. Nelson, G. Silverberg and L. Soete (eds) *Technical Change and Economic Theory*, London: Pinter.

Freeman, Chris and Louça, Francisco (2001) *As Time Goes By: From the Industrial Revolutions to the Information Revolution*, Oxford: Oxford University Press.

Freeman, Chris and Perez, Carlota (1988) 'Structural Crises of Adjustment, Business Cycles and Investment Behaviour', in G. Dosi, C. Freeman, R. Nelson, G. Silverberg, and L. Soete (eds) *Technical Change and Economic Theory*, London: Pinter.

Friedman, Benjamin (2001) 'Comment to O. Blanchard, and J. Simon, "The Long and Large Decline in U.S. Output Volatility" ', *Brookings Papers on Economic Activity*, vol. I, 172–3.

Friedman, Milton (1953) *Essays in Positive Economics* Chicago, IL: University of Chicago Press.

Frisch, Ragnar (1933) 'Propagation and Impulse Problems in Dynamic Economics', *Essays in Honor of Gustav Cassel*, London: Allen and Unwin.

Fullbrook, Edward (2003) *The Crisis in Economics*, London: Routledge.

Galbraith, James K. (1997) *Created Unequal. The Crisis in American Pay*, New York: The Free Press.

Galbraith, James K. (2004) 'The American Economic Problem', *Post-Autistic Economics Review*, no. 25, 18 May, 25–28, http://www.btinternet.com/~pae_news/review/issue25.htm (5 June 2005).

Garegnani, Pierangelo (1983) 'Notes on Consumption, Investment and Effective Demand', in J. Eatwell and M. Milgate (eds) *Keynes's Economics and the Theory of Value and Distribution*, London: Duckworth.

Gerrard, Bill (2002) 'The Role of Econometrics in a Radical Methodology', in S.C. Dow and J. Hillard (eds) *Post-Keynesian Econometric, Microeconomics and the Theory of the Firm, Beyond Keynes*, vol. I, Cheltenham: E. Elgar.

Ghosh, Atish and Phillips, Stephen (1998) 'Warning: Inflation May be Harmful to Your Growth', *IMF Staff Papers*, vol. 45, no. 4, December.

Godley, Wymne and Izurieta, Alex (2002) 'The Case for a Severe Recession', *Challenge*, March–April, 27–51.

Goodwin, Richard (1951) 'The Non-Linear Accelerator and the Persistence of the Business Cycle', *Econometrica*, vol. 19, 1–17.

Goodwin, Richard (1990) *Chaotic Economic Dynamics*, Oxford: Oxford University Press.

Gordon, Robert J. (2000) 'Does the "New Economy" Measure up to the Great Inventions of the Past?', *Journal of Economic Perspectives*, vol. 14, no. 4, 49–74.

Gordon, Robert J. (2002) 'Technology and Economic Performance in the American Economy', *NBER Working Paper*, no. 8771, February.

Greenspan, Alan (1999) 'Testimony of Chairman Alan Greenspan Before the Committee on Banking and Financial Services', *U.S. House of Representatives*, July 22, http://www.federalreserve.gov/boarddocs/hh/1999/July/testimony.htm (accessed 27 March 2001).

Greenspan Alan (2001) 'Opening Remarks', Proceedings of a *Symposium on Economic Policy for the Information Economy*, sponsored by the Federal Reserve Bank of Kansas City, Jackson Hole, WY 30 August–1 September.

Griliches, Zvi (1994) 'Productivity, R&D and the Data Constraint', *American Economic Review*, vol. 84, 1–23.

Grossman, Gene M. and Helpman, Elhanan (1991) *Innovation and Growth in the Global Economy*, Cambridge, MA: The MIT Press.

Hahn, Frank (1982) *Money and Inflation*, Oxford: Blackwell.

Hall, Peter and Preston, Paschal (1988) *The Carrier Wave: New Information Technology and the Geography of Innovation 1846–2003*, London: Allen and Unwin.

Hall, Robert (2001) 'Comment to O. Blanchard, and J. Simon, "The Long and Large Decline in U.S. Output Volatility" ', *Brookings Papers on Economic Activity*, vol. I, 172–3.

Harcourt, Geoffrey C. (1981) 'Marshall, Sraffa, and Keynes: Incompatible Bedfellows?', in C. Sardoni (ed.) *On Political Economists and Modern Political Economy: Selected Essays of G.C. Harcourt*, London: Routledge.

Harcourt, Geoffrey C. and Riach, Paul A. (eds) (1997) *A 'Second Edition' of the General Theory*, 2 vols, London: Routledge.

Harrod, Roy (1937) 'Mr. Keynes and Traditional Theory', *Econometrica*, vol. 5, January, 74–86.

Harrod, Roy (1951) 'Notes on Trade Cycle Theory', *Economic Journal*, vol. 63, June, 61–75.

Hausman, Daniel M. (1992) *The Inexact and Separate Science of Economics*, Cambridge: Cambridge University Press.

Hausman, Daniel M. (2001) 'Tendencies, Laws and the Composition of Economic Causes', in U. Mäki (ed.) *The Economic World View. Studies in the Ontology of Economics*, Cambridge: Cambridge University Press.

Haynes, Michelle and Thompson, Stephen (2000) 'Productivity, Employment and the IT Paradox: Evidence from Financial Services', in R. Barrell, G. Mason and M. O'Mahony (eds) *Productivity, Innovation and Economic Performance*, Cambridge: Cambridge University Press.

Heipertz, Martin and Verdun, Amy (2004) 'The Dog that Would Never Bite? What We Can Learn from the Origins of the Stability and Growth Pact' in F. Torres, A. Verdun, C. Zilioli and H. Zimmermann (eds) *Governing EMU. Economic Political, Legal and Historical Perspectives*, Fiesole: European University Institute.

Hodgson, Geoffrey M. (1998) 'The Approach of Institutional Economics', *Journal of Economic Literature*, vol. 36, no. 1, 166–92.

Hodgson, Geoffrey M. (1999) *Evolution and Institutions: On Evolutionary Economics and the Evolution of Economics*, Cheltenham: E. Elgar.

Hodgson, Geoffrey M. (2001) *How Economics Forgot History. The Problem of Historical Specificity in Social Science*, London: Routledge.

Hodgson, Geoffrey M. (ed.) (2003) *Recent Developments in Institutional Economics*, Cheltenham: E. Elgar.

Hodgson, Geoffrey M. (2004a) 'Is it All in Keynes's General Theory?', *Post-Autistic Economics Review*, no. 25, 18 May, 21–24, http://www.btinternet.com/~pae_news/review/issue25.htm (accessed 14 April 2004).

Hodgson, Geoffrey M. (2004b) *The Evolution of Institutional Economics. Agency, Structure and Darwinism in American Institutionalism*, London: Routledge.

Holland, John H. (1995) *Hidden Order: How Adaptation Builds Complexity*, Reading, MA: Addison Wesley.

Hollingsworth, Rogers J. (2000) 'Doing Institutional Analysis Implications for the Study of Innovations', *Review of International Political Economy*, vol. 7, no. 4, Winter, 595–644.

Issing, O., Caspar, V., Angeloni I. and Tristani O. (2001) *Monetary Policy in the Euro-Area: Strategy and Decision-Making at the European Central Bank*, Cambridge: Cambridge University Press.

Jacobson, Jonathan (2001) 'Do We Need a "New Economy" Exception for Antitrust?', *Antitrust*, Fall.

James, Jeffrey (2001) 'Information Technology, Cumulative Causation and Patterns of Globalization in the Third World', *Review of International Political Economy*, vol. 8, no. 1, Spring, 147–62.

Jameson, Frank (1992) *Postmodernism, or The Cultural Logic of Late Capitalism*, London: Verso.

Jarsulic, Marc (1997) 'Keynesian Business Cycle Theory', in G.C. Harcourt and P.A. Riach (eds) *A 'Second Edition' of the General Theory*, London: Routledge, vol. I.

Jones, Derek C. (ed.) (2003) *New Economy Handbook*, Amsterdam: Academic Press.

Jorgenson, Dale W. and Stiroh, Kevin (2000) 'Raising the Speed Limit: U.S. Economic Growth in the Information Age', *Brookings Papers on Economic Activity*, vol. I, 125–235.

Kaldor, Nicholas (1940) 'A Model of the Trade Cycle', *Economic Journal*, vol. 50, 78–92.

Kaldor, Nicholas (1957) 'A Model of Economic Growth', *Economic Journal*, vol. 67, December, 591–624.

Kaldor, Nicholas (1961) 'Capital Accumulation and Economic Growth', in F.A. Lutz and D.C. Hague (eds) *The Theory of Capital*, London: Macmillan.

Kaldor, Nicholas (1981) 'The Role of Increasing Returns, Technical Progress and Cumulative Causation in the Theory of International Trade and Economic Growth', *Economie Appliquee*, vol. 34, 593–617.

Kaplinsky, Raphael (2001) 'Is Globalization All it is Cracked Up to Be?', *Review of International Political Economy*, vol. 8, no. 1, Spring, 45–65.

Katz, Lawrence and Krueger, Alan (1999) 'The High-Pressure U.S. Labor Market of the 1990s', *Princeton University Industrial Relations Working Paper*, no. 416.

Kelly, Kevin (1998) *New Rules for the New Economy: 10 Radical Strategies for a Connected World*, London: Penguin Books.

Keynes, John Maynard (1936) *The General Theory of Employment Interest and Money*, London: Macmillan.

Keynes, John Maynard (1937) 'The General Theory of Employment', *Quarterly Journal of Economics*, vol. 52, 209–23; reprinted in J.M. Keynes (1973) *The General Theory and After. Part II: Defence and Development* in the *Collected Writings of John Maynard Keynes*, vol. XIV, London: Macmillan.

Keynes, John Maynard (1973) *The General Theory and After. Part II: Defence and Development* in the *Collected Writings of John Maynard Keynes*, vol. XIV, London: Macmillan.

King, John E. (2002) *A History of Post Keynesian Economics Since 1936*, Cheltenham: E. Elgar.

King, John E. (2004) 'A Defence Of King's Argument(s) For Pluralism', *Post-Autistic Economics Review*, no. 25, 18 May, 16–20, http://www.btinternet.com/~pae_news/review/issue25.htm (accessed 14 April 2004).

Kitson, Michael and Michie, Jonathan (2000) *The Political Economy of Competitiveness*, London: Routledge.

Klamer, Arjo (1995), 'The Conception of Modernism in Economics: Samuelson, Keynes and Harrod', in S. Dow and J. Hillard (eds) *Keynes, Knowledge and Uncertainty*, Cheltenham: E. Elgar.

Klein, Joel (2000) 'Put trust in Antitrust', *Wired News*, May 16.

Kose, Ayhan, Prasad, Eswar S. and Terrones, Marco E. (2003) 'Financial Integration and Macroeconomic Volatility', *IMF Working Paper* WP/03/50.

Krugman, Paul (1997) 'Speed Trap. The fuzzy logic of the "New Economy" ', *Slate – The Dismal Science*, 18 December.

Krugman, Paul (2000) 'Can America Stay on Top?', *Journal of Economic Perspectives*, vol. 14, Winter, 169–75.

Krugman, Paul (2001) *Fuzzy Math*, Cambridge, MA: The MIT Press.

Kumar, Krishan (1995) *From Post-Industrial to Post-Modern Society. New Theories of the Contemporary World*, London: Routledge.

Kuttner, Kenneth N. and Mosser, Patricia C. (2002) 'The Monetary Transmission Mechanism: Some Answers and Further Questions', *Federal Reserve Bank of New York Economic Review*, vol. 8, no. 1, May, 15–26.

Kydland, Finn E. and Prescott, Edward C. (1982) 'Time to Build and Aggregate Fluctuations', *Econometrica*, vol. 50, November, 1345–69.

Langlois, Richard N. (2001) 'The Vanishing Hand: The Changing Dynamics of Capitalism', *The University of Connecticut, Canter for Institutions, Organizations and Markets*, September.

Lawson, Tony (1985) 'Uncertainty and Economic Analysis', *Economic Journal*, vol. 95, 909–27.

Lawson, Tony (1997) *Economics and Reality*, London: Routledge.

Lawson, Tony (1998) 'Tendencies', in J. Davis, W. Hands and U. Mäki (eds) *The Edward Elgar Companion to Economic Methodology*, Cheltenham: E. Elgar.

Lawson, Tony (2003) *Reorienting Economics*, London: Routledge.

Leijonhufvud, Axel (1997) 'Macroeconomics and Complexity', in B.W. Arthur, S.N. Durlauf and D. Lane (eds) *The Economy as an Evolving Complex System*, SFI studies in the sciences of Complexity, 2 vols, Reading, MA: Addison Wesley.

Levy, Robert A. (1998) 'Microsoft and the Browser Wars', *Policy Analysis*, no. 296, 19 February.

Liebowitz, S.J.H. and Margolis, S.E. (1999) *Winners, Losers, and Microsoft*, Oakland, CA: The Independent Institute.

Lipsey, Richard and Bekar, C. (1995) 'A Structuralist View of Economic Change', in T. Courchene (ed.) *Technology, Information and Public Policy*, Kingston, ON: John Deutsch Institute for Study of Economic Policy.

Louça, Francisco (1997) *Turbulence in Economics: An Evolutionary Appraisal of Cycles and Complexity in Historical Processes*, Cheltenham: E. Elgar.

Louça, Francisco (2003) 'The New Economy and Economic Cycles', in D.C. Jones (ed.) *New Economy Handbook*, Amsterdam: Elsevier.

Lucas, Robert E. (1981) *Studies in Business Cycle Theory*, Cambridge, MA: The MIT Press.

Lucas, Robert E. (1989) 'On the Mechanics of Economic Development', *NBER Reprints*, no. 1176.

Lucas, Robert E. (2002) *Lectures on Economic Growth*, Cambridge, MA: Harvard University Press.

Lyotard, Jean François (1984) *The Postmodern Condition: A Report on Knowledge*, Minneapolis, MN: University of Minnesota Press.

McCloskey, Deirdre (1986) *The Rhetoric of Economics*, Brighton: Wheatsheaf.

McConnell, Margareth M. and Perez-Quiros, Gabriel (2000) 'Output Fluctuations in the United States: What Has Changed Since the Early 1980's?', *American Economic Review*, vol. 90, no. 5, 1464–76.

Mäki, Uskali (1986) 'Rhetoric at the Expense of Coherence: A Reinterpretation of Milton Friedman's Methodology', *Research in the History of Economic Thought and Methodology*, vol. 4, 127–43.

Mäki, Uskali (1992) 'Friedman and realism', *Research in the History of Economic Thought and Methodology*, vol. 10, 1–36.

Mäki, Uskali (ed.) (2001) *The Economic World View. Studies in the Ontology of Economics*, Cambridge: Cambridge University Press.

Mandel, Michel (1996) 'The Triumph of the New Economy', *Business Week*, 30 December.

Mandel, Michel (1997) 'The New Business Cycle', *Business Week*, 31 March.

Mankiw, Gregory (2001) *Principles of Economics*, 2nd edn, New York: Harcourt College Publishers.

Mankiw, Gregory (2003) *Macroeconomics*, 5th edn, New York: Worth.

Marglin, Stephen A. and Schor, Juliet B. (1990) *The Golden Age of Capitalism*, Oxford: Oxford University Press.

Martin, William and Rowthorn, Robert (2004) 'Will Stability Last?', *CESifo Working Paper Series*, no. 1324, November, http://ssrn.com/abstract=622601

Minca, Claudio (ed) (2001) *Postmodern Geography. Theory and Praxis*, Oxford: Blackwell.

Minford, Patrick (1997) 'Macroeconomics: Before and After Rational Expectations', in B. Snowdon and H. Vane (eds) *Reflections on the Development of Modern Macroeconomics*, Cheltenham: E. Elgar.

Minsky, Hyman (1975) *John Maynard Keynes*, New York: Columbia University Press.

Minsky, Hyman (1982) *Can 'It' Happen Again? Essays on Instability and Finance*, Armonk, NY: M.E. Sharpe.

Mueller, Antony P. (2001) 'The New Economy. Bubble or New Era?', contribution to the *Third Conference of the Association of Historians of the Austrian Tradition in Economic Thought*, Pisa (Italy), 24–6 May.

Nell, Edward (2002) 'Notes on the Growth of Demand', in M. Setterfield (ed.) *Studies in Demand-Led Growth*, Cheltenham: E. Elgar.

Nelson, Richard R. (1993) *National Innovation Systems A Comparative Analysis*, Oxford: Oxford University Press.

Nelson, Richard R. and Sampat, Bhaven N. (2001) 'Making Sense of Institutions as a Factor Shaping Economic Performance', *Journal of Economic Behaviour and Organization*, vol. 44, no. 1, 31–54.

Nordhaus, William D. (2002) 'Productivity Growth and the New Economy', *Brookings Papers on Economic Activity*, vol. II, 211–65.

North, Douglass C. (1990) *Institutions, Institutional Change, and Economic Performance*, Cambridge: Cambridge University Press.

North, Douglass C. (1991) 'Institutions', *Journal of Economic Perspectives*, vol. 5, no. 1, Winter, 97–112.

O'Brien, Richard (1992) *Global Financial Integration. The End of Geography*, London: Pinter.

Obstfeld, Maurice and Taylor, Alan M. (1998) 'The Great Depression as a Watershed: International Capital Mobility in the Long-Run', in M.D. Bordo, C.D. Goldin and E.N. White (eds) *The Defining Moment: The Great Depression and the American Economy in the Twentieth Century*, Chicago, IL: Chicago University Press.

OECD (2001) 'Productivity Manual: A Guide to the Measurement of Industry Level and Aggregate Productivity Growth', Paris.

Oliner, Stephen D. and Sichel, Daniel E. (2000) 'The Resurgence of Growth in the Late 1990s: Is Information Technology the Story?', *Journal of Economic Perspectives*, vol. 14, no. 4, Fall, 3–22.

Pasinetti, Luigi (1981) *Structural Change and Economic Growth*, Cambridge: Cambridge University Press.

Perez, Carlota (1986) 'Structural Changes and Assimilation of New Technologies in the Economic and Social System', in C. Freeman (ed.) *Design, Innovation and Long Cycles in Economic Development*, New York: St. Martin's Press.

Perez, Carlota (2002) *Technological Revolutions and Financial Capital. The Dynamics of Bubbles and Golden Ages*, Cheltenham: E. Elgar.

Phelps, Edmund S. (1990) *Seven Schools of Macroeconomic Thought*, Oxford: Oxford University Press.

Popper, Karl R. (1979) *Objective Knowledge*, 2nd edn, Oxford: Clarendon.

Prasch, Robert E. (2000a) 'Complexity and Economic Method', in D. Colander (ed.) *Complexity and the History of Economic Thought*, London: Routledge.

Prasch, Robert E. (2000b) 'Integrating Complexity into the Principles of Macroeconomics', in D. Colander (ed.) *The Complexity Vision and the Teaching of Economics*, Cheltenham: E. Elgar.

Preston, Paschal (2001) *Reshaping Communications*, London: Sage.

Prigogine, Ilya and Nicolis, Gregoire (1989) *Exploring Complexity*, New York: Freeman.

Pryor, Frederic L. (2000) 'Looking Backwards: Complexity Theory in 2028', in D. Colander (ed.) *The Complexity Vision and the Teaching of Economics*, Cheltenham: E. Elgar.

Quah, Danny T. (1999) 'The Weightless Economy in Growth', *The Business Economist*, vol. 30, no. 1, March, 40–53.

Reati, Angelo (2001) 'Discussion of Bassanini et al. Knowledge, Technology and Economic Growth: Recent Evidence from OECD Countries', in J. Smets and M. Dombrecht (eds) *How to Promote Growth in the Euro Area*, Cheltenham: E. Elgar.

Rennstich, J.K. (2002) 'The New Economy, The Leadership Long Cycle and The Nineteenth K-Wave', *Review of International Political Economy*, vol. 9, no. 1, March, 150–82.

Rifkin, Jeremy (2000) *The Age of Access: The New Culture of Hupercapitalism Where all life is a Paid-For Experience*, New York: Putnam.

Roach, Stephen (2003) 'America e i danni collaterali dell'export di occupazione' *Repubblica*, 22 September.

Robinson, Joan (1956) *The Accumulation of Capital*, London: Macmillan.

Rodriguez, M. João (ed.) *The New Knowledge Economy in Europe. A Strategy for International Competitiveness and Social Cohesion*, Cheltenham: E. Elgar.

Romer, Christina D. (1999) 'Changes in Business Cycles: Evidence and Explanations', *Journal of Economic Perspectives*, vol. 13, no. 2, Spring, 23–44.

Romer, Paul M. (1986) 'Increasing Returns and Long-Run Growth', *Journal of Political Economy*, vol. 94, no. 5, 1002–37.

Romer, Paul M. (1990) 'Endogenous Technical Change', *Journal of Political Economy*, vol. 98, no. 5, 71–102.

Rosenof, Theodore (1997) *Economics in the Long Run: New Deal Theorists and Their Legacies, 1933–1993*, Chapel Hill, NC: University of North Carolina Press.

Rostow, Walter W. (1990) *Theories of Economic Growth from David Hume to the Present, with a Perspective on the Next Century*, Oxford: Oxford University Press.

Rutherford, Malcolm (2001) 'Institutional Economics: Then and Now', *Journal of Economic Perspectives*, vol. 15, no. 3, Summer, 173–94.

Ruttan, Vernon W. (2001) *Technology, Growth, and Development. An Induced Innovation Perspective*, Oxford: Oxford University Press.

Samuelson, Paul A. (1939) 'Interaction Between the Multiplier Analysis and the Principle of Acceleration', *Review of Economics and Statistics*, vol. 21, no. 2, 75–8.

Sardoni, Claudio (ed.) (1992) *On Political Economists and Modern Political Economy: Selected Essays of G.C. Harcourt*, London: Routledge.

Schotter, Andrew (1981) *Economic Theory of Social Institutions*, Cambridge: Cambridge University Press.

Schumpeter, Joseph (1939) *Business Cycles: A Theoretical, Historical and Statistical Analysis of the Capitalist Process*, New York: McGraw Hill.

Schumpeter, Joseph (1954) *History of Economic Analysis*, Oxford: Oxford University Press.

Sent, Esther-Mirjam (1998) *The Evolving Rationality of Rational Expectations: An Assessment of Thomas Sargent's Achievements*, Cambridge: Cambridge University Press.

Setterfield, Mark (2002) 'Introduction', in M. Setterfield (ed.) *Studies in Demand-Led Growth*, Cheltenham: E. Elgar.

Setterfield, Mark (ed.) (2002) *Studies in Demand-Led Growth*, Cheltenham: E. Elgar.

Shackle, George L.S. (1967) *The Years of High Theory*, Cambridge: Cambridge University Press.

Shapiro, Carl and Varian, Hal (1998) *Information Rules. A Strategic Guide to the Network Economy*, Harvard: Harvard Business School Press.

Shiller, Robert J. (2000) *Irrational Exuberance*, Princeton, NJ: Princeton University Press.

Shiller, Robert J. (2004) *The New Financial Order: Risk in the 21st Century*, Princeton, NJ: Princeton University Press.

Simonazzi, A. (2003) 'Innovation and Growth: Supply and Demand Factors in the Recent US Expansion', *Cambridge Journal of Economics*, vol. 27, 647–69.

Smets, Jan and Dombrecht Michel (eds) (2001) *How to Promote Growth in the Euro Area*, Cheltenham: E. Elgar.

Soete, Luc (2002) 'The Challenger and the Potential of the Knowledge-Based Economy in a Globalised World', in M.J. Rodriguez (ed.) *The New Knowledge Economy in Europe. A Strategy for International Competitiveness and Social Cohesion*, Cheltenham: E. Elgar.

Solow, Robert M. (1956) 'A Contribution to the Theory of Economic Growth', *Quarterly Journal of Economics*, vol. 70, 65–94.

Solow, Robert M. (1997) 'Is There a Core of Usable Macroeconomics We Should All Believe In?', *American Economic Review, American Economic Association*, vol. 87, no. 2, 230–2.

Sonneschein, Hugo (1972) 'Market Excess Demand Functions', *Econometrica*, vol. 40, 549–63.

Stiglitz, Joseph (1987) 'The Causes and the Consequences of the Dependence of Quality on Price', *Journal of Economic Literature*, vol. 25, 1–48.

Stiglitz, Joseph (2002a) *Globalization and Its Discontents*, London: Penguin Books.

Stiglitz, Joseph (2002b) 'The Roaring Nineties', *The Atlantic Monthly*, October 2002, 1–14.

Stiglitz, Joseph (2003) *The Roaring Nineties: Seeds of Destruction*, London: Penguin Books.

Stiroh, Kevin J. (2000) 'What Drives Productivity Growth?', *Federal Reserve Bank of New York Economic Policy Review*, vol. 6, March, 37–59.

Stiroh, Kevin J. (2003) 'Growth and Innovation in the New Economy', in D.C. Jones (ed.) *New Economy Handbook*, Amsterdam: Academic Press.

Stock, James H. and Watson, Mark W. (2003) 'Has the Business Cycle Changed?', Proceedings of a *Symposium on Monetary Policy and Uncertainty: Adapting to a Changing Economy*, sponsored by the Federal Reserve Bank of Kansas City, Jackson Hole, WY, 28–30 August.

Storper, Michael (2000) 'Globalization and Knowledge Flows: An Industrial Geographer's Perspective', in J.H. Dunning (ed.) *Regions, Globalization, and the Knowledge-Based Economy*, Oxford: Oxford University Press.

Talalay, Michael, Farrands, Chris and Tooze, Roger (1997) 'Technology, Culture and Competitiveness. Change and the World Political Economy', in M. Talalay, C. Farrands, Chris and R. Tooze (eds) *Technology, Culture and Competitiveness. Change and the World Political Economy*, London: Routledge.

Talani, Simona (2004) 'Governing EMU: The European Central Bank between Growth and Stability', in F. Torres, A. Verdun, C. Zilioli and H. Zimmermann (eds) *Governing EMU. Economic, Political, Legal and Historical Perspectives*, Fiesole: European University Institute.

Tamborini, Roberto (2004) 'The "Brussels Consensus" on Macroeconomic Stabilization Policies: A Critical Assessment', in F. Torres, A. Verdun, C. Zilioli and H. Zimmermann (eds) *Governing EMU. Economic, Political, Legal and Historical Perspectives*, Fiesole: European University Institute.

Teece, Daniel J. and Coleman, Mary (1998) 'The Meaning of Monopoly: Antitrust Analysis in High Technology Industries', *Antitrust Bulletin*, vol. 43 (3–4), September, 801–57.

Thirlwall, Anthony P. (2002) *Nature of Economic Growth: An Alternative Framework for Understanding the Performance of Nations*, Cheltenham: E. Elgar.

Togati, Teodoro Dario (1998) *Keynes and the Neoclassical Synthesis. Einsteinian Versus Newtonian Macroeconomics*, London: Routledge.

Togati, Teodoro Dario (2001) 'Keynes as the Einstein of Economic Theory', *History of Political Economy*, vol. 33, no. 1, Spring, 117–138.

Togati, Teodoro Dario (2004) 'The New Economy and Economic Policy in the Euro-zone', in F. Torres, A. Verdun, C. Zilioli and H. Zimmermann (eds) *Governing EMU. Economic, Political, Legal and Historical Perspectives*, Fiesole: European University Institute.

Toporowski, Ian (2000) *The End of Finance*, London: Routledge.

Torres, Francisco Verdun, Amy, Zilioli, Chiara and Zimmermann, Hubert (eds) (2004) *Governing EMU. Economic, Political, Legal and Historical Perspectives*, Fiesole: European University Institute.

Turner, Alan (2001) *Just Capital. The Liberal Economy*. London: Macmillan.

Tvede, Lars (2001) *Business Cycles. From John Law to the Internet Crash*, London: Routledge.

Varian, Hal (1997) 'Versioning Information Goods', http//www.sims.berkely.edu (21 March 2001).

Varian, Hal (1998) 'Markets for Information Goods', http//www.sims.berkely.edu (21 March 2001).

Vercelli, Alessandro (1991) *Methodological Foundations of Macroeconomics: Keynes & Lucas*, Cambridge: Cambridge University Press.

Vercelli, Alessandro (1997) 'Keynes, Schumpeter and Beyond: A Non-Reductionist Perspective', in G.C. Harcourt and P.A. Riach (eds) *A 'Second Edition' of the General Theory*, London: Routledge, vol. II.

Verspagen, Bart (2000) 'Economic Growth and Technological Change: An Evolutionary Interpretation', *ECIS Working Papers*, no. 00.12, Eindhoven Centre for Innovation Studies, Eindhoven University of Technology.

Verspagen, Bart (2002) 'Structural Change and Technology. A Long View', *ECIS Working Papers*, no. 02.13, Eindhoven Centre for Innovation Studies, Eindhoven University of Technology.

Viskovatoff, Alex (2000) 'Will Complexity Turn Economics into Sociology?' in D. Colander (ed.) *Complexity and the History of Economic Thought*, London: Routledge.

Weber, Stephen (1997) 'The End of the Business Cycle?', *Foreign Affairs*, vol. 76, no. 4, 65–82.

Western, David (2004) *Booms, Bubbles and Bust in the US Stock Market*, London: Routledge.

Wible, James (2000) 'What is Complexity?', in D. Colander (ed.) *Complexity and the History of Economic Thought*, London: Routledge.

Williamson, Oliver (1985) *The Economic Institutions of Capitalism: Firms, Markets, Relational Contracting*, New York: The Free Press.

Winkler, Bernhard (2004) 'Stability and Growth: The Role of Monetary Policy and the Policy Actors in EMU', in F. Torres, A. Verdun, C. Zilioli and H. Zimmermann (eds) *Governing EMU. Economic, Political, Legal and Historical Perspectives*, Fiesole: European University Institute.

Winnett, Adrian (2004) 'Growth and Productivity in the New Economy', in *NESIS: Final Report. Conceptualisation and Analysis of the New Economy*, University of Bath.

Woodford, Michael (2001) 'Monetary Policy in the Information Economy' Proceedings of a *Symposium on Economic Policy for the Information Economy*, sponsored by the Federal Reserve Bank of Kansas City, Jackson Hole, WY, 30 August–1 September.

Zarnowitz, Victor (1999) 'Theory and History Behind Business Cycles: Are the 1990s the Onset of a Golden Age?', *Journal of Economic Perspectives*, vol. 13, no. 2, Spring, 69–90.

Index

agents: interaction 63; perception of
  'time' 129
Aghion, P. 30, 59, 269
Alexander, J. 50
Amariglio, J. 52, 270, 273
America: Institutionalist economics 77;
  model based on deregulation and free
  markets 137; stock market bubble 179
anti-deterministic view 64
antitrust policies 174
Archibugi, F. 1
Arena, R. 144, 150, 276
Arestis, P. 183, 250, 252, 281, 283–4
Argentina, recent crisis in 177
Argyrous, G. 114
Aristotelian views 84
Arrow, K. 269
Arrow–Debreu model 21
Arthur, B.W. 9, 18, 59, 67–8, 70; model of
  belief formation in stock market 88
artificial intelligence, models of 63
Asia, liberalization of capital markets
  in 182
Asimakopulos, A. 23–5, 31, 109, 111–13,
  215–16, 219, 221, 268
Atkinson, R.D. 142, 144
attractors 28, 35, 206, 269; see also
  equilibrium
Audretsch, D.B. 131–2, 134, 139, 141,
  154, 165–6, 174, 176, 276, 278
Auerbach, A.J. 3
Austrian school 60

Backhouse, R.E. 75, 159–62, 203, 270–1,
  275, 280–1
Baily, M.N. 2–3, 31, 122, 127, 129, 138,
  141, 145, 151–4, 156, 159, 161–2, 164,
  168, 171, 174–5, 232, 235, 267,
  279–80, 283

Baker, D. 3, 167, 169–70, 180–1,
  208, 281–2
Banerji, A. 3, 138, 152, 161, 170, 179,
  267, 279
bank debt to marketable debt, shift from
  152
bankruptcy 209
Barro, R. 196, 200, 208
barter 90
Barthes, R. 53
Basu, S. 275
Baudrillard, J. 270
Bauman, Z. 52
Baumol, W. 59
Beck, U. 267
Becker, G. 16; 'imperialist' approach 29
Benthamite calculations 100
Bernanke, B.S. 3, 170
Bibow, J. 248
Blanchard, O. 3, 54, 121, 128, 133, 141,
  143, 145–6, 149, 152, 160, 170–1, 173,
  189, 192, 206, 222, 234, 250, 252–3,
  257, 271, 275, 279, 281, 283–4;
  macroeconomics 19
Blaug, M. 160, 162
Blinder, A.S. 133, 140–2, 276–8
Boggio, L. 33
Boland, L. 98
Borio, C. 151, 280
Bortis, H. 25
Boyer, R. 2, 41, 45; and Regulation
  school 37
Boylan, T.A. 50–1, 79–80, 84, 86, 273
Brecht, B. 50
Bresnahan, T. 31
Bretton Woods system 137, 167, 219; of
  fixed exchange rates 166
Brock, W.B. 67, 69, 249, 271–2
Brussels School approach 271

Brynjolfsson, E. 143–4, 153, 162, 278
business cycle 2, 28, 128; in four decades after Second World War 177; monocausal theories of 121
butterfly effect 27

Calvino, I. 10, 120, 126; labels 9–10, 117, 121, 127, 223, 259, 263, 267
Cambridge: Keynesians 26; UK, flexible saving-ratio model 25; US, variable capital-ratio model 25
capital: market liberalization 209; in public investment in R&D 200
capitalism: history, five paradigms 38; market economies, rich 136; past stages of 119
Caserta, M. 89
Castells, M. 120, 143
catastrophic outcomes 109
causality: issue and role of ICT 122; 'map' of all mechanisms 80; variables 95
Cecchetti, S.G. 152
central banks 167; behaviour of independent 166; power 168
Chick, V. 15, 31, 50, 78, 89, 106, 215–16, 243
Clarida, R. 3, 170
'Classics', key differences from Keynes 94, 102, 104
Clinton administration 180; boom on supply side 181; deficit cut 171; increase in taxes 181
Cohen, S.S. 2, 120, 124, 132, 136, 141–2, 152–3, 162, 175–6, 181, 255, 267, 276–9, 282
Colander, D. 9, 58–64, 67, 69, 88 249, 271; law of complex systems 272
Coleman, M. 144
collective bargaining 266
Comim, F. 9, 59, 63, 68, 88, 272
communications networks 142
Comor, E. 133, 276
competition/competitive: intensity due to globalization 133, 145; and inter-firm coordination 175
complex adaptive systems 63
complex dynamic systems 60
complexity theory 9, 50, 58, 77; current 59; elements of 'realism' 63–4; general equilibrium model 61; inductive approach 67–70; institutions as generating functions of complex patterns 76–8; key steps in

simplification strategy 79; stability 68; vision of economy in 58–60
complementarity view 64–7
computerization of economy 38
Comte, A. 50
constant elasticity of substitution (CES) production function 62
Cooper, R. 242
'coordination', concept of 35
Cornwall, J. 220
corporate governance, patterns of 136
corporate investment, underestimated in 1990s 202
corporate prosperity, adoption of alternative criteria for assessing future 156
Court, R.H. 142, 144
Crafts, N. 59
creation of value 150
creative destruction 132, 146, 199
credit contracts 154
Crocket, A.D. 156, 280
cross-cultural comparison between Japan and US 277
cross-national production system 132
crowd-in effects, weak 179–80
Cubist revolution 50
Cullemberg, S. 51–4, 120, 133, 150, 270–1, 273
cultural institutions of third sector 282
cycles 110; instability 132, 149

data collection 158
David, P. 31
Davidson, P. 17, 90–1, 93, 137, 182, 196, 229, 268, 273, 284
D'Avolio, G. 152, 155–6, 173, 217
DeLong, J.B. 2–3, 6, 20, 124–6, 131, 141–3, 148–50, 153, 163, 165, 170, 173–7, 222, 267, 279, 282; and Summers, insights on NE 125
DeMartino, G.F. 131–2, 135, 137, 139, 273, 276
Denzau, A.T. 100, 102–3, 105–6
deregulation 141; and financial innovation 154, 201
Derrida, J. 270
Descartes, R. 50
determinism 52
Dornbusch, R. 267
Dosi, G. 35
Dow, S. 15, 17, 22, 50–6, 75, 78, 128–9, 158–60, 190, 240, 268, 270–5, 280, 284

duality 52, 110
Dunford, M. 135
Dunning, J.H. 27, 131–3, 136, 144, 146, 148, 276, 279
dynamics: general economic theory of 70; versus structural simplification 61–2

Eatwell, J. 25
ecological approach 271
economic/s: advanced mathematical tools 159; as cumulative and linear processes 16; dynamic behaviour of systems 258; factors, interrelations among 121–3; fluctuations 190–2; natural science, analogies 59; in NE 162; scientific nature of 71; theory, crisis in 6, 49
The Economic Consequences of the Peace 276
E-conomy 120
economy, 'normal' working of 188–90, 214
E-culture 120
effective demand, principle of 260, 264
Eichengreen, B. 3
Elam, M. 41
elasticity of employment, higher 145
electrification 38
e-money 168
Enlightenment and its positivistic methodology 50
E-polity 120
equilibrium: concept of 16; level of income 214; without structural change 15
E-society 120
essentialism 53, 105
Europe 122: definition of macroeconomic stability 249; increased need for skilled labour 145; stability pact 172, 183; and US, rapidity and effectiveness of decision-making 173
European Central Bank (ECB) 169, 207; strategy of 178, 281, 283
European Monetary Union policy rules, inflation 250
Eustace, C.G. 149–50
evolutionary paradigm 35; and complexity theory in economics 48
exchange rates, fixed 266
expenditure cuts, instability due to 180

Federal Reserve System 169, 170, 173, 179, 208, 281
Feldstein, M. 208

Feustré, A. 144, 150, 276
feudalism 90
financial assets 148
financial investment decisions, private, 134
financial markets: channel for transmitting shocks across borders 136; development of 141; erratic behaviour of 155, 202; experiment 67; faster development in NE 151, 201
Fine, B. 7, 16, 29–30, 33, 197, 268
First World War, global integration before 131
fiscal incentives to saving 265
fiscal policy: as anti-cyclical instrument in NE 171; and exchange rate policy 168; ineffectiveness, reasons for 170; pragmatic 171–3; rules in NE 170–1, 179; and structural policy in NCM 208–9; tight 252
Fischer, S. 121, 271, 275
Fisher, I. 18, 54, 159, 216
flexibility and inclusion 175
Fordism 42
forecasting: attempt to improve 160–1; problems 163
formalism 51–2; values in economics, role of 159–60
formalization 158; as standard of presentation of all types of economic analysis 159
Foster, J. 88
fragmentation of structural conditions 134–5
France 136
Freeman, C. 1, 3, 7, 15–16, 28, 35–40, 43–5, 50, 145, 235, 275, 277, 284
free-market: orientation of NCM 209; policies 173
Freud, S. 50
Friedman, B. 152, 168, 177, 273, 280–1; on gap of theory and real phenomena 85–7; k-percent regime 207; monetarism 86; predictive success of economic theory 86; quantity theory of money, version of 17, 128
Frisch, R. 16; 'stick and rocking horse' metaphor 19
Fulbrook, E. 49
full employment as condition for flexibility 181

Galbraith, J.K. 77, 180–1
Garegnani, P. 25
GDP: growth 169; volatility 128

general equilibrium: analysis 60; 'deep' parameters of 192; economics, tradition of 15; influence of post-modernism 54
General Purpose Technologies (GPTs) 30
General Theory 23, 89, 91, 99, 212; basic interdependence between economic agents 101; causal variables in 95; criticisms of 107; generality of 90; insights on dynamic analysis 109; neglect of technology 43; scope of 93; *see also* Keynes
Germany 136
Gerrard, B. 273
Gerschenkron, A. 277
Ghosh, A. 284
Gilder's law 129
global inefficiencies 156
global inequality in income and wealth distribution, greater 139
globalization 15, 45, 119–20, 128; in age of ICT 131–2, 134, 138–9, 195; era of full deregulation and 176; negative externality effects 133–4
global stability 72–3
global uncertainty 147
'global' versus 'local' imperfections 216–19
Godley, W. 21, 138, 154, 172, 240, 267, 280
'Golden Age' in period from 1945 to 1973 220
Gold Standard 151, 166; demise of 148
Goodwin, R. 24, 26–7, 59; *see also* Kaldor–Goodwin model
Gordon, R.J. 2–3, 37, 120–1, 124, 128, 141–2, 144, 151, 153, 159, 267, 282
governance of world economy 229; problems 137–8, 197
grand theory 70
Great Depression 250, 277
Greenspan, A. 128, 143, 152, 168, 170, 179, 275, 278
Grossman, G.M. 30
growth accounting exercises, performance of 121, 123
growth models, limitations of 31
growth theory: endogenous 196; mainstream 32; *see also* New Growth Theory; Old Growth Theory

Hahn, F. 21, 85, 205; alternative general equilibrium model 54; view, limitations to 22
Hall, R. 151, 156, 202, 281

Hansen, A.H. 8, 24
Harcourt, G.C. 26
Harrod, R. 8, 24, 32, 220, 268; and Keynesian growth theory 23, 25; model 25, 268; and non-linear dynamics 31
Hausman, D.M. 86, 272
Hayek, F.A. 59, 64; notion of spontaneous order 271
hedonic price indexes 159
Heipertz, M. 252
Helpman, E. 30
Hempel, C. 50
herd behaviour 224
Hicks' *Value and Capital* 83
Hitt, L.M. 143–4, 162, 278
Hodgson, G.M. 50, 58, 76–7, 84–5, 90, 92–3, 96, 98, 104, 106–8, 271–3; definition of 'general theory' 91
Holland, J.H. 272
Hollingsworth, R.J. 76, 273–4
household, greater heterogeneity in structural conditions 147
Howitt, P. 30, 59, 269
human capital 197; formation of 266; greater investment in 144
Hume, D. 50
Huyssen, A. 52

Ibsen, E. 50
ICT (Information, Communication and Technology) 2; capital stock 143; deregulation and 154, 198; diffusion of 226; dynamic equilibrium 23; factors of 125; globalization 135; instability 40–1; key factor in creation of global society 131; plurality of models 136–7; problems 135, 205; products, rapidly falling prices of 143; in reasoned history approach 40; revolution 124; scope for data collection and analysis 159; sources of revolution and US advantage 282; stability, greater flexibility of goods market 143–4; synchronization or coordination between firms 144; time and space-shrinking technology 144; wage differential between skilled and less skilled workers 147; weaker notions of dynamic equilibrium 13
ideas as 'information goods' 153
IMF 182
income distribution 175, 191, 201; alternative models of 25–6; effects, adverse 181, 210, 221, 253, 256;

Pareto's Law of 272; unequal 139, 233, 236

individuals: and countries, growing interdependence between 227; in NE, growing interdependence of 196

industrial policies protecting national industries 176

inflation targeting 167; failure 178–9; in NE 168

inflation targeting rule (ITR) 206–7, 209, 251

Information, Communication and Technology *see* ICT

information technology *see* ICT

instability: cyclical 132, 149; endogenous since Second World War 251; expenditure cuts and 180; ICT 40–1; source of 'subjective' qualitative change and 119; structural 69; tax cuts and 181

institutions: differences among countries 123; exogenous data 105–6; granting stability, positive role of 77; historically contingent 106; historically specific 105; reciprocal influence between economy and 124; role of 39

intangibles/goods 148; building 181; importance of 239

intellectual property rights 124

interest rates, raising 170

international competition 195

international institutions 182

Internet 1, 120, 141; potential of 158

investment: 'boom and bust' model 235; in physical and human capital and R&D 265

IS-LM 78

Izurieta, A. 21, 138, 154, 172, 240, 267, 280

Jacobson, J. 174

James, J. 138

Jameson, F. 53, 120, 136, 270–1

Japan 122, 136; liquidity trap 180; recent crisis in 177; reform, stability pact 183

Jarsulic, M. 23, 25–7, 29, 215–16, 219–20, 229, 268

jobless recovery 138

Jorgenson, D.W. 142

Kaldor, N. 24, 26–7, 32, 59, 230, 277; technical progress function 269

Kaldor–Goodwin model 27

Kalecki, M. 24, 268

Kaplinsky, R. 131, 139, 196

Katz, L. 145, 233

Kelly, K. 2, 49, 193

Keynes, J.M. 28, 31, 50, 59, 64, 100, 217, 268, 276; account of expectations 99; alternative to psychologism and institutional determinism 104; beyond 113–15; broader notion of essence 100–3; Classics', key differences 94, 102, 104; complexity theory 88–90; critique of accelerator hypothesis 31; critique of econometrics 43; effect 190, 199; essentialist conception 102; 'inversion' 105–6; macroeconomics 54, 106; stability 108–9; theory, Davidson's view 91; *see also General Theory*

Keynes analysis: aggregate function 92, 96, 98, 101; of business cycles 23, 215–16, 219–20; capitalist dynamics 111, 260; context of 'light theory' 93; dynamic, limitations of 215; equilibrium 212–13; expectations 98; fluctuations 216–17; informal dynamic method 109–12; limitations 7–8, 113; long-run trends 220–1; stability of NE, policy implications 263–6; static equilibrium 24; theory for US in 1930s 93; versus standard dynamic approaches 108

Keynesianism/Keynesian 90; demand policies of 1960s 165; 'disequilibrium' counterparts 204; dynamic stability 261; globalization 226, 229; institutionalists 60; interpretation of NE 221–4; macroeconomics 55, 213; macro model 79, 81, 214; monetary and fiscal policy 167; principles 208; scenario, generality of 259–61

Keynesian model 236, 252; conventional methods and indicators 245; erratic behaviour of financial markets 240–3; fiscal policy 252–4; intrinsic limits of pragmatism 248; liberalization and deregulation of capital markets 256; management by numbers 244–5; nature of contemporary knowledge 234–6; new discretionary policy stance 249–50; non-linear macroeconomic models 29; predictive failures 246–7; specific features of NE 224–5; structural policies and rules for markets 255–7; technological change and labour market flexibility 231–2; widening gap between theoretical and empirical progress 246

Keynesians, New 201, 217, 222, 225, 283

Keynesians, Old 222

Keynesian theory 6; generality of 11; lightness 237; multiplicity 226; New Economy 212; precision 244; rapidity 230; visibility 248

Keynes model 88; deregulation and financial innovation 239–40; distinction between primary and secondary variables 93–5; growth as condition for stability 248; heuristic 283; macro and institutions of modern economy 106–8; monetary policy 250–2; quality issue 237–9; wage flexibility, dynamic versus static analysis 232–4

King, M. 24–6, 90, 168, 268, 271, 273

Kitson, M. 135–6

Klamer, A. 51, 270

Klein, J. 174

knowledge 197; capital 154; commodity in NE 150; contemporary problems due to nature of 146; non-price mechanisms through diffusion of 228

Kondratieff, N. 36–7; cycles 36, 39, 41, 71; tradition, theoretical requirement of universality in 37

Kose, A. 2

Krueger, P. 145, 233

Krugman, P. 3, 59, 141–2, 161, 171, 180–1, 278, 282

Kumar, K. 50, 52, 54, 120, 136, 143, 270, 280

Kuttner, K.N. 281

Kuznets, S. 36

Kydland, F.E. 192

labour: market flexibility 211, 232; new division of 132; relations 136; skills 154

laissez faire 69

Langlois, R.N. 143

Latin America, liberalization of capital markets in 182

Lawson, T. 15, 17, 49, 58, 80, 85–6, 97–8, 102, 128, 159, 271, 273–4, 280

Leibowitz, S. J. 187, 267

Leijonhufvud, A. 89; paper on relation between macroeconomics and complexity 71

Levy, R.A. 174

liberalism 53

liberalization: of capital markets 182; of international trade and investment 226

lightness 117, 120, 148; in age of ICT 149; in complexity theory 61; in NCM 200–2; negative factors of 201; potentially negative effects of 152

light theory 57–8, 60–1

Lipsey, R. 31

Louçã, F. 1, 3, 15–16, 28, 35–7, 40–5, 50, 71, 192, 216, 281

Lowe, P. 151, 280

Lucas, R.E. 21, 83, 94, 127, 188, 196, 200, 203–4, 206, 213, 268, 275; critique 203; definition of business cycle 126, 128, 191; equilibrium method 188, 274

Luhmann, N. 72; system theory 271

Lyotard, J.F. 52–3, 270

Maastricht Treaty 171

McCloskey, D. 50–1, 55, 271, 273

McConnell, M.M. 2, 149

McGrew, D. 275

macroecology approach 271

macroeconomics: aggregates, critique of 38; data 5; instability *see* instability; paradigms, two basic 81; problems beyond inflation 179; stability *see* stability; theories and features of NE 263–4

macro models: basic, primary and secondary variables in 95–6; and interpretations of complex patterns 78–9

Madden, G. 242

Maddison, A. 37, 45

Maki, U. 86

Mandel, M. 151, 267

Mankiw, G. 189, 196–7, 222

marginal efficiency of capital (MEC) 216

Marglin, S.A. 219

Margolis, S.E. 187, 267

markets: concentration 199; for cultural artefacts, growth of 150; expectations, role of benchmark for 161; forms and macroeconomic outcomes 236; limits of setting rules for 181–2; rule for NE 173–5; spillovers 217; unification 132–3

Marshall, A. 29, 59, 274; distinction between short-run and long-run equilibrium 97

Martin, W. 3, 170

Marx, K. 87; theories of 36

Marxism 53, 70

mass commodification 120

mass production 42

measurement 158; problems 161–2
Menger, C. 84, 273; method of
   isolation 85
mental models 102–3; shared 105
meta-interpretation of NE 80
Metcalfe's law 129
methodological individualism 76, 106, 263
Michie, J. 135–6
Microsoft case 174
Milgate, M. 25
Military and Civilian research,
   government funded 282
military expenditure 172
Mill, J.S. 16, 80, 84, 273; 'empirical laws'
   definition 272
Minca, C. 271
Minford, P. 187
Minsky, H. 13, 26, 216, 239–40; changes
   in agents' confidence 284
Mitchell, W. 6, 10, 77
modelling problems 162
modern capitalism 93, 148; 'fundamental'
   institutions of 124
Modern Economy (ME) of 1930s
   considered by Keynes 232
modernism 50–2; commandments of 51;
   'official', and post-modernism,
   divergence 47, 52
modern micro-foundations literature 236
Modigliani, F. 94
Mokyr, J. 270
monetary policy: lack of general model to
   guide 178; in NCM 206–8; pragmatic
   169–70; rules 166–9
monetary targeting 166–7
monopolies 174–5; in high-tech
   industries 199
Moore's law 5, 129, 141, 153
moral hazard 179, 209
morphogenesis 40
Mosser, P.C. 281
motorization 38
Mueller, A.P. 142
multiple equilibria, notion of 69
multiplicity 117, 120, 131; in NCM 195
mutual influences between institutions/
   culture and economic factors 119
Myrdal, G. 277

NAIRU (Non Accelerating Inflation Rate of
   Unemployment) 145, 169, 208, 252, 281
national economies: foundations of
   distinctive growth 136; reduced
   autonomy of 135

National System of Innovation 39
NCM (new classical macroeconomics)
   54, 128; business cycles 224;
   explanatory power, general limits
   of 193; fluctuations 223; greater
   deregulation and flexibility 265;
   information, faster transmission of 198;
   instability problems 209–11;
   institutional detail, neglect of 197;
   literature 208; mathematization of
   economics 203; models 55; and NE
   187, 195; 'positive' policy moves 265;
   technological change, effects of 198,
   230; *see also* NE
NE (New Economy) 1–4, 56, 129,
   212–13; acceleration of key trends
   128–30; acceleration of positive
   feedbacks 142–3; alternative
   scenarios of 185; commodification
   149; complex phenomenon 258;
   'deep' parameters 188; definition
   117, 119; dynamic stability of 261;
   economic and socio-institutional
   spheres 123–6; five empirical laws
   of 130; flexibility in labour market
   144–5; general view in NCM 192–4;
   impact on standard methodology and
   policy-making 129; information
   technology effects 49; interdisciplinary
   perspective 120; key factors 120–1;
   Keynesian model and specific
   features in 224–5; 'lightness'
   concept 128; macroeconomic theories
   185; measurement, modelling and
   forecasting techniques 161;
   micro–macro features 126–8;
   network effects in 143; stability of,
   Keynesian approach and policy
   implications 263–6; standard laws
   of exchange rates 284; structural
   trends or empirical laws of 114;
   US and 136; visibility 166;
   see also NCM
Nell, E. 13, 114, 243
Nelson, R.R. 39, 59, 77
neoclassical theory 13, 16–17; analysis,
   causal variables 95, 97; and Keynesian
   concepts of equilibrium 112;
   limitations of 6; macro model 83–4,
   190; macro paradigms 79; mechanisms
   of self-interest and competition 87;
   methodology, key aspects of 15; model
   of notion of general equilibrium 83;
   paradigm 81

neo-modernism 47, 49, 55–7; building of
 scenarios 258–9; role of empirical
 evidence 57; three-step modelling
 strategy 259
neo-Ricardians 25
neo-Schumpeterians 35, 37–8, 41–3
new classical macroeconomics *see* NCM
New Classical theorists 21
New Economic Paradigm 193
New Economy *see* NE
New Growth Theory (NGT) 7, 29–32,
 222; models 34; notion of steady-state
 balanced growth as equilibrium 30
New Institutional Economics 76, 106
new 'light' products, value of 150
Newtonian mechanics 60
Nicolis, G. 27, 59
Nietzsche, F. 50
nihilism 56
Non Accelerating Inflation Rate of
 Unemployment *see* NAIRU
non-conventional economists 59
non-linear dynamics 26–9, 61, 268;
 networks, adaptive 63
Nordhaus, W.D. 153
North, D.C. 9, 77–8, 100, 102–3, 105–6

O'Brien, R. 276
obsolescence: of knowledge, faster 199; in
 NE 145
Obstfeld, M. 275
OECD 153, 159
O'Gorman, P.F. 50–1, 79–80, 84, 86, 273
Okun's Law 67
Old Growth Theory (OGT) 29
Oliner, S.D. 143
'outsourcing' strategy across borders 132

Pasinetti, L. 24–5; contributions to the
 theory of growth in a multi-sector
 economy 25
patent applications in US 141
path-dependence 58
Patinkin, D. 94
Perez, C. 3, 35, 38–45, 71, 145, 235, 270,
 275, 277, 284
Perez-Quiros, G. 2, 149
Phelps, E.S. 51, 281
Phillips, S. 284
Phillips Curve 205; instability 67
Pigou effect 190, 215
Pirandello, L. 50
pluralism of complexity 60

policy: increasing innovation 266; low
 interest rates 151; making in NE 165;
 moves 45; pragmatic, limits of 182–3;
 rules, limits of general 177; slow 183
political economy, laws of 84
Popper, K.R. 99; 'world-3' conception 99
post-modernism: criticism 75; features of
 52–4, 270; implications for economics
 54–5; incontrovertible merits of 55; last
 phase of capitalism 120; limited impact
 on economics 56
Prasch, R.E. 9, 17–18, 59–60, 64, 68–9,
 77, 88, 101, 268, 271–2, 277
precision 117, 120, 128; in NCM 202–5
pre-Depression era 281
prediction 158
Prescott, E.C. 192
Preston, P. 38, 41–2, 52–3, 270–1; TEP
 approach 269
price formation, endogenous, in artificial
 financial world 67
Prigogine, I. 27, 59, 68
privacy 124, 175
product differentiation 146–7
production: factors, accumulation of 266;
 functions 121, 123
productivity: growth 141–2; rise in 198
property rights and responsibilities, new
 definition of 175
protectionist measures 176
Pryor, F.L. 9, 59–60, 70–3, 75, 79, 134
psychological factors 105
psychologism 105; critique of 98
public expenditure 197; cutting 252
purchasing power parity theorem 123
puzzle metaphor 79

Quah, D.T. 144, 150
quality of goods, problems in 152–7

R&D 266; capital 154; key source of new
 knowledge 154; spillovers 30
rapidity 117, 120, 140; in NCM 198–200
'rational bubble' approach 242
Rational Economic Man 100–2
rational expectations hypothesis 227
rationality 274
Reagan, R. 172; effects of cuts carried out
 by 181
real-balance effect 199
Real Business Cycle (RBC) theory 192;
 model 206
reasoned history, theory of 35–7

Reati, A. 17
Regulation school 45
Rennstich, J.K. 136, 145
research and development *see* R&D
research strategy to account for complex
  dynamics 37
Ricard, D.: comparative advantage
  principle 196; equivalence view 208
Rifkin, J. 106, 143–4, 147, 150, 156, 165,
  177, 180–1, 282
Roach, S. 138
Robbins, L. 85
Robinson, J. 24, 26, 32, 59
rocking-horse metaphor 16
Romer, C. 3, 170, 177, 267, 281
Romer, P.M. 30, 222; model, three
  elements 269
Rosenberg, A. 203
Rosenof, T. 8
Rostow, W.W. 1
Rowthorn, R. 3, 170
Ruccio, D.F. 52, 270, 273
Russell, B. 50
Rutherford, M. 77
Ruttan, V. 25, 30–1, 34

Samuelson, P.A. 24, 26, 51, 94, 101, 222
Santa Fe Approach (SFA) 59, 72, 271;
  a priori stability assumption, lack of 68;
  complexity 272; conceptualization of
  duality and structural instability 69;
  explanatory power, lack of 73; failure to
  account for complex patterns 71–3;
  focus on complex historical patterns
  74–5; 'light theory' underlying 74;
  limitations to 70; meta-model 74;
  model 63–4; stability 74; systemic
  dynamic laws, lack of 70–1; *vis-à-vis*
  standard theory 73
Santa Fe Institute 9
Sargent, T.J. 268
Sawyer, M.C. 183, 250, 252, 281, 283–4
Say's Law 189, 214
Schoenberg, A. 50
Schor, J.B. 219
Schotter, A. 76
Schumpeter, J.A. 26, 28, 39, 44, 59, 274;
  view of *General Theory* 44, 92; view of
  innovation 43; vision 119
Second World War 219; growth in trade
  since 131
security 175; rules for 277
self-interest 115

Sent, E.-M. 22, 268
September 11, 2001 147
Seravalli, G. 33
Setterfield, M. 32–3, 89, 222, 230, 268
Shackle, G.L.S. 59, 98, 235
Shapiro, C. 143–4, 279
Shiller, R.J. 2, 151, 155, 241; irrational
  exuberance thesis 156
shocks 197, 206
short-termism 156
Sichel, D.E. 143
Simon, J. 3, 59, 128, 143, 149, 152,
  170–1, 173, 279, 281
Simonazzi, A. 154
simplification strategy 79
simplified propaedeutic 31
Sims: inductive approach 129; time-series
  analysis using vector autoregression
  (VAR) 275
simulation of dynamics on computer 62
skilled labour shortages 146
Smith, A. 59, 87, 269
Smith, M.D. 153
social capital 181
social trust 181
social welfare 136
society, general theories of 70
Soete, L. 35, 150
Solow, R. 32, 222, 278; diminishing
  marginal productivity of capital 268;
  model 17, 20, 32
Sonnenschein, H. 268
speculation or 'irrational exuberance' 202
Sraffa, P. 59; critique of neoclassical
  theory 26
stability 15; alternative approaches to 13;
  analysis 47; article of faith 17–18;
  assumption 191; definition for Europe
  249; instantaneous equilibrium model
  112; limitations of assumption 18;
  macroeconomic 74; in mature economies
  134; and monetary policy rules 167–9;
  New Economy 79, 117, 262; pact in
  Europe 171, 254; and tax cuts 181
standard analytical methods 47
standard macro models 84; gap between
  pure theory and actual phenomena
  84–5; study of growth and cycles 16
standard theory 123; limitations of 84;
  negative outcomes 19; 'pure' market
  system 112; Rational Economic Man
  100–2; two features of 121
'static' macroeconomic models 78

steam-powered mechanization 38
Stiglitz, J. 3, 137–9, 155, 169, 171, 175, 177, 182, 217, 222, 240, 252, 267
Stiroh, K.J. 30, 132, 142, 150, 152, 154, 159, 201
Stock, J.H. 3
stock options 156
Storper, M. 134–5, 196, 276
Strindberg, J.A. 50
structural change: and instantaneous equilibrium 74; without equilibrium 35
structural complexity, dimensions of 75
structural policies, pragmatic 176
Stuttgart School approach 271
Summers, L.H. 124–6, 131, 141–3, 148–50, 163, 165, 173, 235, 267, 279
supply-side free market policy 165
synchronization or coordination between firms 199
systemic failures 177

tacit knowledge 139
Talalay, M. 131
Talani, S. 169
Tamborini, R. 222
tax cuts 168, 171–2; instability due to 181
Taylor, A.M. 275
technical and organizational innovations 38
Techno-Economic Paradigm (TEP) 3, 35, 37–9, 275; complementary social, institutional and economic factors 38; dangers of disregarding macroeconomic equilibrium 42–5; interactions and complementarities, analysis of 38–40; limitations, dangers of technological determinism 41–2; 'long-wave' phenomena 39
technological change 128; in age of ICT 140–1
technological determinism 16
technological unemployment 146
technology 119; shock, favourable 198
Teece, D.J. 144
theory, patterns 67
Thirlwall, A.P. 17, 24–5, 32, 222, 228, 230, 269
Tinbergen's study on statistical testing of business cycle theories 23
Tobin's q 283
Togati, T.D. 99, 252, 274
Toporowski, I. 152
trade, terms for developing countries 139
trade unions 141, 234

Trajtenberg, M. 31
transformational growth, theory of 13
Treasury view in Britain 170
Treatise of Money 43
trust and interpersonal relations 153
Turner, A. 135, 149
Tvede, L. 15–16, 19, 26–8, 32, 215–16, 269

uncertainty: global economy 176; growth prospects 163; potential growth rate 178
unification of markets 195
US 136, 176; advantage, institutional sources of 124; dollar 137; economic transformation 124; economy, imbalances 240; economy, virtuous cycle 138, 141; energy companies and telecoms group, recent scandals 155; and Europe, more flexible fiscal policy 17, 171; growth in capital services 142; increased need for skilled labour 145; key regulating mechanisms 137; productive basis, shrinking 138; recent moderation of business cycle 170; recession after terrorist attacks 172

value and capital, broader concept of 150
van Gelderen, J. 36, 40
Varian, H. 143–4, 153, 279
Veblen, T. 77, 270, 277
Vercelli, A. 4, 7, 17–19, 26–8, 127–8, 188, 191–2, 203, 216, 268–9, 274–5, 283
Verdun, A. 252
Verspagen, B. 35, 38
'vertical' simplification 127
visibility 117, 120, 165; in NCM 205–6
vision of economy in complexity theory 58–60
Viskovatoff, A. 9, 16, 18, 58, 71–2, 77, 136–8, 161, 271–2, 277
volatility of financial markets 155
Von Tunzelmann, G.N. 270
vulnerability, increased 133

Walrasian equilibrium 21, 218
Walrasian markets 21
Walrasian paradigm 83
water-powered mechanization 38
Watson, M.W. 3
Weber, S. 2
Weber, M. 50
weightlessness 119, 148
welfare 266; state 171; system 180

Western, D. 242, 284
Wible, J. 59–60, 64, 88, 271–2
Wicksell, K. 16
Williamson, O.E. 76
Winkler, B. 206–7
winners and losers 228; growing distance between 196
Winnett, A. 153
Winter, S. 59, 77

Woodford, M. 151, 168; on Central Banks in NE 281
WTO 176

Young, A. 269

Zarnowitz, V. 3–4, 20, 133–4, 155, 217, 280, 282
Zysman, J. 142, 153, 175–6